Political Parties in Industrial Democracies

POLITICAL PARTIES
in
INDUSTRIAL
DEMOCRACIES

IMAGINING THE MASSES

Harmon Zeigler

University of Puget Sound
and
University of Washington

 F. E. PEACOCK PUBLISHERS, INC.   *Itasca, Illinois*

Cover photo by Robert Amft

To
Pat, Michael, Amanda, Jim, Charlie
Rose, Esther, Tim, Justin, Poppie, and Chloe

Contents

Preface

This book grew out of my curiosity about "American exceptionalism," that collection of attitudes and institutions said to make the American political system so unlike any other as to render comparison tenuous. Of course, comparisons between the United States and other industrial democracies abound, and the dissimilarities between "us" and "them" are not difficult to unshroud. They are recounted in some detail in the pages that follow.

There is, however, a larger question. It is especially appropriate as the United States—in the 1990s—has entered one of its cyclical periods of popular cynicism. But this time, coupled with the cynicism is an economy in peril and a political system ill equipped to make the difficult choices required to prevent further deterioration. It is a system that has been re-formed relentlessly so as to depict the American bias against organizations. Can a political system designed and redesigned for inefficiency and fragmentation avoid paralysis?

The other industrial democracies, with less committment to individualism, once were told by their scholars to "Americanize," that is, to substitute the fluidity of hyperpluralism for the rigidity of organizationally structured politics. One rarely hears this plea nowadays. To Americanize now means to substitute glitz for substance, to stress personality over ideology.

This comparative analysis contrasts an unstructured, free-floating political system with those with only limited tolerance for political entrepreneurship. The contrast is well phrased by Donald Granberg and Sören Holmberg, who invite us to imagine a situation in which two groups of people, randomly selected and uninformed about art, are asked to evaluate works of art. The first group sees slides of several paintings that differ only modestly from each other. Furthermore, the transparencies are out of focus, and people's attention is constantly being diverted by more appealing distractions. The second group examines transparencies of paintings that are appreciably different. They are projected sharply and there are few diversions. If one asked the members of the first group questions about art, there would be only one conclusion: people know and care virtually nothing about it. The first group is intended to portray the United States; the second, almost any European industrial democracy. Members of the second group would obviously yield substantially different levels of information and understanding.

I am indebted to two generous and severe critics, John Keeler and David Olson. Keeler, presumably harboring some latent inclination toward masochism, read the entire manuscript twice, and each time proved to be appropriately compulsive. As his own research amply shows, he is among that small group of scholars who write elegantly and with subtle humor, and who eschew trivia to address consequential issues. At the University of Puget Sound, Michel Rocchi worked with me tirelessly on languages, and David Sousa guided me through theoretical problems that I had not considered. I also profited from conversations with Klaus Hansen (Germany), and with Pierre Muller and Thierry Vedel (France).

At Peacock, Leo Wiegman joins David Estrin (Longman) and Irving Rockwood (Dushkin) in that tiny band of editors that read manuscripts (as opposed to menus), and provide felicitous and pertinent criticism.

1.

Introduction

This book is about political organizations, political parties, and interest groups. Political parties in democratic systems are organizations whose primary purpose is to elect candidates in order to control the personnel and policies of government. Interest groups are formal organizations that try to accomplish their goals through influence on public policy. These descriptions are abstract; in practice, the functions of political parties and interest groups are much less clearly defined.

WHY THE PEOPLE MUST BE MANUFACTURED

The argument is simple: people are not especially interested in politics, and for good reason. Politics appear remote to the central personal problems of daily life. But political processes and public policies can influence how satisfying and rewarding daily life is; sometimes directly, more often indirectly. As Alan Ehrenhalt, recalling Walter Lippman (whose *Phantom Public* embodies the idea of inventing the people), reflects: "Life is too short, work is too hard, and leisure too precious for the average citizen to spend more than a small fraction of his time gathering information about the people whose names confront him on the ballot each election year."[1] The premise of democracy is that, while many of us do not care about politics, we are the best judges *individually* of how things ought to be. None of us need be an expert in economics to recognize hard times. People want to be happy and secure, and government ought to do what the people want. But how does a government find out what they want? Herein lies the problem of democracy, especially with the large, industrial democracies of today.

The Key Role of Political Organizations

Without political organizations, the task of finding out what the people want is beyond reach. The American culture, the American tradition, has difficulty with this notion. Strong populist currents elevate the common person to the level of political sophisticate, *requiring* that he or she vote often. A resident of England, in a typical five-year period, has four opportunities to vote (local council, county government, Common Market referenda, and House of Commons). The typical American could have voted 165 times (thirteen for city offices, forty-nine for county offices, forty for state offices, thirteen for national offices, and fifty referenda) in the same period of time.[2]

Thus, the American political culture deliberately maximizes the opportunities for individuals, without organizational intervention, to control policy or personnel. In doing so, it assumes too much. The outcome is predictable: Americans know less and vote less than citizens of other industrial democracies. The fault is not so much with the voters as with the election system, which requires more knowledge of politics and government than is reasonable. As Lippman lamented, "[The voter] has been saddled with an impossible task and . . . is asked to practice an unattainable ideal. Few people, perhaps fifteen percent, follow politics closely. Consequently, most votes that we cast . . . are stabs in the dark."[3] As Arthur Seldon explains:

> The most endlessly discussed, and most extravagant of space in the press and of time in broadcasting, is politics; its meetings, conferences, party caucuses and personalities. The least discussed are the nonpolitical activities that many more people enjoy far more: domestic interests, artistic pursuits, charitable works, fraternizing with friends or doing nothing at all—all ways of using leisure time that mystify the political people and mislead them into seeing non-political people as irresponsible, uncooperative or unpatriotic.[4]

Voters are not stupid; they are just more intent on controlling their immediate environment. As Thomas Hobbes puts it: "A plain husband-man is more Prudent in the Affaires of his own house, than is a Privy Counselor in the Affaires of other men."[5] When that immediate environment becomes politicized, so do the voters. In England, where the management and funding of the National Health Service have moved to the center of the domestic agenda, the opposition Labour Party has used by-elections (special elections held to fill parliamentary vacancies) to underline its opposition to the Conservatives. In Monmouth, a special election became a referendum on the National Health Service; Labour won easily, and surveys revealed that the National Health Service was the voters' principal concern. A political organization, the Labour Party, used this win, and in so doing, kept the debate about health care at the top of the agenda. If there had been no strong political organization, such constraints would have been impossible. Political organizations provide shortcuts to "the people." When properly functioning, they reduce information costs to individuals and to elite decision makers. Individuals who may not see the utility of keeping up with politics should be able to find a political party or interest group that will do this job for them. Yet, these organizations are not, whether by design or by "natural law," democratic. Parties and interest groups are not run by the members; they are managed by a permanent bureaucracy. European parties make no pretenses about their lack of democracy (even the German ones, with democratic procedures mandated by the Basic Law, do not hold primary elections). But American individualism has a difficult time accepting the idea that nondemocratic institutions can serve as a link between leaders and followers, thus creating "more democracy." The unique institution of the primary election that allows voters to nominate a party's candidate can be taken as the latest American effort to overcome Michel's "Iron Law of Oligarchy" ("He who says organization says oligarchy") by removing political organizations from the flow of influence between rulers and the ruled.[6]

Previously, during the reform movement at the turn of the century, much of local politics was made nonpartisan. The same impulse, the bias against organization, is at work. In Europe we find virtually no nonpartisan elections. Parties run candidates in city, state, and national elections: "In the states and cities across America . . . parties make little difference. Candidates for all sorts of offices are perfectly capable of going on about their business without them. . . . Who sent us the political leaders we have? There is a simple answer to that question. They sent themselves."[7]

What is needed is stability in political organizations. One needs to know that being loyal to the Democratic, Republican, Christian

Democratic, or Labour parties will yield reasonably comparable images of the good life from year to year. Consider a tax accountant. All of us, if we had the time, inclination, and expertise, could file our own income taxes. But many of us prefer to use an accountant. As long as the results are satisfactory, we do not change accountants. We also could repair our own cars (indeed some who find taxes too complex find automobiles more accessible), but mechanics know more and, as long as the car performs, we are not inclined to change mechanics. Modern politics in democracies depends upon organizations to perform the political roles of accountants and mechanics.

The emphasis on organizations does not deny the vital role of dynamic leadership. Franklin Roosevelt, Charles de Gaulle, Margaret Thatcher, Ronald Reagan, and François Mitterrand surely loom large in any discussion of modern democratic politics. Rather, the focus on organizations asserts that whereas individuals come and go, organizations persist. Whereas individuals are easily deluded about the wishes of the people, organizations should be efficient in *linking* elites and masses. When the titans pass from the scene, the organization should not deteriorate; rather, it should recruit new titans. The best illustration of the relation between individual and organization is Margaret Thatcher and the British Conservative Party. She guided it three times to victory but was *not* the party, as she learned when she was replaced as party leader and prime minister.

Although the removal of a sitting prime minister by her or his party is unusual, the subordination of individual to organization is not. European political parties have identifiable party leaders who serve as the voice of the opposition, responding to government initiatives, proposing alternatives, and the like. These leaders are likely to be in office for at least one or two elections; thus, voters know who they are and the party is given personification. Neil Kinnock in the United Kingdom, Björn Engholm in Germany, and Jacques Chirac and Valéry Giscard d'Estaing in France serve the role of party leaders in opposition. Who leads the American opposition? Since the Democrats control the legislature and the Republicans the presidency, *where* is the opposition party? Can a sitting president be a member of the opposition? Surely not. Therefore, are Tom Foley (Speaker of the House) and George Mitchell (Senate Majority Leader) coleaders of the opposition? What about defeated Democratic presidential candidates? As Alan Ehrenhalt says of the latest, "He was not, in anything but the nominal sense, anybody's standard bearer. That point is underscored by the rapidity with which he lost any national influence in the Democratic party after his defeat."[8] Perhaps a successful Democratic presidential candidate could serve as the voice of the opposition. Jimmy Carter, who won the presidency in 1976 and lost it four years later, suffered the same problem as did Dukakis: "Having been nominated and elected to office without any organizational allies in the Democratic party....The door was open and he walked in."[9]

David Broder addresses impermanence and stability by comparing two often-defeated political parties. He selects the British Labour Party, which lost three times in a row to the Conservatives, and the American Democrats, who lost three times in a row to the Republicans:

> The difficulty is that the Democratic Party has no mechanism for speaking as a party; it has no policy voice....The lack of a policy voice is one of the chronic problems for the out-party in America....When Britain's Labour Party lost for the third straight time in 1987, its leader Neil Kinnock invited party officials at all levels to review Labour's message. The process...led Labour to dump some damaging policies...and has won the party new credibility with the voters. The [American] Democrats have lost three in a row, too, but they have no machinery for asking themselves where they went wrong or figuring out what they might say differently. They do not even have a policy voice.[10]

Broder reflects on the Democrats' lack of a consistent tax policy. President Bush proposed a reduction in the capital gains tax (upon profits from the sale of stocks or bonds). The chairman of the Democratic National Committee, Ron Brown, wanted the Democrats to "draw a line in the sand" and defeat the president. However, the chairman of the Democratic Congressional Campaign Committee (in the House of Representatives) spoke and voted for the Bush proposal. A group of Senate Democrats prepared a tax bill that National Chairman Brown found "only marginally less offensive" than the President's proposals. So what do the Democrats think? On the other hand, President Bush felt so unattached to his domestic agenda that he fought only weakly for his tax. Unlike Reagan, Bush is an active participant in his administration, but he finds foreign policy more interesting than domestic matters. The domestic agenda, therefore, lies unattended because Bush, as an *individual*, can ignore it. No European prime minister could do so. Indeed, in France, where the president, like President Bush, is intrigued more by foreign than domestic matters, the prime minister is in command of the domestic agenda.

Now consider the response of the German Social Democratic Party to a proposal by Chancellor Helmut Kohl that the Basic Law be amended (requiring a two-thirds vote in the legislature) to allow German troops to become more active in multinational military exercises, such as the 1990–91 war in the Persian Gulf. Thus, as Kohl's governing coalition does not have two-thirds of the vote, the opposition party would have to agree. Meeting in Bremen, the Social Democrats declined. Engholm's statement was made at a party meeting, not at the Bundestag. So what allows him to assume that the Social Democratic members of parliament will agree and not defect to the chancellor? They will not because party unity is assumed. Chancellor Kohl assumed as much when he issued a statement regretting the decision. It never occurred to him to lobby Social Democratic members of parliament. At about the same time, the Democrats in the American House of Representatives passed a civil rights bill that the president intended to veto. Although the vote was 273 to 158, a substantial margin of victory, the outcome was a setback for the Democratic leadership, because the votes in favor of the bill fell 17 short of the number needed to override a veto. The coalition in favor consisted of 250 Democrats and 22 Republicans. In opposition were 143 Republicans and 15 Democrats. Thus, 37 members of the legislature defected to the other side. There are 264 Democrats in the House, 26 short of the two-thirds required to override a veto. Even if the Democratic Party had gotten a "European" level of support from the rank and file, Republican defections would be necessary.

POLITICAL CULTURE AND POLITICAL ORGANIZATIONS

Political culture dictates somewhat how willing a polity is to subordinate the individual to the organization, a necessary condition for effective linkage, for representative democracy. European societies are less individualistic than is the United States:

> [A]lmost without exception European observers have focused upon egalitarianism, openness, absence of social hierarchy, suspicion of political authority, and belief in popular sovereignty as critical characteristics distinguishing American from European politics.[11]

European public opinion is more collectivist (see below) and European budgets more committed to welfare than are American ones. European education is less individualistic, more inclined toward the values of the meritocracy. "Political culture" is a vexatious idea, but few would argue that the American culture and institutions are not more individualistic than those of Europe. The simple measure of legislative party discipline alone shows American legislators as entrepreneurs and European ones as cogs. One would expect that pub-

Table 1.1   Country Variations in Preference for Freedom or Equality

	Equality	Freedom
United States	20%	72%
United Kingdom	23	69
France	32	54
Italy	45	43
West Germany	39	37
Japan	32	37

lic opinion is a crude approximation of these organizational ideologies. This is the case. Beginning with the distrust of royal authority engendered by the American Revolution, and enhanced by the American belief in popular control of government, American values lean more toward freedom (from authority) than do European ones.[12] The proportions preferring either freedom or equality are displayed in Table 1.1.[13]

The proportions that believe it is the government's responsibility to reduce income differences are displayed in Table 1.2.

Elite attitudes, while more sympathetic to equality, reflect mass beliefs. Elites in the United States, in comparison with those in Sweden and Japan, are more disposed to oppose income distribution, and "no American [elite] group occupies the position of the left groups in Japan or Sweden. . . . In Japan and Sweden, where leaders demonstrate greater commitment to community than to individualism and a greater deference to the state, we also find greater acceptance of a positive government role."[14]

The American culture, in other words, rejects the idea that political organizations are necessary for political democracy. The people need no intermediaries. European culture, less individualistic, is less optimistic about the faculties of the common man. Thus, European political parties are hierarchically organized and firmly in control of the leadership; American parties are loosely organized and well beyond the control of anyone. European interest groups are more likely

Table 1.2   Country Variations in Belief in the Governmental Obligation to Reduce Income Differences

Italy	81%
Netherlands	63
United Kingdom	63
West Germany	56
Australia	42
United States	28

to be engaged in a "corporatist" arrangement, by which they participate as privileged partners in policy or implementation. American interest groups are engaged in a wide-open fight for influence and access. And European governments diminish direct popular control by reliance upon parliamentary government. Rather than directly electing a president, most European elections are for a legislature, which, in turn, selects the prime minister.

Collective Leadership Versus Individualism: The Role of Institutions

The combination of more structure and institutionalization of political parties and interest groups with parliamentary government is summed up well by the idea of *collective leadership and collective responsibility*. A prime minister and his or her cabinet are directly accountable to their parliamentary party. The members of the parliamentary party are accountable to the party organization. Consequently, personality is less a variable in assessing the performance of governmental elites than it is in the individualistic United States. There are strong and weak prime ministers: the United Kingdom's Winston Churchill and Margaret Thatcher are regarded as more dominant than Clement Attlee, Harold Wilson, or current Prime Minister John Major. West Germany's Konrad Adenauer's personal power has yet to be equaled by his successors. But the range within which this personal power is applied is limited by collective principles and institutions. *Governments* (i.e., executives) are much more powerful than an American president, as there is no separation of powers. But *individual leaders* are more institutionally constrained. They have less power within the executive branch, but far more power *vis-a-vis* the legislature. The point is well made by considering the proportion of executive-sponsored bills that are enacted into laws: 97 percent in the United Kingdom; 87 percent in Germany; 74 percent in France; 73 percent in Japan; and only 33 percent in the United States. Richard Rose explains:

> An American president has a far more difficult task in managing government than do [European] counterparts. Congress really does decide whether bills become laws, by contrast to the executive domination of law and decree-making in Europe.[15]

The import of parliamentary government is to allow concentration of power, checked by the electorate. The intent of presidential government is to separate power, checking elite ambition by countervailing elite ambition. The strength of a European prime minister is not measured by his or her ability to negotiate legislation through parliament; rather, strength is measured by the boldness of policy proposals and tenacity to harness a political party's energy. A seemingly trivial law shows well the difference between deliberately fragmented and consciously concentrated power. The United Kingdom, in addition to having parliamentary government, also has a unitary relation between national and local governments. The John Major government moved quickly to rid Britain of pit bull terriers. The law required all such animals to be destroyed or neutered and kept on a leash and muzzled. If we try to imagine a national law banning pit bulls in the United States, the difference between the two political cultures becomes apparent.

European and American Political Economies

European governments are more intrusive. For example, while 34 percent of the American Gross National Product (GNP) was attributed to government spending, European government spending accounts for about 45 percent. While Americans complain about taxes, their tax rates are substantially lower than European rates. The highest tax rate in the United States is 31 percent, compared to 40 in the United Kingdom, 53 percent in Germany, 57 percent in France, and 50 percent in Japan (see Appendix). And the money is spent with attention to different priorities. About 40 percent of American health expenditures are public, compared with about 75 percent in Europe. Subsidies to industry, which amount to about one-third of 1 percent of the GNP in the United States, average 2 percent in Europe (see Appendix). Americans complain about bureaucracy, but European bureaucracies are bigger. Not only are a higher proportion of people employed publicly in Europe than in the United States but also central government employees exceed state and local employees in number. The opposite is true in the United States (see Appendix).

A noteworthy example of the American and European industrial strategy is Airbus Industrie, a German, French, British, and Spanish consortium. These governments have invested about $8 billion of public revenues in Airbus, trying to make it competitive with America's Boeing. The American trade representatives routinely and vigorously complain about these subsidies to little avail. The European response points out that there are *de facto* subsidies, because Boeing is a major defense contractor. The United States spends much more for defense than do the European countries. Philosophical differences aside, Airbus seems to be poised to capture a substantial portion of the market. In 1988 Airbus sold 15 percent of the world's passenger jet aircraft, while Boeing enjoyed a market share of 59 percent. In 1990 Airbus advanced to 34 percent while Boeing declined to 45 percent.

THE EUROPEAN VIEW OF AMERICAN GOVERNMENT

Often European assessment of the American government finds it wanting. Richard Rose, an American who has spent most of his professional life within British universities, especially identifies with this view.[16] He does not mean that the American government can never undertake concerted action, but rather that when it does, a charismatic personality rather than a political party deserves the credit. Speaking of Ronald Reagan, whose tenure they regard as, on balance, a successful one, Paul Peterson and Mark Rom conclude "that the President had the ability to guide the federal government decisively should be praised by both liberals and conservatives, because it shows that an active president can effectuate change."[17] They speak mostly of Reagan's first term. In 1986 the Democrats regained control of the Senate and the Iran-Contra scandal damaged his popularity substantially, if only temporarily. His "box score" after that was disappointing. For the remainder of his term, fewer than half of his proposals to Congress were approved, and his budgets (an essential tool for influencing policy) were scornfully tossed aside.

A different president, with a different style, merited this somber assessment: "After two years in office, the point at which most presidents have their most significant domestic achievements already behind them, Bush had little to show."[18] Rose, comparing the United States with Europe, seeks a government institutionally capable of managing.

> In seeking to exercise influence on subgovernments [that is, combinations of interest groups, bureaucracies, and legislative committees], the basic problem of the President is simple: there is no government there. The President does not have in his own hands the authority to override the preferences of subgovernments in the name of broader national interests....Parliamentary systems have subgovernments too...but in a parliamentary system there is government as well as subgovernments.[19]

Theodore Lowi explains the dilemma of show without substance: "The more a president holds to the initiative and keeps impersonal, the more he reinforces the mythology that there actually exists in the White House a 'capacity to govern.' "[20] Lowi means that Presidents are, at best, opportunists and facilitators rather than policy leaders. Good facilitators (e.g., Franklin Roosevelt and Ronald Reagan) exercise leadership "at the margins."[21]

There is a cruel contradiction at work. In a country whose legislatures and bureaucracies are said to be under siege from interest groups and political action committees, the presidency is not. It is relatively free of ensnaring and entangling group alliances in governing. Presidents and their staffs are less accessible to interest groups; their campaigns are less dependent upon interest groups for money (with partial public financing). Presidents normally serve eight years (the post-war average is five-and-a-half years, but that will increase with Republican hegemony), but congressmen stay as long as they wish. Interest groups operate best in the deep confines of Congress. But presidents cannot use their relative independence from interest groups because their power, in comparison to that of Congress, is in decline. Lester Seligman and Cary Covington explain the "presidential paradox":

> Developments in the presidential election system [primaries] and in the general governing context [increased fragmentation] have made the process of translating electoral support into a governing coalition more difficult. The striking consequence of these developments is that at a time when the scope of the president's responsibilities has expanded, the bases of his political support have become less reliable.[22]

Presidents "struggle to get control of the government," but "few of them succeed."[23] How many other industrial democracies are plagued by the inability of the putative leader to gain control? Possibly Japan, where prime minister Toshiki Kaifu was generally regarded as having less power than his predecessors due to his weakness within the ruling party. When coalition governments are necessary, as in Italy, the reputed leader, the prime minister, is also more constrained by the need for bargaining with coalition partners.

But, in both these cases, there is *somebody* with whom bargains can be struck and obligations honored. In Japan, Kaifu's selection as prime minister was a fluke, necessitated by the Liberal Democratic Party's need to find somebody untainted by scandal. However, he proved more resourceful and resilient than was anticipated and clung to his job tenaciously. Even were he to remain a pure figurehead, the LDP's power brokers, Shintaro Abe and Shin Kanemaru, certainly are not: somebody is in charge.

In Italy, where governments are formed and dissolved with monotonous regularity (about every ten months), the country's reputation as lurching from crisis to crisis is belied by the durability and power of political parties. As LaPalombara concludes: "No one can doubt that political parties are in control of the country."[24]

"Cohabitation" in France did not result in the president failing to gain control; rather, he ceded domestic policy to Jacques Chirac, who was in control (at least more than an American president). British prime ministers may lose influence in cabinet disputes, but the collective cabinet does not suffer *vis-a-vis* Commons. Parties do make a difference: "American political parties were rarely helpful [in enabling a president to control the government] when they were relevant and potent. They would be even less valuable today with their potency on the wane and their relevance to the task of governing very much in doubt."[25]

A frequently used measure of an American president's success, his "batting average" with Congress, is a meaningless statistic for most European parliamentary systems. Its meaninglessness is accentuated for France, where the separate election of a president makes it possible for an opposition coalition to command a legislative majority. The prime minister, chosen by the president, must negotiate with Leaders of this coalition. Therefore, Michel Rocard became known for the "methode Rocard," the cultivation of opposition leaders. Edith Cresson, his successor, regarded as more ideologically committed to the socialist left than was Rocard, explains that she must govern "closer to the center than I would prefer." However, the task is not as difficult in France as in the United States, because party leaders can negotiate with confidence that the rank and file will not abandon them.

Another way of comparing the two governmental systems is to consider the fates of two leaders who were deposed without an election: Richard Nixon and Margaret Thatcher. Nixon, tormented by an almost paranoiac fear of enemies, resigned rather than face successful impeachment for obstructing justice, a criminal act. His resignation, nevertheless, dragged on for months as a fascinated America watched him slowly wrenched from the presidency. The resignation of a president will remain for many politically attentive Americans the central event of their lives. Margaret Thatcher committed no greater sin than to convince a majority of the back bench of the Conservative Party (those Conservatives not serving in the government) that she would lead the party to defeat in the next elections. Thatcher's resignation took a few weeks to negotiate and created no more than a temporary sensation. The Iron Lady who "accumulated more personal power than any peace-time prime minister in history"[26] was dispatched by her own party.

Current President George Bush is regarded as experienced and seasoned; current British Prime Minister John Major is said to lack "bottom" (the knowledge gained from years of service). Bush and Major have been in public life for about the same number of years, even though Bush is much older than Major. Bush entered politics in 1967; Major in 1968. Bush went directly to Congress, served as permanent representative to the United Nations, head of the U.S. Liaison Office in Beijing, and director of the CIA before becoming vice-president and, in 1989, president. Major served in the Lambeth city council from 1968 to 1971, went to Parliament in 1979, served in a number of junior ministerial posts, became chief secretary to the Treasury in 1987, foreign secretary in 1989, and, his penultimate post, chancellor of the exchequer. Of course, the Lambeth* city council is not the center of power in Britain, nor is the seventh district of Texas likely to capture much time on CNN; but Major's national experience can surely contest Bush's.

THE ENDURING DILEMMA: LINKAGE

Both the European and the American schemes are intended, however indirectly, to provide linkages between rulers and the ruled. The European model assumes that collective decisions most in harmony with mass wishes are best achieved by limiting, channeling, and constraining individual choice. The American model assumes the reverse. Both, however, must "invent the people."

The political-governmental process, representing mass opinion, devising programs in keeping with the main contours of this opinion, and facing the consequences of misrepresentation, is the topic of this book. Accordingly, it examines party organizations, interest groups, and the process by which they "invent the people."

The Impermanence of Individualism

The American process wants the people to invent themselves; the European process wants the (nondemocratic) parties and interest groups to invent them. Realistically, the American process allows individuals, or entrepreneurs, to invent their own people and, when they depart office, forget them. To Alan Ehrenhalt, Gary Hart is the purest example of the American process of self-nomination, with his

---

*Lambeth, a working-class area on London's edge, is the subject of the song, "The Lambeth Walk," in the West End and Broadway musical comedy, Me and My Girl.

"underlying individualism, the untethered quality of his life. . . . The crucial task of the self-nominee is to *manufacture issues and constituencies.*"[27] The issue becomes not one of inventing the people or speaking for them; rather, the issue is making the inventor a corporation or an individual entrepreneur. Just as small businesses fail at many times the rate of corporations, so do the people invented by entrepreneurial politicians disappear with them.

American individualism pervades all levels of government. As presidential aspirants invent people and issues, so do the less visible participants. Consider the Senate Democratic Policy Committee established in 1946. Invented by those committed to strong parties, the Committee was intended to "formulate overall legislative policy."[28] In fact, it has not." The Senate policy committees. . . have done little to increase party cohesion and have not contributed much to policy accountability. . . . The purpose and character of the Democratic policy committees has been shaped by the preferences of the individual majority leaders."[29] George Reedy, a former director of the Democratic Policy Committee, explains that "in practice the Senate Democratic Policy Committee became *whatever the floor leader wanted it to be.*"[30]

The American President and the American Culture

Similarly, presidential scholar Richard Neustadt describes the institution of the presidency as having "reflected the strengths and weaknesses of the man holding it."[31] Even with a personal staff much larger than that of the leaders of other industrial democracies, the American "Second Republic" is "a plebiscitary republic with a personal presidency":

> Having been made a star by the selection process and the structure of the office, the president must personally shine so brilliantly and generate so much gravity that the rest of the Washington universe will revolve in an orderly fashion around him.[32]

Perhaps the best symbolic illustration of this cultural difference is the gasp that invariably emerges from my classroom students when they watch question time at the British Parliament on the C-SPAN television channel. The prime minister simply walks in and sits unnoticed, awaiting the harsh test from the opposition. In contrast, an American president enters Congress like Hannibal, to the obsequious deference owed to royalty. Lowi's description of the transformation of Jimmy Carter from a self-deprecating and modest aspirant to a symbolically regal president is frightening.

Table 1.3   Percent Believing that the Moral Practices of Various Occupations Are Excellent or Good

23	Labor union leaders
33	Federal government officials
34	Stockbrokers
35	Corporate board members
37	State and local government officials
38	Advertising executives
39	Corporate executives
42	U.S. senators and representatives
43	Lawyers
48	Military leaders
51	Media news reporters
57	Supreme Court
57	Bankers
65	President
69	College professors
74	Average workers
75	Scientists
76	Small business proprietors
76	Physicians

Source: Adapted from Gary King and Lyn Ragsdaale, *The Elusive Executive* (Washington, D.C.: CQ Press, 1988), p. 368.

Carter began enlarging himself, in the promises he made and the rhetoric with which he made them. . . . His vocabulary became more and more inflated and his references more and more personal. . . . He was distinctly modern in making them immensely large and intensely personal.[33]

The American president receives more veneration and possesses less power than European heads of state: "He is the nation's spokesman, the personification of the nation—the closest thing Americans have to a royal sovereign. Upon his election he and his family dominate the news in America."[34]

Because American presidents conduct extensive personal campaigns and make hyperbolic promises—phrases generally in pithy, memorable sound bites ("It's Morning in America," or "The Magic of America")—people expect that they will work miracles; that they will simultaneously reduce unemployment and inflation, strengthen national defense, and reduce the cost of government.[35] The Americans elect a "king, high priest, and prophet."[36] Table 1.3 shows American veneration.

These rankings reveal much about American culture. The president is alone among government officials or employees in garnering a majority vote of confidence. Federal government officials (civil servants), venerated in Europe and Japan, are mistrusted by Americans.

Average people are among the most admired; small businessmen (perhaps symbolizing the American economy) are more admired than are corporate executives. Ordinary workers have, in the opinion of Americans, more integrity than any government official, including the president. Americans also expect their presidents to be exemplary in their personal lives by living pure and clean and setting an example, like royalty. Presidents must provide not only political salvation but moral cleansing as well: "The President is expected to personify our betterness in an inspiring way, to express in what he does and is (not just what he says) a moral idealism which, in the public mind, is the very opposite of 'politics.' "[37] When a president does not behave as expected, as is often the case, the shock is profound: Nixon's profanity and vulgarity, as revealed by the Watergate tapes, generated outrage. How Americans would respond to Edith Cresson's remarks that "they [the Japanese] sit up all night thinking of ways to screw the Americans and Europeans" can only be surmised. Even scholars are appalled at John Kennedy's astonishing sexual promiscuity. Reeves writes of John Kennedy that:

> Kennedy abused his high position for personal gratification. His reckless liaisons with women and mobsters were irresponsible, dangerous and demeaning to the office. . . . Had Kennedy lived to see a second term, the realities of his lechery and his dealings with [mobsters] might have leaked out while he was still in office, gravely damaging the presidency, debilitating his administration and severely disillusioning a populace which, no matter how jaded it seems, looks to a president with hope for reassurance and leadership.[38]

Between one-fourth and one-third of Americans object to a president's not belonging to a church, using tranquilizers, using profanity, having seen a psychiatrist, or wearing jeans in the oval office.[39] Jimmy Carter's symbolic populism was ill designed to suit these expectations. But Carter, incorrect in his judgment about the appropriate symbols, still understood the necessity of symbolism. He bounced up the stairs to Air Force One and handed his garment bag to an attendant, as would any ordinary traveler. However, the garment bag was empty.

Children—more in the United States than in Europe—come to believe that great presidents, great men, made America rich and strong. Encouraged by a media obsession with personality, Americans expect their presidents to be personally responsible for the resolution of the nation's problems.

Gallic Excess

European heads of state do not have such an opportunity, although the French presidency comes close. Since there have only been four presidents in the Fifth Republic, it is too early to say if this office will attain the majesty of the American presidency. Three of the four presidents—Charles de Gaulle, Valéry Giscard, and François Mitterrand—have been distinctly image conscious and regal in bearing. Mitterrand has the closest affinity to the Gaullist tradition. He is aloof, enjoys pretending to be above politics, and has a taste for public martyrdom and adoration, as did de Gaulle. Like de Gaulle, he has developed a court of lackeys and a fanatical following, and encourages "tontonmania" (Tonton, his nickname, is the term of endearment for "uncle"). In recent years his character on the "Bebête" show has been referred to as "God." A French president's public presentation of self is as ostentatious as an American president's. Mort Rosenblum describes Giscard's arrival in Guinea:

> [The Concorde] rolled up, its nose sloping elegantly downward. A blue, white, and red flag flew from the cockpit. Everyone, soldiers, witchdoctors, and president, watched transfixed....The message had been delivered. *Vive la France.*

When Giscard was defeated and Mitterrand, more egalitarian in policy, became president, he, too, went to Guinea: "Mitterrand was forty-five minutes late, as was his habit, and people grew restless in the steaming heat. Then a glint of sunlight caught the approaching aircraft. Same Concorde. Same blue, white, and red flag in the cockpit window. And same reaction from the crowds. Socialist, schmocialist: *Vive la France.*"[40]

But French media do not probe Mitterrand's personal life; his long-time affair with Prime Minister Edith Cresson is little more than café conversation, not outrage. Opposition politician François D'Aubert did, however, call Cresson's appointment as prime minister "Pompadourian," referring to the Marquise de Pompadour, Louis XV's mistress and "favorite."

But humor and moderate backstabbing are not outrage and calls for resignation. Cresson, a glamorous extrovert, was named in a 1983 *Paris-Match* survey as one of twenty women (and the only politician) with whom French men would like to have an "aventure amoureuse."[41] However, her high rating may be a quirk in the French idea of beauty. In 1991, in an interview she gave four years earlier (but does not remember), she is alleged to have said that about one-fourth of English men were homosexuals and the remainder "were not interested in women." The import of her remarks was taken to mean that there was something culturally or biologically wrong with English men. Her complaint: "When strolling about in London men in the streets don't look at you. When you do this in Paris, men look at you." Thereupon the House of Commons entertained the motion: "This House does not fancy elderly French women."[42]

This cavalier attitude toward one's personal sexual preferences has no parallel in the United States, where the media delve relentlessly. Cresson, on another occasion, remarked that she regarded extramarital affairs as "amusing." By "amusing" she intended to say "interesting," or "diverting." One of the most amusing, in the sense of "funny" affairs was Valéry Giscard d'Estaing's early morning collision with a milk truck. Driving to the Elysée Palace after a late-night tryst, he ran head-on into a milk truck; but nothing was ever said about Giscard's poor driving. (How often does an American president drive himself?)

Americans have a more thoroughly developed sense of moral outrage (see Appendix). Nearly all Americans believe in God; and only 8 percent of Americans say that their belief in God is not very important in their lives. No European country approaches this level of religious commitment, except possibly Ireland. Five times as many Americans attend church at least once a month as do Japanese, and nearly twice as many Americans as do West Germans. While other effects of this American religiosity are difficult to identify (teen birth rates, for example, cannot be explained by this category), Americans are certainly more judgmental and moralistic than any of the European nations. Sixty-five percent of all Americans condemn homosexuality as unjustifiable. The next highest in this category are the Japanese at 52 percent, and no other population is above 50 percent. Sixty-four percent of Americans believe that extramarital affairs can never be justified. Besides the United States, only the United Kingdom squeaks in above 50 percent on this issue, and the French come in at a "shocking" 25 percent. For a nation supposedly based on freedom and equality by people escaping persecution, Americans are an intolerant and judgmental lot when it comes to private lives. A good example of the culture clash between the lenient Europeans and the censorious Americans occurs over smoking. There are few restrictions on smoking in Europe. Many hosts will routinely offer smoking material after a meal, and some of the genuinely memorable restaurants maintain a selection of cigars. French visitors, coming from a highly regulated society to the United States, known for its emphasis on individual liberties, are shocked by the intolerance of smoking.

I have encountered only one restaurant in Paris, "L'Ecluse," a chain of wine bars widely advertised in travel magazines, that has a no-smoking section. I watched with rueful amusement one night as a Parisian lit up, Americans protested, and the waiter treated them as if they were insane (an analogue would be objecting to jaywalking in New York)!

American Party Organizations as Chimeras

Another example of the degree to which institutions conform to the expectations of individuals is American party organizations, with rules changing frequently to aid or hinder a particular candidate. In 1984 backers of Walter Mondale hoped to benefit from the "super delegate" and "super Tuesday" rules, installed to benefit mainstream candidates. *Super delegates* were uncommitted delegates chosen because of electoral or party status, rather than by primary election. They preferred Mondale to Gary Hart. Super Tuesday (the South as a regional primary) was supposed to lift Mondale as it had Carter. It backfired and probably will disappear. In 1988 Jesse Jackson, seeking to parlay his delegate strength into the vice-presidency, settled for rule changes making his 1992 nomination more likely. Democratic primaries will allocate delegates by proportional representation rather than winner takes all, and there will be fewer super delegates. These constant rule changes, inevitable in the era of candidate-centered politics, further weaken the role of the party organization. As James Ceaser explains:

> The Democrats have altered their national party rules in an important way for each contest from 1972 through 1984. This instability has an unhealthy effect. The knowledge that the rules could be changed led prominent contenders to use their influence in the rules-writing process. Not only were the politics of the system candidate driven, but so too were the rules of the system itself.[43]

Fiddling with primary elections is an activity that does not engage the Democratic National Committee, but rather aspiring candidates. In 1975 Jimmy Carter, seeking to win an early engagement with George Wallace, persuaded Florida not to move its primary to a later date. In 1978 Carter's White House (*not* the Democratic National Committee) talked Mississippi, South Carolina, Oklahoma, Georgia, and Alabama into moving their primaries to March to get the president off to a good start. The Reagan operatives had a similar strategy in 1976: persuade South Carolina to hold its (first) primary earlier than other southern states, enabling Reagan to defeat, and thus demoralize, John Connally.[44] Rules are designed for candidates, not by the party organization and, therefore, "The National Democratic Party will be largely defined by its choice of Presidential nominee."[45]

Although American political parties fund only a small portion of a candidate's total electoral expenses, even fundraising is directly tied to candidates rather than to the party organization. "Soft money," designated as "party building," usually goes to registration and to get-out-the-vote efforts during the campaign. When parties lack attractive candidates, even the soft money is hard to get. In 1992, while the Republicans were easily raising money, the Democratic Party had no clear idea who its nominee might be. Democratic funding sources—as distinguished from those tied to a particular candidacy—remained passive. One such group, Impac, a consortium of Democratic party fundraisers, disbanded.

> Once there was an organization, but no longer. Thirty years ago, the party was anchored between presidential elections by the Democratic National Committee....Democratic national chairmen and chairwomen enjoyed great political power in their own right.[46]

Imagine the American response to John Taylor, a British Conservative Party candidate for Parliament in Cheltenham, a wealthy town that the Conservatives have won since 1950. Taylor, a black London attorney, was personally selected by party leader and Prime Minister John Major to try to broaden his party's base. Until chosen by Major, Taylor had never been to Cheltenham in rural western England. Once selected, Taylor went there every weekend. The local party members toyed with a rebellion, but the retiring member of Parliament (MP), Sir Charles Irving, rallied the party faithful around Mr. Taylor's candidacy. To select a candidate is to possess organizational power; American political parties do not have such power.

CONCLUSION

To simplify matters greatly at the acceptable risk of ignoring significant exceptions, we can say that American political culture is egalitarian, open, and individualist. In Germany and France, children's names require local government approval to prevent a parental whim from leading to future embarrassment. So "Zowie Bowie" would not have made it. Nor does "Schroeder," a common last name in Germany, which, since its appropriation as a first name by the

Beethoven-obsessed young pianist in the *Peanuts* comic strip, is prohibited in Germany. So are "Woodstock," "Pushkin," and "Hemingway." Can you imagine the American reaction to such an assault upon the individual?

The European political culture is elitist, closed, and collectivist. Consider the status of women (see Appendix). On a scale of 0 (unequal) to 100 (completely equal), American women score 83, compared with the European average of 76. American women discuss politics more than European women, and the difference between the proportions of women and men who discuss politics is smaller in the United States than in Europe. America has more divorces, and fewer traditional families, than does Europe, reflecting its more egalitarian approach to sexual equality.

American education sends twice as many to college, since it does not segregate on ability or impose national tests. As a result, Americans are also less literate, and our high school graduates invariably appear in a poor light compared to their European counterparts (see Appendix). The use of national tests, common in Europe and Japan, is still a controversial item in the United States. If one needs a concrete example of the differences between our egalitarian and their elitist education, consider these questions from the national high school examinations:

> France: "Explain the evolution of the debt of the developing countries. From whom are they borrowing?"
>
> Britain: "Unbelievably naive or a dogged man of principle: which verdict better characterizes the conduct of Woodrow Wilson from 1917 to 1920?"
>
> Germany: "St. Just was a close confidant of Robespierre. Discuss the role and significance of Robespierre later on in the Revolution. Both the American and French revolutions were world historical events. Choose one of the two and discuss its significance."

In American legislatures, state and national, inexperienced newcomers develop their own personal constituencies and issues, independent of political party organizations. As Herbert Gans writes:

> People hope [that organizations] will pursue the relevant values as if they were individuals, although few are surprised when this is not the case. As a consequence people distinguish between immoral organizations and moral individuals in them...whenever possible...they search for moral individuals in organizations with which they must deal.[47]

Table 1.4   Differences Between the European and American Systems

	United States	United Kingdom	France	West Germany
Government type	Separation of powers	Parliamentary	Mixed parliamentary	Parliamentary
	Federalist	Unitary	Unitary	Federalist
Party system	Weak	Very strong	Moderately strong	Strong
Interest groups	Extreme pluralism	Structured pluralism	Weak corporatism	Moderate pluralism
Electoral rules	Plurality	Plurality	Majority/ plurality	Proportional representation/ plurality

In Europe even experienced legislators, unless they are members of party policy committees or the cabinet, have little influence on policy. American politicians are, in the best American tradition, individual entrepreneurs. European politicians are more willing to abandon personal preferences to collective goals. American politicians nominate themselves; European ones are selected by party leaders.

Although American political parties were never as strong as European ones, they were once more influential than they are now. How can one talk about different political cultures, when "American exceptionalism," in its current extreme form, is a product of the last three decades? There is no clear answer. One suggestion is that American individualism is a slow, relentless pressure against hierarchy. Thus, gradually the institutions of hierarchy crumble. The Senate, once named by state legislatures, became popularly elected. The electoral college, once a legitimate selector of presidents, became a rubber stamp. Party machinery has followed the same path. Once presidents were chosen by a congressional caucus; then Andrew Jackson's revolt shifted power to state organizations. Finally, the reliance upon the primary election reduced the state party organizations to auxiliaries to personal organizations.

The differences between the European and American systems are displayed in Table 1.4.

These countries represent well the kinds of differences in political and governmental systems that we seek in comparing political organizations. Britain and West Germany are true parliamentary governments, with the executive selected from the majority (in Britain) or a majority coalition (in Germany) in the legislature. The United States is, of course, the best (and only) example of genuine separation of powers among the industrial democracies. France elects a president independently of the legislature, but allows him to dissolve the National Assembly and appoint and remove a prime minister. In Germany some instances of separation of power occur. Germany has a federal system, making it possible for opposition parties to build strength beneath the national level. The second house in the parliament, the Bundesrat, is appointed by the state governments. After a series of victories in state elections, the opposition Social Democrats were able to name a majority of members to the Bundesrat. For the first time since 1982, a portion of the national government was not controlled by the majority coalition—the Christian Democrats and Free Democrats. Now considered normal in the United States, divided government in Germany in 1991 threatened Germany with the debilitating deadlock that has characterized American government. Several government bills were blocked in the Bundesrat. In France, with a separately elected president, the national government experienced a divided party rule similar to that in Germany; the opposition coalition regained control of the National Assembly in 1986, and a prominent opposition leader, Jacques Chirac, became prime minister.

The electoral rules differ substantially. In the United States and England, a plurality ("first past the post") wins in legislative and presidential (in the U.S.) elections. In France, legislative elections must be won by a majority on the first try; if not, there is a second ballot in which a plurality wins. In French presidential elections, a majority (and thus a run-off) is required. In Germany, part of the legislature is elected by plurality and another part by proportional representation, in which a party's legislative seats are directly in proportion to its share of the popular vote. Missing among the countries is a pure proportional representation scheme. Italy will be used to illustrate this method. Additionally, Italy and Japan employ modes of candidate selection that are needed to round out the available options and thus will be considered in sections dealing with party organization. Other countries, Sweden, Denmark, Canada, and Australia, come in for more topical, less sustained treatment.

West Germany, like the United States, has a federal division of authority between state and national government, while France and Britain are unitary (legal power is concentrated in the national government). Unrepresented, however, is the strong mode of corporatism. Switzerland, a strong corporatist country, will serve as the case study here.

The theme of the book dictates its organization. The subject, political parties and interest groups, is one that compels attention. As will be underlined in greater detail later, these two principal kinds of political organizations are interposed between rulers and ruled for the purpose of *representation*, or *linkage*. In the chapters that follow, I examine political parties and interest groups with a view toward explaining a paradox: these organizations need not be internally democratic to contribute to regime stability. The journey takes us through the role of political parties in recruiting candidates for public office, campaigning for their election, and regulating their behavior in office. Interest groups do not ostensibly engage in these efforts; rather, they supplement political parties by offering a different basis of representation.

In comparing the United States with the other industrial democracies, I hold up a system with a powerful inclination against intervening organizations to those with equally strong biases against political entrepreneurs. The conclusion asks the awkward question, so what? Do strong political organizations provide strong linkage? Do they provide policy stability?

CHAPTER **2.**

Inventing the
People

Paolo Fabbri, who discourses at the Sorbonne at the Institute of the History of the French Revolution, is among the best lec-
turers on the idea of "the people." Fabbri avows there aren't any
people; that "the people" is a phrase invented and used by whomever it suits for whatever cause they intend. His case in point is the
French Revolution, although the use of "the people" is omnipresent,
irrespective of cause or ideology.

Fabbri argues that, at least in the eyes of the leaders of the Revolution, those who liked the monarch or went to church were simply
not "the people." As a result, the revolutionaries destroyed as many
of those (non) people as they could. The French revolutionists were
inventing the people.[1] The Roman *populus*, a term denoting those subject to the government, became *le peuple*, small businessmen, gro-
cers, artisans, workers, servants, peasants, or "the poor" (*le petite
peuple*).

THE SEARCH FOR THE PEOPLE

Political philosophers wish to maintain this distinction, arguing that
there is the idea of the people as conveyed in "government of the

people, by the people, for the people," and in the Marxist-Leninist throwback to the French Revolution, with people becoming *some* people (the proletariat and its allies). Even so, the distinction is facile, for irrespective of usage, "the people" describes a phantom.

A few years before Robespierre invented the people, the colonists in the American Revolution did precisely the same thing. They invented the *idea* of the American people: "...it is the Right of the People." Given their political philosophy, the authors of the American Constitution probably thought of people in a decidedly exclusive sense. Like the Greeks, the American constitutional architects did not regard slaves as (political) people.

Still, at least if we give legitimacy to squatters' rights, revolutionary causes have more of a stake in the phrase. As Richard Pipes sees it, the finest people inventors were the Bolsheviks, who took their text from the French[2]:

> Nowhere is this penchant for creating one's own reality more apparent and more pernicious than in the intelligentsia's conception of the people. Radicals insist on speaking for and acting for the people (sometimes described as the popular masses) against the alleged self-seeking elite in control of the state and the nation's wealth. In their view, the establishment of a just and free society requires the destruction of the status quo. But contact with the people of flesh and blood quickly reveals that few if any of them want their familiar world to be destroyed: what they desire is satisfaction of specific grievances, that is, partial reform, with everything else remaining in place. It has been observed that spontaneous rebellions are conservative rather than revolutionary, in that those involved usually clamor for the restitution of rights of which they feel they have been unjustly deprived: they look backward. In order to promote its ideal of comprehensive change, the intelligentsia must, therefore, create an abstraction called the people to whom it can attribute its own wishes.[3]

One colorful exception to the rule is Fidel Castro. "When we speak of the people," he wrote, "we do not mean the conservative elements.... The people we counted on in our struggle were these: 700,000 Cubans without work...500,000 farm laborers...400,000 industrial workers...100,000 small farmers."[4] In good Marxist fashion, Castro limited the range of the people to the proletariat. His explicitness was unusual.

The American "People": From Andrew Jackson to Jesse Jackson

However, inventing the people is not an activity confined solely to revolutionaries. The American populist tradition, too, has its special "people." For Thomas Jefferson, "people" were agrarian land-owners, urban dwellers being "sores" and "cankers"; Andrew Jackson kept the farmers in his definition, but expanded "the people" to include cankers and sores; that is, urban artisans and mechanics. The turn of the century progressives forgot the original agrarian component and defined their people as the urban working class.[5] Each definition added and subtracted. Andrew Jackson's people, for instance, were emphatically not blacks or Indians. Jackson was absolutely driven about Indian removal and cultivated racial intolerance in elections with the finesse of a Bilbo, Duke, Talmadge, or any of a number of southern populists—racists.

In recent history, one of the best examples of inventing the people comes from the United States. From the passage of the Civil Rights Act in 1965 until the resignation of Richard Nixon in 1974, the slogan "power to the people" rocked (or at least created the impression of rocking) American college campuses. "The people," in this case unquestionably did not include the rich, and not many of Andrew Jackson's people either. This embodiment of the people had at its core the exact category banished by Andrew Jackson and delineated by Jesse Jackson. Does that mean that the rich were not people? Of course not. It means merely that they are a part of a different group of people.

In 1991 Congress, in considering more revisions to civil rights legislation, attempted to overturn judicial decisions making it difficult for those seeking relief from discrimination in employment to win. President Bush had vetoed a similar bill the previous year, alleging it to have established a quota system for hiring and promotion. In denying Bush's allegation, Representative Don Edwards (Democrat, California) explained that "the people's rights are being denied." A few weeks later, when Utah's legislature passed a tough antiabortion law, Karrie Galloway, Executive Director of Planned Parenthood of Utah, announced a court challenge: "This really has come down to the legislature and the governor vs. the people." As James Morone, with commendable understatement, concludes, "It was not obvious who belonged to the community of the people and who did not. ...The image of the people and their shared interest has been constructed in many fanciful ways."[6]

POLITICAL ORGANIZATIONS AND INVENTING THE PEOPLE

Inventing the people is what political organizations do best. Without political organizations, the emotionally bracing phrase "of the people, by the people, for the people" would be *completely* without meaning. Edmund Morgan observes that:

> Sober thought may tell us that all governments are of the people, that all profess to be for the people, and that none can literally be by the people. But sober thought will tell us also that the sovereignty of the people, however fictional, *has worked.*[7]

Furthermore, without political organizations to constrain individualism, inventing the people ("linkage" in the language of political science) becomes, at best, haphazard. James Burns sets forth the thesis that individual leadership, without a firm grounding in political organizations, is inadequate.[8] Individual leaders, no matter how enlightened or benevolent, invent the people to suit their images and needs. The point about individuals and organizations as inventors of people is well put by David Broder:

> In the last 40 years, we have seen the steady decline of the political party organizations that *once served as links between local citizens and governments at all levels*. Do elected officials no longer hear or heed what citizens think? It is largely because the political networks, from precinct captains to county and state chairmen, that *once carried the message*, no longer exist.[9]

"The People" have not always had a voice in government. For thousands of years in China, the Emperor ruled not because the people approved but because he claimed to be the Son of Heaven. The same can be said of Western kings who claimed to rule by divine right. If no linkage between rulers and ruled existed, as was true in those times, there could be no "people." The job of political organizations is to make the fiction of "the people" credible. Other justifications for governing—superior intelligence or training, an obligation to serve—need other fictions. Bureaucrats, especially European ones (and American educational administrators), today assert claims that require no "people" to justify their authority. They, like Marxists, claim to know the people's needs even if the people do not:

> The task of leaders is not to put into effect the wishes and will of the masses. . . . The task of the leaders is to accomplish the interests of the masses. Why do I differentiate between the will and the interests of the masses? In the recent past we have encountered the phenomenon of certain categories of workers acting against their interests.[10]

Leaders of political organizations do not invent people cynically. They invent them by the *act* of speaking for them. One level of invention is to romanticize the people, a common error made by those who earn their living by writing about public affairs. View this critique of a recent made-for-TV movie about Lieutenant Colonel Oliver North:

> The man portrayed in the CBS movie "Guts and Glory: The Rise and Fall of Oliver North" was a cartoon caricature of the man I knew and worked with....The title alone was prejudicial. Most viewers have probably forgotten that the original use of the "rise and fall" phrase belongs to Gibbon's history of Rome. Many may associate it only with William L. Shirer's history of the Third Reich.[11]

Most viewers had not forgotten about Gibbon; they had never heard of him. Nor did they associate the title with Shirer. The author was inventing people because she needed more justification. It is not enough to say, "I think CBS was playing fast and loose with the facts." One must affirm that the people have been deceived.

Another journalist invents people who "desire a foreign policy that is didactic or therapeutic, instructing and curing difficult regimes." It is safe to surmise that "the people" who are said to want a didactic foreign policy are different folk from those in whose name the "power to the people" campaign was waged, or even the same people that were lied to about Oliver North. They are a different people, invented for a different purpose. They are also different from the people invented by Chairman of the House Agriculture Committee Congressman E. (Kiki) La Garza: "the unique nature of agriculture—the lengthy production cycle, dependency on the weather, susceptibility to price swings, etc.—justifies a certain level of government involvement."[12]

Yet another set of people appears in Debra Saunders' indictment of the American Democrats. The Democrats lost because the American people understood their agenda too well. They may elect Democrats to Congress, but they know that Democratic presidents mean big government, huge tax hikes, and mushy foreign policy.[13] Presumably, her people aren't La Garza's, since they appear to possess radically different philosophies.

Politics and Everyday Life

Max Weber's apt depiction of most people as "occasional politicians" fits well with this colloquy.[14] Most of us vote (at least occasionally), and sometimes even argue about politics. More often than not, however, our waistlines, credit limits, bank balances, and love lives extract more anxiety and contentment than do the public policies that so vex our leaders. Every so often, however, there are no people. They need to be invented. Just as the divine right of kings provided legitimacy for earlier governments, "the people" legitimize today's governments. Edmund Morgan clarifies:

> Government requires make-believe....Make believe that people *have* a voice or make believe that the representatives of the people *are* the people....The fiction that replaced the divine right of kings [the people] is our fiction, and it accordingly seems less fictional to us.[15]

LINKAGE

Political scientists call inventing the people a *linkage*. Political organizations link people with policy, and elites with masses. The linkage may be one of *policy, personnel,* or *process.*[16]

Policy Linkage

Policy linkages are the most crucial as well as the most conceptually and empirically demanding. For this linkage to occur, five conditions are indispensable:

1. Competing parties must offer clear policy alternatives.
2. Voters must be concerned about policy.
3. Election results must clarify majority preferences on these matters.
4. Elected officials must be bound by the positions they assume during the campaigns.
5. Elected officials must have the institutional power to implement their commitments.[17]

An extraordinary quantity of conceptual skill and energy is asked of elites and masses. Elites must develop, refine, and articulate visions of the good life. Presumably, each party's aspirations must be sufficiently distinct from the others', making it apparent to voters that alternate futures are, while not necessarily mutually exclusive, at least worthy of commitment.

The Quandary of Change and Stability.   Additionally, the discrete futures should not be so variant that they appear revolutionary. If all hell breaks loose, provided the other side wins, any continuity of policy will be lost and the decision costs of elite replacement will be too great. Elites—partisan activists—sometimes *believe* that all hell will break loose, especially during the heat of a campaign. However, campaign rhetoric disguises a durable consensus in the industrial democracies. Thus Joseph and Mildred Schlesinger praise France:

> The Fifth Republic's most impressive accomplishment is its solution to the problems of political parties that plagued its predecessors. Unlike its predecessors, the Fifth Republic has a party system capable of performing the basic task asked of parties in a democracy—the production of alternative stable governing majorities.[18]

The authors compress policy linkage into a single task: recurrent stable majorities; that is, the replacement of a government that didn't satisfy with one that might. This is a difficult line to tread. Socialist and conservative parties in Europe can nationalize or privatize a bit, but they can hardly abandon all connections with the antecedent policy. Major rhetorical breaks with the past in England in 1979 or France in 1981 are just that. The problem of understanding change is a serious one, especially when ideologically driven candidates like Ronald Reagan, Margaret Thatcher, and François Mitterrand win with commitments to major change. (Mrs. Thatcher, when asked what she intended to change, responded: "Everything, I intend to change everything.") John Keeler, defining reform as either a substantial redirection or reinforcement of previous policy, shows that, at least initially, reform occurs. Mitterrand, a Socialist, extended the nationalization of France's already heavily nationalized industrial section; Thatcher, a fierce opponent of public ownership, began an equally ambitious privatization program.[19]

Moderately different programs to realize the same goals are more valence (affect or symbol) than not, but European political parties are infinitely more programmatic than those in the United States or Japan.[20] William Crotty calls American parties "nonideological, nonprogrammatic, and nonissue oriented," while European ones are "ideological, programmatic, and issue oriented."[21]

Thus, while all hell does not break loose in Europe when one party replaces another, there is some discernible difference. In the United Kingdom, had the Conservatives not won in 1983, there would have been, according to Richard Rose, marginally less unemployment, marginally more economic growth, and about a 3 percent higher rate of inflation.[22] Can one describe what would have been different had not Ronald Reagan won in 1980? Possibly a smaller budget deficit without the tax cuts; surely less money wasted in lost-cause foreign policy schemes. Certainly, there are idiosyncratic behaviors associated with each presidency: Richard Nixon's mental instability and Watergate; Lyndon Johnson's megalomania and Vietnam; Ronald Reagan's disassociative habits and the Iran-Contra scandal. Different people would have reacted differently. Reagan's exchange of domestic spending for a vast military buildup, based upon his belief in "the evil empire," certainly held the headlines for several years.

But what endures? The dramatic accomplishment of the largest tax reduction in U.S. history was followed in 1986 by a tax reform based on a different philosophy. The 1981 tax laws reduced business taxes and the top rates of individual income taxes. Once this legislation was in place, Reagan proposed the elimination of tax shelters. The winners in 1986 were the poor, because the new law doubled the personal deduction; the losers in 1986 were businesses, the big winners in 1981.[23] Because the 1986 tax legislation is often regarded as the single exception to Reagan's loss of the domestic initiative, it is noteworthy that it was a U-turn from the 1981 legislation. Not only did the 1986 tax legislation help the poor, but Reagan could not cut back on welfare programs, the "safety net" that he promised to honor. There were marginal changes in 1981, but the Democrats in the House and Senate sustained the safety net. The net was not expanded, but it did not disappear. Thus, "as dramatic as Reagan's successes were in his first year, they were not followed by comparable domestic policy successes during the remainder of his administration."[24] Not surprisingly, while taxes as a proportion of the gross national product declined slightly, overall government spending increased during the Reagan years. Reagan made some changes, largely incremental, and largely accepted by the Democrats.

But the tax cuts and budget deficits were approved by a Democratic House and Senate. So which *political party* do you blame or praise? Additionally, there was never a Democratic alternative. In addition to the cooperation by House Democrats, Jimmy Carter repeatedly called the welfare system a "disgrace." Both candidates favored a smaller role for government in economic life, and Carter's statements were "surely in a more conservative than liberal direction."[25] Nevertheless, Carter lost support among moderate voters and among weak liberal voters. In spite of the tenor of his remarks, he gained among the strong liberal voters.

The Fairness Issue and the Reagan Presidency.   The Reagan presidency provides a good opportunity for making the point about the impotence of political parties, and the largely symbolic consequences of the presidency. The most widely heard charge in the post-Reagan years was that, because of his tax cuts, the rich got richer and the poor got poorer. This was the central theme of Kevin Phillips' "briefcase book," *The Politics of Rich and Poor* (so called because of its popularity with Democratic members of Congress).[26] He writes, "The share of wealth held by the 'super-rich'...has risen sharply in the last decade after falling for forty years."[27] Forty years ago the super-rich had either 19.3 percent or 22.7 percent. In 1983 they had 26.9 percent. Rather than "falling for forty years," the percentage rambled up and down: increases were recorded in 1956, 1965, and 1983. The biggest decrease was from 1972, when Nixon was elected; the latest rise occurred in 1976, when Carter took office. Another distinct surge was from 1962 to 1965 (Kennedy-Johnson). So there is no trend, much less one that would operate to the Democrats' advantage.

Income distributions do not vary with the election of Democrats or Republicans. Phillips, in talk-show appearances, drew our attention to a *Times-Mirror* survey, *The People, the Press, and Politics 1990*, which showed a tripling (from 18 to 51 percent) since 1957 of those who believe the Republican Party has become the party of "the rich and monied interests."[28] However, the *Times-Mirror* subsequently issued an erratum; the actual increase was from 18 to 21 percent. Phillips conceded that as the Democrats are now popularly regarded as incapable of governing, they could not exploit this weakness. But he did not mention a question more directly related to his thesis. Respondents were asked about the statement, "It's really true the rich get rich and the poor get poorer." The percentage completely agreeing increased only modestly, from 31 percent in 1987 to 38 percent currently. For once, "the people" have a firm grasp on reality.

A much more reliable book on this subject, Frank Levy's *Dollars and Dreams: The Changing American Income Distribution*, does not support Phillips' thesis.[29] Written so that, in David Broder's words, "Even a journalist can understand him," Levy says, "From 1947 to 1969 income inequality across families declined modestly; from 1970 to 1979 it increased modestly, and from 1980 to 1984 it increased more sharply. But the most obvious feature of postwar family *income distribution was its stability*."[30] Levy's Gini Coefficients (measuring deviation from "perfect equality," or 0) declined from .38 in 1947 to .35 in 1969 and climbed to .39 in 1984.[31] Have you ever seen a better example of stability? Phillips, who cites Levy's book, ignores Levy's central finding. Furthermore, the "Reagan aftermath" could be renamed the "Nixon, Ford, Carter aftermath," since, again, the pattern, albeit modest, began a decade before Reagan took office.

Levy also says, "Unlike the stability of the family income distribution, the income distribution of unrelated individuals shows a modest trend toward greater equality throughout the postwar period. This reflects the growing number of prime-age workers who live as unrelated individuals."[32] Levy, of course, corrects for taxes, in-kind government, private benefits, and family size, and concludes that forty years ago the richest quintile earned 39.3 percent, whereas in 1984 it earned 36.8 percent of total national income. He does find that in 1979 the richest quintile earned 34 percent, thus supporting the moderate inclination mentioned before.

At the other end of the scale, the poorest quintile went from 5.8 percent forty years ago to 7.3 percent. The proportion of income going to this group peaked in 1979 (8.7 percent). Levy asserts that two factors influenced this most recent shift: (1) the 1981 tax legislation reduced rates, but did not change exemptions and deductions much, and (2) the inflation that started in 1978 had totaled 48 percent by 1984. Thus, the lowest quintile paid more taxes because its income exceeded its exemptions and deductions. The tax system had already become less progressive over the 1970s.[33]

While the Democrats could follow Phillips into his call for a populist rebellion, how would they (and he) explain the impact of the inflation (1978) and the Democratic support for the 1981 tax changes? How about the long-term trend away from progressive taxation? Taxing and spending responsibility has not been surrendered by the House Democrats.

Less populist, simple-minded inquiries show that there are factors that operate without even the most remote pretense from government of its ability to control them. Among the more inelastic are: (1) the growth in female headed families; (2) the exacerbation of the income gap between older and younger men (because the size of the baby-boom cohort and because younger workers no longer have a substantial educational edge over older workers); and (3) the rise in two-earner families *and* no-earner families. Two-earner families reflect the rise of women's labor force participation (in the top two quintiles, 60 percent of the families have two earners; in the bottom quintile, 44 percent of the families have *no* earners).

Entirely consistent with these findings is the 1990 Census Bureau's annual report on poverty. Noting that "income distribution has become somewhat less equal over the past 20 years" (so much for Phillips's claim that inequality has "risen sharply in the last decade"), the report said the reasons for the rise in inequality are "not entirely clear," and suggested: (1) growth in elderly population; (2) an increase in the number of people living alone; and (3) the escalation of female-headed families.

So there is no sharp increase in the gap between rich and poor; the slight rise since 1984 is a consequence of a multitude of factors, most of which are beyond anybody's reach. The current rise in superrich income is the *fifth* example of the phenomenon since 1922

(1929: Hoover; 1939: Roosevelt; 1956: Eisenhower; 1965: Johnson; 1983: Reagan). In fact, with the tax legislation of 1986, which sacrificed business tax preferences, favorable treatment of capital gains, and tax shelters for wealthy taxpayers, Reagan could stake a claim to "populist conservatism," in the George Wallace tradition, since the poor were the biggest winners, and the rich the biggest losers.[34]

If we look at comparative data, the "populist rebellion" comes into sharper focus. The U.S. government reduces inequality by 14 percent, second only to the United Kingdom. And proportionally, we have fewer billionaires than West Germany. Our Gini Coefficients are hardly excessive. Indeed, they are lower than those of France and West Germany, where government reduces income by 4 and 9 percent, respectively. Since Phillips can hardly assert that Reagan had something to do with income distribution in other industrial democracies, he should admit that income distribution does not respond to the whims of an American president:

> The popular notion that miserly government welfare and social insurance payments caused the increase in inequality [that is, the modest one reported by Levy] is untrue; aggregate government transfer payments did not decline in the 1980s (in any event these payments have little to do with overall income distribution). Nor is there any evidence that income taxation has any significant effect on the distribution of income. Before-tax and after-tax income distributions are nearly identical.[35]

The problem is not uniquely American (British and French policy also have their U-turns), but our weakened parties, decentralized Congress, and separation of powers generate more paralysis than is true in the other industrial democracies:

> Although the President was able to check the growth of safety-net programs, he was not able to really cut them back; the outcome was to stabilize the programs as they had evolved by 1980. Except for marginal changes made in 1981, a Democratically controlled House and a combination of Democrats and moderate Republicans in the Senate fought vigorously to sustain safety net programs....Democrats were unable to expand the safety net, but the Reagan administration...could not reduce them or change their design.[36]

There were losers beyond businesses and the rich. Programs that had lost their support among Democrats in Congress—energy, the environment, transportation, housing, law enforcement, scientific research, health education, employment training, and aid to state and local governments—saw their proportion of the budget decline from 24 to 15 percent in 1980. These are genuine changes, but they required the collaboration of the Democrats. These programs will edge their way back.

Can Anybody Find Our Rascals? Within a few weeks after the 1990 budget was approved, the Congressional elections followed. The budget had raised taxes, even though President Bush had pledged "no new taxes" during the 1988 campaign. He had changed his mind. Media hype abounded: "Throw the rascals out." But which rascals? The President did not need to seek reelection. How about those members of Congress who had gone along with new taxes? Ah, here are some rascals. Yet, many members of the president's party—including Minority Whip Newt Gingrich of Georgia—voted against the budget because it included new taxes. Most Democrats— the "opposition"—supported the budget. But they trashed Bush and the Republicans for refusing to "soak the rich" (they referred to a wholly symbolic surtax on millionaires).

Then Bush, seeking to help his Republican colleagues in their efforts to be reelected, for whatever reason, hit the campaign trail. He lambasted as irresponsible the Democrats who had supported and enacted the budget, while campaigning for Republicans who had opposed it. So, assume a rational voter. Assume further that this voter, wishing to cast a sane vote, had followed the budget vote closely. Which party, or which candidate, would our voter select? A voter splenetic over the budget mess would have no clear choice. Therefore, 96 percent of incumbents were returned to office. I am not suggesting that voters, frustrated by governmental fragmentation, throw up their hands in despair. Since most of them cannot identify the party in control of the Senate or House, and because, when it is explained, they generally like separation of powers, such a supposition makes little sense. The point is simply that even if voters were informed and angered by fiscal irresponsibility, they could not locate and, hence, retroactively punish the guilty.

Some scholars have given up trying to compare American presidential elections with European ones and have, for good institutional reasons, used congressional elections instead.[37] One could hardly expect Americans to see significant differences between the two major parties, and indeed they do not. Actually, with consummate good sense, they do not care one way or another about them.[38]

Reagan, Thatcher, and Dissimilar Stable Majorities

Consider the rise to prominence of Ronald Reagan. Reagan won because he was a congenial man, and because so many people disliked Jimmy Carter. One cannot claim that Carter was disliked without any policy justifications. The energy crisis, the hostage catastrophe, and double-digit inflation certainly did not help. Even Reagan, after his first two years in office, was dreadfully low in the polls because the economy had not turned around. Still, unlike Reagan, Carter was stiff, without a discernible sense of humor, and maddeningly self-righteous. Presumably, had things gone swimmingly, he would not have lost his bid for reelection. Supposedly, had things not improved immensely for Reagan, he would have lost in 1984.[39] None of this has anything to do with the shifts to the right that supposedly existed in the electorate.

Now consider British Prime Minister Margaret Thatcher. Although Mrs. Thatcher's monetarist domestic policies attracted comparison with Reagan's ideology, her personality remains altogether different. Mrs. Thatcher was decidedly *not* pleasant. Nor was she popular, being surpassed only by Edward Heath among postwar prime ministers in *un*popularity.[40] However, she had to persuade only the Conservative members of Parliament to elect her. Although Mrs. Thatcher was more disliked than most prime ministers, she was not exceptional. British prime ministers do not achieve the pinnacles of adoration that American presidents expect. The average level of support for prime ministers is 46 percent, compared with 53 percent for American presidents. Mrs. Thatcher's average, 40 percent, was lower than that of any American president, yet she led the party to three successive victories.[41] Her career shows the soundness of Richard Rose's assertion:

> The focus of media attention upon party leaders is mistakenly treated as evidence that party competition has been reduced to competition between the personalities who lead the parties. This is not so. Voters form their judgments of parties *before* a particular politician becomes its leader. . . . Conservative supporters tend to support whoever is conservative leader, and Labour supporters to like whoever is elected Labour leader. . . . In America, by contrast, a much larger proportion of the electorate chooses a candidate without regard to party label.[42]

Nonetheless, a key ingredient in the Thatcher defeat was the multitude of surveys showing that were she replaced (by either John Major or Michael Heseltine), the Conservatives would regain their lead over Labour. Yet, contrary to American counterparts, after she was replaced, the coalition that supported her did not disintegrate. The contrary occurred. She lost the leadership to John Major for several reasons. She was unwilling to recant on the community charge, or poll tax, which imposed (theoretically) a local tax on all citizens despite income. Even her supporters called it "the worst tax reform in Britain's history."[43] She was also intransigent about constitutional reform (devolving power to the regions, changing the voting system from plurality to proportional representation, reducing government secrecy), and furious about the direction of European unity. But Major is a "Thatcherite" and was her choice for a successor had she been allowed to finish her third term of office.

The United Kingdom's strong party discipline does not produce clones. Major, given the sobriquet "Mannock" (a contraction of his name and Labour leader Neil Kinnock's, derived from the earlier "Butskell," a contraction of Conservative "Rab" Butler and Labour's Hugh Gaitskell) by *The Economist*, allowed Cabinet Minister Michael Heseltine full authority to jettison the poll tax. Bush, aware of the futility of continuing Reagan's funding of the Nicaraguan Contras, dropped them like hot potatoes six months after inauguration. It is, however, probable that a Conservative Party power shuffle would result in less of a policy shift than a change in the American Executive would cause within his own party.

Reagan left office as he entered, beloved of the people. He suffered major erosions in popular affections because of the Iran-Contra scandal, but bounced back easily. The British electorate presumably does not care whether its prime minister is pleasant. More properly, since the electorate does not directly elect the prime minister, it does not really matter if it likes him or her or not. Again, there is no point in reaching for extremes; the Conservatives also win because the opposition is, seemingly permanently, divided between Labour and the Liberal Democrats. Also, under Thatcher, the Conservatives had been consistently trailing Labour in the polls; but once she was replaced, the Conservatives (temporarily) shot past Labour. Personality is not *entirely* unrelated to a party's electoral fortunes. For the American electorate, image is really all there is. Mrs. Thatcher, saying the same things in the same way to an American electorate, would have been clobbered (One need hardly add that Reagan would never have been elected Conservative Party leader, nor would he have lasted six months in Mrs. Thatcher's workaholic environment.)

The Myth of the Policy Mandate. A similarity that both leaders share is that neither could point with any legitimacy to a policy *mandate*. The American electorate did not shift to the right to elect Reagan, and the British electorate is hardly Thatcherite stylistically.[44] As Ivor Crewe and Donald Searing conclude:

On the issues connected with the core Thatcherite values of strong government and discipline—immigration control, trade union reform, the
death penalty, crime, pornography—the electorate held Thatcherite positions before the Conservative party did....By appealing on these
grounds Mrs. Thatcher served her party, as Disraeli did a century earlier, by discerning potential supporters as the sculptor discerns an angel
in a block of marble.[45]

Crewe and Searing get right to the matter: could anyone, other
than the most shameless sycophant, declare such things about
Reagan? Surely not. Morris Fiorina, noting that "mass attitudes toward public policy issues have long been known to be ill-formed and
unstable," asks no more than a less articulate shift toward conservatism during the Reagan years. But the shift is not there. Compare
Fiorina on Reagan with Crewe and Searing on Thatcher:

There is little doubt that conservative elites are brimming with self-
confidence while liberal elites are full of doubt and disillusionment....
But there is good reason to believe that recent years have seen considerably more change on the elite level than in the mass electorate. There is
always some information in the electoral signals, but it typically is over-
interpreted and misunderstood by overreactive elites.[46]

It is easy to see how the myth of the conservative shift in American politics became popular. The electorate was trying to put the economically disastrous Carter years behind it and needed to hear that
its government was really changing its ideology. The fact remains,
however, that no conservative shift actually occurred. Most intriguing is Wattenberg's discovery that most people had no idea of what
had or had not happened during the Reagan years. He remarks
about the "startling lack of knowledge" and a "distressingly low
level of public information."[47] The evidence that caused his distress is
this: less than 30 percent of those interviewed were aware of the
spending cuts in funding for the environment, assistance to the
poor, and education. All told, less than 2 percent both knew about
and approved these cuts!

Table 2.1 shows the distribution of the American population on a
seven-point scale, so designed that a minimum of sagacity is required. A respondent does not have to explain anything, merely select a number from most liberal (1) to most conservative (7).

Plainly, there has been no shift in the American voters' preference for conservative or liberal candidates, since there was little shift
in ideology during the Reagan revolution. As Richard Niemi, John
Mueller, and Tom Smith conclude: "There has been remarkably little
change in the distributions over the past fifteen years, despite the

Table 2.1   Liberal or Conservative Self-Identification (percent)

	1	2	3	4	5	6	7
1976	2	13	12	37	15	13	2
1980	2	8	14	40	18	12	3
1984	2	9	12	39	19	13	3
1988	2	12	13	35	17	15	2

"Filtered" on whether or not respondent had given thought to his or her answer:

	1	2	3	4	5	6	7
1976	1	7	8	25	12	11	2
1980	2	6	9	20	13	13	2
1984	2	8	9	23	14	13	2

Source: Adapted from Richard G. Niemi, John Mueller, and Tom W. Smith, *American Public Opinion* (New York: Greenwood Press, 1989), pp. 19-21.

Reagan victories on an explicitly conservative agenda and the success with which George Bush painted Michael Dukakis's liberalism as a strongly negative feature."[48] Political parties, if they are responsible, can reduce information costs and allow people to behave as if they cared about politics. But this does not occur in the United States, where political elites so closely conform to Selden's characterization. Thus, when the "filter" was used to ascertain ideology, about one-fourth did not know or had not thought about the matter. ("Filtering" is the process of isolating those for whom ideology is a meaningless term.) Even when people think about politics, which is rare and usually during recessions, international confrontations, and (less so) elections, they do not concentrate their minds on political parties. On more explicit, less abstract, measures of belief, the Reagan revolution is equally a bust. For example, in 1978, 19 percent wanted the government to reduce income differences. An unnoticeable decline of 2 percent occurred in 1980 when Reagan won the election, but rebounded to 21 percent when he won again in 1984.[49] Even those who discern a shift to the right in 1980 find a shift to the left four years later when Reagan was reelected.[50] In fairness to the American voter, European voters are, while more informed and sophisticated, willing to adopt a supple posture concerning ideology. Thus, Mitterrand's "socialist" triumph in 1981 was followed by the famous "U-turn" three years later, when he became a Monetarist like Thatcher in England and eventually won reelection in 1988. Even Europe's most famous ideologue, Margaret Thatcher, did not author a revolution in popular ideology.

Why Mrs. Thatcher Lost.   Even with the simplicity of a parliamentary system, policy linkage is illusive. In parliamentary systems, especially with a "first past the post" vote-tallying method, policy linkage seems more assured. A plurality of voters in a majority of districts elect a political party that, because it has a legislative majority, selects a prime minister.

Yet, recent evidence suggests that the British electorate not only did not move as far right as previously thought, but may now be moving farther left than it was to begin with. Ivor Crewe writes:

> Between 1974 and 1979 the electorate grew slightly more conservative about pornography, modern teaching methods, racial equality, sexual equality, and the availability of welfare benefits. But between 1979 and 1987 public sentiment reversed direction. The proportion of social conservatives fell by 33 percent on "the availability of welfare benefits," 14 percent on "changes toward modern teaching methods," 11 percent on "attempts to ensure equality for women," 10 percent on "nudity and sex in films and magazines," 8 percent on "the availability of abortion on the N.H.S.," and 4 percent on "challenges to authority." Over a similar period support for the return of capital punishment—surely the core of authoritarian populism—fell by 12 percent.[51]

As powerful as Margaret Thatcher, or any British prime minister, was, she had no more control over her voters than any other modern politician. Like every prime minister before her, she could only get away with so much before the electorate would vote her party out of power. This is precisely why the Conservatives replaced her. Survey after survey showed the Conservatives trailing Labour, with Thatcher as prime minister. *Without* her, the Conservatives enjoyed a substantial lead. Conservative party leaders who appear to be dragging the party to defeat find themselves relegated to the back bench. Mrs. Thatcher's alleged strong grass-roots support was not a factor. Little party democracy was involved, since the decision to remove her was made by the parliamentary party, with only slight regard for the opinions of constituency parties. Loss of *cabinet* support was fatal. Because Mrs. Thatcher never had much public support (that is, support beyond the members of the Conservative Party), a populist appeal would have been pointless.[52] Winston Churchill encapsulates the role and risks of the Conservative Party leader:

> The loyalties which centre upon number one
> are enormous. If he trips, he
> must be sustained. If he
> makes mistakes, they must be covered.
> If he sleeps
> he must not be wantonly disturbed.
> If he is no good
> he must be *poleaxed*.[53]

Mrs. Thatcher's defeat bears some resemblance to John Kennedy's 1960 election, in that party loyalty was a major factor in both events. Surveys showed Richard Nixon to be more popular than Kennedy, but the Democratic party leadership nominated Kennedy anyway. Nixon, more popular, lost because of party loyalty among Democratic voters, who at that time enjoyed a healthy lead over the Republicans.[54] Today, Nixon would not have lost. If England's politics were as candidate-centered as those in the United States, Thatcher would never have become prime minister. That she was removed by a cabal of old boys is, therefore, poetic justice.

The European Analogue to the American Obsession with Personality. In the United States the most important political qualification is personality. France has a system in which personality is almost as pivotal to electoral success as it is in the United States. As in the United States, France has an independently elected executive. Valéry Giscard d'Estaing, French president during the late 1970s, won initially as much for his telegenic persona as for his policies. He lost, not because of disillusionment with "advanced liberalism," but because he had become aloof and arrogant, and because the national economy had become stagnant (as was true everywhere except in Japan). François Mitterrand, who defeated Giscard, won not solely because of socialism but because he appeared sensible and reasonable. His reelection ratified his position as "tonton" ("uncle"), above the struggle and dignified. While there was some ideological support for Mitterrand's traditional socialism in the first election (1981), it evaporated quickly even as his personal popularity continued through his 1988 victory.

When reading of French politics, one encounters "Gaullism." This is understandable. After all, there is a Gaullist party, basking in the nostalgic glory of Le Grande Charles, father of the Fifth Republic; but there is also "Rocardism." Rocardism? Michel Rocard was the youngish Socialist prime minister. Why does he rate an "ism"?[55] Even more excessive is the appearance of the neo-Rocardians. Raymond Barre, prime minister under Giscard, coined "Barrism," the relentless pursuit of economic growth.

Or consider Jacques Chirac, Gaullist leader and mayor of Paris, about whom *Le Figaro* writes, "The neo-Gaullist planet is about to transform itself into a vague collection of stars more or less distanced from the others. But the center of gravitation remains the mayor of Paris."[56]

Clearly, in the French system, personality is a part of the process. In France, as in America, there is a thriving cottage industry
among intellectuals on the subject of the decline of the legitimacy of
the political system.[57]

Although one hears grumbling about the Americanization of
politics throughout Europe, only in France has a semblance of our
media hype been achieved, because it has the only directly elected
president in Europe.

Perhaps the most trenchant comparison of the two systems is
that of their most recent scandals. In the United States, the Reagan
administration sanctioned an arms-for-hostages exchange, by which
Americans held hostage in the Middle East would be returned in exchange for weapons to be sold to Iran. The proceeds from the weapons sale went to fund the Nicaraguan Contras, in defiance of
congressional stipulation that no such money be spent. The entire
scheme was hatched without the support or participation of the established foreign policy bureaucracy. Oliver North, like Ronald
Reagan, viewed bureaucracy as part of the problem. The entire operation was conducted by an obscure shadow government, accountable only to itself. No cabinet official, either from defense or state,
was ever accused of participation; at worst, they were blamed for
their lukewarm and ineffective opposition.

The French *Rainbow Warrior* affair, while equally embarrassing,
was the opposite of the Iran-Contra scandal in origin. In 1985 two explosive charges sank the *Rainbow Warrior*, flagship of the Greenpeace
movement, as it moored in New Zealand in preparation for a protest
against French nuclear tests at Muruoroa. After initial silence and
denials, Prime Minister Laurent Fabius admitted France's guilt. The
head of intelligence was fired and Defense Minister Charles Hernu
took full blame and then resigned. Two French agents were sen-
tenced to ten years in prison. The usual press speculations were that
Prime Minister Fabius, and possibly even Mitterrand, knew and approved of the sabotage; but Giscard's muted "my country, right or
wrong" kept the issues from exploding. Irrespective of the extent of
knowledge by the president and prime minister, the *Rainbow Warrior*
affair was bureaucratic in origin and collective in resolution. A minister of defense, not a "cowboy" like Oliver North, was held accountable. Perhaps most importantly, the *Rainbow Warrior* affair was
effectively covered up and forgotten.

Finally, even with the French obsession with personality, one
does not encounter the lusty search for intimate detail that has come
to typify American media. In 1987 Gary Hart's affair with Donna

Rice ruined his chances for the Democratic nomination, in 1991 *People* magazine reported on Senator Edward Kennedy's inappropriate sexual behavior at a popular Washington restaurant, La Brasserie. In the same year, his brother John's sexual exploits were paraded before us in far greater detail than ever before (David Niven's wife complained that the president eschewed foreplay). Mrs. Reagan's alleged affair with Frank Sinatra was front-page news, and even Dwight Eisenhower's wartime dalliance with Kate Summersby was resurrected (including Ike's "difficulty in consummating the affair"). Are American politicians unusually immoral or are European ones more shielded in their personal lives? Surely the latter is true. European politicians are no less likely than American politicians to "play the field," but one looks in vain for biographies that recount sexual exploits.

At a less erotic but equally personal level, the American media now makes stories out of public figures' propensities for crying. In this enterprise they are aided by the politicians themselves. From Bush, in 1988, we hear, "Did you know that we had to sit there and watch a child wrenched from our hearts in six months of cancer, knowing that she was going to die?" In 1991 Bush told a gathering of Southern Baptists that he had "prayed and cried" before sending Americans into battle against Iraq. Public crying is virtually *de rigueur*, but Bush need not have divulged his most personal moments, and would not have done so had he not seen some political advantage in so doing. Few, if any, European politicians share such occasions.

Policy Linkage and Meaningful Choice

Elections are meant to provide a voter with "meaningful choice," and the instruments by which such preference is accomplished are political parties. Unless the choice is to be purely idiosyncratic— solely due to whomever is running—parties should provide some sense of continuity. They should be larger than the personalities that, at a given moment, symbolize or represent them publicly. The point is not a sententious one. Presumably there was some discernible difference between, for example, Michael Dukakis and George Bush.

Although there was almost nothing of substance in their deplorable campaigns, one can spot the occasional dissimilarity of opinion; Bush was opposed to abortions, Dukakis was not. Bush supported Reagan's Contra policy, Dukakis did not.

But what has any of this to do with political parties? During the campaign, the most often-mentioned issue was crime. An American President's role in crime and law enforcement in a federal system is minimal. Rather, Bush, like his Republican predecessors, contributed to the *politicization* of crime, but not to a feasible solution.[58] After the inauguration, the most often discussed issue was the deficit, a topic rarely encountered during the campaign. Crime in our federal system is largely a state and local matter, and Bush, as president, promptly put it on hold—along with most other aspects of the domestic agenda. On the matter of furloughs for prisoners, for example, only 8 percent of all prisoners are in federally administered prisons. Thus the president, even if he had an unconstrained hand, which he does not, could make at best a tiny dent in the furlough program.

The Meaning of Meaningful.   Meaningful is, admittedly, an ambiguous word. That which is meaningful to a passionate Dukakis supporter or an equally zealous adherent of President Bush might seem like so much bumwad to me. Is the choice necessarily greater in countries with competitive systems—those with regular changes in personnel because of elections? The answer depends on perception. Consider American political parties. They are highly competitive; neither party enjoys an electoral monopoly for very long. In the recent past, the election of Franklin Roosevelt in 1932, and his three subsequent reelections, caused thoughts about the destruction of the Republican Party. Notwithstanding, the Republican Party maintained its roots in state government and recovered with the election of Eisenhower in 1952. With three consecutive presidential victories since 1980, it has created the same kinds of misgivings about the Democratic Party. Still, the Democrats have maintained a base in the House of Representatives, and regained control of the Senate in 1986. Still, only one-third of post-World War II presidential elections have been won by the Democratic nominee.

Obviously, American elections provide for at least some change of governing personnel. But what about changes in policy? Both parties share the same fundamental ideology to a greater degree than occurs in European parliamentary democracies. Because both parties believe in the sanctity of private property, a Democratic victory does not result in the nationalization of major industry; nor does a Republican defeat mean the dismantling of the Tennessee Valley Authority and the U.S. Postal Service. Both parties' most visible spokespersons are committed to a free-enterprise economy, individual liberty, limited government, majority rule, and due process of law. Besides, since the 1930s both parties have endorsed public-oriented, mass-welfare domestic programs such as social security, fair-labor standards, unemployment compensation, graduated income taxes, countercyclical fiscal and monetary policies, and government regulation of utilities. Lastly, both parties' activists and elected officials have supported the basic outlines of American foreign policy since World War II, including anticommunism, military preparedness, the North Atlantic Treaty Organization (NATO), and even the Korean and Vietnam wars.

Rather than promoting competition about national goals and programs, American parties reinforce social consensus and limit the area of legitimate political conflict. The two major parties are not *identical* in ideology. Their positions show nuances of differences. Republican leaders are conservative on domestic policy, whereas Democratic leaders are liberal.

Additionally, the social bases of the parties are slightly different. Both parties draw support from all social groups, but the Democrats draw disproportionately from labor, Jews, Catholics, and blacks. The Republicans draw disproportionately from rural, small town, and suburban Protestants, business interests, and professionals.

Partisan rhetoric and media exaggeration sometimes create the impression that the election of a Republican—Reagan, for example—is revolutionary. This is not so. Vigorous partisans feel more passionately about their beliefs than do most people; therefore, Democratic and Republican activists describe themselves in much more ideologically combative terms than most of us. "The people" are decidedly neutral about their political parties; most have neither strong likes nor dislikes. We just do not think about them very much.[59]

Do Voters Care About Policy?

Voters, then, must care about policy—the *second* condition for policy linkage. Otherwise, parties would be silly to run campaigns based on issues. Even with the simple device of "left-right" self-placement, one can see some response to consumer demand. Without asking more than a response to symbols, voters should be able to discern whether they are "left" (egalitarian, committed to popular participation, dedicated to the welfare state) or "right."

European voters are more likely to understand the left-right distinction and to place themselves somewhere on a continuum between the extremes than are American voters.[60] In the United States, the relative meanings of the terms *left* and *right* are subject to much debate, and consequently, their use is less meaningful.

In Europe, especially in France, left and right have an essentially institutionally legitimated status, almost like class or party. The French addiction to the terms might be explained by the fact that they originated from the French habit of seating nobility to the King's right in the assembly.

Left and Right and the French Malaise.   Surveys routinely assign voters and candidates to the left or right categories. The matter will be addressed in some detail later. Even so, Americanization has become the code word for shoddy politics, while a different problem has produced yet another "malaise politique." This putative ennui has nothing to do with ideology, the French obsession notwithstanding. It is described in left-right terms, but the reality is more complex.[61]

The current malaise, which "spares neither the left nor the right," is said to be a consequence of the same old faces, as much as a decline of interest in the center, mainstream parties.[62] With proper tintinnabulation, the government's Planning Secretariat published a massive analysis, asking why the French, individually and collectively, "view tomorrow with fear." The "malaise" talk became all the rage in December 1990, when Michel Noir, who had enthusiastically participated in a center-right unity movement, resigned from the RPR (Rally for the Republic). Unable to dislodge Jacques Chirac as the leader of "the right," Noir, the ambitious young mayor of Lyon, claimed that:

> France is sick, sick of seeing politicians of all colors dedicated to their favorite game of internecine battles for power, sick of crises in justice, education, safety and health, sick that France no longer holds its historic role on the international stage.[63]

Had Noir been able to zoom to the top, he probably would have been less convinced that the French were sick (he, too, invents people: sick Frenchmen). Noir's freelancing is the French way. Like all ambitious French politicians, Noir wanted his own organization, or at least his personal faction.

But he faced powerful intra-RPR rivals: Edouard Balladur and Alain Juppé (Chiracians), and Charles Pasqua and Philippe Sequin (passionate nationalists of the old Gaullist school). Concerning union with the UDF (Union for French Democracy), Noir wanted total merger; the Chiracians wanted a federation; and the hardliners wanted nothing. Noir saw the principal opponent as Le Pen's Front National; the others feared the Parti Socialiste. Noir wanted a broader-based, Mitterrand-style movement, while the others still wanted to respond largely to the aspirations of the right.[64]

On the left, the same complaint was heard: a group of Parti Socialiste deputies put the blame for the French Malaise on the "progressive Americanization" of French public life. *Progressive Americanization* is "growing individualism, the impoverishment of the state, the omnipotence of television, untempered consumer spending, and the power of lobbies."[65]

That sounds pretty much like the United States, does it not? A typical French lament (writing about the 1988 elections) is:

> Jamais auparavant on n'avait assisté dans l'Hexagone [France] à pareille mobilisation d'experts de tout poil.... [les] réalisateurs vedettes de la télévision, [les] photographes célèbres, [les] comédiens parmi les plus populaires...[les] chanteurs engagés mais aussi [les] spécialistes du listing, [le] démarchage, [la] promotion, [la] marketing, ainsi naturellement que les papes des sondages. [Never before have we seen in France a parallel mobilization of experts of all varieties...star TV directors, popular actors, committed singers, but also specialists in electoral lists, quick sales, promotion, marketing, and naturally the popes of surveys.][66]

But the nub of the malaise disputation is that the same people have been running the parties for decades. Giscard, Chirac, and Mitterrand have dominated their parties and have worked assiduously to prevent the emergence of a natural successor. Therefore, the abortive movement toward right unity was doomed from the start. Thus, truly radical politicians, like Jean Marie Le Pen, and truly shocking riots, like the student rampage of 1990, jarred French opinion leaders much as the 1960s and 1970s shocked the American political establishment. The French governing class worried about European integration and German unification, but among the masses, immigration—the golden issue of the extreme right—is much more important.[67] Is the issue one of responsiveness? Perhaps. A socialist deputy complained that "all the institutions built over the past forty years are in crisis and are therefore incapable of responding." The fight is about people, personality, and opportunity.

PERSONNEL, NOT POLICY

Here, the opportunities for linkage are more restricted, but less difficult to attain. If one wants to be involved in politics, either as an activist or as an elected official, the party should be there with money, training, opportunities for experience, and the like. These formidable obstacles mean, of course, that few will be recruited. Either party

membership is small, as happens in European politics, or meaningless, as in the United States.

American Parties and Personnel Recruitment

American political parties do not recruit energetically prospec-
tive members of their party. There is no reason for them to do so. If
all it takes for someone to become a Democrat is self-declaration (a
notoriously weak commitment), why bother spending money on
such party "members"? It is much more cost effective for parties to
spend their money on increasing short-term party identification
than it is to try to increase permanent membership in the party. Why
waste money trying to increase party membership, when the goal is
to persuade voters to identify with a candidate when they step into
the voting booth?

American parties also provide no incentive for an individual to
devote herself or himself to the service of her or his party. Even if one
chooses to devote his or her life to working for the Republican party,
for example, there is no guarantee that one will be rewarded for that
service. The party cannot guarantee that any individual will be its
nominee for public office, unless it has control over the nomination
process. Because candidates in the United States are nominated
through the primary election system, the party cannot reward one
person's efforts—no matter how valuable his or her contributions. If
advancement is the goal, it is better for an individual to devote himself or herself to a candidate rather than to a party. The candidate
who wins is more likely to reward another's efforts than is the party.
The party, after all, has nothing meaningful with which to reward.

In the European democracies, party membership is weightier.
One cannot become a member of the Conservative party in the
United Kingdom by simply saying, "I am a Conservative." Nor can
one become a member of the Christian Democratic Union or of the
Social Democratic Party in West Germany by announcing general
agreement with their goals. Instead, one must pay membership
dues, attend party meetings, and participate in the political decision-
making process. While this greatly reduces the number of people
who are active in political decision making, it also ensures that those
who are involved are committed to their party's policy programs.

If the only way to advance in politics is to climb inside the party,
the importence of political parties will be much greater than if political newcomers can easily rise to power. There is no chance that an
outsider, like Ronald Reagan or Jimmy Carter, could have risen to
prominence in European politics without first serving his or her

party. Neither Carter nor Reagan had served in national office; neither had been a lifelong party activist. Compared to the prereform
presidents (those that were elected initially before the widespread
adoption of primary elections to nominate presidential candidates),
they were amateurs. If these notables would have been also-rans in
Europe, what can we contend about Jesse Jackson or Pat Robertson?
Candidate recruitment in the European democracies comes from
within the party.

Compare Carter and Reagan with Margaret Thatcher; François
Mitterrand, president of France; or Helmut Kohl, chancellor of Germany. Thatcher was elected to Parliament in 1959 and served in the
Edward Heath government as secretary of state for health and science; thirty years after her entry she became prime minister. François Mitterrand was elected to the National Assembly in 1946 and
participated in several Fourth Republic cabinets before becoming the
leading opponent to Charles de Gaulle and his successors as first
secretary of the Parti Socialiste. He became president thirty-five
years after winning his first political office. Kohl joined the Christian
Democrats at age seventeen, earned his Ph.D. in political science at
Heidelberg, served in the Rhineland-Palatinate parliament (1959-
1969), and as that state's minister-president (1969-1976) before becoming leader of the opposition in the Bundestag in 1976 and
Chancellor in 1982—all twenty-three years after his first political office. Jimmy Carter was elected to the Georgia State Senate in 1963,
became governor in 1971, and president of the United States five
years later. Reagan became governor of California in 1967 and president of the United States in 1980, thirteen years after first political office. As Robert Nisbet ruefully laments:

> Fascination with the amateur steadily widens in America—amateur in
> the sense of unprepared or inexperienced. We scorn professionality in
> appointments of such officials ranging from the Librarian of Congress to
> Secretary of State. A Martian might think experience in national and in-
> ternational affairs the first requirement of the Presidency. Not so, for we
> fairly regularly and confidently elect Coolidges, Kennedys, Carters and
> Reagans to the White House as if there were a positive advantage in be-
> ing ignorant or inexperienced in national and international politics. . . .
> The first thing an amateur does when elected to the White House is ap-
> point fellow amateurs.[68]

Britain's Prime Minister John Major seems decidedly American,
having entered Commons in 1979 and the government in 1986. Major, a parvenu by British standards, began his career a meager two
years after George Bush, the unsurpassed American insider, began

his! (and attained his land's highest office two years later than did Bush). Their "elapsed time" is identical, but their political cultures are not.

PROCESS

Process is the most difficult linkage to obtain. A process link occurs when the members of the political party have a direct influence on the decisions that their party makes. Often this is confused with the mere ratification of decisions made by the party's leadership. Ratification of decisions provides only the illusion of linkage, and not linkage itself.

American political parties attempt to make a process link in their national political conventions. Their success at attaining this link, however, is questionable. It is true that in the Democratic National Convention, delegates selected by each state vote to *influence* what form the party platform will take. It is *not* true that in the Democratic National Convention, delegates selected by each state vote to *decide* what form the party platform will take. The difference seems inconsequential, but it is assiduously important.

In 1988 the top two delegate winners among Democrats during the primary election season were Michael Dukakis and Jesse Jackson. During the convention, much emphasis was put on what influence Jackson would have on the party's platform. The bargaining sessions that decided how significant that influence would be occurred not in front of convention delegates but behind closed doors in meetings between Dukakis staffers and Jesse Jackson loyalists. Delegates to the convention merely ratified decisions that were made by the candidates and their staff members; they did not make the decisions on their own.

Political Parties and the Mandate as Process:
The Mischiefs of Personality

More obvious examples of process linkage gone awry are the national conventions themselves. The conventions mean nothing, as they no longer decide anything of importance. Due to state-by-state primary elections, each party's nominee is known well before its national convention, and unless "partying" is considered a valuable part of the democratic ideal, the conventions are expensive fluff. The 1988 conventions furnished evidence of this. During the Democratic National Convention, a major news organization printed a script of one day's events during the convention. The script outlined when "spontaneous" demonstrations were to be held, who was to hold them, and how long they should last. The script also ensured that "significant" events only occurred in times that the convention was receiving national television coverage. Here, the process linkage is clearly more of an image than a reality.

British political organizations deal with this problem in two separate ways. The Conservative Party, as led by Margaret Thatcher and John Major, is content to allow the process linkage to be a weak one, as it is in the United States. The Labour Party of Neil Kinnock, however, is in the process of modifying the link in an attempt to eliminate the consolidation of power that now exists within the Labour Party's upper echelons.

Labour Party members and officials meet yearly to establish the party platform for the coming year. Possible positions are discussed and debated, and then a vote is taken among those present to determine where the Labour Party will stand on a given issue during the coming year. Currently, about 50 percent of those votes are cast by only a few people. This process is called the block vote, and Neil Kinnock is doing his best to abolish it.

Many Labour Party members are passive members; their dues are deducted from their salary if they are a member of a labour union. Active Labour members can participate directly in the annual Labour Party conference. But labour unions currently have the authority to vote for their passive members in huge block votes. A direct consequence of this power is that the process link appears to lose some of its meaning. The link is not directly with the people, but rather with an intermediary. While this is really no worse than a direct link, it gives the impression of being unfair. Neil Kinnock has taken the position that the block vote should be abolished, or, at the very least, significantly modified to diminish the influence held over his party by British labour unions. Whether he will be successful in his attempt to reform the Labour Party remains to be seen. Even if Kinnock is successful in his efforts, it should not be said that the process link will be stronger in the Labour Party than in other political parties. The truth of the matter is that the process link will still be mainly a myth. The only difference is that more people will be participating in the tale.

It is precisely because Labour insists on more intraorganizational accountability that Kinnock has been driven mad in his need to move the party to an electable center. Raised on the antinuclear hard-left politics of Wales, Kinnock knew polls: he believed no "radical" Labour policy—one that unilaterally renounced nuclear weapons—

could unseat the Conservatives. However, unlike Bush on Nicaragua, Kinnock was not free to change Labour's position on a whim. Rather, he had to wade into the unions, grapple with Militant Tendency and other intraparty antinuclear factions, and then win at the annual conference. Before changing from Labour's suicidal postures, Kinnock had to construct a coalition within the party consisting of Labour Members of Parliament (MPs) who had served in previous Labour governments and "soft-left" Labour MPs who, like Kinnock, understood that winning an election was a necessary precondition to the implementation of their policy aspirations.

Kinnock is the leader of a political party, as was his longtime opponent, Margaret Thatcher, who guided the Conservative Party to three consecutive victories. When the *party* tired of her, it promptly replaced her. These examples contrast with the French and American experiences to the advantage of the British insofar as policy linkage is concerned. Both Thatcher and Kinnock as *personalities* fall well below Reagan, Mitterrand, and Chirac. Glittering personalities detract from linkage, especially when they are unconstrained by a political organization. All American presidents are unconstrained. French right-wing politicians are largely so. However, lesser party members (legislators) are not. Mitterrand is only slightly more constrained. Once elected, he abandoned much of the sacred Socialist dogma, and his reelection was largely personal.

Linkage is thus fractured by George Bernard Shaw's cynical avowal that government is the art of the organization of idolatry. "The people" do not identify with abstractions, but with personalities. But unless a political system develops beyond its great men, linkage becomes improbable. James Burns's accurate description of French center-right political parties (and American parties as well) is an exemplary manual for the eradication of linkages: "The leadership of French parties... has long been noted for its freewheeling independence, doctrinal suppleness, and flair for private political enterprise."[69] The French electoral system, like the American system, provides for the separate election of the president, and encourages the same sort of adoration the American electoral process fosters. Pure candidate domination is "a recipe for irresponsible, unaccountable performance in office."[70] Mitterrand's second election (1988) shows how far the cult of personality has come in France (see Table 2.2).

In 1981 Mitterrand won with most voters not caring much about his personality, a characteristic of left voters in general. The right, as expected, conducted its usual personality pageant. But next time Mitterrand, having jettisoned most of the *Parti Socialiste* program,

Table 2.2   Voter Motivations in 1981 and 1988 in France

Candidate Choice	1981		1988	
	Personality	Policy	Personality	Policy
Communist/left	26%	70%	36%	52%
Parti Socialiste (Mitterrand)	35	62	74	23
Center-right	74	19	78	20
RPR	62	36	68	26
Total left	34	63	68	28
Total right	69	27	71	26
Total electorate	51	44	68	27

Source: Adapted from Jérôme Jaffré, "France au centre, victoires socialistes," *Pouvoirs*, 47 (1988), p. 173.

won because he was personally popular and reassuring. His personal appeal spilled over to the Communist voters, who reported more interest in personality than they did in 1981. But he did not appeal, of course, to the right voters, who always view elections as soap operas. Mitterrand won because he was "judged to be more able to direct the country, to unify France, and to defend France in the world"; hardly words to inspire a programmatic presidency. As Jérôme Jaffré explains, "The voters, especially the Socialists, considered the choice to be dictated by personal considerations rather than programmatic ones."[71]

The more an election favors personality over policy, the less likely are its chances of becoming a policy mandate. By creating presidential election systems—allowing for the election of a president independent of a legislative majority—France and the United States have taken the lead in the politics of personality.

France and England: Political Party Organizations in Gear. In 1989 a former Klansman, David Duke, became a Republican nominee for the Louisiana state legislature. Both President Bush and Republican National Committee Chairman Lee Atwater said that Duke was not really a Republican (as if a few thousand votes in New Hampshire made Bush a real Republican). The truth is that Duke was as much a Republican as any other who had entered and won a Republican primary election—and he told the president so. Duke, emboldened, was back in 1990 running for the Senate, building a network for a George Wallace-type run for the presidency, and "thus far GOP poobahs haven't figured out how to get Duke out of their hair."[72] Exactly who the "poobahs" were was not specified. It is a natural, almost irresistible urge to think of parties as organizations with some control over their destinies: Who are the Democrats going to nominate?

The Republican party is not alone in its otiose demeanor. The same fate befell the Democrats in Illinois, in even more outrageous fashion. Several followers of extremist Lyndon LaRouche won the nomination of the Democratic Party to several minor state offices, causing Illinois gubernatorial candidate Adlai Stevenson, Jr., to respond pretty much as had President Bush. His reaction earned much the same kind of response. The LaRouche followers pointed out that whoever wins the primary earns the right to the title. Stevenson had no choice but to agree, and to withdraw from the Democratic Party ticket and create the Solidarity Party. He finished second to Republican James Thompson. The Democratic Party, to whose name the phrase "no candidate" was appended, collected 7 percent.

Compare the Duke and LaRouche fiascos with the Gaullist Rally for the Republic in France. In response to the serious threat posed by the far right, the RPR mayor of Grenoble urged voters to support a Socialist candidate in the run-off election, reasoning that the Socialist—albeit a political enemy—was, as they say in America, the lesser of two evils.

Not so, responded party leader Jacques Chirac, who began expulsion proceedings. The mayor also proposed a "republican front" to "block the extremist candidate and work for the republican candidate," who, in this case, was a Socialist. As the far right National Front candidate (for mayor of Villeurbanne, a town of 100,000) defeated the RPR candidate in the first round, the only option for the run-off was the Socialist or the National Front. Alain Juppé, spokesman for the RPR, explained: "It's a question of putting things back in order. The wings of the party must contribute to the debate of ideas, not create contradictions. A minimum of political coherence is necessary."[73] The day that an American political party begins expulsion proceedings is the day that proponents of the rejuvenation of American political parties can be taken seriously. When an American politician can emulate Harold Wilson, then talk of party resurrection can be taken seriously. Wilson threatened a Labour MP:

All I say is "Watch it." Every dog is allowed one bite, but a different view is taken of a dog that goes on biting all the time. If there are doubts that the dog is biting not because of the dictates of conscience but because he is considered vicious, then things happen to that dog. *He may not get his license renewed when it falls due."*[74]

WHAT MANNER OF PEOPLE DO POLITICAL ORGANIZATIONS INVENT?

Political organizations, both parties and interest groups, invent their people with more or less distinctness, depending on the official and unofficial rules of the game, the political culture and history in which they operate, and the goals they espouse. Interest groups have the advantage because most of them are more narrowly focused than political parties and, thus, are more likely to strike a responsive chord.

The precision with which organizations invent their people also hinges on the reach of their representative ambitions. If an organization wants to speak for the people, then the task is doable only rhetorically. Interest-group representation has one major advantage over political party representation: rarely do charismatic and evocative personalities, unconnected to factions or sets of demands, manufacture them. Personalities are less a factor. When powerful personalities do appear, the same problems for inventing the people occur. Ralph Nader's people are invented with abandon and impermanence. Nader himself survives longer than many of our more ephemeral politicians, but his people are as imaginary as Gary Hart's. One of Nader's aides explains: "Because Ralph is self-sustaining, he is responsible only to his own conscience. The others aren't—they're in the middle of a web of interests, and have to compromise their ideals to protect present income or future sources."[75] Nader's web of organizations begins with the Center for the Study of Responsive Law, and extends to thirty-four satellite organizations, many with no actual membership. Others are funded by members (e.g., the Trial Lawyers for Public Justice Foundation). The Trial Lawyers Public Justice Foundation collects annual fees that range from $1,000 to $10,000. Trial lawyers support Nader because they have a mutual interest in preventing legislation limiting damage awards (contingent fees are usually 30 to 40 percent of damages). Who are the people that Nader invented?

But Nader is an exception. Most interest group politics are routinely organizational. Inventing the people should, therefore, be less difficult than it is for political parties. Organizations are created by entrepreneurs; they do not spring up spontaneously. They must sell services to potential members who, in turn, must make a more tangible commitment (money) than is required of the people invented by Gary Hart.

If an organization has a subset of the people in mind, the task becomes even less daunting. Everyone is a consumer, but not everyone is a businessperson. Every businessperson is not an importer. All importers are not wine importers. There are the British voters, Conservative or Labour supporters, Conservative and Labour *members*, Conservative and Labour leaders of constituency associations, and Conservative and Labour members of Parliament. It is a good deal less difficult to invent the members of the Wine Importers Association and the Conservative parliamentary party than it is to invent "the people." To the extent that cultures encourage organizational *exclusivity and monopoly*, the task of invention becomes more manageable.

However, when interest groups seek a broader constituency, their ability to invent people with precision is impaired. In the United States, interest groups must lobby more than in Europe, where interest group-government interactions are more institutionalized. When groups try to generate massive letter writing, they sometimes reach beyond their membership. For example, the Association of American Railroads designed a campaign in favor of strict weight limitations on trucks based on a widespread fear of big trucks, rather than on the fact that trucks and railroads are economic competitors. The American Trucking Association wanted relaxed restrictions so that heavier and longer trucks could compete with railroads. TV viewers were shown a mother and her two children as a triple-trailer truck bears down from behind, filling the rear view mirror with its giant headlights and grill. The railroad-sponsored legislation was approved in the Senate, establishing the first national government intervention in the regulation of trucks, a task that had been left to the states for three decades. Who, then, were the people invented by the Association of American Railroads?

INTEREST GROUPS AND INDIVIDUAL CHOICE

Interest groups are formal organizations that seek to influence public policy in democratic polities. This is all they are; to become more precise is to become more specious. Other definitions, using phrases like "shared attitudes," "cohesion," or even "representation," can be shown to be wrong. Furthermore, one distinction often made that is plainly out of date is that whereas political parties try to elect their nominees, interest groups are content to influence the elected. This is certainly the case in the United States. Political action committees—interest groups—are more active in the electoral process than are political parties. And many of the classifications of groups, being the product of the American political science culture, assumed a free and open individual choice (conditions that are modified in corporatist political systems).

Rather than plunge into the morass of definitional debate (one is reminded of Fidel Castro's pathetic remark that "we must correct the errors we made in correcting our errors"), it is better to provide a simple definition. Start with the organization's rationale for existence (as opposed to the individual's motives for joining or continuing membership). Is the rationale economic or not? I do not suggest a simple yes or no answer, as many groups combine emotionalism with economics, both in linear and in parallel fashions. For instance, the Veterans of Foreign Wars frets about the inadequate treatment of veterans in hospitals *and* about flag burning. Another way of distinguishing among groups, akin to the economic or noneconomic foundation for the organization, is whether or not the rationale is occupational. In this case, the Veterans of Foreign Wars is a nonoccupational group, since one cannot earn a living as a veteran. Some may be owners of used car lots. They might very well feel threatened more by Ralph Nader's reforms (such as those requiring all defects in cars to be posted) than by the occasional burst of anti-American fervor.

One's beliefs about abortion, or indeed, about the proper intrusive role of the state in the private affairs of citizens, are not predicted by occupation. Noneconomic, nonoccupational organizations may find that their membership is disproportionately concentrated in certain occupational categories (groups seeking full and open abortions attract college-educated, employed women), but the cause is not a matter of direct, individual, economic concern. Nonoccupational organizations are sometimes called "ideological," meaning that their goals are of little economic interest to their members. The Sierra Club's membership does not sell camping equipment; the National Rifle Association does not consist solely of owners of sporting goods stores. Here again, the scope of the goals is consequential. Does the organization seek to end federally funded abortions or to "get the government off our backs"? These kinds of distinctions guided Murray Edelman to his yet-to-be challenged essay on group goals.[76]

Finally, and somewhat dependent upon the above, is the setting forth of the scope of group goals. Are they narrow and specific, or garbled and shapeless? Does an organization seek the repeal of a tax on luxury private boats or lower taxes?

Interest groups are indigenous to open societies. However, their methods of organization, their claims upon their members' loyalties, their techniques of asserting their demands, and their success in fulfilling their goals vary with the political culture in which they operate. The two modes of political culture most often used for the understanding of interest groups are pluralism and corporatism.

Pluralism

Put most simply, pluralism is:

> [T]he belief that democratic values can be preserved by a system in which (1) there are many competing interest groups, (2) public policy is determined through bargaining and compromise, and (3) voters can influence policy by choosing among parties and candidates.[77]

Interest groups are the linchpin of pluralist theory. They move from unavoidable evils in the mind of James Madison, writing in the 1780s, to agents of connection for the pluralists, an important transformation. At the very core of pluralist theory is the belief that *individuals* can best convey their needs and wants to the government through concerted group activity. In a large, complex society one stands little chance of being heard—much less of affecting the governmental decision-making process.

When many people who share a particular concern coalesce, however, pluralist theory holds that their collective opinion will speak with more strength than the sum of their individual voices. Thus, pluralists view interest groups as channels through which people realize the democratic ideal of legitimate and satisfying interaction with government: "Voluntary associations are the prime means by which the function of mediating between the state and the individual is performed. Through them the individual is able to relate...effectively and meaningfully to the political system."[78]

Robert Dahl writes that "[autonomous organizations] are...necessary to the functioning of the democratic process itself, to minimizing government coercion, to political liberty, and to human well-being."[79] This proposition is radically different from that of Madison, who praised the potential of the new American government to "break and control the violence of faction" and to control the "mischiefs" of factions.[80]

Voluntary associations can also be political parties, but the term more often describes interest groups. Organizationally, their role is as vital as that of parties; they provide linkages, and invent the people. They become even more essential in the United States as politi-

Table 2.3   Identification with Social Groups (percent "feeling close")

	1972	1984
Middle-class people	52%	77%
Young people	44	62
Elderly people	41	59
Whites	39	62
Blacks	15	28
Women	33	59
Farmers	26	47
Southerners	15	27

cal parties slip in their ability to link. The conventional wisdom is that when one linkage organization declines, the other will take its place. In the American states, governments with strong political parties are less afflicted with powerful interest groups. The opposite is also true: where groups are powerful, parties are impotent. Michael Wattenberg asserts that the same thing is happening in presidential politics. As partisan attitudes become weaker, as parties become institutionally less relevant, interest groups fill the vacuum. We then need to keep in mind the strong individual need for the reduction of information costs earlier in the chapter. The most influential analysis of American voting behavior, published in 1960, well before the demise of political parties, warned that "the psychological economy of the individual demands parties as an organizing principle, and if bereft of this, there might be much more straightforward dependence on other groups for guidance."[81] Interviews taken in 1972, and repeated each election, show that individual needs for psychological economy are operative, channeled toward social groups, only some of which are, of course, formally organized. (See Table 2.3)

Wattenberg believes that "groups are replacing parties as organizing objects." If so, then the implications are profound, for interest groups are no more accountable to their members than parties are to theirs. Nor are groups allotted any quasi-official status; they must gain access, and they must lobby. They have not yet begun recruiting candidates, although they might. They are no worse than political parties in inventing their people, but surely they are no better. Indeed for Senate Democrats, the *second* most influential agent of recruitment, other than family and friends, is unions![82]

Corporatism

Before corporatism can be discussed, it must be defined, which is no easy task:

> Corporatism...is a system of interest representation in which the constituent units are organized into a limited number of singular, compulsory, noncompetitive, hierarchically ordered and functionally differentiated categories, recognized or licensed (if not created) by the state and granted a deliberate representational monopoly within their respective categories in exchange for observing certain controls on their selection of leaders and articulation of demands and supporters.[83]

Corporatist schemes are meticulously coordinated. In corporatist countries:

> Important aspects of public policy are made after consultations approximating negotiations between government and "monopolistic" interest groups with the exclusive right to represent employers and unions. Government generally plays an active role in shaping economic development through plans for the economy as a whole or individual sectors. ... The economic interests speaking for employers or unions should have a high degree of *influence*...in shaping government policy. Governments turn as easily to the leaders of employers organizations or the unions and perhaps more frequently than they turn to legislators or parties for advice, permission and approval in undertaking major policy changes.[84]

The government sculpts and molds interest-group operation. Nonetheless, there are degrees of coordination. Some systems—Switzerland, Japan, Austria, Norway, and Sweden—are corporatist on a polity-wide basis. Others—West Germany and possibly France—are more corporatist in some economic sectors than in others.[85]

The pivotal challenge of pluralism is representation, while the central problem of corporatism is coordination. Pluralism sacrifices efficiency for amplified and comprehensive representation; corporatism forgoes expanded and inclusive representation for efficiency. But is the trade-off either necessary or desirable? Is representation more successful in pluralist systems, and is the business of government more efficient, for the benefit of all, in corporatism? Put in the language with which the chapter began, interest groups in corporatist environments have an easy time inventing the people; indeed the universe is limited almost by fiat. Interest groups in pluralist processes not only must engage in competition to define the people but once they have defined them, they must try to keep them in the fold. Nevertheless, as they are necessary—with political parties—for the proper functioning of the polity, their attention to these tasks is vital.

Problems with Pluralism

Critics of pluralism assert that the very organizations said to provide a linkage between rulers and the ruled are themselves undemocratic. Because pluralist theorists place interest groups at the vortex of their argument, the oligarchic nature of formal organizations was once thought to be damning. One such critic writes that "the voluntary associations or organizations that the early theorists of pluralism relied upon to sustain the individual against a unified omnipotent government have themselves become oligarchically governed hierarchies."[86] According to this school of thought, the idea that an undemocratic organization can serve a democratic purpose is nothing short of absurd.

Yet, this criticism is facile, and even distorts the pluralists' point of view. In reality, pluralism never claimed that mass participation was necessary or even possible. Nobody has ever successfully refuted Michels' thesis that large-scale organization and democracy are incompatible, even if some organizations have rules that regularize leadership replacement. The American Bar Association went to eighty-eight ballots in its sixty-one-member nominating committee to select a presidential nominee to be submitted to the 480-member House of Delegates in 1991. The Ralph Nader conglomerate is, on the other hand, a one-man show. The Internal Revenue Service has no record (required for nonprofit status) of Nader's headquarters, the Center for Responsive Law, or for seventeen of the eighteen other Nader organizations (Public Citizen, Trial Lawyers for Public Justice Foundation, Clean Water Action, and so on). But the American Bar Association and the Nader consortium are distinguished by the structure and bureaucratization rather than by elite rule, as opposed to membership rule.

Competing elites, a phrase often used by pluralists, decidedly encompasses the idea of the undemocratic organization serving a legitimate representative function. Since pluralists accept the fact that most people are not active in politics, competing elites act in their stead. The passive masses cheer them on, applaud their victories, and punish their failures, like an enlarged House of Commons. Competing elites provide "indirect representation." Thus, pluralists must either accept this absurd premise or abandon their theory.

THE DECISION TO PARTICIPATE

A more serious (and more valid) criticism of pluralism is the assertion that the reasons for joining a group, long assumed by pluralists to be political, are not. Pluralism accepts, without really giving different possibilities much thought, the idea that people join groups to attain public policy aspirations. Therefore, "interest groups are associations of individuals who share a desire for a contested political good.[87]

The Problem of Choice

Pluralists attribute more political interest to potential group members than is supported by the evidence. The mere existence of a joint interest in a collective good (shared attitudes) is not a sufficient condition for rational people to unite in organized group activity, or for an individual to join an existing group, unless the potential group is very small. Such persons will realize that if others organize, the value added to the group by their membership will be insignificant. Also, since the good in question is collective (policy choices ratified by public bodies are collective), people will benefit from an organized group's acquisition of the good regardless of whether they participated in the process by which it was obtained.[88] This problem is best known as the problem of the "free-rider."

The Free-Rider Problem. The notion of the free-rider has long been considered in most economic theories, but only recently has the free-rider taken a prominent position in political discussions as well. The free-rider gets something for nothing—a conclusion that economic theory cannot assimilate. A favorite instance of this problem is the U.S. Defense Department. As taxpayers, we all pay to support our armed forces so they may defend America from all threats, foreign and domestic. This is a collective good, as everyone benefits equally. Yet, if one family on your block does not pay their taxes, the military is not likely to protect all houses on your block except theirs. Your neighbors are obtaining something for nothing, while everyone else must pay more to make up the difference. Before you become too excited about the idea of not paying taxes and becoming a free-rider yourself, remember that your neighbors are also at risk of prosecution for tax evasion—a cost that may outweigh the benefit of being a free-rider. The benefits of not facing jail time for tax evasion while still receiving the advantages of your tax dollars are part of the advantages you gain in paying your taxes.

Because group membership is *never* without a price for the individual, no rational person will incur the costs of organizational participation unless (1) the anticipated payoff resulting from such participation is appreciably higher than the probable payoff resulting from nonparticipation and (2) the payoff exceeds the costs of group membership. If those two qualifications are not met, it would be more beneficial to be a free-rider, or not to become involved at all. These arguments are in keeping with what we know about people's interest in politics. For most people, joining a group is a marginal act not easily manipulated by organizational incentives.[89] While there is an active strata of the politically active and aware, most people are less interested in politics than in their everyday life. When the two coalesce, political activity may momentarily occur, only to cease when the intersection recedes.[90]

Collective and Selective Goods.   The everyday life versus political commitment dilemma is addressed by the distinction between *collective goods* and *selective benefits* mentioned briefly above. The former are goods that cannot be distributed selectively (i.e., to some people but not to others). The latter are benefits derived from membership in an organization and thus can be denied to nonmembers. Members of the American Association of Retired People (AARP) cannot deny to nonmembers the benefits of universal health insurance, for which the organization lobbied. But they can deny to nonmembers reduced rates on pharmaceuticals, travel, and insurance, which the AARP makes available, through mass-purchasing arrangements, only to its members. Thus, rational retired persons (more accurately people aged fifty or more) would not join for benefits that they will enjoy without membership; they can be free-riders.

Implications for Pluralism

The implications of one's personal motives in joining an organization for pluralism are substantial. How can organizations be the link between members and government if people join to gain selective benefits? If people join the AARP to get discounts on prescription medicine, can they be regarded as a political constituency when their lobbyist testifies on a complex social security problem? If their lobbyist took a position contrary to that of a majority of members, would they instruct the lobbyist to stop? If he or she did not, would they resign from the organization?

> We can see that a group's formal membership is not a valid indicator of its political support. . . . Formal membership suggests that the group is successful at selling selective incentives, not that it is politically popular. Indeed, since selective benefits have nothing whatever to do with the group's goals, there is no guarantee that any dues-payers agree with those goals. What could be further from pluralist preconceptions?[91]

**Table 2.4   Main Reasons for Initially Joining and Renewing
Interest-Group Membership**

Type of Group	Initially	1st renewal	2nd renewal
Occupational			
Trade (n = 267)			
Lobbying	35%	22%	20%
Services	20	18	21
Sense of obligation	19	12	8
Social interaction	26	48	—
General (n = 539)			
Lobbying	24%	29%	19%
Services	31	41	44
Sense of obligation	11	5	6
Social interaction	34	25	31
Nonoccupational			
Citizens (n = 301)			
Lobbying	19%	21%	11%
Services	9	7	5
Sense of obligation	45	41	53
Social interaction	24	31	31
Single-issue (n = 124)			
Lobbying	51%	61%	60%
Services	2	1	2
Sense of obligation	38	36	38
Social interaction	9	2	—

Source: Adapted from Harmon Zeigler, *Pluralism, Corporatism, and Confucianism: Political Association and Conflict Regulation in the United States, Europe, and Taiwan* (Philadelphia: Temple U. Press, 1988), p. 64.

The Return of Political Man?   Recent research has undermined some of those suppositions. In many organizations, selective benefits are the primary reason for joining, but in others there is a genuine political commitment. Doctors may join the American Medical Association (AMA) to receive selective benefits, but women may join the National Organization of Women (NOW) because they wish to support its programs and because they enjoy the emotional nourishment. Table 2.4 breaks down the reasons for joining and renewing interest-group membership into occupational and nonoccupational groups, each group with two subdivisions.

The decision to *renew* membership may be dissimilar to the decision to *join* an organization. Persons deciding to renew their memberships in the AARP will likely know more about the organization than when they originally joined—more about the organization's lobbying efforts, more about the services it offers, and more about the organization's other members. Generally, selective benefits become more important as membership is renewed. This ranking would seem to give lobbyists more freedom as there is less checking on the lobby as time goes by. Yet, because new members know less than veteran members about an organization's policy aspirations, they, too, are a weak source of constraint.

Only among single-issue groups does lobbying remain the most significant reason for membership renewal; more typical are the social interaction and services-based renewals that compose 72 and 75 percent of occupational groups second renewals. The sense of obligation felt by citizen-group members is admirable, but it, too, has little to do with restraining lobbyists.

A superb epitome of the individual's mixed motives and the difficulty of organizational response is the National Rifle Association (NRA).

Originally a sporting organization that offered selective benefits (discount ammunition, marksmanship training and competition, and the like), the NRA altered directions when, due to the assassinations in the 1960s, serious attempts at gun control began. Known rightly as intransigent for many years, NRA lobbyists began enduring defeats at the state level (especially significant was California, where a law requiring the registration of semiautomatic assault weapons produced widespread protests), and could not prevent national legislation from outlawing private ownership of fully automatic machine guns. As a result, a spirited insurgent faction within the NRA has attacked its leadership for spending too much money on sportsmen's activities (selective benefits) and not enough on assertive political action. Faced with an abrupt dip in membership—enrollment dropped by more than 120,000 in the first eight months of 1990—the NRA sought to resupply its membership roster with such offers as free "shooter's caps," and the opportunity to enter the "win a Winnebago" sweepstakes. Furthermore, despite its aggressive reputation, NRA's membership has declined about 500,000 during the past five years. Evidently, lobbying has not been a sufficient incentive for joining or renewing membership. In the media age, the NRA has found it expedient to press celebrities—principally Charlton Heston—into recruitment service, apparently to little avail (James Whitmore had more success for the AARP).

Perhaps the most significant aspect of the intense exploration of individual motives for joining and renewing membership is that the concept of the economic person is too simple. People join and remain in political organizations for myriad reasons. Some organizations (e.g., citizens groups) attract people who are genuinely concerned with political reform. Others, such as trade associations, attract those with a more personalized vision. When people join groups for political reasons, inventing them is easy. They invent themselves and group leadership needs only represent them correctly and efficiently.

Single-issue groups are the best example of people who know what they want. There is little room for traditional bargaining and negotiating among the competing and cooperating elites said to characterize American pluralism. The NRA's problems stem directly from the fact that its people really do not want *any* gun control. Its leaders quite naturally find at least some merit in the opposition's arguments. "Pro-life" (antiabortion) organizations are unlikely to compromise on an issue of such moral ferocity. If they do, their people will abandon them. Turnover in single-issue groups is massive, as passion fades. But turnover does not make inventing the people more difficult, for the new recruits are ideological clones of the departed.

Problems with Corporatism

Corporatism's problems do not involve individual motivations for joining. Nor do they involve the ability of the organization to speak for its members. Rather, they are embedded in a complex definitional problem. And inventing the people is less a problem than is excluding them. Corporatist systems routinely are accused of freezing out important, but economically marginal, categories of people.

The earlier, simplistic views of corporatism were obtuse and resistant to empirical affirmation.[92] More systematic studies have developed a manageable understanding of the phenomenon. John Keeler, a leading authority on corporatism in France, outlines the dynamics of strongly pluralist and corporatist arrangements and invites us to array governments along a continuum. His scheme is shown in Figure 2.1.

Keeler and others interested in empirically testable measures of the degree of corporatism suggest a *continuum* rather than an absolute classification. Keeler's continuum is:

Strong Pluralism	▶	Structured Pluralism	▶	Weak Corporatism	▶	Moderate Corporatism	▶	Strong Corporatism

Countries, as Keeler demonstrates about France, can vary in corporatism by economic sector. France is typically regarded as among the more pluralist of European political systems. From 1958 through 1981, France moved from strong pluralism to structured pluralism in the labor sector, from structured pluralism to moderate corporatism

	Strong Pluralism	Strong Corporatism
Role of the state in shaping the pattern of interest intermediation	The state plays no active role, serving as a broker vis-a-vis competing interest groups.	The state plays a very important role as an architect of political order, acting to bolster an official client group.
Nature of group-state interaction in the public policy-making process	Groups attempt to influence policy by lobbying decision-makers. No groups are *formally* incorporated into the policy process.	The *official clients* benefit greatly from biased influence, structured access, and devolved power. *Nonofficial* groups lobby (see strong pluralism).
Nature of intragroup (elite-member) relations	Group leaders respond (imperfectly) to member demands. Groups "defend" their members against the state.	Elites unresponsive to member demands; leaders enjoy "immunity" through state protection. Groups acts as "transmission belt" between members and the state, mobilizing members in support of policy and disciplining dissidents.
Nature of intergroup relations	Groups compete for membership and influence without state interference. Members join and remain in an organization because of the attractiveness of incentives.	The *official client group* enjoys an enormous competitive advantage, as the state provides it with resources or even makes membership compulsory. *Nonofficial groups* receive no such resources and may even be repressed.

Figure 2.1   An outline of the dynamics of strong pluralist and corporatist arrangements.

in the business sector, and from structured pluralism to strong corporatism in the agricultural sector. In comparison, West Germany's corporatist arrangements "expanded and later contracted in response to changing economic and political conditions."[93] Thus, while France became more corporatist, West Germany became less so.[94]

However, general patterns do allow an imperfect placement on the continuum. Just as the United States (even with the microcorporatism of the iron triangles) is conceded by others as the locus of the most pluralist democracy, Austria and Switzerland are rarely challenged as among the most corporatist of the industrial democracies. Japan, with an intricate mode of concert between business and

System	Examples
Strong pluralism	United States
Structured pluralism	United Kingdom
Weak corporatism	France
Moderate corporatism	West Germany
Strong corporatism	Austria, Switzerland, Japan

Figure 2.2 General patterns allow imperfect placement on the continuum.

government, does not include labor in the corporatist bargain as do European systems. One expert on Japan has argued that due to the Liberal Democratic Party's virtual monopoly on political power, to regard Japan as corporatist is to "render the theory almost meaningless."[95] Unquestionably, Austria's labor dominated corporatist arrangement differs from Switzerland's business driven one,[96] but no two countries are identical. Without doubt the United Kingdom's pluralism is very different from that of the United States. Even with these subtleties, few would argue with the assertions shown in Figure 2.2.

In the chapters that follow, the political party and interest-group systems that have been sketched here will be examined as they invent the people: how they recruit candidates, how they contest elections, how they govern.

3.
Political Parties and the Obligation of Choice

Political parties are organizations that provide voters with a sense of symbolic identification with their candidates; that is all. We are often wont to assert that they are more; that they "nominate candidates,"[1] that they "seek electoral and nonelectoral authorization from the public,"[2] and so on. That is not correct in the United States; it is true only in the other industrial democracies.

Political scientists attach great importance to political organizations, especially political parties. Most of them believe that if government is ever going to do what "the people" want, political parties will be the agent of responsiveness. Western political scientists, almost all of whom believe in the idea of democracy, think that political parties are a prerequisite for a successful democracy. Without parties, they argue, democracy would be doomed. Therefore, when they read, "There is no need to dwell on the evidence of party decline; it is all around us," they recognize the seriousness of this claim. Theodore Lowi touches gingerly but candidly upon our American dilemma:

> Nothing about the present American party system warrants the respect it receives. Presidents need a party and have none. Voters need choices and continuity and rarely have either. Congress needs cohesion and has

little. Although almost everyone recognizes that party organizations in the United States have all but disappeared, especially from the national scene, they nevertheless assume that this is merely a momentary lapse. ...But the moment of lapse is now three or four decades in duration.[3]

Because political parties are central to theories of pluralist democracy, political scientists cannot dismiss them lightly. James Reichley proclaims: "Both parties are moving toward the model of tightly structured programmatic parties common in other Western democracies."[4]

But our parties have no control over who can join them or represent them. From a European perspective, there are no political parties in the United States. One such scornful dismissal comes from Britain: "How could [the American political party] lose power when it never had any?"[5] But earlier European observers found a strong party impulse in elections, if not in government. Lord Bryce wrote in 1895: "In America the great driving forces are the parties. The government counts for less than in Europe, the parties count for more. ... Party feeling has generally been stronger in America than in England, and even now enforces a stricter discipline."[6] James Bryce could not know that the American impulse to destroy organization would reduce party organization to the status of "competing interest group" less than a decade later. (In an unobtrusive measure of party status, the National Journal's *Capital Source,* which lists most public and private offices in Washington, includes the Democratic and Republican National Committee under "Interest Groups.")

There are, however, still Democrats and Republicans. "People," albeit without much precision, have images of our two major political parties. Democrats are said to speak for "people like me," while Republicans toady to "the rich," in the popular parlance.

American parties exist symbolically if not organizationally. In spite of mighty efforts at obfuscation, voters still are guided somewhat by their party identification. Warren Miller shows that there are fewer strong partisans now than three decades ago; but there are more today than in 1976, the low point of partisan identification. Since then, partisan feeling is enjoying a bit of a renaissance.[7] In 1988, 81 percent of the voters in the presidential election were partyliners (they voted for the candidate who matched their party identification), up from 67 percent in 1972. However, the proportion of party liners in House of Representative elections is less resilient, causing Morris Fiorina to conclude:

> Party identification in the population was a stronger correlate of voting in the 1930s and 1940s than it is today. Although the increased indepen-

dence of the electorate has clearly been exaggerated, . . . there has been a general weakening in the strength of partisanship. In addition there has been a decline in the capacity of partisanship to "structure" the vote. . . . Even those who report that they are strong partisans are less likely to support their party's candidates *across the board* than they were a generation ago.[8]

Something similar has taken place in other industrial democracies, of course, but the vote remains more structured. Because France is most often compared with the United States due to its independently elected chief executive and a fixation with personality, it is instructive to learn that 12 percent of those who voted for the *Parti Socialiste* in the 1986 legislative elections voted for center-right candidates in the 1988 presidential election. Two percent of the center-right voters in the 1986 legislative elections voted for the *Parti Socialiste* candidate, François Mitterrand.[9] In Germany, where there are two ballots for the federal legislature, 12 percent changed parties.[10] In the United States, about one-fourth of the electorate votes for the presidential candidate of one party and the congressional candidate of the other.[11] However, as the United States has many more opportunities to vote than do other industrial democracies, there are more opportunities to split tickets. The total percentage of those who voted for Democrats for some offices and Republicans for others is much higher than the proportion splitting its votes in national elections. In 1960 about one-third divided their allegiance; in 1988 *two-thirds* did.[12] Political parties are weaker than they once were, and they are now—as they have always been—organizationally and symbolically weaker than in Europe. A longer view reveals how much has changed about the American voter. Table 3.1 presents the proportion of variance explained by a state's aggregate vote in three kinds of election combinations. In the 1900s one could predict 85 percent of the variance of state votes for the House of Representatives by knowing its vote for president. That is, a reliable prediction of a state's vote for its congressional delegation could be made simply by knowing its vote for president. In the 1980s this information would have been no help at all; the two votes were virtually independent.

THE SUBSTANCE AND SHADOW OF AMERICAN POLITICAL PARTIES

Both parties have national committees that are generally quite busy, but do little of substance concerning the essential task of political

Table 3.1   **Decline of the Relationship between Votes in Three Electoral Combinations**

Decade	President-House	President-Governor	President-Senate
1900s	85%	82%	
1910s	54	74	84%
1920s	40	70	55
1930s	44	64	65
1940s	65	75	82
1950s	63	60	67
1960s	26	20	26
1970s	16	31	4
1980s	14	3	13

Source: Adapted from Martin Wattenberg, *The Rise of Candidate-Centered Politics* (Cambridge, Mass.: Harvard U. Press, 1992), p. 37.

parties: deciding who earns the imprimatur. They (especially the Republicans) have been trying; candidate seminars are all the rage, and there are some tentative efforts toward candidate recruitment. Nonetheless, they do not nominate candidates. As Paul Herrnson, in an otherwise ebullient tribute to the return of the parties, concedes: "Most candidates for elective office in the United States are self-recruited and conduct their own nominating campaigns."[13] More importantly, parties do not *reject* them. Again from Herrnson, "[Party organizations] have explained that 'negative recruiting' is rarely practiced."[14] Herrnson's interviews show the same thing: "The decision to run for office is *extremely personal.*"[15] The parties are not invisible, only weak. Herrnson's data are instructive on this point. He asks candidates to rate the influence of various agencies in their recruitment. The scores can range from 1 (no influence) to 5 (great influence). Although there is some variation (to be described shortly), we can see the average rates by all candidates in Table 3.2.

The table describes feeble parties. Among the Democratic candidates, unions and interest groups are judged more influential (for House candidates) than or equally influential (for Senate candidates) as the Democratic National Committee. Among both sets of contestants, the local party was more influential than the national party organizations. These data hardly argue for a resurgence of parties, and do not support the oft-claimed nationalization of party organizations.[16] The table does support, modestly, another bit of conventional wisdom: Republicans have a more vital party organization than do Democrats. This proved to be true when Republicans were challenging Democratic incumbents in competitive districts. Here the estimate of influence for the Congressional Campaign Committee was

Table 3.2   Candidates' Estimate of Influence in Recruitment

	Democrats		Republicans	
	House	Senate	House	Senate
Family; friends	3.7	3.8	4.1	3.8
Local party	2.2	1.5	2.3	1.6
State party	1.8	2.0	1.8	2.0
National committee	1.5	2.0	1.8	2.1
Cong./Senate campaign committee	1.5	2.3	2.0	2.7
Unions	1.8	2.0	1.7	1.6
Interest groups	1.8	2.0	1.7	1.3
PACs	1.4	1.4	1.6	1.6

Source: Adapted from Paul S. Herrnson, *Party Campaigning in the 1980s* (Cambridge, Mass.: Harvard U. Press, 1988), pp. 8, 112.

3.1.[17] These variations aside, candidates do not regard parties as the origin of their political careers. Herrnson opines that "some congressional candidates may be only slightly cognizant, or even unaware, of the effects that party activity had upon their decision to run for office....It is extremely unlikely that many candidates were fully aware of what their national or other party organizations did 'behind the scenes' to pare down that field of potential candidates."[18] But Herrnson explains that "negative recruiting" is rare. Also, what is one to make of his equation of the alleged deep background efforts to clear hurdles (negative recruiting) with the candidate's own recruitment? If winning candidates are unaware of party influence, what is to enable the party to influence their behavior in office? Finally, how does one refute a claim for which there is no evidence? All the evidence says otherwise, so either we accept it or explain it away.[19]

Once the nomination process is over, the most intensely personal part of recruitment and election ends. What happens to parties when families and friends recede? When it's time to raise money, from which sources do candidates believe it comes? (See Table 3.3.)

Here we find evidence for the belief that paties are gaining ground: Republicans regard their Congressional or Senate campaign committee as providing the most help. Democrats, true to their image, are more beholden to interest groups. Candidates of the party that has held a majority in the House of Representatives since 1953 regard unions and political action committees as more helpful than political parties in raising money.

What about the issues, said to have become relics of the past in the media age? (See Table 3.4.)

Table 3.3   Candidates' Assessment of Help in Fundraising

	Democrats		Republicans	
	House	Senate	House	Senate
Local party	1.8	1.5	1.8	1.8
State party	1.6	2.4	2.0	2.8
National committee	1.6	1.8	2.2	2.0
Cong./Senate campaign committee	2.5	2.8	3.1	4.0
Unions	2.8	3.0	1.1	1.0
Interest groups	2.4	2.6	1.8	1.8
PACs	2.7	2.4	2.4	2.4

Source: Adapted from Paul S. Herrnson, *Party Campaigning in the 1980s* (Cambridge, Mass.: Harvard U. Press), pp. 97, 116.

From the candidates' point of view, not much is happening here; perhaps the technology of campaigning is more important. The Republican Congressional Campaign Committee is, again, the exception. The Democrats are more influenced by unions and interest groups than by their party. The fact that *nobody* helps much with the issues means either there aren't any or another agency (possibly family, friends, personal reflection) should have been included as an option.

Among the other aspects of the campaign—its general management, polling, advertising, turning out voters, and so on—political parties play a more active role. Among Republicans, party organizations are more important than other agencies in each activity with the exception of supplying campaign workers, where the interest groups are more important. Among Democrats, the party is regarded as less significant. It is more important in overall campaign management, but less important in developing advertising. The

Table 3.4   Candidates' Assessment of Help in Issue Development

	Democrats		Republicans	
	House	Senate	House	Senate
Local party	1.4	1.1	1.4	1.7
State party	1.2	1.3	1.4	1.2
National committee	1.7	1.5	1.9	1.5
Cong./Senate campaign committee	1.8	1.9	2.6	2.1
Unions	1.8	1.8	1.1	1.1
Interest groups	1.9		1.5	
PACs	1.5	1.3	1.5	1.1

Source: Adapted from Paul S. Herrnson, *Party Campaigning in the 1980s* (Cambridge, Mass.: Harvard U. Press), pp. 93, 114.

Table 3.5   Comparison of Candidates' Estimate of the Influence of Parties and Groups on Campaigns. Scale: from 1 (not important) to 5 (extremely important)

Activity	Estimate of party influence	Estimate of group influence
Campaign management	1.7	1.2
Issue development	1.6	1.5
Advertising	1.9	1.6
Fundraising	2.3	2.2
Polling	2.4	1.7
Getting out the vote	2.4	1.8
Recruiting campaign workers	1.9	1.8

Source: Adapted from Paul Herrnson, *Party Campaigning in the 1980s* (Cambridge, Mass.: Harvard U. Press), pp. 84–119.

party is no more important than interest groups in conducting surveys, conducting get-out-the-vote efforts, and in recruiting campaign workers.[20]

These party efforts are taken as evidence of the return of the political parties; not as organizations that recruit and discipline candidates, but as intermediary organizations. While not influencing who runs, they provide help to those who are selected. Parties are, therefore, one of a variety of agencies upon which candidates rely. Are "party organizations having greater influence in nearly every area of campaigning than are PACs, unions, or any other political organizations besides the candidates' own campaign committees"?[21] Herrnson's data lend scant support to this conclusion (see Table 3.5). He considers a variety of possible campaign activities, but usually the assessment of candidates shows that they see little difference between the political parties and the interest groups.

On the scale administered to the candidates, 1 to 5, neither political parties nor interest groups do very well, and the difference between them is not significant. As Herrnson says, the candidates' personal campaign committees are more important. Even the minor differences disappear if we consider the propensity of organized groups to support incumbents. Take the House Democratic incumbents, for example. Their general estimate of group influence is 2.0, while their universal appraisal of party influence is 1.6, not a significant or major difference. But they are in the reverse direction of the minor differences reported by Herrnson. Since the Democratic incumbents enjoy a reelection rate in the mid-to-high 90-percent range, there is little parties can do but work with them. "Reselection" procedures (required by the British Labour Party) are out of the question, as in most political parties in industrial democracies.

We should also understand that to speak of "the party" is to simplify the complex relationships among the national legislative campaign committees, the national committees, and the state and local party organizations. Herrnson's data show that, of all the party organizations, the national legislative campaign committees are regarded as the most important. On the crucial issue of fundraising, Senate candidates give their legislative campaign committees a resounding average score of 3.4, a significantly higher rating than that given for any other party organization. Of this development, Frank Sorauf and Scott Wilson write:

> Greater powers of incumbency have joined with a greater ability to fund the electoral politics of the legislative party. The result is... greater autonomy for legislative parties—greater freedom to frame their own campaign themes and strategies, to set policy-making agendas and positions, *without interference from the party organization.... It is not the whole political party, but only a part of the party that is strengthened.*[22]

Much of the literature about the return of the parties addresses shifts of power within party agencies, rather than the strength of parties in comparison with other contenders for influence, as Sorauf and Wilson conclude. Herrnson says, for example, that national organizations are "stronger, more stable, and more influential than ever in their relations with state and local party committees and candidates."[23] The data are uncertain on this point, however. The Senate and House campaign committees are more influential than state and local committees, but the Democratic and Republican national committees are not.

But what about state and local parties in their own politics? Since the United States and Germany are the leading examples of federalism among industrial democracies (Canada, Switzerland, Austria, and Australia also are federal), one might expect more vigor here. American local politics are still under the influence of the turn-of-the-century reformers, who sought a "nonparty" politics. Two-thirds of American cities hold nonpartisan elections. There are regional variations (eastern cities are more partisan), and beneath the nonpartisan guise sometimes lurk stable factions. Still, compared to European local politics, where parties are strong and coordinated by central authority, American local politics is only weakly partisan. Local politics, with the traumatic destruction of the urban machines, provide "the most obvious instance of party decline."[24] There are strong state parties (measured by staffing, budgets, fundraising, and so on; not measured by candidate recruitment), where nonpartisanship has less impact. Cornelius Cotter and his associates estimate that about half of the existing state party organizations are strong.[25] David Mayhew's more sober assessment (including the requirement that the organization "regularly tries to bring about the nomination of candidates for a wide range of public offices") finds a dozen states with strong party organizations.[26] When researchers ask the state and local party activists what they do, the results are impressive: two-thirds claim participation in candidate recruitment for Congress.[27]

Because of their variety, state and local political party organizations are difficult to generalize about. In about a dozen states, there is evidence of "traditional party organization."[28] One can find evidence of resurgence or decay. Alan Ehrenhalt says that "in the states and cities across America, where elections are fought and won, parties make little difference."[29] Samuel Patterson says that "state parties matter. They have an effect on the nomination of candidates."[30] However one assesses them, state parties, local parties, and national parties are not what they once were. In 1963 Charles Clapp quoted a congressman recounting that "every two years [the organization] designates the whole ticket."[31] By the 1970s Richard Fenno found that "only two of eighteen members studied were originally recruited by the local party organization. And eight began their careers by challenging the organization. . . . In only two or three cases is there an integrated working relationship between the congressman's personal organization and the local party organization."[32] Institutional barriers abound: in only nine states do party conventions help select candidates. Parties can make preprimary endorsements in twenty-two.

The strength of one unit of the party at the expense of others is unrelated to the strength of the entire party (in comparison with other political organizations). The parties can provide campaign technology and services, even if their role in financing campaigns is minor.

One enterprising example of the new accommodation that political parties have made with interest groups is found in the career of Tony Coelho. Understanding that political action committees (PACs) had more money to spend than party organizations, Coelho, Chairman of the Democratic Congressional Campaign Committee, pressured PACs into giving money to Democrats. (One wonders how much pressure was necessary, as PACs prefer incumbents, and Democrats are incumbents.) Nonetheless, Coelho inserted the party into the financial picture. Coelho, the former chairman of the Democratic Congressional Campaign Committee, claimed that his organization could "turn the PACs off."[33] Coelho was forced to resign in the aftermath of the Jim Wright scandal, but he and Wright are widely credited with serious efforts to reassert the role of the party in congressional voting. That both are now gone is perhaps the best testimony to the resistance such centralization efforts can incur. Wright and Coelho were vigorous builders of the party organization (often cited by political scientists as evidence of the return of the parties), and tried to rein in the growing independence of the rank and file.[34] Had Coelho's party defended them, they could have ridden out the ethical storm. (Wright correctly pointed out that, even in the sensitive post-Watergate era, his behavior was hardly exceptional.) However:

> The fall of Jim Wright marked a climax to fifteen years of changing relations between Congress and its leadership, years in which members by and large ceased to ask what they could do for the leaders and began to ask what the leaders could do for them. Forcing Wright's resignation... was the inevitable action of members of Congress whose investment in their political careers, and determination to protect that investment, left them feeling no real choice.[35]

Although political party organizations, especially the Democrats, are always running out of money, they are raising more, and brokering more.[36] As party contributions are minor (4 and 9 percent in the House and Senate, respectively), and PAC contributions substantial (40 percent in the House and 20 percent in the Senate), the party organizations would have to do a prodigious amount of turning off to affect the flow.

Instead of actually nominating candidates, American political parties lend party legitimacy to those who have won primary elections, extravaganzas over which the parties, as organizations, have little, if any, control. Occasionally, party leaders disown the results of primary elections, but only with the true impotence of the helpless. They have no voice in the matter. Surely E. E. Schattschneider, who understood power, would be appalled. In 1942 he wrote: "The nominating process...has become the crucial process of the party. The nature of the nominating procedure determines the nature of the party; he who can make the nominations is the owner of the party."[37]

In the United States, all it takes to become a Democrat or a Republican is to say, "I am a Democrat" or "I am a Republican." In half of the American states, if you register to vote, you declare a partisan affiliation. You may honor it or ignore it, and many undeniably ignore it. Most, therefore, do not bother to change their registration if they change their minds. William Keefe explains:

> In effect, anyone who considers himself a Democrat is a Democrat; anyone who considers himself a Republican is a Republican....No obligations intrude on the party member. He can be a member without applying for admission, a beneficiary without paying dues or contributing to campaigns, a critic without attending meetings, an interpreter without knowing party vocabulary, an apostate without fearing discipline....The typical American is insensitive to the claims, problems, and doctrine of his party. His principal participation in party life is through the act of voting—sometimes for his party and sometimes not.[38]

Asked if he was a member of President Bush's party, rock star Bon Jovi replied: "Yeah. I'm mainstream."[39]

"Theirs and Ours"

Herein lies a crucial difference between our political parties and the parties in other countries. For example, to become a member of the Labour Party or Conservative Party in the United Kingdom, one must pay dues to the party. The same requirements apply to political parties in West Germany, France, Japan, and Switzerland. These dues allow one to participate in the decision-making process of his or her party. If an individual does not pay the dues, then he or she cannot claim to be a party member. If one does not pay one's dues or comply with the beliefs held by the party, he or she will not be nominated to run for office. This framework gives party leaders a voice in who can represent them, and what their party will stand for; something not found in the United States. As Austin Ranney explains:

> Both parties have become little more than passive arenas within which the real political actors—groups committed to particular candidates and issue positions—contend for the nominations. The prizes are the two parties' labels, but the parties no longer control who bears them.[40]

Facing Reality

The subversion of political parties in the United States has been a bitter pill to swallow for American political scientists. Some, following Ranney, concede their ruin. Donald Matthews, comparing the United States to Norway, concluded that leadership selection by party organization has been "vastly weakened" by "the erosion of the parties, the emergence of TV, shifts in the policy agenda, the reduction of uncertainty by political polling, misguided efforts to reform the parties and election financing."[41]

Others find political parties to have reasserted their claim to power. Larry Sabato and Paul Herrnson are fine examples.[42] Both document that political parties are spending more money, hiring more staff, and taking more interest in candidate recruitment. Still, irrespective of these efforts, most American candidates are self-starters and conduct their own campaigns at the local, state, and national levels.[43] According to Austin Ranney, no matter how many candidate seminars they hold, American political parties do not control their nominations: "Candidate selection in the United States is by far the most inclusive and least party controlled in the world."[44] Ranney offers more tenable appraisal:

> There are today no officers or committees in the national parties who can regularly give nominations to some aspirants and withhold them from others. To be sure, in many states party committees and leaders often publicly endorse particular primary candidates, and my impression is that those endorsed win more often than they lose. Yet it is equally common for party organizations to make no endorsements or other visible efforts to support particular aspirants; and even when they do it is not unusual for a well-known and well-financed "outsider" to beat them.

In less elegant, but equally precise, language, New York's Boss Tweed is reported to have said, "I don't care who does the electing as long as I do the nominating."[45] The American distrust of organizations naturally extended to urban machines, and primary elections were consciously intended to lessen allegiance to parties. Therefore, "American party organizations [are] the first—and still the only—ones in the world to have the nominating function taken away from them."[46]

Lowi is emphatic on this point. Either parties control nominations or they are not parties: "[Political scientists] agree on the litmus test of party organization vitality: control of nominations."[47]

The significance of candidate nomination is even more important for American parties than for European ones. Our parties have always been more pragmatic, focused on elections, rather than programmatic, focused on policy. Lord Bryce's exploration of late nineteenth-century American politics shows his understanding of the need for organization and his admiration of the American party organizations:

> Since the parties, having of late had no really distinctive principles, and therefore no well-defined aims in the direction of legislation or administration, exist practically for the same purpose of filling certain offices, and carrying on the machinery of government, the choice of those members of the party whom the party is to reward, and who are to strengthen it by the winning of offices, becomes the main end of its being.[48]

Sabato's agenda for renewal of parties sounds like the economists' agenda for America's return to a competitive role in the international economy (rebuild the infrastructure, increase savings rate, eliminate the deficit, make education internationally competitive): "Increase the parties' capacities for policy formulation...leave nominating method to the parties...increase potential for coattails and strengthen executive party leadership...expand patronage and other rewards for party work."[49]

How one accomplishes these laudable goals is unclear. Those whose careers are self-propelled would be reluctant to change. House Republican Whip Newt Gingrich led a successful Republican majority in the House against the President's 1990–91 taxing and budget reduction programs. Republican Senator Richard Lugar's trips to the Philippines undercut Republican President Reagan's support (misguided though it was) for President Marcos, contributing to Marcos' departure. Bush fared no better with the independent-minded Lugar. He and two other Republican Senators broke with Bush over the Star Wars antimissile defense system. As ex-Republican representative Perkins Bass explains:

> When I was in Congress, we had a lot of party discipline. There's no discipline I can see today. [Pointing to the Republican rank and file rebellion against the budget agreement, he says:] Congress can't take on the ...tough budget choices, because there's no discipline.[50]

The numbers support Bass's impression. At the turn of the century, in slightly less than half of the votes taken in the House of Representatives, 90 percent of the Democrats voted against 90 percent of the Republicans. This rigid division is rare now, occurring perhaps 5 percent of the time. David Brady describes party influence in an earlier era:

> Both the U.S. House of Representatives and the Senate at the end of the nineteenth century were partisan, centralized, and hierarchical. The Congressional majority party...was controlled by a small number of

leaders who occupied both party and committee leadership positions, thus making power centralized and hierarchical in that members *took their cues from these party leaders*. . . .More than half of all roll calls. . . were 90 percent of one party versus 90 percent of the other.

Thus, political scientists adopted a less rigorous standard, settling for simple majorities. Using this standard, the decline in party line voting is equally severe, even if it occurs more frequently. At the turn of the century, about 70 percent of the votes aligned a majority of one party against a majority of the other. Now, about half of all recorded votes are party line. The trend is downward. Every now and again, as during the Reagan years, party-line voting increases, but these are slight peaks in what has been a consistently downward trend.[51] Additionally, even when party-line votes do take place, they are the result of natural disposition rather than explicitly formulated party policy. Lowi makes that distinction between party regularity, which—given the relaxed standards of American political scientists— still happens, and party organization and discipline, "of which there is none."[52] As James Ceaser concludes:

> For many Europeans, the role American parties play in governing is so minuscule as to invoke no more than a contemptuous dismissal. Yet, like creatures who inhabit dark regions, American analysts claim to detect glimmerings that go unnoticed by their foreign brethren.[53]

Two such glimmerings, the centralizing efforts of Jim Wright and the surge of party-line voting in Congress during the Reagan years, have already abated. Wright is gone, abandoned by his party, and the party-line vote in the House is back in its accustomed 40-percent range.

Entrepreneurial policy-making does not contain a risk of going too far, of generating unseemly publicity. Thus, Speaker of the House Jim Wright and Christopher Dodd, a member of the Senate Foreign Relations Committee, speaking only, as Stephen Kinzer says, as "sympathetic members of Congress," told Nicaraguan President Daniel Ortega that a relaxation of the repression of dissent in that country might persuade Congress to vote against further aid to the Contras.[54] No *organizational* limitations on Wright's behavior existed; he was accountable only to himself. So were these Democrats, who supported President Bush's plans to negotiate a free-trade agreement with Mexico: Senate Majority Leader George Mitchell; Labor and Human Resources Committee Chairman Edward Kennedy; Senate Finance Committee Chairman (and former Democratic vice-presidential nominee) Lloyd Bentsen; Senate Judiciary Committee Chairman Joseph Biden; House Majority Leader Richard Gephardt; House Ways and Means Committee Chairman Dan Rostenkowski; and the chairman of the Democratic Congressional Campaign Committee, Vic Fazio. Party discipline can hardly be enforced when the party's titular leaders support a Republican president.

Thus, the presence of the party in governing is as diminutive as is its presence in selecting candidates. Again, American parties differ in kind, not degree, from European parties and from prereform American parties. Other political parties have intraparty factions or coalitions. But only in the United States do factions within *both* parties combine to set policy.[55] European legislative parties are strong, as were earlier American parties. Cross-party coalitions do not occur in Europe and were rare in the United States. The American legislative parties, however, have evolved to a structure in which "cross party coalitions are strong and parties are weak and/or unimportant."[56]

The problem of linkage, of inventing the people, is exacerbated when political parties do not exercise constraint over individual political urges. For example, who do we blame for the savings and loan crisis in the United States? This infamy, without doubt the most costly financial scandal in the history of the United States, was due to the "deregulation of the banks at both the federal and state levels between 1980 and 1983."[57] Now we know when it happened, but who did it? When casting about for villains, the *New York Times* found them everywhere: Congress (Democrats) and the presidency (Republican) both were involved. The Democratic House of Representatives was as enthusiastic as the Republican president.[58]

As for the electorate, Sabato believes it does not "seem to be hostile toward the parties."[59] Maybe, but a plurality (39 percent) declares no preference, making this group larger than either Democrats (33 percent) or Republicans (28 percent). Unlike Sabato, the *Los Angeles Times-Mirror* surveys have found that:

> In the years since 1987 . . . both parties have declined precipitously in the public's estimate. . . . The conundrum paralyzing our politics today is that this perceived affinity [for the Democrats as more concerned with "people like me"] cannot overcome the Democrats' image as a hapless party uncertain of its calling, while the Republicans' management skills cannot erase their popular perception as the tool of the rich. . . . Since 1987 there has been a significant upswing in feelings of mistrust of political leaders, disillusionment with politics and feelings of powerlessness.[60]

Distrust and alienation are, arguably, preferred to the numbness and disinterest that Martin Wattenberg discovered. The percentage of respondents neutral toward both parties climbed steadily from 13 percent in 1952 to 37 percent in 1980, before declining to 30 percent in 1988. The percentage positive toward one party and negative toward the other displayed a similar pattern, declining from 50 percent in 1952 to 27 percent in 1976, and rebounding slightly to 34 percent in 1988.[61] Neutrality (irrelevance) is as troublesome as the fraying of party identification, if not more so. It is not that party loyalty does not constrain voters; rather, voters simply do not care. The dismay occurs because proponents of strong parties, and of the return of such parties, place the obligation squarely upon the voters: "If the two party system is to play a more central role than it has for decades, then the voters must come to understand that a candidate's party affiliation will have an impact on the performance of that candidate in office."[62] But voters do not believe that party influences behavior in office, and they are not inaccurate. Furthermore, voters do not want party to influence officeholders. Martin Wattenberg asserts that "the most potentially damaging attitude to the political parties future...is the large percentage of the population which sees little need for the parties altogether." His illustration of his point is portentous:

Interviewer: Is there anything in particular you like about the Democratic Party?
Respondent: No.
Interviewer: Is there anything in particular you don't like about the Democratic Party?
Respondent: No.
Interviewer: Is there anything in particular you like about the Republican Party?
Respondent: No.
Interviewer: Is there anything in particular you don't like about the Republican Party?
Respondent: No.[63]

It is just as well. In 1992 both parties were dead broke, the money having passed into the hands of the PACs. Both national committees were laying off staff, and faced mountains of debt.[64] Where they spent their money remains a mystery, since only about 4 percent of the campaign bills for House elections and 9 percent of those in the Senate are paid by the parties.[65] Like many bureaucracies, presumably they spend it on auxiliary activities that have become central to the organizations rather than the candidates. In 1988 the Democratic Party's various units reported spending about $120 million and the Republicans more than twice that much. But only about 5 percent went into campaigns.

Specialists in European government sometimes inadvertently reveal how silly these claims are. Jürg Steiner writes of the powerless Swiss political parties that:

> The freedom of choice that the Swiss system permits the voter obviously weakens the party's control over its candidates, and thus party discipline may be as low as in the United States. While a Swiss party *still controls whether a candidate gets listed,* it cannot determine a candidate's chances of election through rank on the list. Once candidates are listed they are on their own. While this system gives great power to the electorate, it also increases the influence of special interest groups.[66]

Swiss political parties, surely the weakest in Europe, nevertheless can control the use of their names. American political parties may adjust, may become holding companies for PACs, but they will not approximate remotely the vision of Frank Sorauf and Paul Allen Beck:

> The national committees are stronger today than at any time since their creation. . . . Stronger too are the congressional campaign committees and the national party conventions. . . . The party electorates respond increasingly to national issues, to national candidates, and to national party symbols and positions.[67]

WHY POLITICAL SCIENTISTS FRET ABOUT POLITICAL ORGANIZATION

How is it possible for two such widely disparate views to exist? This book asserts that American parties are much less influential than they once were. Herrnson and those who agree with him declare that they have never been more vibrant. One is reminded of the Monty Python skit about a parrot, obviously dead, that the pet shop owner keeps insisting is only sleeping.

American political parties exist as bureaucracies and centers for activist symbolism. Herrnson can point correctly to examples of national party committees imposing a procedure on an unruly state party organization. So what? These machinations are of interest to activists, political junkies, future candidates, and political scientists who interview activists. As does Herrnson, they become caught up in trivia. In 1988 the Washington state Republican delegation to the national convention cast its vote for Pat Robertson. Where are those delegates now? In 1991 the "same" Washington State Republican

Party filed a court challenge to the ballot title and summary of an initiative that would limit contributions to candidates and provide some public funding of campaigns. Did the party activists who supported Robertson know or care about what their party was doing? They did not, because they had captured the party, used it, and discarded it when their champion was dispatched.

Certainly, there are isolated examples of party recruitment. As Gary Jacobson explains, "Scattered instances of party control over congressional nominations can still be found."[68] He gives the example of John Fary, who represented Illinois's 5th District (in Chicago). In 1982, after serving the party faithfully for three terms, he was told to retire. He refused, ran in the primary, and was soundly beaten.

> Fary's tale is noteworthy because it is so far from normal. The party organization's influence on congressional nominations varies but is generally feeble. Few congressional candidates find opposition from the local party leaders to be a significant handicap; neither is their support very helpful. The nomination is not something to be awarded by the party but rather a prize to be fought over (when it seems worth having) by freebooting political privateers.[69]

Herrnson prefers "selective but noteworthy" impact upon recruitment, but the data do not support a conclusion different from Jacobson's.[70] Herrnson shows that Republican candidates regard party organizations as more active in recruitment than do Democratic candidates. But even here, the Republican candidates regarded party as a less important source of recruitment than family and friends.[71]

Nonetheless, as noted above, the Republicans are trying harder than the Democrats. Jacobson notes that the absence of an incumbent gives the Republicans an ideal opportunity. Since incumbents so rarely lose, the House Democrats have enjoyed a majority since 1953. (In contrast, the British Tories have organized the government since 1976; the German Christian Democrats since 1983; and in France, control of the National Assembly has gone from the right to the Socialists in 1981, and back to the right in 1986.) Jacobson explains that "electoral disintegration" (i.e., diminishing association between election results and different elections) is an especially frustrating development for Republicans:

> If straight ticket voting were still the custom and the choice were determined by the top of the ticket, Republicans would by now be in control almost everywhere, not least in Congress. The disaggregation of election outcomes across offices has allowed the Democrats to survive, even

prosper, at other electoral levels despite nominating a string of presidential losers.[72]

The disaggregation explanation for the unusual durability of the Democrats makes good sense. If people really wanted the Republican hegemony to extend to Congress, they would elect Republicans, especially in open seats. This reasoning is the Republicans' and they have made the most of it: "Republican officials have given top priority to identifying and recruiting attractive, talented prospects."[73]

This propensity for scouting talent is especially apparent in the South. Illustrative of the Republican effort in the South is the national party's continued frustration over David Duke. When he showed an interest in the Republican nomination for governor, the Republicans persuaded the incumbent governor, a Democrat, to "become" a Republican. Called "operation open door," the national and state Republican party organizations have found ambitious politicians confronting "crowded paths to power within the Democratic party."[74] Promised an easy nomination in the less jammed Republican primaries, and with the assurances of substantial financial support in the general election, Republican organizations discovered a treasure trove of candidates who had "already won." Twenty of forty southern Republicans in the 101st Congress had once been Democrats.[75] How many of the members of European parliaments were once members of the major "enemy" party?

However, when an open seat becomes available because a Democrat is not seeking reelection, the Republicans have not been able to plunder many of them. Democrats and Republicans have about the same level of success in taking seats away from each other, in spite of the Republicans' sophisticated and expensive candidate schools: Since 1982 Republicans have won about one-fourth of the seats held by Democrats, and Democrats did the same to Republicans. One cannot argue that incumbency is the only thing in the way of Republican hegemony, as the Republicans who organize the campaign schools would like to believe. (If it were, why do not more Republicans win when there is no incumbent?) In any case, because the Republicans are doing more than, and achieving about the same results as, the Democrats, the importance of party organizations is doubtful, beyond sheer activity. Indeed, Jacobson shows that there has been a notable drop in the proportion of challengers with prior governmental experience in the 1980s. Only 12 percent of the challengers had previous experience in 1988, compared with 21 percent from 1946 to 1986. But—and this finding cuts to the heart of the party renewal argument—Jacobson suggests that "one reason for the Republican party's inability to advance in the House...may be its failure to field candidates of sufficient quality to take full advantage of favorable conditions."[76] Unless one assumes that the Republican Party strategists are incapable of interpreting election results, we must conclude that they can do nothing to improve the quality of their candidates because they do not control their use of the party name.

Speaking of the Republican effort, Jacobson provides an assessment of consequences: "Expanded national party involvement in campaigns has not, at least yet, shifted the focus away from individual candidates and back to parties....[Campaigns] are best understood as ventures undertaken by individual political entrepreneurs in a decentralized political marketplace."[77]

Incumbency, according to Jacobson, is a powerful inducement to entrepreneurial behavior, to the development of a personal organization: "About half of those [voters] identifying with the challenger's party have deserted their party's candidate in contested elections involving an incumbent." Eighty-nine percent of Democratic voters voted for the Democratic nominee when he or she was an incumbent; only 45 percent did so when he or she was a challenger. For Republicans, party loyalty is more substantial, with 93 percent sticking with the party when an incumbent is running and two-thirds doing so when the Republican is a challenger.[78] Incumbents are immune to a party's bad fortune: 78 percent of the Republican incumbents survived Watergate and Nixon's resignation, and 89 percent of the Democrats survived the Reagan landslide.

Parties are indeed vigorous, but their energy is an internal matter. Leon Epstein explains that "the long-established national party organizations have been strengthened *not as nominating authorities* but in other roles where they had traditionally been weak" (that is, *vis-a-vis* local and state organizations).[79]

Even in the arcane areas of party rules, which generally engage only political junkies, the minor roles of the party organization are apparent. The trivial impact of the party organization is especially evident in "the politics of structure" (when and how to hold primary elections). Minnesota wanted to move the primary date forward to gain the advantage of publicity. The Democratic National Committee objected (there was not much else it could do) and threatened the Minnesota delegation to the national convention with loss of discount hotel rates. Minnesota held the primary when it wished, and withheld the results (with exit polls being what they are, who cared?). California, bursting with people, wanted an early primary, too, but the state legislature could not agree upon a date. Therefore, the state party opted for a plan by which a third of its delegates are to be selected at caucuses three months before the primary election in that state. In contrast, today the chairman of the Democratic National Committee is "one voice among many, often saying contradictory things."[80] Indeed, the chairman of the Republican National Committee may be even less than that. As is customary, President Bush named his personal campaign manager, Lee Atwater, as chairman of the Republican National Committee. Atwater's death created a dilemma: nobody of any stature wanted a job that was surely to be subordinate to the President's own organization during the 1992 campaign. Ultimately, after the job was turned down by drug czar and former Secretary of Education William Bennett, among others, it went to Clayton K. Yeutter, a former undersecretary in the Department of Agriculture.

But national parties do, in fact, fight with state parties, raise money, conduct candidate seminars, and in general, keep busy. Still, we are in a candidate-centered era.[81] In the age of the entrepreneurial candidate, political parties, or any other political organizations not controlled personally by the candidate, have limited electoral impact. How does one become a politician?

Alan Ehrenhalt has shown that, rather than needing political party endorsement or support, people who are willing to spend money and time incessantly can win.[82] We live in an era of self-nomination, and no amount of party busywork can change that. As Ceaser concludes: "Parties provide more services, but they do not control the key function of nominating."[83] David Duke and the Illinois LaRouche followers may have been exceptional in their ideology, but not in their methods. In an open system, full-time campaigners can win because of sheer determination and nothing else.[84]

There are many examples of the Duke and LaRouche phenomenon: people who want to hold public office and keep at it until they do. William Keefe, noting the LaRouche example, reflects that "the primary has increased the probability that candidates with different views on public policy will be brought together in the same party. Whatever their policy orientations, the victors in primary elections become the party's nominees, perhaps to the embarrassment of other party candidates."[85]

Ehrenhalt uses the example of Concord, California, to make his point that self-selection permits extreme selective perception in "inventing the people." In this conservative, blue-collar town that consistently voted for Republicans, all five city council members are liberal Democrats who enacted a comparable worth program, subsidized a rape-crisis center, set childcare fees on developers, and fed the homeless in city parks. The people invented by these city council members were obviously not those who preferred Republicans. So the rule, not the exception, is Duke and LaRouche:

> In our era of debilitated political parties, Washington is run by 536 individual political entrepreneurs—one president, 100 senators and 435 members of the house—each of whom got here essentially on his own. Each chooses the office he seeks, raises his own money, hires his own pollster and ad-maker and recruits his own volunteers.[86]

The discrepancy between this book and those who find rejuvenated political parties is easily resolved. This book's view is that of Boss Tweed. Parties must control who uses their name. Lord Bryce's admiration for American politics in the nineteenth century was based on his respect for the parties' abilities to control their nominations. His remarks show the transformation of the American system from party-centered to candidate-centered:

> That no American dreams of offering himself for a post unless he has been chosen by his party [is due to] the notion that the popular mind and will must be in all, that the people not only create the office-bearer by their votes, but even designate the persons for whom the votes may be given.[87]

Bryce's people were not those invented by individual entrepreneurs, but rather the members of the party organization. His political theory invented a people for whom self-nomination would be an encroachment upon their right to say whom they will consider. Bryce finds majorities in collective decisions, and believes individual self-selection to be destructive to popular, majority will:

> The theory of popular sovereignty requires that the ruling majority must name its own standard-bearers and servants, the candidates, [and] must define its own platform. Were it to leave these matters to the initiatives of candidates offering themselves, or candidates put forward by an unauthorized clique, it would subject itself to them, would be passive instead of active, and would cease to be worshipped as the source of power. *A system for selecting candidates is therefore not a mere contrivance for preventing party dissensions, but an essential feature of a matured democracy.*[88]

The "revisionist" view is more generous. Intraparty organizational power shifts (from state organizations to national ones for the Democrats and increased national funding by the Republicans) are more important for them than for me. In particular, I see no relationship between internal power shifts and party *strength*. I agree with Ceaser that "party nationalization and party strength are best regarded as distinct concepts."[89] Ceaser adds that the trends toward centralization have now abated, and that the remaining centralizing

tendencies actually *weaken* parties by enabling "outsiders to dominate the candidate selection process."[90]

Wattenberg shows how damaging the free-market ideology can
be. Willie Horton, while imprisoned in Massachusetts (the state
where Democratic nominee Michael Dukakis was Governor), was
given a furlough and ran berserk, raping and killing. As a result, he
became a vivid symbol of the campaign. George Bush proudly announced that he was tough on crime, and would never let something
like that happen while he was in control. Coverage of Bush's relentless assault on Willie Horton never asked the obvious question:
What portion of furloughs are from federal prisons, and therefore
presumably subject to some of Bush's jurisdiction? A trivial 8 percent!

Noting that the issue of the furlough for Willie Horton was first
introduced in the Democratic primaries, Wattenberg goes on to
prove that disunity during the primary election season damages
Democratic chances in the general election: "The public comes to see
more conflict in the party than really exists and is led to doubt
whether the party label means anything. . . .With party organizations less institutionally relevant, they are less salient in the public
mind, and therefore the party symbol no longer serves the unifying
function it once did."[91] Ironically, the public is under the impression
that political parties are stronger today than in the past![92] How to re-
vitalize parties when they are regarded as already strong is a dilemma that bothers Wattenberg, as well it might. A solution for the
problem of public misperception probably is not forthcoming. But a
solution to academic misperception is possible.

Consider the careers of Franz Schoenhuber, leader of the Republican Party in Germany, and Jean-Marie Le Pen, leader of the French
National Front. As leaders of extreme right political parties, neither
could make any headway with the mainstream conservative parties
in their countries. The French UDF and RPR did agree to second-
ballot deals with the National Front in 1983, but refused cooperation
in 1988. By restoring the earlier electoral rules, that is, abolishing
proportional representation, the two leading right-wing parties succeeded in disabling the National Front. In Germany, the Republicans
remain beyond the pale. No possible collaboration with the Christian Democrats exists. Thus, Schoenhuber and Le Pen—both intelligent, dynamic, charismatic, appealing politicians—had no access to
the legitimating label of a major party and, consequently, began to
lose influence. There was no open door for either.

Now compare these candidates with American Democrat Jesse
Jackson and American Republican Pat Robertson. Robertson, in the
Iowa caucus, finished ahead of the eventual nominee, George Bush,

and won the Washington caucus. In both states, Robertson used his "invisible army" of evangelicals to swamp the caucuses and win. His chances for the nomination, which at first improved substantially, diminished with the sex scandals of fellow evangelist Jimmy Swaggart. In addition, Robertson's blatantly false claim that Russian missiles were in Cuba made him appear silly, and he drifted back into the pack. Jackson's "invisible army" executed the same maneuver in the Michigan caucus, using intense support in the place of numbers. (With a 3-percent turnout, this strategy is sensible.) He won caucuses in Alaska and Vermont with the same tactics. Both Robertson and Jackson were free to inhabit the party organization, even though the people they invented were unrepresentative of the larger bases of party support. Jackson continued to do well in areas with large black populations, but Robertson lost his people—white fundamentalists and evangelical Christians denied him a majority.[93] Le Pen and Schoenhuber, as marginal to the aspirations of most voters as were Robertson and Jackson, could not appropriate a major party. They had to stand on their own two feet.

How, then, are we to assess American parties? They do not have much influence in the crucial job, naming candidates, and they have modest influence in other, less important areas. Candidates recruit themselves and develop their own issue positions. Thus, Ceaser speaks of the movement to "reform the reforms" (i.e., to moderate the impact of the antiorganizational movements of the 1970s). Such a movement "remains...limited and tenuous." He adds that "while party leaders have pressed this case at the elite level, they have been unwilling to challenge reform openly at the level of mass politics or demonstrate the democratic character of stronger parties."[94] He believes that the battle to return parties to their rightful role as linkage agents (inventing the people) must be waged here.

The task is daunting. We saw earlier that political parties are losing their grip on the popular imagination, but that, ironically, people *believe* them to be stronger than ever. The belief that one should vote for the candidate rather than the party is pervasive. Larry Sabato found 92 percent claiming to "always vote for the person who I think is best, regardless of what party they belong to."[95] There is, of course, a filter. Many who claim to ignore party conveniently discover that the most qualified candidate happens to be campaigning under the banner of the party to which they owe nominal allegiance. Finding out which party this is has become more difficult than in the past, when candidates routinely mentioned party. Today, they rarely do.

William Crotty, no addle-headed dreamer, speaks well for his colleagues when he avows that political parties:

- organize and coalesce public coalitions behind candidates and policies in accord with their views;
- nominate and seek to elect a nation's political leadership;
- hold leaders accountable and responsive to the electorate;
- provide voters with competing, realistic alternatives on issues of public policy which
- allow the citizen to control the direction of policy;
- educate the population on the limits of governments, and duties of citizens;
- limit elite power by providing an alternative elite; and
- establish coherent government policies.[96]

It seems that parties and interest groups are the only things between us and the Gulag! The list explains why political scientists want so much for American political parties to become more vigorous. A noted scholar writes:

> Political parties, with all their well-known human and structural shortcomings, are the only devices . . . that with some effectiveness can generate countervailing collective power on behalf of the many individually powerless against the relatively few who are individually or organizationally powerful.[97]

A more compelling task could hardly be imagined; but, is it *really* true that political parties are the only organizations between autocracy and us? Perhaps not, but they are said to be a necessary condition if politicians are to look over their shoulders. We must then ask the new American political parties: how well do they invent the people; how well do they execute the vital task of linkage; how well do they achieve Crotty's agenda? The parties have "successfully adapted to contemporary politics."[98]

Like all organizations that survive, political parties in the United States have adjusted their goals and methods. They do not control nominations, nor do they dominate or regulate their candidate's campaign, and, if successful, his or her behavior in office. They *do* help candidates with the technology of campaigning and have about the same degree of influence as do interest groups. Candidates select themselves: "The primary obstacle to nomination is no longer an elite. The obstacle is now a physical one, a personal one. The aspiring candidate no longer needs to worry much about what important people think of him. He needs to worry about whether he has the stamina or desire to make it through the gruelling work that lies ahead."[99] He will need some help, some of which parties and other organizations provide.

The Herrnson research does not ask candidates about the services they regard as most important, but it is reasonable to assume that raising money is among them. Here, groups and parties are about equally influential; both, however, cluster toward the low end of the scale. But even in this modest role, we should understand that the "party committees have not yet tied spending in campaigns to the candidate's position on issues, program, or ideology or to the candidate's record of support for party positions. . . . If one employs the ultimate test—the control of the content and strategy of the campaign—the parties are still some distance from the kind of party control they had between the world wars."[100]

Lord Bryce's description of nineteenth-century British political parties, ironically, matches today's American parties: "An organization which exists, like the political associations of Britain, solely or mainly for the sake of canvassing, conducting registration, diffusing literature, getting up courses of lectures, holding meetings and passing resolutions, has little or no power."[101] English parties became strong and American parties became weak. If "he who can make the nominations is the owner of the party," then American parties are owned by individual candidates[102]:

> The classic functions of party involve recruitment, nomination, and campaigning. Today's parties are unable to dominate any of these activities, and often their impact is negligible. American politics in the media age is thoroughly candidate-centered. For most offices, major and minor, most of the time, candidates are on their own in making the decisions that count. No party organization or leadership tells them when to run, how to run, what to believe, what to say or (once in office) how to vote. Candidates may tolerate party nudging on some matters while they welcome party money, technical assistance, and services. And they receive them, especially on the Republican side, where a well-developed national system is in place for raising funds and providing services to candidates and state party organizations. But it is unmistakably the candidates who decide what to make of their party membership and party connections—both in and out of government. And no one, including party leaders and party committees, can do much about it. In jurisdictions where American parties have more than ordinary importance, they are essentially facilitators, helping candidates who wear their label to do better what they generally would do in any case.[103]

Each candidate is free to invent his people as he sees fit and America has, as Richard Rose puts it, a "no party system."[104]

4.
Party and
Recruitment

In the last chapter the failure of American parties to recruit and screen candidates emerged as their most serious inadequacy. This reasoning is against the view holding that a party is no
more than "any group, however loosely organized, seeking to elect
governmental officeholders under a given label."[1] American parties
do this, but so do interest groups. American labor unions generally
try to elect people with the label "Democrat." If political parties are
to be more than just another group, then they must control nominations. Except in the United States, they do. Government leaders rise
from the ranks of the footsoldiers in the political parties. The quality
of political leadership is heavily influenced by the recruitment and
selection process employed by political parties. All such leaders have
paid their dues, and in understanding them, we need to understand
the nature of the payment.

Figure 4.1 outlines the characteristics of successful legislative
candidates.

In all countries except the United States, successful candidates
have a background in party affairs. Other than incumbency and
above average social status and education, party is the constant ingredient.

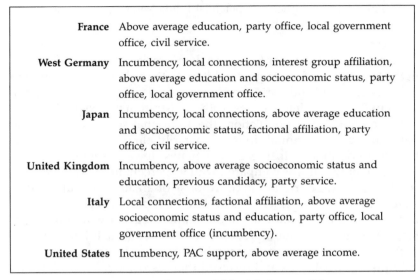

Figure 4.1 Characteristics of successful legislative candidates.

Yet, how political parties undertake their recruitment varies substantially, from the locally centered British style to the completely nationalized Japanese mode. Candidate recruitment, the secret garden of politics, is the pivotal obligation of political parties.[2]

Those countries using local committees are: Australia, Belgium, Canada, Denmark, Finland, France, Ireland, Norway, Sweden, Switzerland, the United Kingdom, and West Germany. Italy alone uses a regional committee, whereas Austria, Israel, Japan, the Netherlands, and New Zealand use national committees.

CANDIDATE SELECTION BY LOCAL COMMITTEE: THE UNITED KINGDOM

The most popular way to select candidates is by local committee. The United Kingdom serves as the most renowned illustration:

> In theory and in practice all British parliamentary candidates are selected by relatively small groups of party members in each parliamentary constituency. All aspiring Members of Parliament (MPs), from the

humblest backbencher to a potential Prime Minister, must first be selected as a candidate by a local party.[3]

As is true in the other European democracies, party membership
in the United Kingdom requires a bit more than showing up. Annual
dues are assessed and party membership cards issued. Because, as is
usual in European democracies, voter registration is designed to register the entire adult population, the additional steps of selecting a
party and paying annual dues customarily eliminates a portion of
the weak identifiers. In the United States, fewer people are registered (about two-thirds compared with 99 percent in the UK), as registration requires a trip to the courthouse or an auxiliary substation.
At registration time, Americans declare their party allegiance. Obviously, in the other democracies, one cannot register with a partisan
tag, since the registration process is automated (much like the census). So in England the party membership includes those who have
paid their annual dues and received their cards.

Party Organization

The two major parties, Conservative and Labour, differ organizationally as well as ideologically.

The Conservatives.   England's Conservative Party has about 2 million
dues-paying members. These members are organized into *constituency associations,* based on the constituencies of Parliament. The constituency associations raise money and recruit members. About half
of them employ a full-time staff. Each local association is given a
quota, a minimum level of funds to be contributed to the national
party organization. Of course, not all the Conservative Party's national funds come from constituency associations. It also receives direct individual contributions and contributions from businesses or
trade associations. Even so, perhaps a quarter of Conservative Party
money comes from the constituency associations. The local associations invariably raise more money than the national party.

The constituency associations, meeting at annual conferences,
offer (at best) advice and suggestions to the Conservative members
of Parliament. The British system (particularly the Conservatives) illustrates a process fundamentally at odds with the U.S. system. Although the local constituency associations select parliamentary
candidates who select a leader, the constituency associations'
choices are constrained by national lists of acceptable candidates.

Members of Parliament, then, are the most powerful component of the Conservative Party.

The Conservative members of Parliament elect a *party leader.* The party leader will become prime minister if his or her party wins. If the Conservatives do not win a majority or cannot form a coalition with another party, the party leader is the leader of the opposition. In 1974 the Conservatives lost the general election. The former prime minister, and still party leader, Edward Heath, was then defeated by Margaret Thatcher. She led the Conservatives in opposition until 1979, when the Labour Party lost a vote of confidence, thus requiring a general election. In the general election, the Conservative Party won, making Mrs. Thatcher England's first female prime minister. Mrs. Thatcher, like all British prime ministers, was "elected" only as a member of Parliament, not as prime minister. She, like all British prime ministers, was elected by two "constituencies." She won a seat in Commons; and she won the party's election to become party leader. This later election, that of the party, made her prime minister. The Conservatives have won twice since 1979. Mrs. Thatcher remained prime minister until 1990, when a party coup removed her, sending her to the back benches and John Major to Ten Downing Street.

The Conservatives, with a majority in Commons, replaced their leader and, therefore, their prime minister. Mrs. Thatcher had remained stubborn in her reluctance to plunge England into a united Europe. In a stunning rebuke, her Chancellor of the Exchequer, Sir Geoffrey Howe, resigned. With Howe's resignation, Thatcher's long-time rival, Michael Heseltine, announced his candidacy for the job of *party leader.* On the first ballot, Mrs. Thatcher fell just short of the required 15-percent advantage. She withdrew, and the second ballot elected Mr. Major. Thus the government was replaced by the vote of a private organization, the Conservative Party (only back-benchers vote).

Howe, a loyal advocate since the beginning of Thatcherism, did not quietly resign. Rather, in Commons he denounced her government without mercy. The speech was devastating. As Mrs. Thatcher listened, she expected a resignation, but did not anticipate the depth of Howe's displeasure. As Howe's speech continued, Thatcher's demeanor clearly showed her shock:

> The tragedy is—and is for me personally, for my party, and for our whole people and for the prime minister herself, a very real tragedy— that the prime minister's perceived attitude towards Europe is running increasingly serious risks for the future of our nation. . . . The time has

come for others to consider their own response to the tragic conflict of loyalty with which I have myself wrestled for perhaps too long.

Michael Heseltine, her most-hated rival in the party, seized the opportunity. Heseltine, who had only several weeks earlier announced that he would not challenge Thatcher, changed his mind when he heard the Howe speech. It was a turning point in the battle for leadership. He needed to persuade a majority in addition to 15 percent of the 372 Tory back benchers that his brand of "wet" Tory politics (ditching the poll tax, pursuing unity with Europe, restoring collective decision making to the cabinet, opting for a more corporatist economic policy) was preferable to Thatcherism. Mrs. Thatcher had to persuade the same audience. On the first ballot, the back bench voted 204 to 152 for Thatcher as party leader, with sixteen abstentions. Her 55 percent, however, required a second ballot, where a simple majority would suffice. Mrs. Thatcher announced her intention to stand on the second ballot.

Yet, in the ensuing days, her cabinet ministers told her that she would lose to Heseltine. Chief whip Tim Renton delivered the same message from the back bench and the junior ministers. She was persuaded that unless she stood down for a unity candidate, the party leadership would pass to the hated Heseltine, a corporatist. After a few desultory Churchillian declarations about fighting on, she learned that more than twenty members of Parliament, while voting for her on the first ballot, would switch to Heseltine on the second. Renton discovered even more chilling news: senior Tories—a clear majority of cabinet ministers—were against her pressing on. Although the ministers pledged their aid, some of her most-trusted advisers told her the truth: either she would step aside or Heseltine would become party leader and prime minister.

Against Heseltine were arrayed Mrs. Thatcher's choice, John Major, and Douglas Hurd, a center-left traditional Tory. Major's image was less clear. The right-wing "no turning backs" thought he was one of them, as did the "wets." Beloved of Mrs. Thatcher, Major had at Treasury persuaded her—where all others had failed—to enter the European exchange rate mechanism. On the next ballot, which requires only a majority, he received 185 votes to Heseltine's 131 and Hurd's 56. He did not earn the required majority. However, his rivals withdrew and eliminated the need for a third ballot. Heseltine, who knocked Mrs. Thatcher out of the job, thus saw the prize slip away (Major made him a cabinet minister).

Had Mrs. Thatcher not withdrawn, she would have ended her career in humiliation. As it turned out, she was made a member of the Legion of Honor (a place became available upon the death of Sir Laurence Olivier), and the Conservatives, trailing in the polls by as many as twenty points, leaped back into the lead.

Mrs. Thatcher, like all prime ministers, entered Commons by way of the constituency committees. Since Conservative incumbents are reselected repeatedly, one must wait for a vacancy before being considered. Most of the new seats will not be winnable. The overwhelming majority of selections, as opposed to readoptions, occur for seats that the party cannot expect to win (and, therefore, the Tories have to beat the bushes for sacrificial lambs).

Weeding Out. When a winnable constituency is available, the competition is keen. The Central Office is responsible for supervising and coordinating the selection of parliamentary candidates. The vice-chairman for party organization maintains the list of approved candidates. *All aspirants for Commons must be on the list,* although occasionally approval after selection occurs.

Although the Conservative Party has been notorious for its lack of attention to the list (with a personal contribution from the aspiring member of Parliament the essential requirement), during Mrs. Thatcher's first term in 1980, the Conservatives became far more rigorous and selective.

A Conservative Party area agent first interviews each candidate before sending the candidate on to the Parliamentary Selection Board of the Central Office. Here, during a weekend meeting, the aspirants are subject to interviews, policy debates, and so on. About one-fourth of the aspirants do not survive. (Some of those who do not make the cut refer to these meetings as "struggle sessions.") Next, the vice-chairman takes a turn at reducing the size of the list, eliminating another 45 or 50 percent. The remaining 30 percent are put on the list to await a suitable constituency. The list normally has about 500 names.

When a constituency association wants to begin the selection process, it informs the area agent, who alerts the vice-chairman, who then passes the word to those on the list. Those interested apply directly to the constituency. Here the aspirants will encounter the selection committee, consisting of the officers of the constituency association and representatives of various party branches (young Conservatives, women's groups, and so on). This committee reviews and selects those that it wishes to interview. For winnable seats, the selection committee must prune down a list of several hundred to about twenty. Those still in the running meet for a half-hour or so with the selection committee. By ballot the committee agrees to a short list of three or four. The shortlisted aspirants next meet with the constituency association's executive council. This meeting is preceded by a social gathering; potential nominees and their wives or husbands mingle. The tension at these gatherings is almost unbearable. The social gathering is followed by a formal meeting. Each candidate speaks for a half-hour, answers questions, and then retires to await the decision. The decision is made by repetitive ballot until one person has a majority. This person is then presented to the entire constituency association, where he or she is endorsed. Occasionally, the executive council will send two names forward, but this is rare.

Jeffrey Archer, a former Conservative Member of Parliament (MP), whose novel *First Among Equals* contains an accurate account of the process, leaves no doubt that Miss Congeniality in a beauty contest is under no more scrutiny:

When Simon and Elizabeth piled out of the car at the market town of Redcorn they were physically and mentally exhausted. The Treasurer's wife took them through to the constituency headquarters and introduced them both to the agent.

"Now the form is," began the agent, "that we are interviewing six potential candidates and they'll be seeing you last." He winked knowingly.

Simon and Elizabeth smiled uncertainly.

"I'm afraid they won't be ready for you for at least another hour, so you have time for a stroll around the town."

Simon was glad of the chance to stretch his legs and take a closer look at Redcorn. . . . As he walked back past the shops in the high street Simon nodded to those locals who seemed to recognize him. . . . They sat on the bench in the market square and read the lead story under a large picture of Simon.

"Redcorn's next MP?" ran the headline.

The story volunteered the fact that although Simon Kerslake had to be considered the favorite, Bill Travers, a local farmer who had been chairman of the county council the previous year was thought to have an outside chance.

Simon began to feel a little sick in the stomach. It reminded him of the day he had been interviewed at Coventry Central nearly eight years before. Now that he was a minister of the Crown he wasn't any less nervous.

When he and Elizabeth returned to constituency headquarters they were informed that only two more candidates had been seen. . . . They walked around town once again. . . .

When they returned a third time to constituency headquarters the fourth candidate was leaving the interview room. . . . "It shouldn't be long now," said the agent, but it was another forty minutes before they heard a ripple of applause.

The agent ushered Simon and Elizabeth through, and as they entered everyone in the room stood. Ministers of the Crown did not visit Redcorn often.

Simon waited for Elizabeth to be seated before he took a chair in the centre of the room facing the committee. He estimated that there were about fifty people present and they were all staring at him. . . .In his dark striped London suit Simon felt out of place. . . .

"Mr. Kerslake will address us for twenty minutes, and he has kindly agreed to answer questions after that," added the chairman. . . .

When he had finished he sat down to respectful clapping and murmurs.

"Now the minister will take questions," said the chairman.

"Where do you stand on hanging?" scowled a middle-aged woman in a grey suit seated in the front row.

Simon explained his reasons for being a convinced abolitionist.

A man in a hacking jacket asked: "How do you feel, Mr. Kerslake, about this year's farm subsidy?"

"It hasn't proved necessary for me to have a great knowledge of farming in Coventry Central, but if I am lucky enough to be selected for Redcorn I shall try to learn quickly."

The next question was on Europe, and Simon gave an unequivocal statement as to his reasons for backing the Prime Minister in his desire to see Britain as part of the Common Market.

Simon continued to answer questions on subjects ranging from trade union reform to violence on television before the chairman asked, "Are there any more questions?"

There was a long silence and just as he was about to thank Simon the scowling lady in the first row, without being recognized by the chair, asked what Mr. Kerslake's views were on abortion.

It was a little after nine when a weary chairman came out and asked all the candidates if he could have their attention. . . ."My committee wants to thank you for going through this grim procedure. It has been hard to decide something that we hope not to have to discuss again for twenty years." He paused. "The committee are going to invite Mr. Bill Travers to fight the Redcorn seat at the next election."[4]

Although the national party's role is crucial at the beginning, it diminishes as the process wears on. Unquestionably, the party will want to assure itself that its leaders, members of the government or shadow cabinet, are protected.

Still, on occasion, constituency associations have been willing to strike a blow for decentralization. Policy considerations are not generally an essential factor, even during the more ideologically charged days of Thatcherism. More folksy considerations are likely to be compelling. Knowledge of the constituency is important. Since Commons nominees do not necessarily live in the district, style, charm, presentation, education, and leadership potential (every constituency wants to have its MP in the government) are terribly important. In the Archer novel, Simon Kerslake's chances are fatally damaged by his wife's unwillingness to live in the district.

While Archer surely knows how the Conservative Party picks its candidates, he perhaps gives the impression of too much idiosyncratic local behavior. The Central Office recruits and trains both the regional and local agents. When one matches career bureaucrats with local volunteers, the imbalance of resources heavily favors the center, not the local parties. The Central Office has been able to *block* the nomination of candidates by constituency associations. The need to do so is rare, since "the Conservative Party is so unified and cohesive that its local associations tend 'naturally' to select candidates who have the leader's confidence without explicit intervention from above."[5]

Tory Traditions and Culture.   Keep in mind the epic contrast with the United States. Presumably, no potential conservative candidate would resemble Sonny Bono (of "Sonny and Cher"), Mayor of Palm Springs, California. In announcing his candidacy for the U.S. Senate, Mr. Bono expounded his philosophy: "I've always been a 'follow-the-yellow-brick-road kind of guy.' " At a briefing at Harvard's Kennedy School for new members of Congress, Representative Scott Klug, a Madison, Wisconsin, Republican elected to the U.S. House in 1990, lamented that lectures on economics were "like taking exams when you're about to get married." He expressed more interest in figuring out how to spend his $475,000 for the eighteen full-time and four part-time aides that will help him. Political parties must be able to say no; European parties can and do. American parties do not, especially to first-termer Klug.

Even if ideology is not terribly important, Tory constituency associations have a good idea of what Conservative MPs should be. (See Table 4.1.)

A more homogeneous lot would be hard to find, and every so often the Conservatives try to create a more diverse pool of nominees. Emma Nicholson, as Central Committee vice-chairman, tried hard to recruit women. John Major dropped out of school at age sixteen and went on the dole. His father was, among other things, a circus trapeze acrobat. Major grew up in Brixton, one of London's seediest areas and scene of vicious race riots during the Thatcher years. He pledged a "classless society" and, under his guidance, a black candi-

Table 4.1   Characteristics of Conservative Party Candidates

Sex	
Male	94%
Female	6
Age	
20–29	9
30–49	63
50–59	21
60+	7
Education	
State school only	19
State school/university	22
Public school only	15
Public school/university	44
University	
Oxford/Cambridge	58
Others	42
Occupation	
Barrister/solicitor	18
Miscellaneous white collar	18
Professions	17
Company executive	16
Independent business	13
Teachers	7
Manual workers	2
University teachers	1

Source: Adapted from David Denver, "Britain: Centralized Parties, Decentralized Selection," in Michael Gallagher and Michael Marsh, *Candidate Selection in Comparative Perspective: The Secret Garden of Politics* (Beverly Hills, Calif.: Sage, 1988), p. 65.

date was selected for a "good" (winnable) seat, Cheltenham, although not without a substantial and embarrassing public protest from the constituency association.

Still, the Conservatives remain, for the most part, white, male, middle class, public school-Oxbridge products. Major is, therefore, a rare find for the Conservatives. Both Thatcher and her predecessor, Edward Heath, were of humble origins, but both went to Oxford.

Shortly after the party bloodletting, Major and his new Central Committee Chairman Chris Patten began the task of rebuilding relations with the constituency associations. Patten called the Tory MPs who had backed Heseltine—always more popular with the back bench than with the constituency associations—to find out if they were having trouble at home. He contacted the troubled associations to stress the need for unity. Some senior party officials counseled Patten to allow prominent anti-Thatcherites such as Mrs. Nicholson to be deselected, but Patten disagreed. However, the senior party members agreed with him on the Cheltenham dispute, and abhorred the behavior of the Cheltenham constituency association members who sought to overturn the selection. In preparation for the election, the Central Committee met with constituency associations and MPs in "red marginals" (targeted by Labour) and "blue marginals" (targeted by the Tories).

Labour.   Britain's Labour Party gives less freedom to its party leader than do the Conservatives. The *party conference,* meeting annually, sets policy by a two-thirds vote. Between conferences, the National Executive Committee is responsible for party policy and organization. The Labour Party's members of Parliament are more active in policy development than are the Conservatives. At party conferences, trade unions, which provide the bulk of the party's money, cast the most votes. The Labour Party, unlike the Conservatives, enjoys a large *indirect membership.* Union members pay through their organizations, rather than directly. Labour has about 5 million affiliated members, but only a handful of direct members. Constituency associations are less important than they are with the Conservatives, since unions can sponsor candidates for Parliament.

Unlike the Conservatives, Labour's constituency associations developed haphazardly, without much central guidance. The party's local efforts went into the unions that, after all, financed most of Labour's organization and efforts. For years, Labour constituency associations were actually local union councils.[6] This arrangement is not surprising. After all, the Labour Party's popular foundation is in the trade union movement. In 1893 the Independent Labour Party was formed from a meeting of trade unionists and socialist societies. By 1900 the Labour Representation Committee, comprising representatives of the Independent Labour Party, the Social Democratic Federation, the Fabian Society, and sixty-five trade unions, was in business. It established a distinct "Labour group" in parliament. In the next general election, the LRC (Labour Representative Committee) became the Labour Party.

Internal Rifts and Institutional Solutions.   Until 1980 the Labour Party leader was elected more or less like the Conservative one, by the Labour members of Parliament. However, a series of intraparty democracy demands, principally from the constituency associations, resulted in an electoral college of sorts (with unions having 40 percent of the votes, and the constituency associations and members of

Parliament 30 percent each). This change caused right-wing Labour leaders to withdraw from the party to organize the Social Democrats. The Parliamentary Labour Party had always been more centrist and moderate than the constituency associations. By creating an electoral college, and diluting the power of the parliamentary party, Labour made it very likely that more radical candidates would rise to the top.

As in the Conservative Party, the Labour Party's leader will become prime minister if his party can win a plurality of seats in the House of Commons. The Labour Party leader is elected to Commons from a constituency, and becomes prime minister by the party's choice.

Labour divides authority between the Labour MPs, the constituency associations, and the unions, giving more voice to rank and file than do the Conservatives. Neither party has a process even remotely similar to our primary elections. Candidates are those whom the *party organization* selects, a process that includes all candidates for Parliament.

Neil Kinnock's selection as party leader in 1983 marked a crucial stage in the struggle for control of the Labour Party organization. As prime minister, James Callahan had of necessity neglected party matters and left the party in disarray when it shifted to opposition in 1979. He was replaced by hard leftist Michael Foot, who was unable to heal the rift between left and right. Kinnock was determined to do so. The left—principally Militant Tendency—introduced the reselection rule, designed to reduce the influence of the parliamentary Labour Party and so enhance the power of the constituency Labour Party. Unlike the Conservatives, Labour required that all incumbent MPs would need to be reselected, a full selection process. Naturally, the Labour Party's new nomination process enhanced its reputation for unruly bickering, as reselection caused frequent intraparty conflict.

The Labour Party has a national list, but divides it into the "A" list (100 or so people sponsored by unions, meaning they will pay most election expenses) and the "B" list (about 300 others who are placed there by the constituency Labour Party; direct applications are prohibited). Membership in either list must be sanctioned by the National Executive Committee. Note two differences between Labour and the Conservatives: (1) Labour discourages self-starting and (2) the national party organization is less active. Labour's list is made up of those sponsored either by unions or by constituencies; rarely will the National Executive Committee refuse endorsement. In practice, the A list is preferable: "Leaving aside those deputies directly put into parliament by the unions, it is altogether rare for a candidate to be chosen if he has not been assured trade union support."[7]

Conversely, when a constituency wants to begin the process—either reselection or selection—National Executive Committee authorization is required. Through its regional representatives, the national party organization schedules nominations, typically seeking to place the hopeless ones first and thus expend weak candidates there. Aspirants, from either list, do not apply directly to the constituency; rather they must be nominated by a local Labour organization—unions, socialist societies, and the like. The nominees are reduced to a shortlist by the Constituency Executive Committee. Here factional conflict, rare among the Conservatives, has been brutal. Up to this stage, no interviews have been conducted. Next, the shortlist is forwarded to the General Management Committee, the local governing body. It may add or delete names, send them to the National Executive Committee, and await validation. Candidate rules are a bit stricter than for the Conservatives: nominees must have been Labour Party members for two years; be members of an appropriate trade union; and agree to abide by the party program. Once vetted, the candidates address the General Management Committee for about thirty minutes. No question and answer period takes place; rather, the General Management Committee moves directly to a vote, continuing until a candidate earns a majority.

Labour does not enjoy the bureaucratic apparatus of the Conservatives, and has not been able to rein in its regional agents. Conversely, the parliamentary Labour Party has an explicit procedure, lacking in the Conservative Party, for "withdrawing the whip" (expulsion from the party). This procedure—meaning the end of a career—has not been applied for thirty years. The parliamentary Labour Party has, nonetheless, vetoed local selection Militant Tendency members.[8]

An excessively rigid process and poor national-local communication or control add to the acrimony of reselection. A small infraction of the rules is used as grounds for appeals, and occasionally for disallowing a nomination. The left factions of the party have been most vigilant in this regard. There have not been many reselections, but most have involved a left-led purge. Ex-Chief Whip Michael Cox was deselected in 1986, for example. Militant Tendency, the organizer of most purges, became much more active in the aftermath of the 1979 Thatcher victory; its goals were to save the party from socialism and keep Kinnock from becoming party leader. Although to the left of the moderates who left the party to form the Social Democrats, Kinnock has moved from the "soft left" to opposition to unilateral nuclear disarmament and to the expulsion of five members of Militant Tendency, no easy task.

Labour's Candidates.   It should come as no surprise that Labour Party nominees are not like the Conservative Party's. (See Table 4.2.)

As both parties allow candidate selection to remain in the hands of small numbers of party activists, "demands have been made from time to time that the process should be widened to involve all party members in the constituency, along the lines of a 'primary' selection in the United States."[9] Nothing has come of these infrequent recommendations, although every so often members have been balloted to help unravel some uncommonly disputatious feud.

The Apprentice Tradition

In Britain, Parliament is the envelope of apprenticeship: British party leaders have spent an average of twenty-five years in Parliament, entering in their youth and appointed to a ministry in the government or the shadow cabinet in middle age. Mrs. Thatcher was elected to Commons in 1959, became party leader in 1975, and, twenty years after her initial election to Commons, prime minister in 1979. She also served seven years in various ministries when the Conservatives organized the government (the average is eleven years). Neil Kinnock, opposition leader, entered Commons in 1970, thirteen years before becoming Labour Party leader.

The Path to the Government.   The British system is one of party responsibility, collective accountability, and sustained apprenticeship. One starts on the back benches, where those who aspire to a government position must begin.[10] The next step is to be selected a junior minister, originally known as "parliamentary secretary." Junior ministers are generally considered as novice ministers, although some junior ministers aim for nothing greater and are given the job in reward for past service as opposed to the expectation of a subsequent government career. Junior ministers, recrudescent of the genesis of the office, spend much time in Commons, rubbing elbows with the back bench and speaking for their department during question time. For the important debates, ministers and the prime minister are at the dispatch box, but for much of the routine question time, junior

Table 4.2   Characteristics of Labour Party Candidates

Sex	
Male	88%
Female	12
Age	
20–29	9
30–49	62
50–59	22
60 +	7
Education	
State school only	45
State school/university	44
Public school only	
Public school/university	12
University	
Oxford/Cambridge	22
Others	77
Occupation	
Teachers	28
Manual workers	21
Miscellaneous white collar	21
Professions	10
Independent business	8
Barrister/solicitor	7
Company executive	1

Source: Adapted from David Denver, "Britain: Centralized Parties, Decentralized Selection," in Michael Gallagher and Michael Marsh, *Candidate Selection in Comparative Perspective: The Secret Garden of Politics* (Beverly Hills, Calif.: Sage, 1988), p. 65.

ministers are given a turn. The marrow of the exchange is to know what you are talking about, as much to impress your own back bench as to score debating points against the opposition: "They know that...a reputation of being unable to answer the arguments with appropriate substance and style may label them incompetent and get them sacked."[11]

Those who endure entertain hopes for a cabinet ministry, but few, of course, succeed. Among the back benchers, 30 percent become junior ministers; of this cohort, 45 percent become ministers, and from this group of ministers, 52 percent become cabinet ministers.[12] In cumulative terms, 4 percent of the back bench develop into cabinet ministers, and it is from the cabinet that prime ministers are drawn.

There are no self-starters here, nor are junior ministers expected to develop individual initiative or ideas. The idea of one of them opposing a government budget, as Newt Gingrich did in the United States in 1990, is unthinkable. As Anthony Trollope explains in *Phineas Finn:*

Now that Phineas had consented to join the Government...he could no longer be a free agent or even a free thinker....Individual free thinking was incompatible with the position of a member of the Government, and unless such abnegation were practiced, no government would be possible.[13]

The dissimilarity with the United States could not be more arresting. Representative Klug, the newly elected representative mentioned above, explained: "I do have a certain entrepreneurial spirit, and I wanted to be the captain of my own ship....In a lot of ways, Congress will be fun." Captain of his ship he undeniably is.

CANDIDATE SELECTION BY LOCAL COMMITTEE: WEST GERMANY

West Germany, with a federal division of authority between national and state governments, allows for experience outside Bonn, just as America allows experience outside Washington.

The similarity is illusory: West German chancellors typically have had *more* state experience and, simultaneously, more national experience than their American counterparts. Chancellor Helmut Kohl built a strong reputation in the Christian Democratic Union by means of seventeen years' experience at the state level. In addition, he was leader of the parliamentary opposition for six years before becoming chancellor. Kohl, called "Der Bär" ("the bear") because of his immense size, is the party man nonpareil. He became a CDU member at age seventeen, while still in high school. At Frankfurt and Heidelberg universities he continued his party service (and earned his Ph.D. in political science in 1958). In 1953 he became a member of the party executive committee for a district association. His first elected office was in 1959, well after he had established his presence in the party.

If ever a system should be democratic, West Germany is the place. Given Germany's antidemocratic past, it is hardly surprising that postwar German politicians took care that public institutions be regulated. Unlike other industrial democracies, especially the United States, German political parties are under the control of formal law. Article 21 of the Basic Law specifies that the internal organization of parties "must conform to democratic principles." To carry out this requirement, the 1967 Party Law requires that parties select their candidates by secret ballot. Not surprisingly, the German law regards the selection and presentation of candidates at elections among the primary defining characteristics of a political party. The parties are left with the responsibility of spelling out the details of the selection process.

The "Party State"

The Basic Law also calls for political accountability within political parties, requiring democratic procedures in making decisions and providing public statements of financing and expenditures. The Federal Republic became a *parteinstaat*. The political parties are central to the governing process because they connect the voters, interest groups, and elites into a coherent process. West German political scientist Kurt Sontheimer claims that "there are no decisions of any importance that have not been brought to the parties, prepared by them, and taken by them."[14]

The 1967 Party Law spells out the role of parties in the usual Germanic detail. Legal guidelines, formal responsibilities, and state money are provided. Parties are institutionalized even more than the United Kingdom's, where the Conservative Party's parliamentary majority can elect a prime minister. The Basic Law requires that political parties "take part in forming the political will of the people." Parties are supposed to take the lead in developing public opinion, not merely responding to demands. The authors of the Basic Law were convinced that Adolf Hitler got the job because of the masses, not the elites. The role of political parties reflects this fear—Madisonian in the extreme—of the masses.

Each major party maintains a large, well-staffed foundation, buttressed by federal funds, to carry out these activities. (The Greens, in a Germanic stroke of precision, have their party headquarters in a former mental institution.) Party foundations pursue public education, conduct research, sponsor international exchange, and so on.

Party Traditions and Organization

The Christian Democratic Union is organized as a federation of state parties, in a deliberate rejection of the more centralized SPD (Social Democratic Party). It was, until his retirement, the personal instrument of Konrad Adenauer, much like the Giscardists and Chiracists in France. Once the last vote was counted, the party "organization" faded away. As Angelo Panebianco explains, "[Adenauer's] situational charisma and development through territorial led together...to a low degree of institutionalization."[15] When "Der Alte" retired, a collective leadership of Bundestag members replaced him. It sought to compete with the better organized SPD with membership drives, expanding from 300,000 party members at Adenauer's retirement to about 2 million today. Party income went from 73 to 300 million deutsche marks.

With the ascension of Helmut Kohl, the party became thoroughly organized. The Federal Executive is the major executive body of the party. It has about sixty members drawn from the cabinet or the *Fraktion*, from the länder officials, and from party leadership. From this committee emerges the "presidium," the inner circle. The party holds semiannual congresses; every two years there is a full party congress when members ratify leadership decisions. Kohl had made the state party more accountable to the national executive. The party is still a party of local big shots. However, the Federal Executive is not elected, unlike the comparable SPD unit. There is little rank-and-file participation. The decision making is sort of a bargain between the presidium, the Fraktion, the state parties. However, since the 1990 all-German elections, Kohl has become Der Alte, constrained more by the necessity of coalition with the Free Democrats than by his own party.

The SPD was a mass party intended to mobilize the masses, using trade unions to lobby for membership to show class solidarity. It has half again as many members as the CDU (Christian Democratic Union), and has youth groups, sports clubs, and the like, to keep the faith. Its membership is the core of its strength, with the biennial convention the supreme party organ. Nonetheless, the SPD has a centralized, highly bureaucratic structure. The Federal Executive and the Presidium run the show; but the Federal Executive is elected by the Party Congress, and the Presidium is elected by the Federal Executive.

Candidate Nominations. Constituency candidates, that is, those listed in the first ballot, must be nominated either by a meeting of the membership of the constituency party or by a meeting of delegates to which the members have assigned the task. Ordinarily, party members delegate the job. The delegate committees are about twenty-five members in size, representing an electorate of about 200 active members, but a much smaller proportion—perhaps 10 percent—of total membership. Those seeking the nomination usually are active for a year or so before the selection is to occur.

Although one would suspect that those selected have earned their spurs, the constituency selection process is always open to the attractive newcomer; the "Eisenhower" who can bring prominence to the party. Ludwig Erhard, the author of the West German economic miracle, who succeeded Adenauer as Christian Democratic party leader and as chancellor, was not even a formal party member when he was elected to the Bundestag in 1949. Generally, the constituency selection is not terribly exciting. Reselection is the rule, and challenges to sitting Bundestag members are rare.

Local reputations are invaluable in securing the initial selection, particularly if the aspirant has held a local party or municipal office. But local constituency selection committees are jealous of their independence, and intervention by regional or national party leaders is, as a rule, dangerous and, therefore, avoided. (Here the difference between West Germany and the United Kingdom is striking.) Legally, both the land and national party executives are entitled to the exercise of a postselection veto. The delegates themselves are typically mid-level party officials, chosen more because of their prominence or activism than because they represent a specified political ideology:

> Delegates are often faced with the product of informal discussions among the party oligarchs within the constituency, in terms of support of a favoured aspirant or a proposal to renominate an incumbent. The *formal* process of selection in a constituency is therefore not surprisingly often merely the benediction bestowed by the party on the outcome of *informal* discussions and decisions which have occurred well before the selection meeting takes place, though the formal procedures guard against undemocratic "railroading" of selection decisions, and may be very significant in a contested selection process.[16]

Although there are examples of challenges to sitting Bundestag members, only a few are deselected. Still, "The idea of instituting American-style primary elections has sometimes been suggested, but rarely, if ever, has such an experiment been instituted for the selection of Bundestag candidates."[17]

List candidates, those appearing on the second, or party list, ballot, are less likely to have to appeal to local elites. They are chosen either by special meetings of delegates of local party organizations or by the Land Party conference. Typically, the selection is done by special delegate meetings. All told, perhaps 25,000 party members, or 1 percent of the total party membership, are involved in the selection of list candidates. Voting is by secret ballot, by descending order; those who are defeated for first or second positions are free to try for lower ones. The Land Party will invariably present a carefully constructed list of nominees. Additional nominations may occasionally come from the floor, especially for the lower-ballot positions. The delegates are sometimes instructed by local party organizations, but they are not formally bound.

As the opportunity for loss of control plagues Land Party chairmen, at least the first five places will have been preselected by the party:

> This is done to make the selection process comprehensible and to give it structure and order, and also to take account of the numerous factors which have to be considered and the informal agreements or long standing conventions which provide for various forms of balance or compromise among the "interests" involved.[18]

The tricky aspect of this process is this: if a party does exceptionally well on the first (constituency) ballot, it is possible that there will be no additional seats to be added from the party lists! Astute Land Party leaders must estimate not only how many votes the party will earn but how many of them will come on the first ballot. A place on the list that is safe in one election might become marginal or hopeless in another. One way around this is for sitting Bundestag members to contest constituencies *and* appear on the party lists. The Christian Democrats typically propose about one-fourth and the Social Democrats about one-third of their candidates in both the first and second ballots. The "double candidates" who win constituency seats are pulled from the party list before the allocation of seats from the list is made. Double candidates are usually prominent party politicians, potential ministers, and the like, that the party, by hook or by crook, intends to keep in the Bundestag. The SPD has taken the first step in requiring that candidates for high position on the list also be constituency candidates; thus, the higher proportion of double candidates in this party.

Another use of the party list is to reward those who contest hopeless constituencies. Free Democrats and Greens generally do not win constituencies, nor do Social Democrats in Bavaria or Christian Democrats in Hamburg or Bremen. This device is especially useful in balancing the interests of the various intraparty factions and groups:

> The SPD especially will insure that trade union representatives are given prominent places....Shipping in Bremen or Hamburg, wine growing in Rhineland-Pfalz, farming in Bavaria and Schleswig-Holstein ...will be included on the Christian Democrat or Free Democrat lists....Their placing on the list will be an indication of concern by the party that these interests are regarded highly...if only in terms of insuring voting support...and perhaps to encourage financial support for the electoral campaign as well.[19]

However, although there is evidence of interest-group-driven corruption in German politics, strong party organization and the emergence of career politicians have reduced interest groups to a position clearly inferior to their role in American or English politics. The parties take care of their interest groups as much out of tradition as from necessity; most candidates will be members of an appropriate interest group. Perhaps half the Bundestag members are affiliated with an interest group.

Scandals and Money Politics.   Still, although scandals are minor by American standards, the German parties have been tainted. The 1982 Flick affair implicated the CDU in illegal corporate funding schemes. The CDU managed to implicate the SPD in the Neue Heimat scandal, linking the party to union shenanigans. In 1987, in Schleswig-Holstein, CDU minister-president Use Barschel committed suicide after his campaign staff was discovered to have used Nixonian "dirty tricks" against the SPD candidate. While one can hardly imagine an American politician committing suicide over dirty tricks, with negative campaign ads becoming a way of life (e.g., the attack ads of the 1980s), the degree of corruption in West Germany was shocking to many West Germans. The Flick Corporation received tax breaks and the Free Democrats (notably), Christian Democrats, and even some Social Democrats received large cash donations. Flick officials gave money *in cash* to party leaders, among them Helmut Kohl.

Regional balance is equally important, and just as rigidly allocated. Each region may be allocated, for example, every fourth ballot position. Then there is social balance. Major parties will have at least one woman in the top five, since those parties have been unable to win many seats in the constituency elections.

Finally, political factions are balanced. Among the political parties that depend almost entirely on second-ballot seats, factional disputes can be vicious. The Free Democrats, when they switch coalition partners, are notorious for purging those who oppose the switch. Concerning the 1983 defection from the Social Democrats to the Christian Democrats, the FDP in Baden-Württemberg kept the first six places away from those who continued to oppose Genscher (the party leader) and the new coalition (see Chapter 3).

The Lessening of Personality

The consequence of this tedious process is to reduce, if not eliminate, personality as a variable in the voting calculus of German voters. They cannot rearrange the list, and probably have never heard of candidates beyond the top positions, and the majority of voters indicate that because of party loyalty they will vote for constituency candidates whom they personally dislike. Generalized party loyalty is *institutionally* sustained in West Germany.

The privileged status of political parties has made them attractive to professional politicians and public servants. Large numbers of civil servants are party members, with the bulk belonging to the SPD. Universities, public research and policy institutions (such as Max Planck), feed the parties their members. About one-third of the Bundestag members are civil servants; another 14 percent are employees of the parties themselves or of closely associated interest groups.

CANDIDATE SELECTION BY LOCAL COMMITTEE AND NATIONAL COMMITTEE: FRANCE

Given the highly personal nature of French politics, and the extent to which political parties are instruments of personal ambition, the degree of organizational control is surprising. Because the *Parti Socialiste* now dominates the left coalition, and, to a lesser extent, the RPR (Rally for the Republic) and UDF (Union for French Democracy) dominate the right, their organizations have taken an active role in candidate selection.

The Rassemblement pour la République

According to RPR statutes, the national organization—principally Chiracist—exercises the greatest share of power. A nomination commission, composed of the general secretary, leaders of parliamentary groups in the RPR organizational network, and invited guests, solicits nominations from the department organizations. After scrutiny and, not infrequently, alteration of the lists, the nomination commission consigns the names to the Central Committee.

The RPR, like the British parties, would often "parachute" candidates, much to the dismay of local party bosses. The local strategy is to agree, solidly, on a list, thus allowing the nationals little discretion. When this is done, and the local leadership is adamant, it usually can hold off the national organization. Sometimes local leaders threaten to make up dissident lists, and periodically they resign in protest. The RPR typically relies on impeachment in such cases.[20] In 1990 it expelled the mayor of Grenoble for supporting a *Parti So-*

cialiste candidate. (Chirac's cohabitation as Mitterrand's prime minister was viewed as less a transgression than an organizational decision, albeit largely controlled by Chirac, and placed the party at the vortex of the governmental process.)

The Union pour la Démocratie Française

Even more than the RPR, the *Union pour la Démocratie Française* is a confederation of disparate semiautonomous factions. UDF party membership comes with membership in any of the confederated associations: *Parti Républicaine, Centre des Démocratres-Sociaux, Parti Radical, Parti Social-Démocrate, and Perspectives et Réalities* clubs. One also can join directly, without membership in a subsidiary. However, these affiliates, under the guidance of the UDF parliamentary leadership, recommend National Assembly candidates to the Political Committee. To avoid chronic feuds, the affiliates are assigned quotas (ninety-seven to the *Parti Républicaine*, fifty to the *Centre des Démocratres-Sociaux*, and so on).

Each department party organization must accede to the quotas. However, the allotments often violate a department organization's priorities, where dissident lists have been constructed (without the draconian punishment of the RPR) and elected. The UDF allows members of the department committee to vote, thus making expulsion more difficult. But votes are not always held, and usually a considerable measure of preselection takes place. The decay in local influence has also been provoked by the UDF-RPR agreements to run common candidates and the need for coordination between the two parties.

The Parti Socialiste

Unlike many of Europe's left parties, the *Parti Socialiste* has always contained an energetic localist element, almost a penchant for the indigenous. It is much more decentralized than either of its two right-wing rivals, with inarguable jurisdiction being assigned to local conventions (with members voting), with the added proviso of departmental organization ratification. While the national organization retains formal power, it normally intervenes only when absolutely necessary (e.g., when Rocardians and Mitterrand's advocates were contesting the party's top spot).

However, the national convention also has annulled the designation of locally selected candidates in retribution for endorsing heretical socialist groups in general elections. And the national organization makes certain that each "courant" within the party is given a fair shake (eighty-one for Mitterrand's followers, twenty-seven for the Rocardians, and so on).

With its tolerance of decentralization, the *Parti Socialiste* has had its share of local insurrections. Because departmental members can vote, rebellions can be easily sparked, even though only a handful of members show up to vote. Without question, the *Parti Socialiste* has more *member* participation than do the right-wing parties.

The Parties' Cores

The right-wing parties have shown a distinct prejudice in favor of civil servants, chiefly graduates of *l'Ecole Nationale d'Administration*. French law allows deputies to retain their local offices while serving in the National Assembly. Like their *Parti Socialiste* colleagues, the right-wing deputies keep their local *"mandats."* The major difference between the right and left is the lack of civil servants from the *"grand écoles"* in the *Parti Socialiste*. Instead, its deputies are more likely to be teachers, especially university teachers. Teachers play an important role in the British Labour Party, too. However, whereas the British Labour Party has been successful in recruiting some working-class candidates, the *Parti Socialiste* has not; a mere 1 percent of its candidates and members of the National Assembly are working class. And, like the right-wing parties, the *Parti Socialiste* has its share of "enarques" in the National Assembly.[21]

Modes of Collaboration.   With France's two-ballot system, we sometimes hear that France has the functional equivalent of the American primary system. The parties of the right and left coalitions present candidates on the first round, and the victor becomes the nominee of the coalition for the second round. The left does this often, but the right-wing coalition has tried to agree on common candidates. A common candidate agreement is difficult for the UDF, given the Gaullist penchant for conquest. The RPR did succeed on occasion by imposing a unique candidacy strategy upon its smaller rival. The UDF preferred the trial run and, in this limited meaning, accepted the notion of a primary election. When Giscard won the presidency in 1978, the UDF contested secure antisocialist seats with the Gaullists. But with Giscard's fall from grace, the UDF began to lean more toward the unique candidacy (and strategic withdrawal) game plan.

The Personal Presidency Redux.   The comparison with the American primary election is more appropriate to presidential rather than parliamentary elections, since in the latter the party organization is heavily involved. But in presidential elections, the ghost of Le grand Charles looms large. Because the political parties are, in essence, vehicles for personal power, their presidential nomination processes are vague. Why worry about nominations when Charles de Gaulle was, after all, *le roi?* The Parti Socialiste endorsed candidates in full-party conferences, but the UDF and RPR just take it for granted that their leader will compete. Therefore, the breakdown in negotiations between the RPR and UDF on presidential nomination procedures was not unexpected, for it created more uncertainty than Chirac and Giscard were willing to accept. The tradition is for self-selection and strong personality. As in de Gaulle's era, the current right depends more upon personality than organization. There is no clearly understood method of securing a party's nomination for president!

Technically, the process of competing for the presidency is almost as easy as the American primary election system. Instead of requiring petitions signed by a designated number of voters, the French stipulate that a presidential candidate secure 500 signatures from elected officials (at any level), residing in at least thirty different departments. Once a candidate has the 500 signatures, he or she is granted free time on television and radio and, if the candidate earns 5 percent of the vote on the first ballot, public finance for the campaign.

Although such nominations are unlikely to survive the first ballot, they do cause problems for serious nominees. For example, they allowed for the rapid entry into the electoral process of antimainstream candidates such as Jean-Marie Le Pen, the rabid nationalist who could never have attracted the patronage of the center right but who finished fourth on the 1988 second ballot with 12 percent. There is a tradition here: Mitterrand, standing for president for the first time in 1965 against Charles de Gaulle, started with no organization and imposed himself on the left, though he did not join the Parti Socialiste until 1971. It was he, as an ambitious self-starter, who "presidentialized" the left. Who, then, "Americanized" French politics? For de Gaulle, Mitterrand, Chirac, and Giscard, "notoriety from past achievements, personality, and a set of favorable circumstances counted far more than organization."[22] Of course, there are gargantuan differences between the two systems. Our outsiders (e.g., Carter) become president, lose, and retire to exile. French outsiders become insiders and stay around. Indeed, that is the complaint of the younger party activists: how much longer will Giscard, Chirac, Mitterrand, and company dominate the headlines?

American outsiders are more Warholian (Andy Warhol, American painter and pop-cult figure, claimed that "everybody is famous for fifteen minutes"). But the problem of ephemeral individuals in the United States should not be confined to outsiders. Insiders are equally impermanent, and thus when they invent people, those whom they invent depart with them. Whatever happened to Jody Powell, John Ehrlichman, Donald Regan, or David Stockman, all at one time said to be at the heart of the American political power structure? Humorist P. J. O'Rourke is funny and correct:

> I prefer to concentrate on systems and institutions, not because people aren't important, but because people are important, in Washington, so briefly. There was a time not long ago when day could hardly break without asking permission from Don Regan, and now, for all I know, he's hosting a talk show in Anaheim. I concentrated on institutions because in order to concentrate on persons I'd have had to keep revising and revising until the moment these pages went to press, and I'd still wind up with a book as dated as a Jody Powell joke.[23]

We should not let O'Rourke's flip style divert us from the fundamental truth of his observation and from pondering its implications. Individuals come and go, but institutions remain. Without institutions, all politics would be personal. As American political parties are the weakest, institutionally, among the industrial democracies, what can we conclude?

There is no American equivalent to the French prime minister, although the two systems both elect a president separately. Power in the American White House is less institutionally based. Some chiefs of staff have been quite powerful; in other cases, they have not. President Carter chose not to have a chief of staff. The key to finding out who is in or out in the White House is locating the persons that the president trusts, irrespective of their formal position. Nevertheless, O'Rourke is right: those once regarded as the vortex of the power structure were unknown before and after their brief tenure. Sherman Adams, Dwight Eisenhower's chief of staff, was a one-term congressman and governor of New Hampshire. It was he who managed Eisenhower's 1952 floor fight at the Republican National Convention. He retired with Eisenhower, and wrote his memoirs in 1961. He was the first of the modern chiefs of staff. Until Eisenhower, the position was regarded almost as clerical. H. R. Haldeman was Richard Nixon's campaign manager. He resigned in the midst of the Watergate scandal, and became a successful businessman in California. James Baker, Reagan's chief of staff until 1985, subsequently became secretary of state. Donald Regan, who took his place, had a long career at Merrill Lynch before becoming Reagan's secretary of the treasury and chief of staff. John Sununu, like Sherman Adams, was governor of New Hampshire before becoming George Bush's chief of staff.

French prime ministers, in contrast, have long public careers before and after serving their terms. Michel Debré was a major theoretician, principal author of the 1958 Constitution, and founder of *l'Ecole Nationale d'Administration*. Georges Pompidou subsequently became president. Jacques Chirac is the RPR leader and mayor of Paris. Raymond Barre is a center-right coalition leader and was an unsuccessful presidential candidate in 1981. Pierre Mauroy and Laurent Fabius had distinguished careers before and after their tenures as prime minister. Fabius headed the 1989 Parti Socialiste slate for the European elections. Michel Rocard is a major figure in Parti Socialiste politics and aspires to the presidency, and Edith Cresson served formerly as minister of agriculture. They have been active in the past, and continue to be so.

PRESIDENTIAL GOVERNMENTAL SYSTEMS: FRANCE AND THE UNITED STATES COMPARED

The only *purely* presidential system among industrial democracies belongs to the United States. Finland has a directly elected president without executive powers, and France has a directly elected president, but with additional accoutrements from the European parliamentary model. Because the French president does have executive powers—substantially greater than those of the American president—it is reasonable to consider these two as the presidential systems and the others as parliamentary.

The similarities between France and the United States are straightforward: both are political systems in which personalities play a major role. French political parties are very much the creation of charismatic figures, and their rise and decline reflect the fortunes of their patrons more than the preferences of the electorate. On the right, the *Union pour la Démocratie Française* (1978) was created by merging the Republican Party with several smaller parties. The Republican Party was formed by Valéry Giscard d'Estaing in 1977 as the heir to the Independent Republican Party, formed by Giscard in 1962 when he and several others abandoned the *Centre National des Indépendants et Paysans,* which effectively was destroyed after Giscard departed.

Among the other parties in the right coalition, the *Centre des Démocrates Sociaux* stands out. Founded in 1976 by Jean Lecanuet, who negotiated a merger with Jacques Duhamel's *Centre Démocratie et Progrès*, the *Lecanuetistes* and *Duhamelistes* became Giscardians in 1974. They subsequently merged and were absorbed by Giscard's UDF. On the left the most powerful personality after Mitterrand is Michel Rocard, who departed, and seriously weakened, the *Parti Socialiste Unifié* to move to the middle. Those who followed him are called *Rocardiens*.

The French priority given to the personal aspect of French leaders is enhanced by the immense power and prestige given to the presidency by the Fifth Republic Constitution, fashioned in accord with the wishes of Charles de Gaulle. Each inhabitant of the office, de Gaulle, Pompidou, Giscard, and Mitterrand, has been intellectually able and politically courageous. And until Mitterrand, no president had faced a hostile majority in the National Assembly. Although the prime minister, partially as a consequence of the first example of divided government and partially because of Mitterrand's penchant for symbolism, is surely becoming more important, Fifth Republic France has been eminently a government by the president.

The "Other" Presidential System

Although the United States also has a presidential system, which is even more obsessed with personality, the contrast with France is stark. American politicians sometimes leave major parties, as illustrated by the southern Democrats recruited by the Republicans. Sometimes they form minor parties or merge with other minor ones, as did Strom Thurmond (States' Rights in 1948), George Wallace (American Independent in 1968), and John Anderson (National Unity in 1980). With few exceptions, minor parties have limited electoral impact. Martin Van Buren ran as a third party candidate in 1848, splitting the Democratic vote and paving the way for Zachary Taylor's election. In 1912 Theodore Roosevelt, denied the Republican nomination, ran as a "Bull Moose" and caused the election of Democrat Woodrow Wilson.

French minor parties have a better chance of cooperating with major parties, merging to become major parties, or extracting electoral concessions than do American minor parties, as they are able to maintain a rudimentary organization (and because of their role in strategic voting). Although some American third parties are organizationally grounded, most are personal factions. John Anderson's

1980 candidacy illustrates the problem. Anderson, a prominent Republican congressman, entered the primaries, lost to Reagan, and then bolted to form the National Unity Party. But the National Unity Party was not really an organization. If no symbolic importance was attached to political parties, Anderson *should* have done well. He looked presidential (handsome, tall, white-haired), and he lined up the usual gaggle of entertainers. However, he earned a mere 7 percent of the vote and faded away. One aspect of the 1980 campaign that is rarely remembered is the consensual decision to allow Anderson to engage in the national debates (with Jimmy Carter and Ronald Reagan) if he could achieve a 15 percent approval rating in the surveys. He was not nominated by an organization. He had no organization, and no "Andersonians" could be found.

French minor parties, too, disappear. The right-wing Poujadist movement of the 1950s vanished along with its leader. But the *Front National*, with a similar ideology, seems more durable. It is backed by a network of organizations, is not short of money, has ten members of the European Parliament, has 137 regional councilors, holds the balance of power in five of twenty-two regions, and has about 60,000 dues-paying members.

No such party could be organized in the United States for cultural and historical reasons. Ironically, American parties are so porous that anyone can claim their imprimatur. But only with that imprimatur is electoral success likely.

Self-Starters in Two Political Cultures

It is the absence of even the semblance of party organization that, ironically, elevates American politicians to center stage for a brief moment in time, only to dispatch them to obscurity when their fling is over. American politicians—even presidents—are "self-employed politicians."[24] They most decidedly *do not* owe their jobs to the party. Thus, even in France where political parties, notably those on the right, are arenas of personal ambition, personalities are more durable.

In the United States the nature of the prepresidential employment was the Congress, before the 1968–72 reforms. The eleven candidates before reform served an average of eleven years in Congress, and five of them had been vice-president. But after the reforms, candidates served an average of only four years in Congress. The recruitment pattern shifted to the states, where Carter, Reagan, and Michael Dukakis served.

Table 4.3   French Prime Ministers' Political Experience Under Giscard and Mitterrand

	Years experience			
	Civil service	Ministry	International	Economic
Raymond Barre	11	6	5	12
Pierre Mauroy			4	
Laurent Fabius	5	3		3
Michel Rocard	8	4		10

Paltry though this experience is in quantity, it is also qualitatively unlike that of European and Japanese politicians. In France, the other presidential system, politicians are not "self-employed." Those who become president or prime minister are likely to have come from the civil service and to have trained at one of several highly selective institutes such as *l'Ecole Nationale d'Administration*. (See Table 4.3 to examine the careers of the prime ministers serving under Valéry Giscard and François Mitterrand.)

Much like the British with public schools (especially Eton, Harrow, Marlborough, Rugby, Winchester, and "Oxbridge") and the Japanese with Tokyo University, French politicians are recruited from a narrow range of institutions. Beginning with the top academic *lycées* in Paris, through *classes préparatoires* to a *grand écoles* (Institute d'Etudes Politiques, l'Ecole Normale Superieure, or l'Ecole Polytechnique), they progress finally to *l'Ecole Nationale d'Administration* (ENA).[25] Among the current crop of French politicians, ENA can claim credit for: Michel Rocard, Jacques Chirac, Valéry Giscard d'Estaing, François Léotard, Laurent Fabius (former prime minister), Jean-Pierre Chevènement (Mitterrand's defense minister) and Pierre Joxe (Mitterrand's interior minister).[26] As Dogan explains, "Half the deputies who graduated from these schools became ministers. The political elite is thus not the fruit of spontaneous generation. It prepares itself long ahead of time—twenty, thirty, or forty years beforehand."[27]

The recruitment process attenuates, to some extent, the obsession with personality so characteristic of French politics. To become president, one must "go public."[28] However, in the United States, going public is all that is required.

Since the campaign reforms of the 1970s, a potential candidate for the American Presidency *must* go public for support, sometimes more than a year before the nominating convention. The candidate then can only hope to obtain the nomination through cultivating widespread public approval. Experience is not the issue; the ability to campaign effectively is.[29]

In France before one goes public, one must have had a career in government: "In order to qualify as a candidate for the Presidency, an individual must first establish a national position in government or in opposition."[30] Giscard spent thirty years in ministerial posts; Mitterrand sixteen years. By contrast, of the three most recently elected American presidents, only one, George Bush, has had any national government experience.

Thus, one cannot say that presidential electoral systems, by themselves, encourage amateur politics, as only the United States practices amateurism. French politicians do go public, but with nowhere near the zeal American politicians do. But, as Richard Rose says, "the American way to the top is very different from the career of politicians in parliamentary systems."[31] The British, West German, and Japanese parliamentary systems illustrate well Rose's conclusion.

CANDIDATE SELECTION BY REGIONAL COMMITTEE: ITALY

Although Italy's government appears chaotic, with resignations occurring more often than in the other parliamentary democracies, its political parties are exceptionally potent. Between 1944 and 1987 the nation endured forty-six governments averaging ten months each, with the longest lasting just over two years. But the illusion of instability is mitigated by powerful political parties. Emerging from the rubble of World War II, political parties preceded the government. By the time of the first postwar election, political parties had truly managed the government for four years, and they retained much of the authority normally given to governments. *Partitocrazia* (rule by party) has remained in place.

The point here is not that Italian parties are more prominent than are parties in the United States, for parties in *all* industrial democracies are stronger than American ones. Rather, the Italian parties, almost in the fashion of the old Marxist one-party systems, link directly with the government. Most prime ministers in the parliamentary democracies, although owing their jobs to the party, do not seek party approval for party initiatives.

Partitocrazia: Italian "Marxist" Party Traditions

In Italy inconsequential distance separates party and government: "The prime minister is normally little more than a figurehead who serves at the pleasure of party leaders, a fact explaining why many ambitious politicians prefer to be party secretary rather than prime minister."[32]

Parties have members, people who pay dues, but fraud in issuing membership cards is widespread, so individual party members count for little else. Unlike parties in other formerly fascist countries, such as West Germany, those in Italy have not forsaken the autocratic structure used by Benito Mussolini's Fascist Party. Power effectively rests in executive committees: the chairman of this body is also secretary of the party. Executive committees are accountable to larger bodies—regional conferences of various sorts—and ultimately to a more broadly based constituent assembly.

However, the leaders select members of the larger committees, and therefore, accountability is sheer formality. So, although Italian politics often appear out of control, the major parties are genuinely in charge:

> *Partitocrazia* is not simply a matter of party control of the levers of governmental power. It extends well beyond to embrace most of the entire social, economic, and cultural life of the country. One of Italy's unique features is the existence of a vast sector of public and semipublic bodies that dominate almost every area of national life: organizations as disparate as giant industries and banks, welfare and charitable agencies, radio and television, scientific and other research institutes, La Scala and other opera houses, the Venice Biennale and other cultural festivals, sport and recreational associations, hospitals and universities....Controlled completely or in party by the state, they are subject to government influence, which in practice means party influence.[33]

Parties also dispense the spoils of office: jobs, building contracts, pensions, loans, franchises, and subsidies. Party constituent associations are thus more than vehicles of candidate recruitment; they are conduits of the disposition of rewards, much like the now defunct American urban political machines.

The Christian Democrats

The Christian Democrats, the approximate analogue to the British Conservative Party, have been the leading vote getters since the war, but never by absolute majority. Christian Democratic pluralities declined incrementally, and in 1976, to continue in government, the party had to establish an informal alliance with the Communists, who had received just about as many votes. In 1983 the Socialist party leader formed a governing coalition, which was disbanded in 1986. A similar fate befell a Christian Democratic coalition in 1989.

The composition of the governing coalition is not as consequential as the party factions. During the raucous annual conventions, faction leaders reach accords on the composition of a cabinet, should they continue in the coalition, which, of course, they will. The party's secretary and leader is chosen at these meetings, and the choice is ratified by the annual congress.

Origins and Organization: A Question of Independence.   At its inception, the Christian Democratic Party was a creature of the Church, much as the British Labour Party was a production of the unions. The Church, for example, furnished a network of Catholic associations, parish organizations, and supplied personnel, frequently local clergy, to bring about separate local party organizations.[34] During this process, the Christian Democrats were overseen by a most prestigious proponent of liberal Catholicism, Alcide de Gasperi, whose role in the Italian Christian Democrats parallels Konrad Adenauer's in the German party. De Gasperi had the added difficulty of being there during the Fascist period, when relations between the Church and the government were complicated. He became Secretary General in 1944, when the National Council was created.

Between conventions, the National Council runs the party. This body, half of which is from the legislature, is elected by the annual congress. There are thirty ex-officio members, mainly faction leaders and regional secretaries who augment the regular 160-person council. Day-to-day party activities are managed by a forty-five-member executive committee, elected by the congress.

Candidate Selection.   Parliamentary candidates are normally selected at the regional or provincial level. The parliamentary constituencies often contain several provinces, making intraconstituency party bargaining a complex affair. Each party will generate a constituency list, containing one name for each parliamentary seat to be filled. As no party will win all the seats, the *preference vote*, a form of proportional representation, is used. The voter chooses a party, then three or four members of that party. If a party wins six seats, for example, those seats will go to the top six vote getters. Candidates need not only party assistance for nomination; more importantly they need party help in winning or placing well in the preference vote. The party is the most eminent source of this help, less so in the Christian Democratic Party than on the parties of the left, mainly the Communist party. In 1991 the system was changed by referendum to allow a voter only one choice.

The Christian Democratic Party, like Japan's Liberal Democrats, is driven by its factions. Candidate selection begins with National Executive Committee (NEC) guidelines, setting out nonbinding criteria (age, seniority, party experience, and so on). The NEC then assigns the number of candidates each provincial party can select for the Chamber of Deputies party list. Concerning the Senate, the NEC generally reserves thirty safe constituencies for party stars. Within these limitations, provincial parties construct their lists. Ordinary members do not participate; rather, the provincial party committee—the governing body—and the provincial electoral commission do the job. The result is one of negotiation between the various factions.

Each province dispatches its list to the appropriate regional committee, which fiddles with the order of candidates. Then the list is sent forward to the NEC. Still, other than the head of the list, the NEC and regional committees infrequently impose an order, expecting that the various factions have been dealt with or the list would not have been directed forward. The head of the list *(capolista)* is the NEC's choice and will be a leading party official and possibly a local dignitary. He is followed by other national party leaders, local party leaders, and incumbent deputies. Finally, the end of the list contains an alphabetical list of the rest of the candidates.

The factions compete both during the party selection process and during the election, where the minority of voters reordering the list is slavishly courted. Factions also grapple for the allocation of the safe Senate seats. These seats can be the nerve center of Promethean struggles, as in 1983, when the Christian Democrats recruited prominent intellectuals, previously uninvolved in party politics, to stand for safe seats in Rome, Milan, Turin, and Naples. Those already in these seats were moved to other safe seats to make room for the new blood.

Other parties, except the Communists, differ only in degree from the Christian Democrats, about which Douglas Wertman opines:

> The DC's candidate selection process is fairly chaotic and disordered, and is primarily a process of negotiation and compromise among the party's factions. The final authority rests with the National Executive Committee, but in practice most Chamber candidates and many Senate

candidates are selected at the provincial level with some regional input.[35]

Durable as it is, the Christian Democratic Party had to survive a serious rebellion in 1990, when two of its younger members proposed referenda that would modify the proportional representation system by electing members of the Senate by plurality. Both the Christian Democrats and Socialists vigorously oppose the referenda, and there is small chance of anything coming of it. Curiously, the Italian reformers model their efforts on the British first-past-the-post system at the same time that British reformers, principally the *New Statesman and Nation* and its pressure group, Common Voice, are demanding proportional representation![36]

The Italian Communists

The Communists can count on the votes of about one-third of the electorate, putting them in second place behind the Christian Democrats. Such strength may appear aberrant in a Catholic country with open elections and a prosperous economy, albeit one in which major institutions are managed by the government. The Italian Communist Party was, however, verifiably independent of Moscow in the days when the U.S.S.R. asserted a claim on European Communist parties, and never notably fierce in its Marxism. It enjoys a reputation (unusual in such a traditionally corrupt and inefficient government) for good management of the numerous cities that have Communist elected leaders, and is generally believed to be the party most antagonistic to the Mafia. Nevertheless, it has not been invited to join a formal coalition.

Its greatest chance for inclusion was destroyed when terrorists killed Christian Democratic leader Aldo Moro in 1978 at the very moment when his party was interested in incorporating the Communists into the mainstream. The Red Brigades, denounced by the Communists, sought to repudiate the Communist strategy of compromise. Moro was not really the target; rather, the moderate Communists were to be exposed as frauds. Nonetheless, the party has sought to associate itself with the various Social Democratic parties in Europe and to eschew Leninism as dogma.

Curiously, given its moderation, it remains Leninist in organization, adhering to the principles of *democratic centralism* (prohibiting open dissent once a policy decision is made). Like other Italian parties, the Communists are not democratic. Candidate selection, party platforms, and the like, are routinely rubber-stamped by a compliant party congress, as true power rests with a seven-member secretariat, headed by the party secretary. Centralization and autocracy do not distinguish it from the other parties, however.

In 1991 the Communists, bowing to the inevitable, changed their party name to the Democratic Party of the Left. Slipping in the polls for fifteen years, the party abandoned the polemics of class warfare and embraced the spiritual leadership of Pope John Paul. Because the Christian Democrats' partners in coalition have always been the Socialists, the new Democratic Party of the Left aspires to appropriate their position. Bettino Craxi, Socialist leader, dismissed the former Communists as "papists."

But the party's spirited passion for discipline is exceptional. Its candidates can count on much more help in gaining votes, and individual campaigns for preference votes are not allowed. Whereas one-third of the Christian Democratic candidates believed their party did nothing to help them, only 4 percent of the Communists' candidates thought that their party ignored them.[37]

THE DURABILITY OF PARTY RULE

In government the strength of the parties is even more apparent. When a coalition disintegrates, an election is not automatically called. The old coalition lingers on as a caretaker until a new coalition is put together. Failing this, an election will be called. The *Partitocrazia* is widely covered by Italian television. Joseph LaPalombara recalls:

> One has the impression of a continuing "summit meeting" among men who may or may not be cabinet members but who nevertheless exercise powers of life and death over them, and over public policies as well. What kind of democracy is this, [reformers] ask, where those who head the political parties, including parties that are supposed to be in opposition, get together outside parliament, or away from the cabinet, and decide by themselves which laws will or will not pass, which government will or will not survive?[38]

However, the nobility of *Partitocrazia* was not lost on Italian political elites when the Radical Party successfully nominated Ilona Staller ("Cicciolina," which means "cuddles," or "little fleshy one"), the country's most notorious porn star, in 1987. (In 1990 she offered to have sex with Saddam Hussein if he would agree to free foreigners in Iraq.) Her name, number forty-nine on the Radical Party list of fifty-four, was placed there on the theory that she might attract votes to the tiny party. Keep in mind the Christian Democratic strategy of attracting nonparty notables, and the tactic is plausible.

The Radical Party is not a party of the absurd, and its choice of Cicciolina was predicated on the premise that, while she would lose, she would give desperately needed publicity to the Radical Party. Radical Party theory has its roots in Adam Smith; it is secular, liberal, and internationalist in outlook. In 1983 the Radicals nominated and elected the leftist Professor Tony Negri, who had been jailed for links with the Red Brigades. The Radicals also named Enzo Tortora, a television personality accused of drug dealing, to a high party post. Negri invoked the immunity available to party and government officials and escaped to Paris; Tortora was arrested and acquitted. But Cicciolina stayed put, much to the chagrin of the women who held high posts in the party. Unlike Negri, who used his immunity to escape, Cicciolina used hers to continue her performances of "Perversion," as she could no longer be prosecuted for violation of the public decency acts. She also voted to send Italian troops to the Persian Gulf in January 1991, in support of the American-dominated war in Iraq. (Perhaps Saddam should have taken her more seriously.)

CANDIDATE SELECTION BY NATIONAL COMMITTEE: JAPAN

The Japanese formula for candidate selection, like the German one, bears a superficial resemblance to the American formula. Here the common component is money: the Japanese electoral procedure is more exorbitant than the American one, and bribery is as blatant. Since the Liberal Democratic Party is as eternal as the Democrats in the American House of Representatives, it also divides itself into factions. Like American parties, the factions are not ideological. In spite of these superficial similarities, Japanese factions are long-lived, unlike the ephemeral, personality-based coalitions that spring up and vanish with each American election.

The utilization of money is also entirely antipodean. In the United States, individual legislators sell favors to political action committees. The renowned "Keating Five" in the Senate took millions from savings and loan miscreant Charles Keating to protect him from a federal investigation of financial impropriety. Legislators, not voters, are bribed. In Japan, voters—much like the recipients of American urban machine largess in the nineteenth century—welcome gifts (payment of school fees, household appliances) for their votes. As is true everywhere except the United States, money largely is raised and distributed by party organizations; for party organizations are genuinely important, even in the money politics of Japan, as in all parliamentary systems.

The Liberal Democrats

Between 1945 and 1955 the Japanese government was controlled by various groups that in 1955 fused to form the Liberal Democratic Party (LDP), which is neither liberal nor democratic. There were some coalition governments with the Japan Socialist Party in 1947–48, but the U.S. Army of Occupation was calling the shots, and such coalitions were in ill repute. Because most rightist politicians had been purged, as in Germany, there was a pressing need for reliable conservatives. Since 1955 the LDP has never been out of power (it ruled in coalition with a tiny conservative fragment, the New Liberal Club, between 1983 and 1986).

Japan's election schema, as we have seen, is unlike any other industrial democracy. It is similar to the prewar "multimember" district system. From two to six (usually three to five) representatives are elected from each district. In spite of multiple representation, each voter gets one vote, a "single, nontransferable vote." That is, voters vote for only one candidate, though there is more than one seat to fill.

Because the number of seats is supposed to be allocated according to population, Japan's immense urbanization should have resulted in reapportionment. As the LDP is stronger in rural areas, it has not redistricted. Sometimes, malapportionment is so severe that it takes five times as many votes to elect a representative in urban than in rural areas. In response to a 1983 court ruling, the LDP added a few urban seats and took a few away from the rural districts, but the structural problem remains unreformed.

Had the Diet (parliament) been fairly apportioned, the LDP would have lost about twenty-seven seats, and the Japan Socialist party would have dropped seven. In 1990 the LDP won 275 seats. As there are 512 seats in the Diet, subtract twenty-seven and the LDP would have 48 percent, not 54 percent. Thus, it would have had to form a coalition with some of the smaller parties, such as Komeito (with which it traditionally cooperated).

The LDP defies reapportionment because it and the farmers have formed an informal alliance that, except for formal institutionalization, resembles the Labour-trade union pact in the United Kingdom. The LDP has traditionally protected farmers by prohibiting the import of rice, though Japanese rice costs about seven times as much as rice imported from other Asian countries and the United States.

The Enduring Survivors.   The LDP runs more than one candidate (it averages 2.6) in many districts. Individual LDP members run against other party members, as well as the nominees of other parties. If voters want to throw out the rascals, they have to go beyond rascal A to rascal B; therefore, the LDP frequently leaves it up to the candidates themselves to sink or swim. Much as in the United States, personality, pork barrel, and bribes are influential. Candidates must form personal support groups to buy votes.

The practice is not precisely like the temporarily mobilized American support groups that roam the primary elections. Rather, it almost resembles the old-style urban machine, but is more personal. Unlike the candidate-centered organizations that run campaigns in American primary elections, the Japanese candidate support groups remain in place. More than half the members of the Diet are the sons of former Diet members, a testament to the durability of candidate organizations. The campaign itself lasts only a month, and is carefully regulated; door-to-door canvassing is prohibited, and the number and location of posters is regulated. (The laws are routinely violated and arrests are made.) Political TV was permitted after 1969. But few ads are allowed, and the media are not a factor.

The LDP emerged as an elite, parliamentary party, an alliance among incumbent legislators who had their own election machines. Like the Christian Democrats in West Germany, the LDP was a concord of local notables. It is governed by an executive committee whose most important member is the party president. The president is, according to the LDP constitution, to be elected by party conventions for a two-year term. However, all but two—Tanaka and Ishibashi—have been ratified in an uncontested vote. Most often the president simply emerges, like pre-Thatcher Tory leaders. The Japanese like to avoid open disputes, and a shoot-out like the Thatcher-Heseltine vote in the United Kingdom in 1990 would be unlikely. Culturally and financially open duels can be costly: in the Tanaka-Fukada contest (1972) the average delegate bribe was about $70,000.

A few reformers tried a two-stage primary election process, with the first stage allowing all party members to vote, with the two highest candidates facing each other in a run-off at the party convention. But the party gave it up after one excessively costly, dreadfully disruptive attempt. Technically, a candidate needs the endorsement of fifty Dietmen to go to the convention; in reality, factional negotiation is how one gets the job.

LDP presidents select their assistants personally. There is a party executive committee, a cabinet-type group that engages in organizational and policy matters, a Policy Affairs Research Council, an extremely large research organization with many committees operating as semi-independent policy groups (Japanese iron triangles). There are also the National Organization Committee, the Party Discipline Committee, the Election Policy Committee, the Public Relations Committee, the Diet Policy Committee, the Finance Committee—all active national committees. In addition, there are the LDP Parliament Group and various publication and training groups situated in the party's impressive headquarters near the Diet in Tokyo.

The Factions.   The real power in the LDP is in the *factions.* They play a major role in the selection of the president and in the funding of parliamentary candidates. The factions, less ideological than those in France, are instruments of personal power. Bradley Richardson and Scott Flanagan write:

> While factions stem from many different sources, such as graduation from common elite schools or espousal of a common ideology or interest, the primary basis for the organization of Liberal Democratic Factions is a personalistic affiliation of rank and file members of parliament with one or another of the party's strongest politicians.[39]

Factional leaders change. Here are three decades of major factional alignments (remember, these are *within* the Liberal Democratic Party):

    1959   Ikeda Sato Kishi Miki Kono
    1982   Suzuki Tanaka Fukuda Komoto Nakasone
    1989   Takeshita Abe Miyazawa Komoto Nakasone

The 1990–91 factions, each named for its leader, are:

    Takeshita   (121)
    Abe   (89)
    Miyazawa   (87)
    Nakasone   (87)
    Komoto   (30)
    Nikaido   (14)

The factions are major avenues to top positions in government; they are also the conduits to Japan's money politics, the most expensive in the world. In 1990 the Liberal Democratic Party spent $1.5 billion, compared to the $400 million spent in 1988 by all candidates for the American presidency. Of this gargantuan sum, about 15 percent was raised by LDP central headquarters by strong-arming major business associations, especially members of the *Keidanren* (Federation of Economic Organizations). About one-third of the amount was raised by individual candidates. The rest, the majority, came from the factions, most from the Takeshita faction, the largest and richest, in spite of the resignation of its leader due to the Recruit (corporate bribery) scandal.

The factions are the channel of recruitment to parliament and into the government. Normally, only faction leaders become prime minister. Only Toshiki Kaifu was not a faction leader. He was there only to guide the LDP out of its financial and sexual scandals. A businessman gave money and stock in the Recruit Company to almost every LDP power broker, and to many of those in the Japan Socialist Party as well. The bribes were for both explicit favors and for future good will, and they were extensive. The LDP replaced the prime minister (Takeshita) with another, untainted member of the Takeshita faction, Sosuke Uno. Not considered important enough for a bribe, Uno had taken solace in engaging geishas for sex. When the LDP lost a politically insignificant, but symbolically important, election to the upper house, Uno was replaced with Kaifu.

Factions establish expense accounts for Dietmen. They meet in plush surroundings, hold seminars, produce internal policy journals, but they are not really ideological; they are personal and social. They are, precisely, engines for the selection of the prime minister. Kaifu comes from the Nikiado faction, which carries little weight inside the party, and was selected only because he was free of scandal. More powerful factional leaders must respect a "decent interval" before they replace him, presumably with faction leader Shintaro Abe.

These sensations create the image, erroneously, of the LDP as a puppet for business interests. While business supplies massive amounts of money to the LDP, its electoral success is more assured because other interest groups—professional, educational, agricultural, and administrative—enjoy close relations with the LDP.[40]

Party Structure.   As Japan's Liberal Democratic Party has won every election for the past three decades, the explanation of party organization will be confined to the LDP. In Japan, except for the Communists, party membership is available to anyone who wishes to join and pay dues. Because, like most people, Japanese find other activities more rewarding, their parties are dominated by professional politicians, principally members of the Diet.

Parties maintain headquarters in Tokyo, with branch offices in prefectures (voting districts) and cities. In theory, annual party conventions decide policy. The membership in the annual confab is limited to two Diet members and two delegates from each prefecture. Every second year, this assembly selects a president and vice-president. If the LDP wins, as it always does, the party president becomes prime minister. Party leaders/prime ministers do not invariably change in harmony with an electoral cycle. A contemporary exchange, replacing Nakasone with Takeshita, was undertaken simply because the party thought it was time for a change, and it wished to keep party traditions alive. Eighteen months later, ruined by the Recruit Company bribery scandal, Takeshita resigned and was replaced by Sosuke Uno, still without an election. A few months later, Uno resigned, to be replaced by way of an LDP ballot by Toshiki Kaifu. Kaifu, aided by an inept socialist opposition, shepherded the party to electoral victory. Kaifu would unquestionably never have been given this opportunity had not the Takeshita faction stumbled.

The Executive Committee is the most powerful LDP organization, consisting of fifteen members of the House of Representatives, seven from the House of Councilors (the other house in the Diet), and eight appointed by the prime minister/party leader. The Executive Committee selects the Diet candidates in cooperation with other national policy committees, often the National Organization Committee, the Diet Policy Committee, and the Party Discipline Committee. The chairmen of these committees, together with the president, vice-president, and chairman of the Executive Committee, are the overarching ruling body. Decisions about LDP Diet candidates take into account local preferences, but are made nationally.

Candidate Selection.   The process begins locally. Prefectural branches propose candidates to the national Election Steering Committee. Like the British Conservatives, the LDP is relaxed about eligibility, and local notables—who can build personal organizations—are favored, even if they are not party members initially. Local notables often augment their personal political machines as a device to attract the LDP; by showing a well-funded organization, a potential candidate becomes more attractive.

The left parties are more selective (as is the British Labour Party), but the LDP is so relaxed that it issues retroactive certificates of nomination to nonparty members who ran as independents and won, proving again that the LDP is hardly an ideologically coherent body.[41] The real competition is between the factions, rather than between the LDP and opposition parties.

As is true of most French political parties, the Japanese LDP is a consequence of a merger between earlier parties, and each group (the Liberal Party and the Japan Democratic Party) retained its symbols and outlook. Since the LDP does not anticipate losing its lock, most factional leaders are more concerned about intraparty balance than possible defeat by an opposition party. The LDP survived in 1989 and 1990, rent with scandal and an unpopular tax. If it can survive these catastrophic events, it can surely fend off opposition challenges.

This process sounds boring, but it is not; intraparty factions are as intensely competitive as Italy's. When the factions resolve their differences, the Japanese government can change executives without an election, as also happens in Italy. And, though the selection process is *technically* centralized, the factions and local machines make it less efficient and more exciting.

The Japanese system resembles the French in that the civil service is the major path to the top: 82 percent of administrative vice-ministers (92 percent of the vice-ministers of the twelve cabinet departments) graduated from Tokyo University.[42] Since about one-third of cabinet ministers have been civil servants, the connection is strengthened.[43] The American elite is far less homogeneous: about 44 percent are from Ivy League universities.[44]

CANDIDATE SELECTION BY PRIMARY ELECTION: THE UNITED STATES

In the United States, primaries are the dominant mode of selecting delegates who will nominate a presidential candidate at their national convention. It would be inconceivable for a person to be nominated without having contested and won the primary elections. In addition, the primary election system ensured the nomination of those who could never have been nominated before the 1968–72 reforms: "Neither George McGovern, the nominee of 1972, nor Jimmy Carter, the nominee and president of 1976 and again in 1980, would—almost could—have been nominated under unreformed rules."[45] For those of us coming of political age in the era of television, any substitute for primary elections seems downright undemocratic. It was not always this way.

Hubert Humphrey was nominated by the Democratic Party in 1968 without having entered, much less won, a single primary election. He was nominated by the national convention, held hostage by retiring President Lyndon Johnson's near obsession that his vice-president be nominated, thus avoiding a repudiation of his Vietnam policy. From 1840 until the ill-fated Humphrey nomination, conventions selected nominees. Delegates to conventions were selected by state party caucuses or comparable organizations. There was no *intraparty* democracy. This period is now regarded with derision as the era of the "smoke-filled room." Between 1912 and 1968 reformers began to propose an alternate method: the presidential primary. The reform movement reached its zenith with Woodrow Wilson's presidency. Wilson proposed a *national primary* to replace the haphazard collection of caucuses, machines, and state primary elections. After Wilson, the nation lost its enthusiasm for reform. By 1968, when Humphrey was nominated, only about one-third of the delegates to either party's convention were selected by a primary, and many of these were chosen in nonbinding primaries.

As New Hampshire Goes?

If there were a national primary, that is, one held in all states simultaneously, no candidate would spend much time or money in New Hampshire. But New Hampshire, because it has the first primary, is more important to the media than New York, and New York's primary in April is more important than California's in June. New Hampshire's exaggerated influence occurs because primaries generate media attention and notions like *momentum*. As experiments in the democratization of politics, primaries are failures. As opportunities for media participation in politics, they are superb.

When New Hampshire's legislature established the primary, it was held in May. The date was changed a few years later to March, to coincide with Town Meeting Day. But the spring thaw impeded drivers on unpaved roads, so the date was set back again, this time to February. Implausible at it may be, these perfectly sensible decisions cast New Hampshire in the media glare as the first test of strength. Until 1972 many candidates bypassed New Hampshire or announced their candidacies after its primary had taken place.

However, with the reform, it became the most critical step, along with the Iowa caucus. In 1984 Iowa and New Hampshire received 32 percent of the primaries' media coverage, even though these two states contained only 3 percent of the nation's population and 3 percent of the delegates selected to either convention. Also, New Hampshire captures what there is to capture of public attentiveness. Before the event, 28 percent of national public samples claim to be following the campaign on television. Immediately after the New Hampshire primary, 45 percent begin to follow the campaigns. While there is some backsliding, interest does not return to its pre-New Hampshire low. (However, the proportion following the campaign in newspapers, after a modest spurt, returns to about 17 percent; thus, about half as many people follow the news by reading newspapers as do by watching TV.[46])

It is fairly obvious that voters make decisions on less than ideal criteria; it would be incredible that they would do otherwise. Besides maintaining "candidate issues" (i.e., questions about personality, integrity, and character rather than about policy or ideas), the media spend most of their time speculating about the horse-race components of the campaign.

Contrary to myth, winning the New Hampshire primary does not guarantee nomination. Since the reform, among Democrats who have won in New Hampshire, only Jimmy Carter became president. Because Republicans have had a near hegemony on the presidency, this circumstance is no surprise. Among Republicans, four New Hampshire winners (Nixon, Reagan [twice], and Bush) have won the presidency. Put another way, every president since reform has won New Hampshire. Doing well there gets a candidate into the next phase of the primary season.

The Trauma of 1968

Ironically, the New Hampshire primary election was a key ingredient in the events of 1968, a year permanently seared upon the memory of those who watched in horror as the Democratic National Convention deteriorated into a police-led assault on youthful protestors. Eugene McCarthy, a Democrat opposed to Johnson's prosecution of the war in Vietnam, entered the New Hampshire primary and earned 42 percent of the vote, a shockingly high showing against an incumbent president. (Actually, Johnson had not bothered to enter, and could have done so only by a write-in vote.) Widely interpreted as a repudiation of Johnson, McCarthy ultimately gave way to another antiwar Democrat, Robert Kennedy, but not before McCarthy had compelled Johnson to announce that he would not seek renomination. But what he *did* seek was the nomination of Hubert Humphrey. As thousands of antiwar protesters descended upon Chicago, Humphrey was cast in an unlikely role as defender of an unpopular war. When the protesters learned that, irrespective of their efforts, Humphrey *was* to be nominated, they rioted. The Chicago police responded zealously and the nation watched the carnage.

The Rise (Again) of the Primary. The Democratic Party took Humphrey's razor-thin loss to Richard Nixon as evidence that the havoc of Chicago could not be repeated. To this end, a party commission,

Table 4.4   Delegates to National Conventions Selected in Primaries: 1968–88

Year	Democrats			Republicans		
	Primaries	Delegates	% of votes	Primaries	Delegates	% of votes
1968	17	983	38	16	458	34
1972	23	1,862	61	22	710	53
1976	29	2,183	73	28	1,533	68
1980	35	2,378	72	34	1,516	76
1984	25	2,431	62	34	1,551	71
1988	34	2,842	68	36	1,771	78

headed by George McGovern (the McGovern-Fraser Commission), proposed an *open caucus* mode of nomination. It resisted the then radical proposal that caucuses be replaced by direct primaries. One prominent political scientist believed that if caucuses were made more accessible, "the demand for primaries would fade away."[47]

As happens when moderates try to abort radical reform, the hope was futile: "Both Democratic and Republican legislators reflected in the general post-1968 reform ethos that supported a more participatory democracy, and what nomination method could be more broadly participatory than a primary?"[48]

The next election saw a majority of delegates chosen by primary election, and by 1988 more than two-thirds were chosen in primaries (see Table 4.4). Even those states that have retained caucuses have found them transformed by television into *de facto* primaries. Once the nominating process was made more visible, it was a natural target for the media. Although controversy has been taken out of conventions, it is very much alive in the primary-election system. Primaries mean media exposure, money pouring into the state, and the horse-race aspect of politics, which is of more interest to the media and to voters than are the issues.

Intimate Dinner Parties Replace the Smoke-Filled Room

Primary elections obviously engage more people than does the caucus system, but not very many more. About one-third of the eligible voters participate. The primary season officially begins in February, but long before that the candidates are raising money, organizing staffs, and planning diverse strategies. These are the times for the political junkies, that small portion of the population who find politics interesting and primaries irresistible. When the season begins, these people select the candidate they wish to work for and start the

Table 4.5   Public Views of Private Behavior

Drinks heavily	90%
Used cocaine in past year	88
Has a serious medical problem	87
Ever cheated on income taxes	80
Used marijuana in past year	76
Ever undergone psychiatric treatment	74
Is a homosexual	62
Ever cheated on college course	43
Has been unfaithful to his wife	28
Are the TV networks:	
Generally objective?	40
Biased?	54
Which way?	
Liberal?	42
Conservative?	22
Democratic?	36
Republican?	28

Source: Adapted from Michael J. Lipton, "Exclusive TV Guide Poll: Campaign 1988 and TV," *TV Guide,* 36 (4), January 23-29, 1988, pp. 3–7.

process of meeting legal requirements and organizing local staffs. Few understand the extent to which this preprimary season is the functional equivalent of the smoke-filled room. In the 1980s candidates were scrounging around for money, consultants, volunteers, and media sustenance three to four years before the first test of strength, the Iowa caucuses in February.

The 1988 campaign of George Bush versus Michael Dukakis provides an excellent example of how ridiculous the primary system has become. Television, always uneasy with abstract ideas, had its dream election: major candidates of both parties were making fools of themselves trying to create the proper *image.* Who could forget Dukakis riding atop his tank, or Bush running from flag factory to flag factory? Besides exploiting these insubstantial occurrences, the media addressed substantial portions of time and energy to probing popular reactions to the behavior and ethics of reporters, rather than to explaining the ideas or preferences of candidates (admittedly difficult because very few offered any). Was Dan Rather a bully picking on George "The Wimp" Bush because he had nothing better to do? Has the public the right to know so much about a candidate's personal life? (See Table 4.5.)

Nelson Polsby provides a cogent summary of the rules of the road for primaries:

1. "Crazes or Manias." The intensity of short-term trends of opinion is amplified. Ollie North shot to the top of the charts as fast as Gary

Hart had done in 1984. Daily surveys by television recorded the adulation of our "national hero," and North tee shirts were hot sellers. A few weeks after his appearance ended, he was forgotten (but not before several candidates, Bush among them, tried to grab on to Oliemania by echoing the President's belief that North was a hero).

2. "Fads or social contagion." 1988 provides a textbook example: wimps, vulnerability, Dan Rather as bully.

3. "Heroes and bums." Politicians must put enormous effort into structuring the ways in which they are presented by and to the news media, since getting caught on the wrong side of something type casts a political figure and makes him fair game. In primaries, candidates with no visible policy disagreements with one another, must resort to describing their opponents stereotypically.

An Unlikely Villain: Eisenhower

Although the widespread use of the primary election has ended party organization, Theodore Lowi reminds us that there was a "pre-primary" villain, the implausible Dwight Eisenhower.[49] He was the first to adopt an antiparty strategy in 1952. With the Republicans seemingly mired indefinitely in minority status, defections from the Democrats were the ticket to success. As Eisenhower was sufficiently apolitical, he had been approached by the Democrats—the popular war hero, rather than a party stalwart was the key. Eisenhower broke party leadership's hold over the nomination and ran a campaign independent from the Republican Party. By successfully challenging delegates selected by party "bosses," the Eisenhower enthusiasts established a precedent:

> But the legitimacy of party leader control over delegates, the legitimacy of the delegate being the "property of the leader," *was already seriously undermined even before the significant spread of selection of pledged delegates by primary elections.*[50]

Adlai Stevenson (Eisenhower's Democratic opponent) followed Eisenhower's lead, as did John Kennedy in 1960. His successful campaign was even more divorced from established party leaders than was Eisenhower's, and he radiated a different kind of equally infectious personal charm. He won the nomination by going outside, using amateurs, defying the professionals; in effect, forcing them to accept him. The cycle was completed after the primaries became the only path to the top: from Richard Nixon's ill-fated "CREEP" (Committee to Elect the President) in 1972, nominees have run their own shows. Jimmy Carter, Ronald Reagan, Michael Dukakis, and George Bush set up personal organizations with almost no communication

Table 4.6   Confidence in the Media

	France	Germany	UK	Spain	US
A great deal; some	48%	42%	38%	46%	69%
Hardly any; none	49	59	60	51	30

Americans also believe that the media are more influential:

Percent believing media influence is large on:					
Judiciary	46	29	40	32	69
Legislature	37	44	40	38	78
Executive	48	46	44	41	81
Public opinion	77	71	80	70	88

Source: Adapted from Lawrence Parisot, "Attitudes About the Media: A Five Country Study," *Public Opinion,* January–February 1988, pp. 18, 60.

with their party's national committees. The position of chairman of the Republican National Committee is not eagerly contested. Normally, it goes to the successful presidential candidate's campaign aides. In George Bush's case, Lee Atwater, the author of Bush's campaign to "make Willie Horton Dukakis's running mate," was given the job. When he became fatally ill, it was offered first to drug czar William Bennett, who refused, and ultimately to retiring Secretary of Agriculture Clayton Yeutter, an unknown. He is, as are all party chairmen, subordinate to the White House. The organization he directs took second place when Bush established his personal reelection committee, which will dictate the use of party funds. As David Broder says, "The president's priorities will prevail—whatever the party or its chairman may wish."[51]

In this behavioral aspect, American presidents resemble their French counterparts. The personal presidency exists on both sides of the Atlantic, and appropriately, in the only two major democracies with separately elected presidents. The most severe contrast is with the United Kingdom, where Margaret Thatcher was removed as party leader and prime minister by the Conservative Party. Without question, the use of primary elections led to "the diminution, the constriction, at times the elimination, of the regular party in the politics of presidential selection."[52]

The Media Culture

America's political culture is the electronic media. Compared to other industrial democracies, Americans watch TV more and trust it more. (See Table 4.6).

The media culture requires a fundamentally different set of rules of the game. Consider the case of Senator Bill Bradley (Democrat, New Jersey). Seeking reelection, he benefited from a $1,000-a-plate dinner attended by Norman Lear, originator of the popular TV show "All in the Family"; Sydney Pollack, director of *Tootsie* and *Havana* (two politically correct movies); Sally Field; Goldie Hawn; and other glitterati. The party, in addition to raising money for Bradley's 1990 Senate campaign, was the beginning of the 1992 presidential season in Hollywood: "Stars commonly believe that their fame and their relationship with their fans give them as legitimate a role in the public arena as the image-obsessed politicians who compete with them for airtime on the evening news."[53]

Given the low status and esteem of politicians in the United States, they are probably right. National, state, and locally elected officials routinely rank among the least trusted and respected, placing ahead of only real estate agents, labor union leaders, stockbrokers, insurance salesmen, advertising practitioners, and car salesmen.[54] The road between Hollywood and Washington has been traveled by ambitious politicians since John Kennedy's alliance with "the rat pack" in the 1960s. Gary Hart routinely supped with Warren Beatty. Today, a serious candidate *must* make the pilgrimage. As for Mr. Bradley, once he arrived in Washington (in 1978), he learned his way around Hollywood:

> During that first Senate campaign he made friends with Michael Eisner, then a young executive at Paramount.... Through Mr. Eisner...the Senator became friendly with Mr. Ovitz [Michael Ovitz, President of Creative Artists Management]. Mr. Bradley now had as his door-openers the two men generally considered the industry's most influential.... Later, Mr. Bradley developed a close relationship with [Stanley] Pollock, who began to work quietly with the Senator to improve his speaking style.... All of these men acquired a deep commitment to Mr. Bradley's cause.... By the time Senator Bradley ceded the state to comedian Robin Williams...it was apparent that a political star was born.[55]

The Media Culture, Ignorance, and Amateurism.   The media culture is ideal for America, with its individualism, its profound distrust of political organizations, its belief in the common people, and its can-do spirit. Reliance upon celebrities to guide us can only be interpreted as a natural response to our distrust of government: bureaucrats may lie, but Meryl Streep does not. They concealed the truth about Alar and apples, but Meryl Streep did not (Alar, a spray, was said to be carcinogenic). She told us about the dangers, which, fortunately, proved to be nonexistent (a lawsuit against CBS's "Sixty Minutes" is pending). P. J. O'Rourke suggested Yahoo Serious as an expert on Star Wars, causing ripples of laughter. However, why is Yahoo Serious less credible than Sissy Spacek, Jane Fonda, and Jessica Lange? They testified before the House Democratic Task Force on Agriculture. They had all starred in movies about farmers, and "both the actresses and the politicos believed that the stars could contribute to Congress's understanding of the complex problems and issues facing the American farmer."[56] In a similar vein, Angela Lansbury of CBS's "Murder She Wrote" made a series of factually inaccurate commercials opposing a California initiative limiting elective office terms. The actress's son conceded that his mother had been misinformed. Celebrities offer simple solutions, because they are shallow and misinformed people. "I've never lived in a more repressive time than what happened during the Gulf" says Susan Sarandon. She adds, "What worries me is that we will have a series of police actions every time people get hip to the fact that there's a savings and loan crisis." Concerned about class divisions, she adds her definition of class in America: "A lot of people in America are embarrassed about who they're with."

With the exception of the United States, entertainers entertain. True, they occasionally find politics interesting. Yves Montand flirted with both left and right politics in France; Vanessa Redgrave is politically active in various left causes in England; and Glenda Jackson became a Labour Party nominee for Parliament. But these exceptions prove the rule.

But standing for office is not a realistic possibility for celebrities, as party backing is required. Movie stars and other notables stand a chance in Italy, but none do in Germany, France, or England (except for Glenda Jackson as a Labour candidate). Elites are differentiated; public life is a lifetime vocation, and fame in one area of life does not transfer to another. Even the business world does not create the necessary credentials. In the United Kingdom, no business leader has been a senior minister since World War II, and only a few "nonpolitical" persons have made it into the inner circles of German politics: "Very seldom can business leaders or popular personalities use their outside success to attain a top-level position of political influence quickly."[57]

In the United States, celebrities propose the idea that hunger can be eradicated by "Hands Across America" or that the election of a Republican Congress will lead to nuclear war (Roseanna Arquette on "Saturday Night Live"), because they do not know any differently.

Why should they? For them, and for us, bureaucracy is the enemy; "people" can solve any problem. Celebrities thus reinforce the anti-organizational biases that are contributing to the disintegration of the political system.

In addition to the cross-fertilization between entertainment and politics, American politics fosters a more sinister kind of celebrity transfer: the Jesse Jackson-Pat Robertson syndrome. Persons conspicuous in "causes"—TV evangelism, civil rights—can use notoriety to achieve instant political fame. Try to imagine either Jesse Jackson or Pat Robertson in a European political system. Does either have the patience to serve an apprenticeship? Obviously, both would be unknown in systems that do not encourage the transfer of resources from one celebrity status to another.

The media culture denigrates expertise, and therefore encourages ignorance. In fact, television *causes* ignorance! The more one watches TV, the less information one possesses. Jackson and Robertson are creatures of the media age.

For good reasons, Americans are excoriated for their ignorance of the most basic political information, their indifference to most issues, and their inability to understand common political concepts. Among the many reasons for this condition is our addiction to television. Not only does TV not contribute to one's ability to understand politics; it inhibits it.[58] Additionally, TV increases the likelihood that one will think about complex political problems in simplistic terms, thus making one vulnerable to the appeal of media stars and Hollywood celebrities, who—as media professionals—also think simply.

Television news reduces the ability of even well-educated people to think about issues in complex terms. This numbing impact results because TV news is entertainment. As Reuven Frank, former executive producer of NBC News, explains: "Every news story should . . . display the attributes of fiction, of drama. It should have structure and conflict, problem and denouement, rising action and falling action, a beginning, a middle and an end."[59] Dan Rather added the idea of "the magic moment." Unfortunately, those who watch the drama forget the details, and have less understanding of the complexity of the issues; those who are not exposed to the drama do significantly better. So the format of news and the charisma of newscasters contributes mightily to the media culture's emphasis on personality and the magic moment. Emotionalism reduces the ability to learn and remember, and TV news is emotional.[60] Connie Chung, commenting on the story of relatives of the victims of a TWA bombing over Greece, said: "And we saw again today, examples we have seen many times, grieving relatives trying to explain what no

one can explain." No one can explain it, behavior is random, unpre-
dictable, so why bother with exploring the causes of violence? Research by the National Institutes of Health reveals that it takes more
skill and concentration to eat than to watch television.

News anchors are celebrities. They are up-scale Madonnas. As
Ted Koppel explains: "At one time I did want to be a news anchor,
but I know I don't have the pizzazz. Apart from their talents as jour-
nalists Peter [Jennings], Tom [Brokaw] and Dan [Rather] are also extremely attractive and have a level of sex appeal I don't have."
Anchors know very little about politics. Here is one conversation
with an anchor that appeared in *TV Guide:* "Who was John Poindex-
ter? 'I'm drawing a complete blank. The president of El Salvador?'
Can you name a member of the Supreme Court? 'The Italian guy—
Scalion.' "

Rather, Jennings and Brokaw, uninformed as they may be, look
good compared to the new generation of newscasters: "Yesterday,
Today and Tomorrow" with Maria Shriver; "Prime Time Live" with
Diane Sawyer; and "Saturday Night with Connie Chung." These
news shows are star vehicles, with the content comfortably within
the shallow limits of celebrity conversation. At CBS, Van Gordon
Sauter introduced the magic moment, the appeal to the heart, as the
theme for news shows. His producers wore "MOMENTS" badges,
and Dan Rather often felt moved to "wonder at the marvels of the
human spirit."

> News stories on CBS tended to become two-minute morality plays, with
> heroes or villains and a tidy moral, to be summed up at the end . . . .
> Moment-hunting was expensive. Every story was expected to have its
> special video eye-catcher, and nobody asked how much it cost to get
> it . . . . Some stories made the air because they contained heart-
> wrenching Moments.[61]

The media culture soaks up celebrity money. If that were all, our political systems could survive.

But that is not all. The media culture encourages celebrity recruitment, not party recruitment, and it gives amplified credence to
the words and thoughts of celebrities. Initially, Hollywood's involvement was not much more than executive commitment, as in any
other business. Motion-picture mogul Louis B. Mayer, for example,
established a connection with Herbert Hoover.

But it was inevitable that the Washington-Hollywood connection
would drop to the level of the glitter, where the actors and actresses
spoon out their empty commitments. As stars replaced studios with
the current "star system," without much studio control, "men and

women of exceedingly limited political sophistication but bottomless ego and self-righteousness arrived at the formulation that in a media culture not merely does fame equal influence, it also equals wisdom."[62] It is natural for people who have realized fame with little effort to regard themselves as eminent. Presumably, Yves Montand, Jacques Brel, Sir Ralph Richardson, Sir Laurence Olivier, and others of equally celebrated status have given occasional thought to politics. But Vanessa Redgrave, champion of the Palestine Liberation Organization, has never testified at Commons about foreign policy.

But it is America's media culture that legitimates them. Ronald Brownstein writes:

> Politicians, their consultants, the disengaged public, and the inexorable demands of television for abbreviated debate have trivialized American politics. We have all lowered the level of discussion to a point where stars can more easily participate. . . . The expanding mobilization of Hollywood for political purposes has to be seen in that modern context of simplified debate, political celebrities, and minute public attention spans. . . . Celebrities have not caused the public to lose interest in politics; but their heightened political use is an understandable response to an uninterested public. Political campaigns and Washington's decisions occupy such a marginal place in American public life today that is is not unreasonable for political strategists to believe they must bribe the public to pay attention by occasionally adorning obscure debates with famous faces. At a time when public debate revolves around personalities who stand as political symbols, it is inevitable that causes will deploy as spokespeople stars who are themselves symbols—of intelligence, empathy, bravery, compassion, desire.[63]

Ed Asner, playing a journalist on television, becomes a muckraker, exposing administration perfidy in Nicaragua. Jessica Lange becomes a defender of the downtrodden before Congress because of her acting jobs. Neither graduated from college. Asner attended the University of Chicago for two years, before making his stage debut at age 24; Lange attended the University of Minnesota briefly. Yet, in the media age, the age of ten-second sound bites (the original thirty-second sound bite was regarded as too verbose), one looks to images, icons that can deliver a message quickly and with feeling.

IMPLICATIONS FOR DEMOCRACY

Is there one best electoral system? All have their strong points and weaknesses. Rather than answer the question Which is best? it may be better to ask What do we want? Table 4.7 provides another cir-

Table 4.7   Turnout in National Elections, 1945–88

1.	Australia	95%	15.	Norway	81%
2.	Netherlands	95	16.	France*	79
3.	Venezuela	94	17.	Greece	79
4.	Austria	94	18.	Finland	79
5.	Italy	93	19.	United Kingdom	77
6.	Belgium	93	20.	Canada	76
7.	New Zealand	88	21.	Ireland	75
8.	Portugal	88	22.	Japan	73
9.	West Germany	87	23.	Spain	73
10.	Denmark	86	24.	Turkey	67
11.	Sweden	85	25.	Switzerland	65
12.	Netherlands	84	26.	India	59
13.	Sri Lanka	82	27.	United States†	53
14.	Israel	81	28.	Colombia	47

* Parliamentary elections during the Fourth Republic, presidential elections thereafter (by universal suffrage since 1965).

†Presidential elections.

Note: The number of elections varies, depending on both the number of times parliamentary democracies call them, and the drift in and out of open elections in some less stable democracies.

cumstance for our consideration when weighing the most effective system—voter participation. Although Abraham Lincoln did oversimplify democracy with his definition, we can hardly have "a government of the people, by the people, for the people" if the people don't vote.

Nonproportional representation systems average 73.4 percent; proportional representation systems average 86.5 percent. The United States is considerably below average even for the lower turnout group, those without proportional representation. The American rate of participation is less than that of India, a poverty-stricken country with a history of political violence. In India, when 53 percent voted in the 1991 parliamentary election, the lowest turnout of any modern presidential election, the turnout exceeded that of the 1988 American presidential election by 3 percent.

Lack of participation aside, is there anything to recommend "ours" versus "theirs"? If we presume that only institutionally democratic organizations can participate in a democratic political process, then the United States is, as most of its citizens believe, the most democratic country in the world. Our culture posits that *any* individual choice is preferable to *any* organizational choice: Primaries are better than constituency associations because more people participate in them. And, if the United States has no peers in the sheer number of electoral opportunities, then surely ours is the model democracy.

Yet, the opportunity to *control* the contours of policy is less apparent in the United States than in the other industrial democracies. If we suspect, as do they, that most people have better things to do than keep up with the vagaries of countless elections, then fewer, more structured choices provide more of an opportunity.

5.
The Institutional
Structure of Choice

Almost from kindergarten American children are taught that Democracy means rule by the people, or as president Abraham Lincoln put it, "government of the people, by the people, for the people." As noted earlier, inventing the people is a task undertaken by all political organizations. Ask any class of undergraduates to name the most democratic country in the world, and—with rare exceptions—they will answer America. The notion of institutional constraint upon individual choice is infrequently contemplated. Traditional political science was largely a study of institutions. As the behavioral revolution captured our discipline, institutions receded in importance. Especially among the pluralists, institutions became largely neutral arenas that ratified interest-group victories. Moreover, institutions make a sizable difference in who wins and who does not. A distinguished contribution of public choice theories is their adamant insistence that the structure of the decision affects its content. As James March and Johan Olsen conclude:

> Political actors are driven by institutional duties as well as, or instead of, calculated self-interest; politics is organized around the construction

and interpretation of meaning as well as, or instead of, the making of choices; routines, rules, and forms evolve through history-dependent processes that do not reliably and quickly reach unique equilibria; the institutions of politics are not simple echoes of social forces; and the polity is something different from, or more than, an arena for competition among rival interests.[1]

Americans especially should be alert to the leverage of institutions, as the American Constitution evinces compelling evidence that James Madison, like a pre-Skinnerian proponent of behavior modification, understood that institutions could constrain behavior. Since Madison's leery image of human nature led him to posit that personal and policy ambition are natural cravings, the correction is to balance desire against desire by creating an intricate system of checks and balances, separation of powers, and federalism. Madison believed, rightly, that by inventing a fragmented government framework, he could protect it against both mercuric swings in public mood and dominance by a single faction. Today, as the only example of separation of powers *and* federalism, the United States government remains a model of frailty, best at inhibiting the mobilization and centralization of power, and worst at establishing autonomy. As discussed in earlier chapters, the thrust of American constitutional design is to sacrifice efficient government to a balance of power. Conflict between the legislative and executive branches is indigenous to the American system:

> The overlapping powers of the two branches, their representation of different constituencies, the contrast of the hierarchical, expert nature of the executive and the decentralized, generalist Congress, and the different time frames within which they operate guarantee that, except in extraordinary circumstances, conflict between them will remain a central feature of American politics.[2]

As we saw in the first chapter, the president's leadership is at the margins of policy, and without partisan control of Congress, its decentralization makes him unable to lead collectively. Under these circumstances, the autonomy of the state, the ability to make and impose a decision irrespective of the external environment is too much to ask. With presidential leadership at the margins, *members of Congress*, individually, are key initiators of policy, but they do not act autonomously; rather, they usually absorb and modify group demands. By design, the American government is more inhibited in mobilizing resources than are less fragmented parliamentary governments: "The resources of American government are small by comparison with governments in other advanced industrial nations."[3]

REPRESENTATION AND CONSTRAINTS
UPON CHOICE

The most elementary institution limiting our individual choice is the mode by which representation is allocated; how do we elect our representatives? The two main electoral systems are either plurality based (the first-past-the-post [a horse-racing term] systems like those of the United Kingdom and the United States, so-called because the candidate with the most votes, majority or not, wins) or some form of proportional representation.

Table 5.1 presents other institutions within democracies that limit personal choice. These institutions include whether the system is parliamentary or presidential, how the executive is elected, how the lower house is elected, the stability of the lower house, whether the system is federal or unitary, and the nation's economy.

With many variations, there are three basic ways of counting votes and assigning representatives: by plurality (the most votes), majority, and proportional representation (representation matched in proportion to votes received).

The Plurality Formula

The candidate with the most votes wins, even if that candidate does not win an absolute majority. Often plurality systems are accompanied by *single member constituencies*, as in the U.S. House of Representatives. The first-past-the-post formula, when combined with laws allowing only one representative per district, effectively mandates two parties. In a winner-take-all competition, with only one prize, the odds of a small party winning are remote. Those countries that use a pure plurality formula—the United Kingdom, the United States, Canada, and New Zealand—have, *at most*, two effective parties.

Japan's Unique Plurality Rule.   A singular use of the plurality rule is Japan: voters can support only one candidate, although the constituency is assigned more than one member. The top three, four, or five vote getters win. The Japanese mutation of the usual plurality rule may be an explanation of its rare stability. If we compare the countries using plurality rules, the consequences of the law are unmistakable. The winning margin in Japan is huge, about twice its nearest competitor, and the same party has won consistently.

Table 5.1   The World's Democracies

	Mode of executive selection	Electoral rules	Legislative independence	National-subnational division of power	Economic system
Australia	P	m	D	f	C
Austria	P	pr	D	u	MC
Bahamas	P	pl	D	u	CS
Barbados	P	pl	D	u	C
Belgium	P	pr	F	u	C
Botswana	P	pl	D	u	C
Canada	P	pl	F	f	C
Colombia	PE,PL	pl	F	u	C
Costa Rica	PE,PL	pl	F	u	C
Cyprus	PE,M	m	D	u	C
Denmark	P	pr	D	u	MC
Dominican Republic	PE,PL	pl	F	u	C
Ecuador	PE,M	m	F	u	C
Finland	P	pr	D	u	MC
France	PE,P,M	m	D	u	MC
West Germany	P	pl, pr	D	f	C
Greece	P	pr	D	u	MC
Iceland	P	pr	D	u	C
India	P	pl	D	f, u	CS
Ireland	P	pr	D	u	C
Israel	P	pr	D	u	MC
Italy	P	pr	D	u	CS
Jamaica	P	pl	D	u	CS
Japan	P	pl	D	u	C
Luxembourg	P	pr	D	u	C
Netherlands	P	pr	D	u	MC
New Zealand	P	pl	D	u	MC
Norway	P	pr	F	u	MC
Papua New Guinea	P	pl	D	u	C
Portugal	P	pr	D	u	MC
Solomon Islands	P	pr	D	u	C
Spain	P	pr	D	u	C
Sweden	P	pr	D	u	MC
Switzerland	P	pr	F	f	C
Trinidad	P	pl	D	u	CS
United Kingdom	P	pl	D	u	MC
United States	PE,PL	pl	F	f	C
Venezuela	PE,PL	pr	F	u	CS

PE = directly elected president with executive powers;
P = parliamentary (parliament selects or approves prime minister);
M = President elected by majority; PL = President elected by plurality.

pr = lower house elected by proportional representation;
m = lower house elected by majority; pl = lower house elected by plurality.

D = Lower house can be dissolved and elections held at any time;
F = Fixed term for lower house.

f = federal system (power divided between state and national government);
u = unitary government (power concentrated in national government).

C = Capitalist economy; CS = Capitalist-Statist Economy (substantial government ownership of production); MC = Mixed Capitalist (substantial government intervention, especially in the provision of welfare and social services).

Table 5.2   Average Winning Margin and Party Changes

Country	Average winning margin	Party changes/elections
Canada	11.4%	3/14
Japan	20.8	0/10
New Zealand	3.8	4/14
United Kingdom	3.8	5/12
United States	10.8	5/10

In the last ten elections, there have been no changes in party control of the government in Japan; in other industrial democracies such changes are more commonplace. (See Table 5.2.)

Yet, even with this huge margin of success, the Liberal Democrats have not won an absolute majority since 1963! Here is how the law gives a major advantage to the incumbent party:

> The system makes it extremely difficult to "throw the rascals out" if and when a high degree of national dissatisfaction develops with the government in power....In a single-member-district system such as prevails in the United States or Britain, a vote *against* an incumbent and his party automatically becomes a vote *for* the challenger and his. Therefore, a shift of a few percentage points within a district can easily alter the electoral result and the party of the representative. In Japan, however, since most candidates receive somewhere between twelve percent and twenty-five percent of the district's vote, even a ten-percent shift in a major party's support usually means only a three- or four-percent shift in the support level of each individual candidate from that party. In some cases, this is sufficient to ensure defeat for one of them, but the potential for the individual elector to vote effectively against the party as a whole is almost nil....Drastic shifts in the balance of party forces are extremely rare.[4]

The Majoritarian Scheme

In this scheme, candidates must win a majority. There are two ways this can be done: either a run-off between the top two candidates occurs after the initial vote or, as in the Australian House of Representatives, Irish parliamentary by-elections, and Irish presidential elections, voters *rank* candidates. If no candidate receives a majority, the last-place candidate is eliminated and those votes redistributed to the second choice candidates listed on those ballots. The process is repeated until one candidate earns a majority.

Table 5.3   Australian Parliamentary Elections

		First preference vote	Seats
1946	Labor	49.7%	58%
	Liberals	32.3	23
1949	Labor	46	39
	Liberals	39	45
1951	Labor	40	39
	Liberals	47	43
1954	Labor	50	47
	Liberals	38	39
1955	Labor	44	39
	Liberals	37	47
1958	Labor	42	37
	Liberals	37	48
1961	Labor	47	49
	Liberals	33	37
1963	Labor	45	41
	Liberals	37	43
1966	Labor	40	33
	Liberals	40	49
1969	Labor	47	47
	Liberals	34	37
1972	Labor	49	54
	Liberals	32	30
1974	Labor	49	52
	Liberals	41	54
1975	Labor	47	28
	Liberals	41	54
1977	Labor	39	30
	Liberals	38	54
1980	Labor	45	41
	Liberals	37	43
1983	Labor	49	52
	Liberals	34	26
1984	Labor	49	51
	Liberals	34	22

Australia: "Everybody's Second Choice."   The principal use of this system is in the Australian lower house; the upper house uses the single transferable vote.[5] The consequences are intriguing: in eight of seventeen elections held since 1946, the Australian Liberal Party, which has almost never won the most *first preference* votes (one of seventeen elections), has won more seats than the Labor party, which usually (fifteen of seventeen elections) attains a plurality of first preference votes. (See Table 5.3.) The Australian scheme rewards everybody's second choice more often than some people's first choice.

Table 5.4   Number of Parties in Plurality and PR Systems

	Number of legislative parties	Number of electoral parties	Shrinkage
Plurality Systems			
Canada	2.4	3.1	.7
New Zealand	2.0	2.4	.4
United Kingdom	2.1	2.6	.5
United States	1.9	2.1	.2
Japan	3.1	3.8	.7
Average	2.3	2.8	.5
Proportional Representation			
Austria	2.2	2.4	.2
Belgium	3.7	4.1	.4
Denmark	4.3	4.5	.2
Finland	5.0	5.4	.4
West Germany	2.6	2.9	.3
Iceland	3.5	3.7	.2
Israel	4.7	5.0	.3
Italy	3.5	3.9	.4
Luxembourg	3.3	3.6	.3
Netherlands	4.9	5.2	.3
Norway	3.2	3.9	.7
Sweden	3.2	3.4	.2
Switzerland	5.0	5.4	.4
Ireland	2.8	3.1	.3
Average	3.7	4.0	.3

Source: Adapted from Arend Lijphart, *Democracies* (New Haven, Conn.: Yale U. Press, 1984), p. 160.

Proportional Representation

Proportional representation (PR) usually means the list system. Whereas it can be made to appear formidably complex, the gist of the plan is that parties present a list of candidates in multimember districts. Voters choose a *party list*. Seats are allocated to each party according to the *proportion* of votes each receives.[6] The intent—usually successful—is to ensure the health of smaller parties. Not only do PR countries have more effective parties, but the shrinkage between electoral success and seats earned is less. A party that receives votes in an election is more likely to be rewarded with seats in government. (See Table 5.4.)

The more equitable transfer of popular support to legislative representation means that those who support third parties or even

**Table 5.5   The Relationship of Seats to Votes:
The United Kingdom (1987)**

	Votes	Seats (actual)	With PR (theoretical)
Conservatives	43%	376 (58%)	275 (42%)
Labour	31	229 (35)	200 (31)
Alliance	23	22 (3)	147 (23)

Source: Adapted from *New Statesman and Nation*, "The Intelligent Person's Guide to Electoral Reform," April 1990, p. 6.

fourth parties have every reason to believe that not only will their vote not be wasted but that the vote will be more faithfully transferred in legislative power. Arend Lijphart has calculated an *index of disproportionality*: the difference between electoral and legislative strength for the two largest parties, averaged for each election. For plurality systems, the index is 6.08; for proportional representation schemes it is only 2.03 (1.00 being most proportional).[7]

Examples of Distortion: England and France.   As we learned, the Australian majority plan is especially prone to distort party representation by using second place finishes. Yet, in the United Kingdom, the Conservative Party has won the last three elections with popularity *pluralities*, usually earning about 42 percent of the popular vote. Notwithstanding, the Conservatives have managed absolute majorities in Parliament. In the first two of three Conservative victories, the party won more than 60 percent of the seats with only about 42 percent of the total vote. The majority was reduced in 1987, but it was still a majority. The reasons for this persistent pattern are simple: the Labour Party can count on only one-third or so of the electorate, but its geographical base is good enough for it to have seats in approximate proportion to its percentage of the popular vote. But the smaller parties, especially the Liberals or the Social Democrats, usually get one-fourth of the popular vote but only a tiny smattering of seats, since their support is not great enough in enough constituencies to win them the *proper* amount of seats. (These two parties ran together in 1987, calling themselves the Alliance, and later they became the Liberal Democrats.) Often the Liberal Democrats finish second to either Labour or the Conservatives, while these two major parties more often finish first or third. Richard Rose's calculations speak volumes about the discrepancy between seats and votes. (See Table 5.5.)

Table 5.6   Popular Vote and Representation: 1988 French
              National Assembly

	1st Ballot votes	Seats	Ratio
Socialists	38%	48%	1.5
RPR (Gaullists)	19	23	1.4
UDF (Giscard)	18	16	1.1
Communists	11	5	0.5
National Front (Le Pen)	10	1*	0.0

*One seat.

Clearly, the Alliance parties and Liberal Democrats have a strong self-interest in changing the rules. When its leading figures were still in Labour, they opposed proportional representation for the same reason: self-interest, as Labour benefited from first past the post. While the Alliance wins about one-fourth of the vote in hundreds of constituencies, Labour concentrates its vote. However, the *New Statesman and Society*, a leader in electoral reform, claims that Labour's leaders are out of touch with the party membership.[8] Under proportional representation, Labour would lose about 13 percent of its seats, fewer than the Conservatives, but still a serious penalty. Under the first-past-the-post system, Labour needs about 44,000 votes per seat; the Conservatives, 37,000; but the Alliance, 334,000. Sixty-two percent of Conservative MPs won at least 50 percent of the vote, as did 52 percent of Labour MPs. However, the Alliance, spread thin, managed a majority for only 14 percent. Similar distortions can be found in France, as seen in Table 5.6.

The French election plan is built on the expectation of the majority. A general election is held. If no one candidate wins a majority of votes, the leading candidates participate in a run-off election—a second ballot. This second ballot, when voters *eliminate* rather than select, places a premium on a party's ability to find friendly allies. Small, unpopular fringe parties suffer while large, centrist ones prosper.

The second ballot allows any candidate with 12.5 percent or more on the first ballot to run, with the winner determined by first-past-the-post rules. In practice, while some candidates who technically qualify remain on the ballot, the institutional pressures to withdraw are substantial. Strategic withdrawals—the *desistement* of weak candidates in favor of those with a better chance—are sometimes negotiated by national party organizations and are known to candidates in advance. This arrangement has prevailed often between the *Parti Socialiste* (PS) and *Parti Communiste Français* (PCF).

The weaker candidate is expected to withdraw. This arrangement punishes the PCF for its strong discipline: about 95 percent of the PCF voters deliver for the PS candidate on the second ballot (in those districts where a left victory seems likely), but only about two-thirds of the PS voters support the Communist candidate.[9] Sometimes, Socialist candidates have not agreed to withdraw, for personal or ideological reasons, and have thus enhanced the probability of conservative victory. The RPR and UDF also have withdrawal agreements and occasional heretics (more in the more decentralized UDF than in the disciplined RPR).

The first ballot, sometimes erroneously likened to an American primary election, assesses the strength of the left candidates, not against the right but against other left candidates.[10] The same is true for right candidates. Will the left be best represented by the *Parti Socialiste* or the *Parti Communiste Français?* Will the right be better served by the Gaullists or the UDF?

The arrangement works best when the main parties of right and left are about equal in nationwide support. In 1988 the UDF and RPR earned 18 and 19 percent of the vote, respectively. Thus the withdrawal of a UDF candidate in Grenoble, for example, can be paired against an RPR withdrawal in Dijon. However, the problem becomes more complex when the parties are not equal, as is true of the *Parti Socialiste* (with 38 percent of the first-ballot votes) and the *Parti Communiste Français* (with only 11 percent). The result is that the PS enjoys the greatest *overrepresentation* while the Communists suffer the most extreme *underrepresentation*. (See Table 5.6.) In 1988 a second ballot was necessary 80 percent of the time.

Denmark: An Epitome of Exact Representation.   By comparing these ratios to those of Denmark from 1984 to 1990 we can see that the French system clearly distorts in favor of dominant parties, as the Socialists' vote-seat ratio demonstrates. The results of Denmark's last three elections are presented in Table 5.7. One obvious consequence of Denmark's exceptionally accurate rendering of voter preferences is the continued necessity for *coalition* governments.

While Margaret Thatcher reigned unhindered in the United Kingdom, responsible only for her parliamentary majority, Denmark was ruled by a coalition of center-right parties. In the 1990 elections, the "winners" were the Social Democrats, who gained fourteen seats since 1988. The party's biggest gain in any election since the turn of the century, it was a personal triumph for the Social Democrats' leader, Svend Auken. Seizing complete command of the party, he made substantial gains at the expense of the left-extreme Socialist-

Table 5.7   **Popular Vote and Representation in Denmark (1984–90)**

	Popular vote	Seats	Ratio
1984			
Social Democrats	31.4%	31.3%	1.0
Conservatives*	23.3	23.5	1.0
Liberals*	12.0	12.3	1.0
Socialist-People's Party	11.4	11.7	1.0
Radical Liberals	5.5	5.6	1.0
Center Democrats*	4.6	4.5	1.0
Progress Party	3.6	3.4	0.9
Christian People's Party*	2.7	2.8	1.0
Left Socialists	2.6	2.8	1.1
1988			
Social Democrats	29.8%	30.7%	1.0
Conservatives*	19.3	19.5	1.0
Liberals*	11.8	12.2	1.0
Socialist-People's Party	13.0	13.4	1.0
Progress Party	9.0	8.9	0.9
Center Democrats*	4.7	5.0	1.1
Radical Liberals	5.6	5.5	1.0
Christian People's Party*	2.0	2.2	1.0
1990			
Social Democrats	37.4%	36.3%	1.0
Conservatives*	16	16.7	1.0
Liberals*	15.8	16.2	1.0
Socialist-People's Party	8.3	8.3	1.0
Progress Party	6.4	6.7	1.0
Center Democrats	5.1	5.0	1.0
Radical Liberals	3.5	3.9	1.0
Christian People's Party	2.3	2.2	1.0

*Coalition members.

People's Party, which lost fifteen seats. However, his electoral triumph did not earn for him the right to govern, for the center-right coalition, whose support declined from ninety-nine to ninety-three seats, renominated Conservative leader Poul Schlüter. The original coalition of center-right parties, the Conservative, Liberal, Christian People's, and Center Democratic parties, was replaced in 1990 by the

Conservatives, the Liberal Party, and the Radical Liberals, whose combined total dropped from sixty-seven to sixty-six seats. However, the Radical Liberals elected to leave the government, leaving Schlüter with a Conservative-Liberal coalition of fifty-nine seats, or ten less than the seats won by the Social Democrats alone. In three successive parliaments, the Social Democrats—the party with the greatest number of votes and therefore seats—had been denied a role in governing.

PROPORTIONAL REPRESENTATION AND ONE-PARTY DOMINANCE

There is yet another consequence of proportional representation, doubtless unanticipated by its authors: all examples of one-party dominance in parliamentary governments occur in proportional representation systems or electoral systems that foster multipartyism (the American Democrats monopolize House elections but not presidential ones).[11] In a system like Denmark's, with three parties routinely scoring in double figures, any of them can remain in a bargaining position indefinitely. First-past-the-post designs, which appear initially to be less equitable, reduce the probability that a party without a majority can still govern for an indeterminate amount of time. By assuring a tighter ratio of seats to votes, proportional representation encourages more stability in governing coalitions, even as the coalition system contains the implicit threat of precariousness.[12]

France: From Majority to Proportional Representation and Back

France furnishes an excellent example of the political consequences of election laws. From the founding of the Fifth Republic until 1985, France used a majoritarian scheme to elect its legislature. The Socialist President, the vulpine François Mitterrand, crammed a proportional representation system through Parliament, theorizing that PR would increase the number of parties in the National Assembly. By enhancing minor party chances, Mitterrand reasoned that the chance of a right-wing landslide in seats (such as that enjoyed by the Socialists in 1981) was reduced by linking seats and votes more closely. His surveys told him that in the 1986 parliamentary elections, his Socialist Party would lose its control of the legislature. Under the majoritarian scheme, the right-wing opposition probably would earn a majority of seats in the Chamber of Deputies. Under a PR plan, more and smaller parties would win seats, alleviating the severity of the Socialist loss. The surveys were right. In 1986 small right-wing parties (principally Jean-Marie Le Pen's National Front) siphoned off enough voters to make it impossible for the two large right-wing parties running in tandem to receive a majority. This scheme was thwarted; the UDF and RPR, with small centrist party support, pieced together a slim majority.

Although the Socialist vote declined to one-third from 38 percent in 1981, the Socialist Party remained the largest in the legislature, but not part of the majority coalition. An additional bit of cunning was at work. Mitterrand wanted to enhance the status of the extreme right, forcing the moderate right to cope with and become bedeviled by extremism at the very moment when the Parti Socialiste was portraying itself (truthfully) as a party of moderation and consensus.

In 1986 the conservatives, with a working majority and a prime minister from their coalition, changed back to single-member districts with no proportional representation. The return to the two-ballot procedure in 1988 destroyed the National Front in the National Assembly (but not with the electorate).

The two-ballot system also reduces the incentives for smaller parties to merge. The RPR has been successful as a primary, first-ballot party.[13] Viewed initially, in the early years of the Fifth Republic, as a rampart against chaos, the Gaullists won more National Assembly seats than the other parties of the right and won more of them on the first ballot. As the Republic became more secure, the Gaullists lost much of their appeal. The RPR tumbled in 1981 while retaining its first-ballot strength. (That is, fewer RPR candidates won, but 60 percent who won did so on the first ballot.)

In contrast, the *Parti Socialiste* candidates rarely won on the first ballot. In 1981, when it realized its greatest victory, only 17.5 percent of its candidates won on the first ballot. The UDF falls between these two prototypical parties. As the small, liberal (nonstatist) right option, the UDF did well on both first and second ballots, merging with other small parties and resisting absorption by the larger Gaullists. As Joseph and Mildred Schlesinger interpret UDF behavior:

> Our analysis reveals a firm basis for [the UDF] resistance to Gaullist pressures to transform a majority coalition into a majority party—a different and potentially more effective mode of winning. Here was a parti-

san organization that appeared to be capable of appealing to some voters as a first, to others as a second choice.[14]

Voter response to the two-ballot opportunity has provided a bonanza for political scientists interested in individual choice and political strategy.[15] Of course, given the opportunity to duplicate their first-ballot choice, most voters do so. If this choice is removed, voters can select another candidate, abstain, or deliberately spoil their ballot. About three-fourths of the first-ballot voters select another candidate. Abstainers, and especially spoilers, are making a choice also. French voters, then, can discern differences between candidates, and select on the basis of these preferences.

Second-ballot voters do not choose on the basis of ideology, the left-right dimension, as much as in accord with partisan sympathies. Voters are able to make a fine distinction between the candidates of neighboring parties. We know of the interminable and Byzantine struggles among French elites. It is arduous to imagine voters knowing or caring, but they do. If they did not, there would be no point to the elaborate strategic withdrawal agreements (as voters would not know of them, they would not honor them):

> Heretics of various sorts have often been treated more harshly than non-believers. . . . By placing certain parties relatively close to one another on the left-right scale, French voters acknowledge the ideological proximity of those parties, but they may look on ideologically related parties with more or less equal favor, while for other voters the perceived ideological proximity of the parties is accompanied by feelings of fear or hostility toward one or another of them.[16]

FIRST PAST THE POST

First-past-the-post procedures reduce the number of competing units; proportional representation encourages fragmentation. The French system is fragmented, but not as fragmented as it was during its brief experiment with proportional representation. As originally phrased by Maurice Duverger, the "simple-majority single ballot procedure favors the two party system."[17] Thus, if the United Kingdom had proportional representation, it would presumably have more political parties, numerically and effectively. These rules of the game do not cause two-party dualism or multiparty fragmentation, but they do amplify or ratchet them.

The multiparty procedure of the Scandinavian countries preceded their adaptation of proportional representation. It is exceedingly improbable, however, that many parties would have remained vigorous without proportional representation.

First past the post does not banish the prospect of effective multiparty competition, though it does make it improbable.

Canada's Problems with Disintegration

In Canada, with first-past-the-post rules, third parties are more alive than those in the United States with the same electoral rules. The Canadian Reform Party, angered at eastern mastery of major political parties, rocketed to popularity in British Columbia and Alberta. The catalyst for protest was the Meech Lake Accord, granting special status to French-speaking Quebec. (The deadline for ratification was June 23, 1990; on June 22, Newfoundland and Manitoba rejected the accords.) The Reform Party lacks designs on a parliamentary majority; instead it hopes to win most of the eighty-eight seats in western Canada and the northern territories and thus gain a balance of power in Parliament.

It is instructive to compare Canada, the United Kingdom, and the United States, where third parties are so weak. All three systems are first-past-the-post, or plurality, but only the United States combines plurality with a presidential, as opposed to a parliamentary, system. Only eleven times in the last one hundred years have third parties gained more than 5 percent of the vote, and no party has managed to do it more than once. The difference is simple: the presidential system in the United States creates a single constituency—the whole country.

In Canada, third parties can develop the same strategy that the Labour Party developed and the regional parties (such as the Scottish Nationalists) emulated in England. Such parties can focus on select constituencies, where they have a good chance of winning. In contrast to the American experience, federal and provincial politics developed separately in Canada, and the issue of which level of government controls key resources is still unsolved.[18]

Gary Marks notes that in the United Kingdom, as the Labour Party was struggling to gain a foothold before the First World War, it managed about 6 percent of the vote. This small percentage gave Labour about forty seats in Commons. In the United States, the Socialist and Farmer Labor parties came up with about the same proportion of the national vote but had nothing to show for it, except an occasional state legislator.[19] Obviously, it takes more than a first-past-the-post procedure to eliminate third parties.

Contributing to the problems of American third parties is the fact that the dominant two parties have no problem in soaking up whatever constituencies third parties can attract:

> The American constitution has created flexible, ideologically diffuse parties that have consistently undercut third parties by incorporating parts of their programs and encapsulating their constituencies. Political parties in the Western European mold...do not exist in America.... Congressmen are uniquely able to represent the varied interests of their constituents without having to subordinate their political stance to national party platforms.[20]

It is hard to envisage how the United States would react to proportional representation, since none of the other ingredients of a legitimate political party system is in place, whether it contains two, three, or more parties.

The American Politics of Indecision

The shapeless nature of American political parties is surely reinforced by the indistinct complexion of American values. In comparison with European electorates, American electorates do not understand the difference between left and right. Whereas upward of two-thirds of European voters can explain the difference, barely half the American voters can.[21] The differences are particularly arresting among the less-educated: in West Germany and the Netherlands, two-thirds of the poorly educated understood the left-right distinction, but in the United States, only about one-fourth did so. Among college graduates, Americans actually do better than Europeans. Since the left-right schema is "not currently institutionalized in the United States," it would be absurd for parties to try to speak ideologically.[22] Ideology is prominent in describing the orientations of European voters; it is much less helpful in comprehending American voters.[23]

So the dilemma continues: parties cannot be genuine political organizations because Americans are uninterested in ideology; Americans are uninterested in ideology because it is uninstitutionalized. The depressing performance of the poorly educated Americans points us again in the direction of "responsible" parties. As the less-educated are without the skills to figure out the complexities of political life, parties can reduce information costs. They do so in Europe, not in America. (See Table 5.8.)

Table 5.8   Understanding of the Left-Right Schema

	Total	Level of education		
		Low	Medium	High
Self-Placement				
Netherlands	87%	84%	94%	93%
West Germany	89	87	92	95
United States	75	55	75	95
Understanding				
Netherlands	66	61	75	83
West Germany	73	67	82	88
United States	58	26	56	90

Source: Adapted from Kent Jennings, Jan W. van Deth, et al., *Continuities in Political Action* (New York: Walter de Gruyter, 1990), p. 210.

The American Politics of Ignorance

Americans are also comparatively uninformed. The questions of information and elections are sure to infuriate. How does one assess information? Why should Americans know who their Congressman is when incumbents win most of the time? Are the differences between and the disciplines within the Democratic and Republican parties significant enough to warrant voter attention? Is it worth the voter's while to keep informed? With hundreds of elections, are not information costs excessive, in comparison with parliamentary systems that require only a few elections during a governmental cycle? If democracy requires an informed electorate, the United States is in trouble:

> Even the basic facts of political history, the fundamental structure of political institutions, and current political figures and events escape the cognizance of the great majority of the electorate. . . . A majority of citizens are unable even to guess at or approximate the *names* of any congressional candidate, including the incumbent, who in many cases has been serving the district for many years. . . . The fact that a consistent majority cannot recall the names of congressional candidates might well be taken as a benchmark of the mass public's interest in politics. . . . Even the most vivid concepts of political life, such as the cold war, are recognized by only a little over half the electorate. Other fundamental concepts of domestic policy, including such basic symbols of policy polarization as the welfare state, are recognized by only one in three citizens; the Bill of Rights is recognized by only one in five.[24]

Seen graphically (in Table 5.9), the American voter's obliviousness is impossible to refute.

Table 5.9   American Voters' Level of Information

Percentage of public that can define terms	Terms or concepts
60	
	Cold war
	Republicans as more conservative
50	
	Tariff
	Private enterprise
40	
	Welfare state
	NATO
	Electoral College
30	
	Bill of Rights
	Three branches of government
20	Liberalism and conservatism
	Public enterprise
10	

Source: Adapted from W. Russell Neuman, *The Paradox of Mass Politics* (Cambridge, Mass.: Harvard U. Press, 1986), p. 17.

Much of the argument against these conclusions is of the sowhat variety. Are we any worse than the citizenry of any other industrial democracy? We are. We need a "culture-free" measure, since American institutions are unique and more complicated than most. With state, local, and national elections, federalism, separation of powers, primary elections, referenda, it is no wonder that Americans are politically retarded.

Proportional representation is trickier to grasp (in implementation if not in conceptual terms) than are plurality rules, but there is no denying that European democracies, being less Madisonian, are easier to understand. The best solution perhaps is to examine knowledge of the United Nations, to which industrial democracies uniformly belong, whose deliberations are given about equal treatment in the various national media. (See Table 5.10.)

Although Americans are aware of the United Nations, they know very little about it. Irrespective of the education level (included because European education is so much more selective), Europeans know more than Americans.

A comparison of American and Swedish voters depicts the disengaged disposition of American voters. (See Table 5.11.)

The "Berelson paradox" to which the article refers is the behavior of American "switchers." Those who change their minds tend to

Table 5.10   Comparative Levels of Information: Europe and the United States

	Had heard of UN	Could name any agency	Could name UNESCO
Europe			
Total	87%	49%	31%
Primary education	80	34	20
Secondary education	90	49	31
Advanced education	87	73	52
United States			
Total	91	29	10
Primary education	77	18	4
Secondary education	90	18	4
Advanced education	98	46	18

Source: Adapted from Klaus Hüfner and Jens Nauman, "Are the Moral and Value Foundations of Multilateralism Changing," *International Political Science Review* 11 (July 1990): 328.

be those who lack interest and information. Therefore, when elections result in a partisan change, those who caused it are the least likely to know what they are doing! In Sweden exactly the reverse is true: those who change their minds are not likely to be either uninterested or uninformed. Swedish political parties are strong, ideologically oriented, and connected to social class. In the United States, however:

> When low involvement voters...indicate an intention to vote for a particular candidate, they may know relatively little about the opposing candidates. They may lack an abiding partisan commitment and their answer to the "intention" question may be somewhat more flippant

Table 5.11   Partisanship and Interest Among Swedish and American Voters (1988)

	Sweden	United States
High-interest partisans	30%	20%
High-interest nonpartisans	21	8
Low-interest partisans	20	44
Low-interest nonpartisans	29	28

Source: Adapted from Donald Granberg and Sören Holmberg, "The Berelson Paradox Reconsidered," *Public Opinion Quarterly* 54 (1990): 542-43.

than it is reflective of a firm decision. . . . The intention-behavior switchers tend to be those who are apathetic and poorly informed.[25]

THE COSTS AND REWARDS OF ELECTORAL RULES

Proportional representation is largely associated with multiparty systems. Because there are no rewards for finishing second, or third, or
fourth in plurality schemes, Duverger's law shows that there is no
reason for political parties to continue to compete. In proportional
representation systems, however, the rewards are ample. In a multimember district with five seats, proportional representation might
produce:

	Vote	Seats
Party A	39%	2
Party B	36	2
Party C	20	1

Under single-member, plurality rules, as in the United States
and United Kingdom, the also-rans would have no seats. The disadvantage is exacerbated in the United States because of presidential
government. The most important symbol of success is the presidency, not a congressional majority. In parliamentary democracies,
smaller parties with no genuine national constituency can hang onto
a bloc of seats and, sometimes, participate in a governing coalition
(as did the Danish Christian People's Party and Centre Democrats,
and, to a lesser extent, the West German Free Democrats).

Winner Take All or Proportional Representation?

By allowing a simple winner-take-all, single-member plurality,
the United Kingdom and the United States attenuate the odds of
third parties translating votes into legislative seats. One can argue
that these rules are unfair, in that these parties are entitled to as
many seats as they can earn in electoral competition. But under
multiparty conditions, small parties also can obtain much more influence than their numbers warrant.

In the United Kingdom, where third parties—Liberals, Social
Democrats, a Liberal-Social Democratic Alliance, and finally the Liberal Democrats—can garner a quarter of the vote, but receive only
about 3.5 percent of the seats, the inequities are apparent. In the
1989 elections for the European Parliament, the "green" parties of

the continent, where proportional representation was used, secured representation; in the United Kingdom, with pluralities, they did not.

Again, the issue of the fairness of plurality procedures was raised. The issue is real, even though there are individual examples that contradict the pattern. Richard Rose estimates that the distortion imposed by plurality or even majority systems is only slightly greater than that of proportional representation systems.[26] Proportionality (the sum of the difference between each party's share of seats and its share of votes, divided by two and subtracted from 100) is ninety-four for PR countries and eighty-six for plurality or majority ones. Yet, the most proportional plurality procedure, the U.S. House of Representatives (94), puts it exactly at the PR average. (See Table 5.12.)

Proportional Representation and Voters' Alternatives.   The matter is less one of fairness than one of choice. Does the electoral system contribute, causally or not, to the number of political parties? One would think so; parties that routinely get a respectable chunk of votes but almost no seats might wither on the vine. Excluding the United States, for "whether the United States Congress has any nationwide parties electing its members is a debatable point," Rose shows the relationship between the rules of the game and the number of political parties.[27] (See Table 5.13.)

As we know, the number of parties is deceptive. Britain does not actually have nine parties. But notice that the largest party rarely can govern without a coalition in the PR procedures, whereas, more often than not, it can do so in non-PR systems. Perhaps a better way to consider an electoral system is to assess the number of "effective parties" in it. Table 5.14 presents an index of the number of parties in a party formula, taking their relative sizes into account.

The average number of effective parties in nonproportional representation systems is 2.6; in proportional representation formulas that number jumps to 3.7. Taagepera and Shugart have shown that the disparity between the number of effective parties, measured by votes, and the number of effective parties, measured by legislative seats, is higher in plurality than in proportional representation systems. (See Table 5.15.)

Thus, assuming the rational voter (i.e., one whose vote is for a political party with which he or she has some ideological, emotional, symbolic, or personal attachment), the chance of placing such a party in parliament is enhanced by proportional representation, but the odds of that party enjoying a *policy* opportunity are largely unre-

Table 5.12   Proportionality of PR and Non-PR Systems

	Index of Proportionality
PR Systems	
Austria	99
Germany	98
Denmark	97
Ireland	97
Netherlands	97
Sweden	96
Iceland	96
Switzerland	96
Finland	95
Italy	95
Israel	94
Belgium	94
Portugal	93
Norway	91
Luxembourg	90
Greece	88
Spain	84
Average	94
Non-PR Systems	
United States	94
Japan	91
Canada	88
Australia	87
Britain	85
New Zealand	80
France	79
Average	86

Source: Adapted from Richard Rose, "Electoral Systems: A Question of Degree or of Principle?" in Arend Lijphart and Bernard Grofman, eds., *Choosing an Electoral System*, (New York: Praeger, 1984), p. 75.

lated to its electoral success. Unless a party becomes part of a governing coalition, its accurate reflection of public preferences will be of little consequence. If a small party, with 7 percent of the votes, receives 7 percent of the seats, it will not control 7 percent of the policy. If this party is included in a governing coalition, its influence will exceed its numerical strength.

The Fragmentation Effect

Tiny parties can tip the balance of power. The West German Free Democrats do so with circadian frequency. In Denmark, the Radical Liberals—a coalition member with 5.6 percent of the electorate's

Table 5.13   Electoral Parties and Single-party Government

	Number of parties	Largest party's share	Largest party wins half (percent of elections)
Non-PR			
Australia	3	43	20
United Kingdom	9	53	91
Canada	3	52	54
France	6	56	28
Japan	6	56	53
New Zealand	3	51	100
Average	5	51	58
PR			
Austria	3	52	45
Belgium	13	20	7
Denmark	9	34	0
Finland	8	26	0
Germany	3	45	11
Ireland	4	45	33
Israel	10	40	0
Italy	12	41	11
Luxembourg	6	41	0
Netherlands	12	31	0
Norway	7	42	0
Spain	10	58	33
Sweden	5	48	8
Switzerland	13	25	0
Average	8	39	13

Source: Adapted from Richard Rose, "Electoral Systems: A Question of Degree or of Principle?" in Arend Lijphart and Bernard Grofman, eds., *Choosing an Electoral System* (New York: Praeger, 1984), p. 80.

vote—held virtual veto power over environmental and security matters. Its ten seats (nearly the same as its percentage of votes), the lowest number in the governing coalition, still gave it substantially more influence than the Social Democrats, not a member of the coalition, with 30 percent of the vote and the largest party in the legislature with fifty-five seats.

The most extreme example of the subversion of the electorate is Israel. Here, where the Labor and Likud parties are locked in a sixty-to-sixty tie, the balance of power lies with Torah Flag and Shas with six. Passionate about strict Judaism, these parties can compel a harsh and unpopular theocracy in exchange for their participation in a coalition.

Table 5.14   Effective Number of Parties in 22 Democracies

	Mean	Low	High	T&R*
United States	1.9	1.8	2.0	2.0, 1.9
New Zealand	2.0	1.9	2.0	3.0, 2.0
United Kingdom	2.1	2.0	2.3	3.1, 2.1
Austria	2.2	2.1	2.5	2.4, 2.3
Canada	2.4	1.5	1.9	2.8, 1.7
Australia	2.5	2.4	2.7	2.8, 2.4
Germany	2.6	2.2	4.0	2.6, 2.5
Ireland	2.8	2.4	3.6	2.7, 2.6
Japan	3.1	2.0	5.8	3.6, 3.2
Sweden	3.2	2.9	3.5	3.5, 3.4
Norway	3.2	2.7	4.1	3.6, 3.1
Luxembourg	3.3	2.7	4.1	3.6, 3.2
France (5th Republic)	3.3	1.7	4.6	4.0, 2.8
Italy	3.5	2.6	4.4	4.5, 4.0
Iceland	3.5	3.2	3.9	4.2, 4.1
Belgium	3.7	2.5	6.8	8.1, 7.0
Denmark	4.3	3.5	6.9	5.8, 5.5
Israel	4.7	3.4	6.0	4.3, 3.8
France (4th Republic)	4.9	4.2	5.9	4.5, 4.1
Netherlands	4.9	3.7	6.4	4.2, 4.0
Switzerland	5.0	4.7	5.5	6.0, 5.3
Finland	5.0	4.5	5.6	5.4, 5.1

*The first entry is based on votes; the second on seats.

Source: Adapted from Arend Lijphart, *Democracies: Patterns of Majoritarian and Consensus Government in Twenty-One Countries* (New Haven, Conn.: Yale U. Press, 1984), p. 122. Final column from Rein Taagepera and Matthew Soberg Shugart, *Seats and Votes* (New Haven, Conn.: Yale U. Press, 1989), pp. 82, 83.

The Complexity Problem: West Germany, Australia, and Italy

In addition to the confusion occasioned by stalemate in parliament, there is the further cost of bewilderment in the electorate. In their zeal to create genuinely fair electoral rules, constitution writers can create some inconceivably complex ways of sending people to a legislature. Consider West Germany and Australia. In West Germany, half of the 498 seats (before unification) in the Bundestag are decided through proportional representation. The rest are elected on a plurality basis. On election day, one votes for one candidate from his or her individual district and for one party. The candidate the voter supports need not be from the same party as the party that the voter supports. In each district, one candidate wins free and clear. Then seats are distributed through a proportional representation basis.

Imagine six seats available through proportional representation in a given state with the following results (on average, each state gets about twenty-five seats through proportional representation):

Table 5.15   Effective Political Parties and Electoral Systems

	Based on votes	Based on seats	Difference
Plurality			
Bahamas	2.1	1.6	.5
Belize	2.1	1.6	.5
Botswana	2.0	1.3	.7
Canada	2.8	1.7	1.1
Dominica	2.9	1.5	1.4
India	3.8	1.6	1.2
Malaysia	2.3	1.4	.9
New Zealand	3.0	2.0	1.0
St. Lucia	2.4	1.4	1.0
St. Vincent and Grenadines	2.3	1.7	.6
South Africa	2.6	1.5	1.1
Sri Lanka	2.8	1.4	1.4
United Kingdom	3.1	2.1	1.0
United States	2.0	1.9	.1
Mean	2.6	1.7	.9
PR or other			
Australia	2.4	2.3	.1
Austria	2.4	2.3	.1
Belgium	8.1	7.0	1.1
Brazil	2.6	2.4	.2
Colombia	2.7	2.6	.1
Costa Rica	2.3	2.3	0
Denmark	5.8	5.5	.3
Ecuador	10.3	6.1	4.2
Egypt	1.8	1.3	.5
Faeroe Islands	5.1	5.0	.1
Fiji	2.3	2.1	.2
Finland	5.4	5.1	.3
France	4.0	2.8	1.2
FRG	2.6	2.5	.1
Greece	2.6	2.1	.5
Greenland	2.5	2.5	0
Guatemala	6.4	5.0	1.4
Iceland	4.2	4.1	.1
Ireland	2.7	2.6	.1
Israel	4.3	3.8	.5
Italy	4.5	4.0	.5
Japan	3.6	3.2	.4
Luxembourg	3.6	3.2	.4
Malta	2.0	2.0	0
Netherlands	4.2	4.0	.2
Nicaragua	2.1	2.0	.1
Norway	3.6	3.1	.5
Portugal	3.7	3.3	.4
South Korea	3.8	2.7	1.1
Spain	3.5	2.3	2.2
Sweden	3.5	3.4	1.1

Table 5.15   Continued

	Based on votes	Based on seats	Difference
Switzerland	6.0	5.3	.7
Venezuela	3.0	2.4	.6
Mean	3.9	3.2	.5

Source: Adapted from Rein Taagepera and Matthew Soberg Shugart, *Seats and Votes* (New Haven, Conn.: Yale U. Press, 1989), pp. 82, 83.

Party	Votes	Div. 1	Div. 2	Div. 3	Total Seats
CDU	8,200	8,200(1)	4,100(3)	2,733(6)	3
SPD	6,100	6,100(2)	3,050(4)	2,033	2
FDP	3,000	3,000(5)	1,500	1,000	1
Green	2,700	2,700	1,350	900	
Total	20,000				6

The number of votes each party receives is then divided by 1, 2, 3, and so on, depending on need. Candidate number one from the Christian Democratic Union (CDU) state party list wins seat number one because his party has more votes than any other party. Candidate number one from the Social Democratic Party (SPD) state party list wins seat two, since his party has more votes than any other remaining total (CDU divided by 2). Candidate number two from the Christian Democratic Union state party list wins seat number three since his party's vote total when divided by 2 is higher than the next highest remaining vote total (SPD divided by 2). Candidate number 2 from the SPD state party list wins seat number four as his party's vote total divided by 2 is higher than the next highest remaining vote total (Free Democrats [FDP] divided by 1). Candidate number one from the FDP state party list wins seat number five since his total divided by 1 is higher than any other remaining total (CDU divided by 3). Candidate number three from the CDU state party list wins the last seat available as his party's vote total divided by 3 is higher than any other remaining total (Green divided by 1).

The actual seat distribution in the 1987 election shows how the German rules of the game provide an advantage to political parties that do not command enough support to win first ballot victories. (See Table 5.16.)

One important qualification of their PR formula is that a party needs to obtain at least 5 percent of the vote nationally, or win at least three seats outright in a plurality decided district to qualify for

Table 5.16   Seat Distribution in the 1987 West German Election

Party	1st ballot	2nd ballot	Seats earned by PR	1st ballots wins	List candidates elected	Total seats
CDU/CSU	52.1%	44.3%	222	169(68%)	54*	223
SPD	40.4	37.0	186	79(32%)	107	186
FDP	2.8	9.1	46	0	46	46
Greens	4.1	8.3	42	0	42	42
Others	0.6	1.3	0	0	0	0
Total	100.0	100.0	496	248	249	497

*One extra seat to the CDU because it won an additional district seat and because it won one more district mandate that it would be entitled to under PR.

Source: Adapted from David P. Conradt, *The German Polity* (New York: Longman, 1989), p. 118.

this redistribution of votes. Then, if the breakdown isn't entirely right, seats can be added to the Bundestag to ensure that fair representation is carried out. Using the pure first-past-the-post (first-ballot) results, the expected distortions occur: the Christian Democrats, with 52 percent of the vote, capture 68 percent of the seats; the Social Democrats endure an 8-percent penalty. However, the adjustment rectifies the distortion: the Social Democrats end up with 38 percent of the seats and the Christian Democrats end with 45 percent. These percentages approximate the proportion of second-ballot votes earned by each party. If first-past-the-post rules were used, the Christian Democrats would not be required to govern in coalition. Their position would be stronger than that of the British Conservatives, who win a majority of seats with a plurality of votes. The Christian Democrats, under plurality rules, would win a majority of votes and a (greater) majority of seats. One could argue, consequently, that the system used by the West German Bundestag is really proportional representation.[28]

In the event that this explanation is confusing, keep in mind the words of Jürg Steiner:

> Surveys show that most West German Voters do not fully understand how their complicated electoral system operates.... Even at the height of any given campaign, less than half of the voters know the precise meaning of the two ballots.... Shortly after an election, even this percentage drops, to roughly one-fifth of the voting population.[29]

The Free Democrats, a small, very influential party, has survived, verily thrived, because of this formula. A partner in the Social Democrat-led coalition from 1969 until 1982, the FDP switched parties and threw its weight to the Christian Democrats, thus electing Helmut Kohl as Chancellor. In the ensuing elections, the FDP, in an "almost pleading tone" urged second-ballot support for the party. Because voters do not understand the two-ballot system, the FDP encouraged the belief that the first ballot, that for the party list, was more important. "Of course," said FDP leader Hans-Dietrich Genscher in 1983, the first ballot should go to a voter's first party choice. CDU voters should, after casting their "important" ballot, give the tiny FDP a few crumbs.[30]

The FDP strategy works. Between 10 and 15 percent of voters switch parties between the first and second ballots. The vast majority of split-ticket voting involves the Free Democrats. Majority party voters, depending upon the coalition, support their district candidate for the first ballot and then cast a second ballot for the FDP list. In 1980, when the Social Democrats were returned to power along with their FDP coalition partners, 36 percent of the FDP vote came from those who voted for the SPD on their first ballot. In 1983, when the FDP bolted to the Christian Democrats, 58 percent of the FDP voters supported the CDU on the first ballot. Without the two-ballot formula and the consequent opportunity to split, the Free Democrats would not secure the 5 percent cut-off or be represented in Parliament, and, therefore, would not be part of the governing Coalition.[31] Bowing to the inevitable, both the SPD and CDU-CSU, when in coalition with the Free Democrats, have encouraged a second-ballot vote for the smaller party.

The Australian plan is even more complex, although it does not use proportional representation. Australian voters, as mentioned earlier, rank candidates on a scale from one to however many candidates are running for that seat (in the example to follow, the candidates would be ranked from one to five). Imagine an Australian election with the following results:

Neville	200
Nigel	150
Ian	100
Trevor	80
Mick	70
Total	600

As Mick finishes last, he is eliminated. Allocate his 70 ballots to the second choices listed. The result:

Neville	200	+0	200
Nigel	150	+10	160
Ian	100	+40	140
Trevor	80	+20	100

Still, we have no majority, so we eliminate Trevor and allocate his 100 votes to the *second* choice on his *initial* ballots, and *third* choice on the 20 ballots he got from Mick. So now we have:

Neville	200	+0	200	+30	230
Nigel	150	+10	160	+15	175
Ian	100	+40	140	+55	195

Because there is no majority, we drop Nigel and give his *initial* 150 to their *second* place choice, the 15 he got from Trevor to their *third* place choice, and the 10 he got from Mick to their *fourth* place choice. Finally, we have:

Neville	200	+0	200	+30	230	+60	290
Ian	100	+40	140	+55	195	+115	310

At last! The winner is Ian, originally in *third* place.

In Italy proportional representation is used for two houses: the Chamber of Deputies and the Senate. Each has identical legislative powers, unlike most parliamentary democracies but like the presidential system in the United States, with its Senate and House of Representatives. The electoral system determines first how many seats each party wins and, second, which candidates from the parties are awarded the seats. The process is not similar to West Germany's, where both plurality and proportional representation are used. But the *consequence*—the opportunity to choose from among party candidates—is analogous. In the Chamber of Deputies, 630 deputies are elected by the *imperiali quota*, or *largest remainder* method, while the Senate uses the more familiar D'Hondt highest average scheme.[32] Unlike the Federal Republic of Germany, the Italians do not impose a floor, or minimum percentage. Therefore, parties with inconsequential vote totals can earn seats in the Chamber, but not in the Senate (315 members), because of the D'Hondt formula and the smaller number of seats.

Voters first select a party and then cast preference votes (usually three or four) for candidates on the party's lists. Voters could select candidates by number rather than name. Especially in the south of Italy, where Mafia influence is regarded as pervasive, election officials were said to change the numbers. Although parties rank their candidates, voter preference decides who will go to Rome. However, in 1991 a referendum limited voter choice to a single candidate. In such a case, a name, rather than a number, must be used.

As in Japan, the party's candidates—many with formidable personal machines—fight for preference votes. In the Senate, there is no intraparty competition because each constituency has one member and seats are allocated on the basis of party percentage. However, in the Chamber elections, most voters do not bother. They simply select a party, thus ratifying that party's ranking.[33]

CONCLUSION

Because elections are pivotal to democracies, the rules by which they are conducted are of major import. The rules structure individual choices, and they enhance and inhibit opportunities. Although individual voting behavior has occupied the center stage in studies of the electoral process, rules *matter*. Without plurality rules, Margaret Thatcher's disruption of the British consensus might not have occurred. Had the Conservatives been allocated seats in proportion to votes, they would have been forced into a coalition. Had Helmut Kohl not been required to form a coalition (as would have been the case with pure plurality voting), he would not have given the foreign ministry to the Free Democrats and might have been more amenable to an active role for Germany in the 1990-91 Persian Gulf War. Electoral rules make it possible for different "people" to be invented.

A vivid example of the importance of rules is Chile.[34] In 1970 the Socialist candidate, Salvador Allende, received 36 percent of the vote; the candidate of the right, Jorge Alessandri, received 35 percent. The Chilean constitution requires the national congress to choose between leading candidates if none earns a majority. Normally, the national congress accepts the leading candidate, as the outcomes have not been as close as in 1970 (the slimmest plurality since 1942). But on this occasion Allende's "mandate" was questionable, as his vote was only a whisker ahead of the second-place finisher and candidate of former President Eduardo Frei's party, the Christian Democrats, who received 28 percent. However, bargaining with the Christian Democrats (combined with bitterly resented United States pressure against Allende and the murder of the Chilean military chief by right-wing extremists) resulted in a national congress vote of 153 to 35 for Allende. With this narrow support base, Allende nevertheless plunged into a vigorous program of social and economic reform, alienating first the military, then the business community, and finally the Catholic Church. These groups acquiesced in a military coup, and a repressive dictatorship ensued.

Allende's government invented a "people" without much legitimacy, and the dictatorship's "people" bore no resemblance to those in whose name Allende waged his socialist reforms. Suppose Chile had used the French majority rules in its presidential election. The odds are that the Christian Democratic candidate, who finished third, would have picked up support from both right and left (since he represented the moderate status quo). Such a government probably would have survived without a military coup.

Of course, one could argue that electoral rules are not the cause of such tragedies. As Rein Taagepera and Matthew Soberg Shugart wisely counsel: "A sound policy can salvage a defective electoral system, while no electoral system can save a policy bent on self-destruction." [35] A less strident Conservative Party in Britain or a more militarily active German government are not the same as a brutal dictatorship. Perhaps Chile would have succumbed to authoritarian rule in any case. Consider the United States. In 1876, a decade after the Civil War, the bitterness of that ferocious struggle lingered. The South, defeated and occupied, wanted desperately to rid itself of the remains of Reconstruction. In 1874, on one of the few such occasions in the nineteenth century, the Democrats won control of the House, to the dismay of Republican President (and Civil War hero) Ulysses S. Grant. In the 1876 presidential election, the Democratic nominee, Samuel Tilden (capitalizing on the Democratic House's exposure of Grant's corruption) won in normally Republican states (Connecticut, New York, New Jersey, and Indiana) and finished with 51.9 percent of the popular vote. He did not, however, become president. Lacking a single electoral vote, Republican candidate Rutherford B. Hayes negotiated a deal with southern conservatives. Hayes agreed, if he became president, to withdraw occupying northern troops from the South. The Democrats agreed to permit a rigged electoral vote count to proceed without obstruction. Thus ended Reconstruction, and the beginning of the southern "Jim Crow" laws. From 1876 until 1954 segregation was enforced rigidly in the South. Without an electoral college, Tilden would have been president. Whether the South would have been able to establish its social and political system based on segregation by race cannot be known. However, we can say that the electoral rules of 1876 delayed for perhaps eighty years the inevitable confrontation of "the American Dilemma." More recently, the elimination of party organizations from the selection of presidential nominees has contributed to the Democratic Party's inability to win presidential elections, thus strengthening the odds of divided government, fragmentation, and paralysis.

Is there a "best way"? First past the post enables Britain to be governed by a single party, but led to civil strife in Chile (the electoral outcome was consistent with PR). Proportional representation often results in coalitions that may be unstable. If stability is a valued goal, proportional representation is the wrong plan. Coalitions exaggerate the role of electorally insignificant parties in policy, and they also strengthen the barrier between voters and government by diffusing accountability. But plurality rules sacrifice representative fairness for a measure of stability. If fairness in representation, in the legislature but not necessarily in the government, is the goal, plurality is the wrong plan. Since the rules of the game are not designed in isolation from the political process (as the French example shows), they may be regarded as indicators of political culture.

6.

An Exploration of Electoral Change

How does one account for electoral change? Following the hopes or expectations of the previous chapters, the preferred explanation is that linkage works: when voters want to change governments, they do. But why do they do it? Has the government failed to deliver on its promises? Has the electorate repudiated the values that it once held in common with the government? Idiosyncratic reasons (the Watergate scandal or the Profumo scandal in England) are inherently less satisfactory: governments make mistakes and pay the price. But what about systematic or long-lasting changes? After all, Watergate's electoral impact was merely to insert one Democrat in a seemingly endless string of Republicans who occupy the White House. When governments change hands, what message is the electorate sending? Do some elections signal a public desire for major policy change, while others merely punish an inept incumbent? Is it possible that the replacement of one ruling party or coalition by another will have a pronounced, durable impact on the shape of public policy?

The common sense answer to this question is "of course." But newly empowered governments inherit dictates from people long dead. Budgets do not begin as though their yesterdays did not matter; the commitments of governments long departed are still being met. New governments take office bursting with enthusiasm for change. How often do the words "new," "beginning," and "change" appear in campaign literature? Rhetorically appealing, such words conceal the force of inertia. Voters find slogans appealing, but radical change to match the slogans is a different matter entirely. When voters hear of a new beginning, they do not link the phrase to concrete examples. For example, successful campaigns are not run on promises to make social security voluntary, as voters quite reasonably expect the bulk of government programs to continue as before. When we also consider that presidents and prime ministers come and go, but bureaucracies remain, then the problem of meaningful change is apparent.

Furthermore, electoral change need not mandate policy change. John Keeler calls policy change in response to electoral change "extraordinary policy making" for good reason. From the perspective of this book, inventing the people, the place to start looking for linkage between elections, public preferences, and policy is in the communication between the leaders and the led during the campaign. Among the many more systematic explanations of electoral change, realignment, dealignment, failed governments, ideological or policy shifts, each can be equally plausible. The phenomenon I seek to explore is *realignment* and the competing expression *dealignment*. Realignment is a major event in the development of linkages between rulers and ruled. New people are being invented by a newly empowered political organization. It is unclear, although the depth of change seems to imply it, that the newly invented people want a radical change in public policy.

Realignment was developed initially in the United States to categorize elections during which a social group moved its allegiance from one party to another. An additional requirement is that the change be somewhat permanent. During realigning elections, there must be a "significant shift in the group basis of party coalitions."[1] Such a permutation is no trivial requirement. For example, suppose that because of incompetent candidates one party so thoroughly disgusted all segments of the electorate that it abandoned the party in droves. This universal move would be significant, but realignment theory does not anticipate a complete rout. Working-class voters defected from the left party—Labour in the United Kingdom and the Social Democrats in the Federal Republic of Germany—while middle-class voters remained steadfast. In 1981 French middle-class voters abandoned the center-right for the Socialists while working-class voters held firm. In the United States, the overwhelming majority flocked to the Reagan candidacy.

Table 6.1   Division of Major Industrial Democracies

	Government	Opposition
United States	Bush (R)-Foley (D)	Foley-Mitchell (D), Lugar (R), Gingrich (R) (?)
United Kingdom	Major (Conservative)	Kinnock (Labour)
Germany	Kohl (CDU)	Engholm (SPD)
France	Mitterrand-Cresson (PS)	Giscard, Chirac, Noir, Le Pen (?)
Japan	Miyazawa (LPD)	

Note: (?) indicates the author's uncertainty as to the politician's position in opposing government.

Of the outcomes, one can be sure: the "outs" became the "ins," and the "ins" became the "outs." Executive exchanges occur every now and again in industrial democracies. In parliamentary democracies, replacement need not follow an election. In the single presidential democracy, one has trouble figuring out who the outs and ins are. Table 6.1 shows the division of major industrial democracies into governments and oppositions as of 1992.

Because the American presidency and majority leadership of the legislature are normally in different hands and the legislative parties have little leverage over their members, one cannot say when one party has taken over the responsibilities of governing. To control the White House is not to control policy. Since neither the Senate nor House of Representatives, normally in the hands of the Democrats, is hierarchically organized by political parties, the phrase *executive exchange* becomes difficult to apply. Richard Rose correctly clarifies the confusion: "The President has his institutions, . . . but the Congress has 'their' institutions. The President can claim greater individual eminence than a Prime Minister, but he is not so central in government."[2]

The matter is explicit in two pure parliamentary systems, the United Kingdom and West Germany, but less so in France's "mixed" system. François Mitterrand and Edith Cresson lead the Socialists, but who directs the opposition? In France, is the executive exchange measured by presidential elections or by the tenure of prime ministers? There is no clear division of labor between prime minister and president. The assumed distinction—the president is responsible for defense and foreign policy and the prime minister manages the domestic economy—is confusing because the 1958 constitution says that "the prime minister is in general charge of the work of government." Besides, the president can usually replace a prime minister when he pleases, and that makes the division of power one-sided. The 1986–88 period of "cohabitation," with a Socialist president and a Gaullist prime minister, did nothing to resolve these ambiguities.

The same lack of clarity in governing and opposing is evident in Japan, where Miyazawa is the nominal leader of the government. But in Japan, there is no genuine opposition.

Except for Japan, there are rotations in the leadership of industrial democracies. For example, in the United States, Ronald Reagan replaced Jimmy Carter in 1980; the United Kingdom converted from Labour to Conservative in 1979; France elected its first Socialist president in 1981; and Germany returned the Christian Democrats to power in 1983. What, if anything, do these elections tell us about mutations in voter preference or possibly alterations in voting alignments?

Table 6.2 looks only at class, not because of any theoretically precise reason, but merely because social class is a variable that is usually recorded, and because realignment, the central theme of this chapter, is well served by these data. The data are for one election before and one after the "critical" one, when one group of rascals was thrown out.

THE QUESTION OF REALIGNMENT

The most unequivocal, most frequently used prototype of realignment is the United States in 1932–36, when masses of voters who had abandoned the Democratic party in 1896 returned to the fold: blue-collar workers and Catholics, estranged by William Jennings Bryan's rural populism, found Franklin Roosevelt to their liking. Blacks, Republican since the end of the Civil War, switched to the side of the Democrats. Thus, the requirement was met. The Democratic coalition, durable for about two-and-a-half decades, was created.

One can distinguish between the sharp, immediate, and thaumaturgic transpositions and slower, less easily discernible, realignments. The Roosevelt coalition was produced more by the mobilization of new voters than the conversion of old ones, for these were the days of partisan loyalty. We should anticipate more conversion today, as partisan loyalties are decaying. The "old style" realignment, where one cohort of voters with strong partisan loyalties was replaced by another cohort of voters (with the same group identification) with opposite partisan inclinations, has been replaced by one in which individual voters change their minds. Thus, they may just

Table 6.2   Elections with a Change of Government: Percentage Voting for the Left

	1974	1979	1983
United Kingdom	1974	1979	1983
Working class	57%	50%	38%
Middle class	25	23	17
United States	1976	1980	1984
Working class	58%	48%	46%
Middle class	50	40	40
France	1974	1981	1988
Working class	68%	67%	74%
Middle class	51	58	58
West Germany	1980	1983	1987
Working class	58%	52%	54%
Middle class*	28	21	13
New middle class†	47	42	31

* Independents; farmers; free professionals.

† Technical; managerial; administrative; service.

as easily change them back. Therefore, *dealignment* replaced realignment as the descriptive tag.

To go beyond self-evident country-by-country differences, I will examine each country's election in detail. The opportunity is rare: three countries indulged in what was widely regarded as radical turnabout. France elected a Socialist, and the United States and the United Kingdom moved to the right. Only in West Germany could one argue for more of the same. I begin with the election of the two conservatives: Margaret Thatcher and Ronald Reagan.

MRS. THATCHER'S REVOLUTION

The election of the Conservative government in 1979 was a consequence of a modest shift in preference from the last election in 1974, which resulted in Labour's last government. (See Table 6.3.)

The surge in conservative support was "convincing if not overwhelming."[3] The size of the vote for the Conservatives was lower than in any other Conservative victory since World War II. However, because of Britain's electoral rules, the swing in seats to the Conservatives was substantial.[4] Meanwhile, the Conservative party had replaced Edward Heath with Margaret Thatcher as its leader. The image that the party sought to put forth in 1979 was dissimilar to that in 1970 or in any other previous election. Like Ronald Reagan in

Table 6.3   The Shift in British Voting Patterns

	Vote distribution	
	1974	1979
Labour	39%	37%
Liberal	18	14
Conservatives	36	44

1980, Mrs. Thatcher was not a very popular or beloved person. But while Reagan's personal popularity exceeded Carter's, polls showed that Labour leader James Callahan was more *personally* popular than Mrs. Thatcher. As noted at the beginning of the book, such an outcome would be unthinkable in the United States, with its deterioration of party loyalty.

Margaret Thatcher and English Decline

In the 1970s the United Kingdom was in the midst of an economic stagnation that focused the attention of intellectuals and divided the country to a degree at least as severe as that which occurred in the United States due to the Vietnam War and the Watergate scandal. No single event triggered the controversy, but its penetration was as pervasive. The "English disease," a phrase that had died down after World War II, popped up in English, European, and American popular accounts of Britain's economic ailments. The English disease—entrenched unions, class-poisoned politics, upper-class disdain for commercial life, loss of empire, and the weakening of economic vitality—moved from the literary and intellectual journals to the tabloids and to the television in 1978–79, the "winter of discontent":

> Mountains of garbage in Leicester Square; ambulance drivers on strike; attendants turning patients away from hospitals; terrorist bombings of gasoline storage tanks; schools closed; striking lorry drivers huddled around makeshift fires; civil servants refusing to work; trains idle; no *Times*; no *T.L.S. [Times Literary Supplement]*; a bewildered prime minister juggling election days; a Trades Union Congress helpless before militant shop stewards; a peppery leader of the opposition [Thatcher] shouting, "Resign." This was the British winter of discontent.[5]

One can find as many causes for the decline as one wishes: intransigent interest groups, especially labor unions; no highly valued entrepreneurial tradition; or the accidental occurrence of empire and industrial revolution simultaneously. All are plausible, but what really matters politically is that by 1979, the decay of Britain was not a debate; it was an accepted fact. The Bank of England warned that "the consequences of failure to arrest the country's industrial decline are likely to become more pressing and more obvious as time goes on. Now condemned to very slow growth, we might even have to accept, if present trends continue, decline in real living standards."[6]

The atmosphere was far different from that surrounding the 1990s American polemic about economic deterioration. In 1970 the decline of England was not mentioned; in 1974 it was debated; and in 1979 it was *accepted*. Who is to blame? For better or worse, voters blame incumbent governments. Labour's record from 1974 to 1979 invited a great deal of blame. Part of a much maligned, albeit largely mythical, "consensus" (the welfare state), Labour's 1974 manifesto sounded decidedly confrontational. It called for a "fundamental and irreversible shift of power and wealth in favor of working people and their families." In line with this way of thinking, Labour proposed the nationalization of ports (relating to the shipbuilding and aircraft industries), the creation of a National Enterprise Board with the authority to purchase private companies, an annual wealth tax, the removal of tax credit for private education, the restoration of union rights with a new Employment Protection Bill, and various other schemes consistent with "moderate socialism."[7]

Labour's Errors

Despite its ambition, Labour faced serious obstacles: a precarious parliamentary majority and a failing economy. Labour endured inflation in the 20-percent range, and compensated by wage increases of comparable magnitude. The need to rein in inflation suggested that Labour confront the unions and its own back bench. The Labour government tried for a social contract. In exchange for repealing the antecedent Conservative government's punitive restrictions, the Labour government hoped unions would voluntarily reduce their pressure for wage increases. During the 1974 campaign, Labour promised to replace the confrontational industrial relations posture of the Conservatives with a more corporatist one, claiming—given its wont—that it could "work with the unions."

Until 1978 the Labour government made good on its pledge. Until then, strikes were infrequent. After 1978 strikes became a way of life, as the Labour-unions accord deteriorated. In 1978 the average urban dweller's everyday way of life was disrupted in seemingly endless progression:

The difficulty of getting to and from work [because of the petrol tanker drivers strike] or because buses and trains were not running, the shortage of basic items in the shops (because lorry drivers were not delivering them), the unemptied dustbins (because the dustmen were on strike), the closing of schools (because the caretakers were, too).[8]

Not only were strikes occurring in rapid-fire succession, they were surrounded by a nastiness, a vehemence, rarely seen in the civil culture of England. Icy roads were left ungritted, accident victims were left unattended, corpses were left unburied. All this brackish conduct was spewed into millions of homes by way of television. Certainly, England was not on the verge of collapse and, as is normal during such "crises," fewer people were seriously inconvenienced than was popularly thought. However, television, as it did in the United States during the urban riots of the 1960s, made the catastrophe real for its viewers.

British voters believed that unions had become too omnipotent. They approved of unions as representatives of the interests of their members, but loathed them as pressure groups. Seventy-nine percent believed that unions had become too powerful. A surge of strikes early in 1979 devastated Labour's standing in the polls. At the end of 1978 Labour led the Conservatives by 2 percent; by February 1979, Labour *trailed* by 15 percent! Within two months the tide had turned irrevocably against Labour. The shift to the Conservatives was most pronounced among the traditional Labour voters: the working classes.

The Anatomy of the Conservative Win

There was an *individual-level* shift, as opposed to mere replacement of one set of partisans by another. Of the 7.5-percent swing to the Tories, 3.5 percent, the single most important component in the change, was attributable to Conservative votes by those who had voted for Labour in the past two elections. Another significant batch of new recruits was from previous nonvoters. Finally, the Conservatives gained votes from those who defected *from* the liberal party (most of whom voted Conservative), and from those who defected *to* the Liberal Party (most of whom were former Labour backers). Replacement—the factor that loomed large in the American realignments—was inconsequential: physical replacement helped Labour, but not enough.[9]

Table 6.4   Percentage Change in Vote Among Various Social Classes,
1974–79

	Conservative party	Labour party
Higher managerial and professional	+ 3	+ 7
Lower managerial and professional	+ 13	– 1
Skilled or supervisory nonmanual	+ 10	– 6
Lower nonmanual	+ 12	– 7
Skilled manual	+ 11	– 5
Semiskilled and unskilled	+ 13	– 9

Source: Adapted from Bo Särlvik and Ivor Crewe, *Decade of Dealignment* (Cambridge: Cambridge U. Press, 1983), p. 85.

The Working-Class Tories.   "Working-class Toryism," the conservative predisposition of the working class so feared by Labour, proved to be that party's undoing in 1979, as Table 6.4 shows.

As Ivor Crewe summarized the election, and unquestionably the entire Thatcher legacy:

> The Conservative vote in the working class . . . grew at a faster rate than in the electorate as a whole, while the Labour vote declined at a faster rate than the electorate as a whole. . . . Quite simply, the Conservative advance over both the long and short term has been entirely within the working class. . . . Thatcherism has fashioned an ideological realignment within the electorate.[10]

Crewe is too sophisticated to leave the matter at rest with such a sweeping remark. Thatcherism was as much a style—an adherence to principle and combativeness—as it was a battery of policy proposals. On some Thatcherite ideas, the electorate had entered a caesura, waiting for someone to express their long-ignored opinions. Mrs. Thatcher's social conservatism—support for the death penalty, immigration control, limits on pornography, trade union reform— was a dominant mood in the electorate well before the Conservatives accepted its dicta. Mrs. Thatcher's right-wing populism was not fashioned to appeal to survey-revealed voter predilections, but rather was a deeply felt personal conviction. In the manner of the American populists, George Wallace, for instance, Mrs. Thatcher said what more consensus-oriented politicians would not. Her privatization program, the denationalization of previously nationalized industries, remained popular with the electorate and was not seriously challenged by the opposition, principally because Labour supporters outstripped the electorate as a whole in moving to the right.[11] But other aspects of Thatcherism—welfare benefits reform, reform of the National Health Service—were never well received. Mrs. Thatcher never really intended a frontal assault on the National Health Service, unlike the nationalized industries. She did not seek to return health care to private control; rather, her intent was to decentralize. Ideology is one thing; political suicide is another.

What has changed? "Everything, I want to change everything," Mrs. Thatcher proclaimed. Obviously, everything did not change. Unions lost much of their corporatist claim to privilege, and major portions of the economy were denationalized. Other portions of her agenda went unfilled.

Unlike Ronald Reagan, who suffered a loss of interest and energy during his second term, Mrs. Thatcher's second electoral success following the Falkland Islands War encouraged her to become more aggressive. Labour suffered devastating losses, and Mrs. Thatcher's leadership of the party—especially when compared to the fractured Labour Party—was more assured. Her personal leadership, while it never enjoyed the surges of American presidents, was respectable. More privatization, more union legislation, and acts restructuring local government ensued. Without doubt, the Thatcher revolution was real and tangible concerning unions and the role of the state in the economy, both of major importance. Furthermore, even though the general role of the government in the economy has not diminished, the Public Sector Borrowing Requirement was in the black when Mrs. Thatcher resigned.

The Employment Act of 1980 restricted picketing, weakened the closed shop, and curtailed union immunities for secondary boycotts. The Employment Act of 1982 further weakened the closed shop, greatly increased the rights of individual workers against union leadership, banned political strikes, and made union funds open to legal action for unlawful strikes. Labour, when it returns to power, will not try to return to a *status quo ante Thatcher*. It is inconceivable that the trade unions could, after Thatcherism, launch another "winter of discontent."

The privatization of industry undoubtedly diminished the role of the government in the economy. Whitehall did not run the gas industry, the telephone service, or British Airways. The reach of the state was reduced. But at a more aggregate level, public expenditure accounted for 45 percent of Gross National Product (GNP) during the Thatcher years, as was the case during the Labour government that she replaced. From the right Mrs. Thatcher endured criticism that the revolution was too timid. These critics wanted privatization of education, the health service, and pensions, suggestions that Mrs. Thatcher rejected.

The important point is that she went to the electorate as a symbol of radical reform and won. Since voters normally are not inclined toward radicalism, why was she acceptable? Put another way, were there circumstances that made her appeal less frightening? The vital ingredient was the extraordinary unpopularity of the Labour government that she sought to replace. Ideology aside, there was the theme of fitness to govern, of statecraft. Later, the Falklands factor enhanced her image for courage and determination.

The economic and industrial relations disasters of the Callahan government, contrasted with the stern-warrior style of Mrs. Thatcher, played a significant role in her success. For instance, among those voters whose personal preference on industrial relations was closest to the Labour Party, 68 percent believed the Conservatives were better able to handle strikes. Ivor Crewe says it best:

> Almost every government defeated at an election...lost authority before it lost office. Governments defeated at the polls forfeit votes for lack of authority, not authority for lack of votes.... Policy and ideology have been mere cloaks for applying a *coup de grace* to a government already crippled by failure, division, scandal, or sheer exhaustion.[12]

So much of the 1979, and subsequent, fulfillment of the Conservative Party was tied to the dominance of the Thatcher personality that a genuine realignment is difficult to imagine. The electorate, once the dust had settled on the 1978–79 winter of discontent and the displacement of the Labour government, lost many of the attitudinal vestiges of Thatcherism. The drift of the Labour Party to the left, not finally arrested until about 1988 by Neil Kinnock, cannot be underestimated. Still, enduring realignments require more, and what appeared to be Conservative hegemony in 1987 was considerably less certain by the 1990s. Mrs. Thatcher has gone, but what of Thatcherism? Not very much existed in the first place. For example, take the very Thatcherite notion of hard work. Why are people poor? Because of circumstances (Labour, Tory wets), or because they lack motivation (Thatcher). Surveys show Thatcherism in the minority. (See Table 6.5.)

There was more Thatcherism in the British population before Thatcher's election than after! This seeming anomaly makes perfect sense. Labour policy had infuriated large segments of the electorate and, for this reason, the Tories attained their mastery. Undeniably,

Table 6.5   **Answers to the Question: Why Are There People Who Live in Need? (Reasons)**

	1976	1983	1989
Bad luck	19%	14%	12%
Inevitable	20	28	36
Injustice	12	36	30
Laziness	50	25	22

Source: Adapted from David Dolowitz, "Has Mrs. Thatcher Changed the Ideological Parameters of British Politics," unpublished, Essex University, 1990.

however, the underlying attitudinal permutation was not there. Unemployment did increase substantially after 1979, probably influencing some attitude change. As the problem became more acute, Britons came to see it as more of a social than an individual problem.

Conservative identifiers are more Thatcherite than Labour sympathizers, but even among Conservatives, perhaps one-third display the attitudinal accoutrements of Thatcherism. (See Table 6.6.)

Mrs. Thatcher's ouster by her party showed at the very least a conviction that the Tories could beat Labour without Thatcherism or Thatcher. As usual, they would require working-class Tories to do so. Mrs. Thatcher surely took solace from surveys showing that while 73 percent thought trade unions were a prominent issue in 1979, the percentage had decreased to 1 percent by 1987.[13] She had shrunk union power, and made unions almost peripheral to the world view of the British public. When Labour returns, will the party risk being branded a puppet of the unions again?

ARE YOU BETTER OFF NOW?

Mrs. Thatcher's overwhelming presence, sometimes compared to Franklin Roosevelt's and the coalition he created, is more appropriately compared to her fellow conservative, Ronald Reagan. Like Reagan, Thatcher was a "conviction politician," not given to insider trading, and attracted to the great turn of phrase.

Carter's Mistakes

Like Thatcher, Reagan challenged a disdained incumbent, Jimmy Carter. Carter's low point in the surveys, an approval rate of 33 percent, matched James Callahan's. Elected in 1976 partially be-

Table 6.6   Answers to the Question: Why Are There People Who Live in Need? (Conservative vs. Labour)

	Conservative	Labour
Bad luck	12%	8%
Inevitable	39	30
Injustice	30	46
Laziness	30	9

Source: Adapted from P. R. Goodby, "The Shift in Favour of State Support," The Guardian, November 14, 1990, p. 21.

cause of the Watergate disaster, Richard Nixon's resignation, Gerald Ford's subsequent pardon of Nixon, and the national revulsion that followed, Carter's government never found its legs. During his first three years, popular endorsement declined precipitously to the same level as Nixon's just before his resignation. Carter did not maintain consistent or effective programs in the losing struggle against inflation (it zoomed from 8 to 14 percent annually). His energy programs were undersold and bogged down in Congress. In the foreign policy arena, he projected an image of weakness and vacillation in the face of Cuban aggression in Africa and Soviet troops in Cuba.

Carter had less success with Congress than had his two Democratic predecessors, Lyndon Johnson and John Kennedy. Much of this miasma was not Carter's fault. He was the first president to face a reformed Congress, with its myriad of subcommittees and loss of party discipline. Congress would make life miserable for future presidents, too; Carter was simply the first.

More portentously for American politics, Carter did not portray an *image of presidential leadership.* Gradually, the media began to portray Carter as weak, indecisive, and unable to control people or events. In 1976 the media had asked only for honesty. Now the media demanded leadership. Carter responded predictably in the summer of 1979; he delivered a nationally televised speech in which he talked of a "national malaise" that was destroying his leadership efforts, notably in the energy field. He spoke of a "crisis of confidence" and tried to project a new image of leadership. In spite of these Promethean efforts, his approval ratings in the polls stayed low. The new Carter image didn't take hold, and Senator Edward M. Kennedy announced that he would challenge the president in the primary elections.

A scenario was building that was reminiscent of Lyndon Johnson's administration. In 1968 predictions of downfall and infamy

Table 6.7   Erosion of Confidence

Year	1964	1972	1976	1980
Trust government only some of the time	54	8	–63	–46
Government run by a few big interests	35	–16	–45	–54
Government wastes a lot of money	5	–33	–73	–60
Quite a few people running the government are crooked	38	23	–30	3
Quite a few people running the government don't know what they are doing	41	15	–7	–30

Note: Entries are the differences between trusting and cynical responses.

were rampant. Johnson, shocked by a poor showing in the·New Hampshire primary (although he won), did not seek reelection in 1968. A similar fate apparently awaited Carter. However, an imbroglio occurred that caused popular opinion to rally around the president. In 1979, during the thick of the political in-fighting, Iranian terrorists, with the sanction of its political and religious leaders, kidnapped and held hostage fifty American diplomats and employees in the American embassy in Teheran. Shortly after that, Soviet troops invaded Afghanistan. Carter's approval ratings leaped upward, as the "rally-'round-the-flag" effect kicked in.[14] However, as the hostage predicament dragged on, Carter's approval plummeted again. A poorly planned, doomed effort to rescue the hostages in the spring of 1980 made Carter look the fool.

The American Malaise

Since 1964, with exacerbations occurring after the Watergate scandal, Americans had been undergoing a confidence crisis in American government. Assassinations of John and Robert Kennedy and Martin Luther King, the quagmire of Vietnam, and Watergate had taken a horrific toll. (See Table 6.7.)

Except for a reversal of the pattern of belief about honesty—Carter's forte—the electorate was thoroughly alienated in 1980. Thus, the times were ripe for Ronald Reagan, either an "amiable dunce" (Clark Clifford) or "ignorant and lazy" (Margaret Thatcher), but decidedly upbeat.

Carter and Callahan: Reagan and Thatcher

The comparison of Jimmy Carter and James Callahan, Ronald Reagan and Margaret Thatcher, is inevitable but vacuous. The British campaign, even with the fascination of the Thatcher ingredient, was far more issue-oriented. Callahan's fate was determined, not by the campaign, but by the "winter of discontent." In the United States, Reagan's lead over Carter was not firmed up until a few weeks before the election; hence campaign events, essentially meaningless in the United Kingdom, were crucial in the United States. The lead changed hands three times during the campaign. The end of the campaign debate sealed Carter's fate.

Reagan's ability to simplify, a quality Carter found difficult to emulate, and Reagan's unforced sense of humor, a quality lacking in Carter, were exaggerated by television during the Carter-Reagan debates. Carter's attempts to appear human were ludicrous and became the source of many campaign jokes. (At one point he revealed that his daughter Amy was intensely concerned about nuclear weapons and disarmament.) Reagan closed with one of the great lines from American politics: "Are you better off now than you were four years ago?" a simple but effective way to end the debate. It was a theme anybody could understand, and Carter's dense, complex presentation was arranged in vivid dissimilarity.

Although one cannot say that the debates won the election, one can surely infer that they ended any hope of a Carter recovery. In such a volatile election, with lead changes every couple of months, had Reagan appeared as ill-informed as he did four years later, he might have lost. The impact of this performance upon the vote can readily be shown. Remember that Reagan earned a scant 51 percent of the popular vote. Twenty-five percent of those who voted Democratic in 1976 voted for him; about 27 percent of the Democrats in 1980 believed Reagan won the debate, and of those who held this belief, 71 percent voted for him! The debates gave people an excuse for voting for Reagan. He did not seem a warmonger, as Carter had claimed. Since the electorate yearned to punish the incumbent, the debates gave it the opportunity; war and peace ceased to be a factor, and the electorate was free to vote for the nice man who meant well: last-minute switches cost Carter about six percentage points, while Reagan gained one!

The Anatomy of Reagan's Victory

The Reagan win was not class based; an overwhelming majority from all segments of the populace bolted to Reagan. (See Table 6.8.)

Table 6.8   **Percent Decline of Democratic Vote by Selected Groups (1976–80)**

Sex	
Males	–15%
Females	–3
Race	
Whites	–10
Nonwhites	–8
Education	
College graduates	–7
High school graduates	–10
Grade school only	–8
Profession	
Professionals and business	–9
White collar	–7
Manual	–12
Age	
Under 30	–10
30–49	–15
50+	–16
Religion	
Protestants	–14
Catholics	–16
Political Party	
Republicans	–2
Democrats	–15
Independents	–8
Geographic Region	
East	–8
Midwest	–7
South	–10
West	–16
Union	
Members of labor union families	–17

Thus the Reagan victory, despite the similar rhetoric, was not an American version of the Thatcher triumph. The American electorate is substantially more volatile. "Straight conversion," changing from the candidate of one major party to another, is less extraordinary in the United States than in the United Kingdom. Sixty percent of the British electorate voted for the same party in 1979 as in 1974; only 44 percent of the American electorate did so. Among the 16 percent that switched from one party to another, most of the change was in the Republican direction; 23 percent of the 1976 Carter voters (about 7 percent of the total electorate) defected to Reagan. The dissimilarity with England is underscored by the fact that most of the English "wobblers" moved only part of the way—to the Alliance (or Social and Liberal Democrats) from one of the major parties.

There is, however, one similarity between the two elections: each was dominated by a single issue, fatally associated with the incumbent. In the United Kingdom, economic descent was symbolized by union might; in the United States, economic decline was symbolized by inflation.

> Inflation remained by far the single most important determinant of the 1980 election outcome, producing a net pro-Republican effect of nearly twelve percentage points....Most impressive is that the Republicans clearly dominated among the switchers, though, as one would expect, the total effect of this group was not quite so high as for those who stayed with the Republicans between 1976 and 1970. Still, almost none of the Carter vote could be accounted for by switchers on the inflation issue; three percent of the Reagan vote, in contrast, was due to this issue.[15]

Elliot is so confident of his analysis that he says, without equivocation, that inflation "accounted for the election outcome."[16] Still, inflation, like union power in the United Kingdom, is a transient matter, presumably not linked to ideology. We should distinguish between an electorate "moving right" and one simply "fed up." In both the United Kingdom and the United States, there was no right turn; voters did not embrace Thatcherism or Reaganism as ideologies. In the United States, because most voters lack the sophistication to do so, it remained for conservative elites to proclaim the "great moving right show." In the United Kingdom, where voters are more ideologically sophisticated, Thatcherism style was more significant than ideological commitment.

Had the electorate been thinking ideologically, Reagan and possibly Thatcher would not have been reelected. In 1980 the policy proximities (the extent to which the electorate agreed with the candidates on the substantive issues) were in Reagan's favor; in 1984 they were not. (See Table 6.9.)

As Reagan won by more of a genuine landslide four years later, it is probable that the issue proximities of 1980 were an artifact of the

Table 6.9   Policy Proximities in 1980 and 1984

	1980	1984
Government spending	+7	-3
Defense spending	+23	-16
Getting along with U.S.S.R.	+17	-2
Government-guaranteed jobs	+16	+3
Help minorities	+22	-3

Entries are the percentage closer to Reagan, minus the percentages closer to Carter.

appeal of his personality. That is, people liked him, and agreed—for the moment—with what they believed he was saying. When he stopped the message, the agreement vanished but the personality *endured*. We see the same phenomenon at work in the personalization of the French presidency.

THE LONG MARCH OF THE LEFT: MITTERRAND AND THE FRENCH SOCIALISTS

In 1981 the Socialists placed their leader, François Mitterrand, in the Elysée Palace, the first Socialist triumph of the Fifth Republic. As the United Kingdom and the United States were moving to the right, France was moving to the left. But as a rightward move is hard to discern, so, too, the French embrace of socialism was more apparent than real.

We begin with the most manifest anomaly: Mitterrand's "left" victory was, like the "right" victories of Thatcher and Reagan, a consequence of his appeal to the "antagonistic" class, in this case, the middle classes. Holding his working-class support, Mitterrand plucked voters from the ranks of the right.

Mitterrand, the Party, and the Center

Mitterrand's appeal should not surprise us. On the surface, the 1981 election was a stark reversal of the mood and bearing of French politics. Only twelve years earlier, the *Parti Socialiste's* presidential candidate, Gaston Defferre, accomplished the lowest vote in the history of the party: an embarrassing 5 percent. Mitterrand's 1981 accomplishment was remarkable: a moribund party and an isolated politician were converted into a majority party with a soon to become "tonton" ("uncle") at its head.

Mitterrand appointed a Socialist government with the doctrinaire Pierre Mauroy as prime minister, dissolved the National Assembly, and in the election a month later led the party to a strong majority. Socialist hopes were high, and they were not disappointed. The Mauroy government sounded exactly like Thatcher's: "everything" was to be changed.

Mitterrand and "His" Party: Left or Center?   To understand why this was, it is necessary to recall once more the Common Program of 1972 by which the *Parti Socialiste* and the *Parti Communiste* staked out collective ideological territory. Both parties agreed to the nationalization of nine companies: Dassault, Roussel-UCLAF, Rhône-Poulenc, Honeywell-Bull, ITT-France, Saint-Gobain-Pont à Mousson, and Compagnie Générale d'Électricité. The commitment to nationalize these companies may sound like a lot. However, even the committed Mauroy fretted about electoral fallout and many others were excluded from the list.

Mitterrand considered these statements of unity to be intraparty minutiae. In 1974 he, now undisputed leader of the Left, ran as a "common candidate of the left," that is, not as the candidate of any of the parties of the left, but the choice of them all. He did not feel himself irrevocably bound by the Common Program. He resigned as First Secretary of the *Parti Socialiste* to make his independence even more obvious, and selected among his advisors Michel Rocard, who led the smaller *Parti Socialiste Unifié*. His performance against Giscard was encouraging; he lost by a whisker, a mere 1.6 percent. He used his prominence, and that of the charismatic, pragmatic, Rocard to deal blow after crushing blow to the extreme left, especially the *Centre d'Étude de Recherches et d'Éducation Socialiste* (CERES). CERES had been a powerful, dogmatic, independent force in left politics. Its leader, Jean-Pierre Chevènement, acceding to a more flexible stance, served as minister of defense in the second Mitterrand government, and resigned in protest to France's participation in the Persian Gulf War. In the 1978 National Assembly elections, another close loss, the *Parti Socialiste* outpolled the *Parti Communiste*, thus legitimating Mitterrand's centrist strategy.

The strategy was given a jolt by the ambitious Rocard, whose movement to the right of the Socialist movement was as meteoric as his discovery by the media. Opinion polls showed Rocard consistently more appealing than Mitterrand and more likely to dislodge Giscard in 1981. Most critical to his accomplishment was Rocard's attraction to centrist voters, annoyed by Mitterrand's acquiescence in the Common Program. Surveys showed that only 32 percent of *Parti*

Socialiste voters endorsed the Common Program; Rocard symbolized, personified, these moods. As D. S. Bell and Byron Criddle explain:

> Rocard was fêted by the broadcasters, being frequently accorded television interviews on such programs as *Cartes sur table,* and it was for both his poll rating and the TV exposure that he was dubbed by Mitterrand's supporters as the media's candidate for 1981. Rocard indeed did have a carefully prepared and elaborate media campaign assembled by an influential back-up team.[17]

Although not the originator of the Americanization of French politics, Rocard was definitely a most enthusiastic practitioner of the art of going public. Hitherto arcane skirmishes between party factions—somewhat akin to the impenetrable disputes between the Bolsheviks and Mensheviks in 1917—now became accessible to the average TV watcher. Americanization envenomed left intellectuals almost as much as Rocard's conversion to the center. In 1968 he was at the barricades; a decade later he was esteemed as a technocrat.

Mitterrand adhered to his alliance with the Communists. Having been the architect of the left-union strategy, Mitterrand seemingly felt compelled to defend it. Also, Mitterrand knew that the French system of intraparty politics had not yet become genuinely Americanized. Rocard was the favorite in the mass surveys, but not among the party activists. Among the left factions, the Communists were regarded as the most disciplined and reliable in adhering to electoral agreements. In a party conference at Metz, Mitterrand's allies trounced Rocard's pragmatism, and Mitterrand emerged as the defender of the socialist legacy. Thus, when Mitterrand declared his candidacy for the party's presidential nomination, and Rocard immediately withdrew, it was only natural to regard Mitterrand as more doctrinaire than he actually was. His leftist orthodoxy was forced upon him by Rocard's challenge. Mitterrand's willingness to share power with Rocard speaks volumes about his pragmatism. The two are not close personally, and Mitterrand replaced Rocard in 1991.

Giscard's Failures: Mitterrand's Reassurances

The 1981 election pitted Mitterrand, the survivor of a brutal challenge, two-time loser, and, ostensibly, defender of left orthodoxy, against Giscard. Initially, he was only the hope of the Socialist and Communist voters who wished ardently to interrupt the reign of the right. Nevertheless, as this was the same hope that had inspired the

Parti Socialiste in the past, the odds of success were slim. On the positive side, Mitterrand was presidential, having symbolized the opposition for at least a decade. His campaign, joined by most factions and past enemies, portrayed him as a *force tranquile* rather than a hell-bent radical.

His inclinations and his campaign were fundamentally different in tone and substance from those of the other presumed radicals, Thatcher and Reagan. He did not want to "change everything." As Howard Machin and Vincent Wright explain:

> Mitterrand presented his own programme (and not the official PS programme) aiming at mobilizing or at least reassuring marginal, moderate voters....He did not attack the Presidency or the institutions of the Fifth Republic but concentrated on those subjects shown by the polls to be Giscard's weakest points—unemployment and his monarchical style. He and his supporters held meetings for, and addressed campaign broadcasts towards, specific groups of business executives—to make promises and concessions (as set down in his programme) and to deny the threats made by Giscard. He emphasized his closeness to ordinary people—and the importance of retaining these contacts as President.[18]

These programs were popular with the left, but also with followers of the incumbent.[19] Mitterrand even managed a little Red-baiting in the American tradition by lambasting Giscard for being the first Western head of state to meet with Soviet leader Brezhnev after Afghanistan and for displaying a favorable review of the Giscard presidency that appeared in *Pravda*. As Roy Pierce and Thomas Rochon conclude:

> Just as the American parties cannot win nationally by mobilizing their partisans alone, so the two main leftist French parties, the Socialists and the Communists, could not together have won a clear majority of the votes cast in 1981 if their only supporters had been people who perceived themselves to be leftists. American parties need to win nonleaning independents at least, and usually some partisan opponents as well, if they are to win elections. Similarly, the French left needs to win considerable support from the *marais*, if not from centrists and rightists.[20]

The Mitterrand *force tranquile* gambit was not a *Parti Socialiste* strategy. Roy Pierce and Thomas Rochon, writing of the legislative elections that soon followed Mitterrand's triumph and gave him a Socialist majority, claim that, "There is, to our knowledge, no evidence indicating that the French Socialists had any particular strategy for winning the blessing of the *marais* equivalent to their strategy for mobilizing the left."[21]

The personal nature of his campaign does not mean that Mitterrand was not regarded as a legitimate alternative to the right, for as France's symbol of opposition—expressly to Gaullism—Mitterrand had earned his spurs. Additionally, the *Parti Socialiste's* programs, irrespective of the pragmatic inclinations of Rocard and Mitterrand, were very much in the ethic of classic French and European socialism. Nationalization (albeit moderate), obligation to the pursuit of economic equity, social reform, moderate nationalism in foreign affairs were programs squarely within the socialist tradition.

The *Parti Socialiste* did not emulate the German Social Democrats who, following the Bad Godesberg conference of 1959, jettisoned Marxism. French *Parti Socialiste* adherents are more left than German Social Democrats, so the electoral risks were not noticeable. Among the general population, left and right claim equal shares; but between them lies the infamous *marais*, the "bog."[22] Much like American voters, this segment of the French electorate is centrist in leaning, but without any definitive understanding of the meaning of ideology. Occupants of *le marais* normally vote more for the right than the left, causing the *France pense à gauche, vote à droite* phenomenon. Since about one-third of those who select an ideology opt for the "extreme center," *le marais* is an inviting target.

Mitterrand's victory was aided by several factors. First, he had the avid support of the Communists, about 90 percent of whom switched to him on the second ballot. In addition, he benefited from the stability of his *Parti Socialiste* and, most significantly, by a hemorrhaging in the Gaullist ranks. In 1974, when Giscard won, about 80 percent of the Gaullist votes stayed put, continuing to support the right in the second election. In 1981, when he lost, only about 78 percent of those votes did so. After all, the "new Mitterrand," "the potential standard-bearer of Gaullist traditions,"[23] was attractive to prominent Gaullists, several of whom encouraged *l'alternance* as a guarantor of the Gaullist heritage. Both Gaullists and Socialists generally support a strong state presence (*dirigisme*), and Mitterrand's nationalism certainly recalled de Gaulle. Viewed similarly, migration from the RPR to the Socialists in the second round is not as big an aberration as it appears at first glance. About 16 percent of Chirac's first round votes went to Mitterrand, and about one-fourth of the votes of the lesser known Gaullists traveled to the left: "Mitterrand polled well in Gaullist strongholds (6.5 points above the left's first-ballot total) because of transfers and first-round abstainers whilst Giscard even lost right-wing votes in these areas."[24] Chirac's obvious distaste for Giscard was, if not fatal, undeniably injurious.

Table 6.10   Success and Failure of Giscard's Policies

	Success	Failure	Don't know
Inflation	5%	88%	7%
Unemployment	12	78	10
Income gap	20	65	15
Strengthening industry	25	42	33
Teaching, professional training	31	48	21
Energy policy	31	41	28
Quality of life	44	38	18
Status of women	59	22	19

Source: L'Express, May 10–16, 1980, p. 70.

Giscard's Image of Inadequacy.   Decidedly, a key ingredient in Mitterrand's achievement (as in Thatcher's and Reagan's) was intense dissatisfaction with the incumbent. After all, Chirac, following his first-ballot defeat, reasserted his opposition to Mitterrand, but damned Giscard with, at best, faint praise. Noting Giscard's scant vote—25 percent "in his own name"—Chirac announced his intention to champion his rival, but urged followers to "vote according to conscience."

Chirac was merely reflecting public opinion, which viewed the Giscard government as a bust. (See Table 6.10.) Only on policies judged peripheral did Giscard do well. On the key economic issues, he was assessed a flop; more importantly, Mitterrand was predicted to be a success. In a 1981 *Le Point* survey, Giscard was given the edge over Mitterrand in foreign and defense policy and monetary policy, but Mitterrand was judged more competent concerning inflation, social justice, and unemployment—all highly salient issues.[25]

Although there was no "winter of discontent" in France, malaise was decidedly near that of Carter's United States. Stifled by the international stagflation, the French economy was languishing, as were those of industrial democracies in general. Additionally, Giscard, like Carter, was not a man of personal charm; not a Reagan who could convince voters that it was "morning in France." Carter aped the common man with informal dress, but he was really regal in thought. He patronized, particularly in his disastrous speech about malaise. Giscard, aristocratic in appearance, manner, and belief, did likewise. He said, concerning his campaign, that it was to be "the most beautiful, the most aesthetic, the most rich in emotion. . . . That is why it will be late and short, that is why it will take hold of the imagination, and that is why it will be the occasion of my reunion with the French people." Although France is noted for its arrogant politicians, Giscard was really too much.[26]

Giscard had lost the public's confidence by September 1980, when those who were dissatisfied consistently exceeded the satisfied respondents. His ratings, as the election drew nigh, were about the same as Carter's at the same point in the election process: about one-third approved of his performance. Giscard suffered the misfortune of being the first president of the Fifth Republic not to be either Charles de Gaulle or his chosen heir. The first non-Gaullist to be elected could certainly anticipate troubles with the Gaullists. The popularity of the two Gaullist presidents never fell below 50 percent; de Gaulle's bottomed out at 53 percent at his lowest point, the loss of his 1969 referendum. Giscard's approval rating, by comparison, remained over 50 percent only for the first half of his term of office. After his spectacular break with Chirac in 1977, the deterioration became irreversible. The slide was ratcheted by Giscard's loyalty to the most disliked (because of his authorship of an unpopular government austerity program intended to combat inflation) prime minister in the Fifth Republic, Raymond Barre.

None of this is to imply that there was no ideology at play; French voters are not American voters. Roland Cayrol has shown that although personal elements persisted as consequential, policies and programs assumed more importance as the campaign wore on. In August 1980, voters gave personal factors much more importance: 65 percent considered personality as more critical than policy, but by April 1981, the gap had narrowed to 54 to 43 percent.[27]

Undoubtedly, French voters coveted a transformation, and Mitterrand promised one. Mitterrand's irony is that he really promised moderate change, in spite of being portrayed by Rocard as a puppet of extremists. Mitterrand did successfully appeal to Communist voters. About 1.5 million of them voted for him on the second ballot, but as we have seen, Gaullists also found him attractive.

The *Parti Socialiste* Legacy

Mitterrand appointed Pierre Mauroy prime minister and dissolved the National Assembly. A month later, the *Parti Socialiste* was comfortably installed as the majority party. But the landslide was short-lived. The first years of Mitterrand's presidency were heady with socialist ideology and policy, although de Gaulle had nationalized the major banks and Renault (because he believed its owner to have collaborated with the Nazis). The new government's economic policies harkened back to the period of Gaullist rule; that is, a strong

Table 6.11   The Performance of the French Economy

	1976–80 Average	1981–85 Average
GNP Growth	3.3	1.2
Unemployment	5.4	8.8
Inflation	10.5	9.4
Budget deficit (%GNP)	0.7	3.0
Percent change of disposable income	2.6	1.1

state. Giscard had been far more inclined toward market capitalism. The surviving private sector banks were nationalized, as well as portions of the insurance industry and twelve industrial concerns, seven of them among France's largest. Measures to bring parochial school teachers under civil service control, to limit the concentration of the press, to reorganize professional education, to mandate participatory decision making in industry (not *autogestion*, or self-management, as proposed by the CERES and other left *courants*), to strengthen trade unions, and to "change everything" occupied the new government for several years.

Given the costliness of these schemes, the massive public expenditures during worldwide recession and their mixed success, the *Parti Socialiste* spent the last four years of Mitterrand's first term "imposing austerity to pay for the spending spree undertaken during its first two years."[28] It slashed public expenditures, limited inflationary spirals in wages and prices. Although these policies had some salutary effect, France's economic track record was not what the *Parti Socialiste* had expected. (See Table 6.11.)

The last years of the Giscard administration also had been economic disasters, which largely explains why the *Parti Socialiste* won. Unemployment was at 7.8 percent compared to 2.6 percent when he became president. Fueled by the oil shock, inflation was raging at 13 percent, and GNP growth had shrunk to 0.5 percent. Mitterrand concluded, however, that socialist dogma was no better solution. This defeat had been presaged by the 1983 municipal elections, in which the left lost thirty-one towns with 30,000 or more inhabitants.

Another disappointment in the 1984 European elections heightened the *Parti Socialiste*'s sense of urgency. Desperation drove Mitterrand to reintroduce a variant of the Fourth Republic's proportional representation system of voting. Given the government's massive unpopularity, Mitterrand hoped to preserve a core of Socialist seats and reduce the odds of a conservative majority in the upcoming legislative elections. Simultaneously, Mitterrand regrouped the party faithful around the center-left, anticipating the necessity for cooperation after the elections.

The Return of the Right.   In spite of Mitterrand's U-turn, the right opposition returned to control in the National Assembly in 1986. Mitterrand named Chirac as his prime minister, beginning the period of "cohabitation." The new government began a process of undoing much of the first two years of Socialist policy: it planned a privatization program of five years, starting with the most solvent firms and then moving to those long dependent on public subsidies. However, the privatization scheme lasted only two years, as Chirac contented himself with conserving the status quo, a course of action suited well to Mitterrand's preferences.

By 1987 the economy was thriving, and, although outshone by the Federal Republic of Germany, France was in a period of sustained growth. French GNP growth was about as healthy as Germany's and, with German unification and its attendant problems, France's economy in the 1990s was actually healthier (see Appendix). Mitterrand was reelected in 1988, but in subsequent legislative elections did not regain a legislative majority. Rocard became prime minister and the accommodation of socialist theory to the reality of the market and international economic constraints became final. Both Mitterrand and Rocard suggested that voters should keep the RPR and UDF deputies at least at their present strength (in 1988), as one party dominance was unwelcome: "Be careful, we don't want too much of a Socialist majority. Don't overdo it." In truth, they got on almost as well with the center-right as with their *Parti Socialiste* diehards. There was no choice. With no majority (neither for the government nor for the opposition parties), the government's "relative majority" needed extension either from the Communist bloc or the center parties to pass legislation. As one disgruntled Socialist deputy complained, "when we look in the mirror we no longer recognize ourselves."[29] Rocard remains, and will always remain, unpopular with the Socialist hard left.

Jérôme Jaffré has shown how convincing this accusation is in Table 6.12. As Jaffré puts it:

> The vote...constituted a collapse of the sociology of the electorate.... Mitterrand lost ground in the traditional Parti Socialiste voting groups: men, public sector employees, non-religious voters. He lost ground in eight regions, situated south of the Loire, in which there is a strong Socialiste tradition....The electoral map is turned upside down.[30]

Table 6.12   The Evolution of Mitterrand's Vote

	1981	1988
Sex		
Male	56%	53%
Female	49	55
Age		
18–24	63	60
25–34	63	63
35–49	51	51
50–64	47	51
65 +	40	47
Profession of head of household		
Farmer	33	35
Blue collar	40	37
White collar	38	36
Intermediate professional	58	61
Higher professional	38	36
Inactive/retired	45	52
Employment of respondent		
Self-employed	33	33
Salaried, public	73	66
Salaried, private	59	60
Inactive/retired	45	53
Education		
Primary	51	58
Secondary	59	51
Technical college	58	56
University	50	49
Religion		
Regular attending Catholic	20	27
Occasionally attending Catholic	40	44
Nonpracticing Catholic	61	58
No religion	88	75
Interest in politics		
A great deal	64	52
A little	51	56
Very little	50	53
None	41	55
Self-classification (left-right)		
Extreme left	98	100
Left	95	97
Center	34	45
Right	6	6
Extreme right	5	3

Source: Jérôme Jaffré, "France au centre, victoires socialistes," *Pouvoirs,* 47 (1988): 168.

Mitterrand's successes were among older, retired voters, Catholic voters, poorly educated voters, those who cared nothing about politics, and those who claimed to be at the ideological center. By the second time around, whatever one might say about realignment or dealignment, the ideological ardor was gone from Mitterrand's presidency and electorate. No party's good fortune better represents Adam Przeworski and John Sprague's seminal conclusion:

> Faced with a working class that is a numerical minority, class-based parties seek support from other groups. They often win this support, but in the process they dilute the salience of class as a cause of the workers' political behavior, and they erode their strength among workers.[31]

THE FEDERAL REPUBLIC OF GERMANY: "DER BÄR" (HELMUT KOHL) TAKES CHARGE

In October 1980, Chancellor Helmut Schmidt's Social Democratic Party-Free Democratic Party coalition bolstered its majority over the Christian Democrats from ten seats to forty-five seats. The Christian Democrats, led temporarily by Franz-Josef Strauss, a Bavarian right-winger, had lost in its third try to replace the SPD as the leader of the coalition. In 1980 speculation about SPD "hegemony" was rampant. In 1983 the Christian Democratic Party was back as the major party in the coalition, with its best electoral accomplishment in twenty-six years. Now it was the Christian Democrats that pundits projected for hegemony, with the specter of the SPD lingering in opposition for the remainder of the century being seriously suggested.[32]

Even with these substantial anomalies, the Christian Democratic Union's 1983 victory has none of the apocalyptic aspect of the other elections discussed here. In October 1982, the Free Democratic Party-Social Democratic Party coalition had come apart, SPD Chancellor Helmut Schmidt lost a constructive no-confidence vote, and Christian Democrat Helmut Kohl became Chancellor, in coalition with the Free Democrats.[33] The Christian Democratic good fortune in the March 1983 elections ratified the coalition shift. Kohl, unable to dislodge the Social Democrats in prior elections, did so because of the Free Democrat defection; once in, he stayed in. Since Schmidt's no-confidence vote is the only instance in the history of the Federal Republic (another no-confidence vote, against Social Democrat Willy Brandt, failed by two votes), the 1983 elections need to be placed within this broader context.

Table 6.13   Vote Shares by the SPD and CDU (1957–83)

	1957	1961	1965	1969	1972	1976	1980	1983
SPD	32%	36%	39%	43%	46%	43%	43%	38%
CDU	50	45	48	46	45	49	45	49

The Maturation of the Social Democrats

The Social Democrats, governing as a partner in the Grand Coalition of the 1960s, gained the chancellorship in coalition with the Free Democrats in 1969. For the first time, the Social Democrats cracked the 40-percent barrier with 43 percent; the Christian Democrats fell about two points to 46 percent. As a result, over the strenuous protests of the Christian Democrats, the SPD and the Free Democrats formed a coalition. In 1972 the SPD actually outpolled the Christian Democrats, but in 1976 and 1980 the Christian Democrats returned to their customary position as the leading party. In spite of their electoral success, the Social Democrats were clinging to command only because of the forbearance of the Free Democrats. (See Table 6.13.)

The Decline and Fall of the SPD-FDP Coalition

Such forbearance became increasingly scarce. The well-liked Willy Brandt, who guided the SPD to its most impressive victory in 1972, resigned in 1974 after the discovery of an East German spy on his personal staff. His successor, Helmut Schmidt, prevailed in 1976 and 1980. But in the latter election, the CDU ran Franz-Josef Strauss, the leader of the right-wing Bavarian Christian Social Union, instead of Kohl; a mistake that alienated CDU voters in other parts of the Federal Republic. Had Strauss not temporarily replaced Kohl as CDU leader, possibly the coalition would have ended sooner.

Schmidt faced dissent within his party, mainly from the left, which objected to his commitment to NATO and to nuclear defense. The new Greens, which had gained seats in several *länder* elections, were nibbling away at Schmidt's left wing. In an unusually cruel remark, Oscar Lafontaine, who favored a shift toward the Greens, opined that Schmidt had the leadership qualities suitable for a concentration camp guard.

The two years between the narrow 1980 win and the 1982 splintering of the coalition were years of rapid deterioration of the West German economy, as was true with the other major economic powers as well (except Japan). Harassed by the Greens, Schmidt also angered his coalition partners by adhering to the SPD line of increased borrowing and higher taxes to restore economic advancement. The Free Democrats desired tax reductions and cuts in public spending. With such a fundamental difference, the wonder is that the coalition survived as long as it did; probably, the Free Democrats would have returned to their more natural ally, had not Strauss proved such an impediment. A coalition between the Free Democrats, a party speaking for entrepreneurial values (as the British Liberals), and the trade union (public employee-dependent SPD) was unnatural. Willy Brandt's *ostpolitik* (an accommodation to a divided Germany) had proved initially attractive to the FDP. Schmidt's more aggressive stance eliminated this inducement.

Strauss's 1980 debacle removed a serious obstacle to the rejuvenation of a more natural coalition between the FDP and the CDU. It was now only a matter of time.

> The tensions between the coalition partners and the internal divisions within the SPD and FDP not only created a public image of discord, drift, decay, and disillusionment; they also led to ineffective and inefficient government decisionmaking, compromises unsatisfactory to both parties, and even to immobility. It was not mere appearance that the SPD-FDP coalition government seemed unable to cope with the economic, foreign policy, defense, and social changes that were challenging the German government...in the 1980s. The collapse of the coalition ...came as no surprise....To many in the coalition parties it came as a relief.[34]

In regional elections, Greens on the left and Christian Democrats on the right gained ground as the FDP degenerated. Although the Free Democrats had polled 11 percent in 1980, they plunged below the requisite 5 percent in Lower Saxony and Hamburg. In West Berlin the SPD, reeling from scandal, plunged to 38 percent (from 44 percent four years earlier) and the Christian Democrats gained control of this major city. The West German Greens earned 7 percent, without question at the expense of the SPD. When surveys showed the Christian Democrats were on the way to an absolute majority in Hesse, FDP leaders there announced their intention to campaign with the CDU.

In Bonn, Chancellor Schmidt sought a vote of confidence as a prelude to a dissolution and election. However, the tactic failed when FDP chairman Hans-Dietrich Genscher and his colleagues resigned from the government and joined with the Christian Democrats in calling for a constructive no-confidence vote. Although the dreaded debacle in Hesse failed to unfold, possibly due to SPD charges of "treason in Bonn," the FDP could not surmount the 5-percent hurdle and the Greens, with 8 percent, held the balance of power. With chaos in the wings, the new coalition elected Kohl as chancellor. New elections were scheduled for March 1983.

The SPD's chances to regain the chancellorship were dealt a major blow by the retirement of the intense, charismatic Schmidt for "reasons of health" (a decade later, he still seems as vigorous as ever) and the ascension to power of Hans-Jochen Vogel, a competent dullard. Kohl, equally dull, would have had more trouble with Schmidt, but with personality neutralized, Kohl was free to project himself correctly as a solid middle of the roader in the Adenauer legacy. The long-time chairman of the CDU-CSU parliamentary faction, former minister-president of Rhineland-Pfalz, failed chancellor candidate in 1976, and now incumbent chancellor, was ready. "Der Bär" ("the bear") was evidently more appealing than Vogel.

Vogel, initially from the Schmidt-led right wing of the SPD, had served as mayor of West Berlin and Munich, and had served as housing and justice minister in earlier SPD-led governments. The SPD platform reflected Vogel's move to the center, in an effort to impede the impressive progress of the Greens. The party pledged a thirty-five-hour week, a massive investment program, improved environmental protection, vocational training for the youth, more public housing, and a reduction of reliance upon nuclear energy. It reaffirmed the pledge to NATO and was ambivalent about the explosive intermediate-range missile issue. Although Schmidt had supported the stationing of cruise and Pershing missiles on German soil, neither party made much of the issue in 1983. With the Greens demanding the removal of the missiles, neither major party wanted to dredge up the deep-rooted fears of nuclear holocaust.

The Kohl government also was careful not to highlight the missiles, preferring instead to accentuate economic issues. Although Kohl was the incumbent, he could hardly have been expected to turn around an economy that had been slipping for nearly eight years. Like France, and unlike the United States or the United Kingdom, there was no galvanizing event, but rather a gradual awareness that the "German miracle" was less miraculous than originally thought.

Between 1976 and 1980 Schmidt enjoyed an international reputation for astute economic management. In spite of the oil shocks, Germany prospered: while the gross income for industrial workers declined in the United States between 1976 and 1980, it grew by 11 percent in West Germany. By 1980 the Federal Republic's GNP per capita exceeded that of the United States. Inflation, contributing mightily to the American misery index, never exceeded 5 percent during this period, and unemployment hovered around 3 percent. But after 1980 the economy went into a tailspin; inflation remained anchored, but unemployment ballooned to 9 percent by 1982. To meet the obligations of the welfare state to the unemployed, the Schmidt government increased public spending and taxes, which by 1982 amounted to 46 percent of GNP. Federal deficits ballooned, as did interest rates, resulting in record business failures.

> By the end of the summer in 1982, relations between several unions and the government were deteriorating, with a public workers' demonstration in Bonn scheduled for October. An atmosphere of doom and gloom pervaded the country, and the consternation, drift, and disarray within as well as between the SPD-FDP government parties became increasingly apparent.[35]

The Myth of the "Hidden Left"

Given the urgency of the economy to the potential electorate, the Social Democratic Party's loss of Schmidt was doubly unfortunate. Not only did voters consistently rank the economy—singularly unemployment—as crucial to their decisions, they also, in spite of the coalition fiasco, held Schmidt in high regard. In unadorned dissimilarity, the party chancellor candidate, Vogel, was inexperienced and unduly influenced by the pre-Schmidt leadership cadre, notably Willy Brandt and General Secretary Peter Gloz. They imagined a "hidden left" to be exploited, much as Franz-Josef Strauss fantasized that the "hidden conservatives" would elect him in 1980. In courting the left, the SPD stressed the new politics issues: the environment, nuclear power, and more independent relations with the United States. The emerging Greens were the target.

By holding the traditional SPD voters, the new middle class (professionals), lower middle-class technical workers, and the blue-collar workers, the SPD envisaged a new majority. The strategy is tried repeatedly and never succeeds. McGovern in 1972 and the British Labour Party in 1983 and 1987 showed that despite the affinity that upper-class left intellectuals have for feminism, environmentalism, and the other core components of the new politics, such issues are not attractive to traditional working-class voters.

And so the SPD campaign, to the delight of the Christian Democrats, emphasized independence from the United States and the importance of the missiles. It largely ignored the electorate's real concern, unemployment, which 88 percent of the electorate ranked as "very important" compared to 76 percent in the last election (1980).[36] However, the environment (48 percent) and relations with

Table 6.14   Major Party Vote by Social Class (1980–83)

	Old middle class		New middle class		Working class	
	1980	1983	1980	1983	1980	1983
CDU	64%	66%	39%	45%	35%	41%
SPD	28	21	47	42	58	52
FDP	7	12	13	6	6	3

the United States (27 percent), the center of the SPD campaign, were much less salient.

The Christian Democrats, having dispatched Strauss and installed the moderate Kohl, enjoyed incumbency without being required to defend the government's economic record. Kohl campaigned on thirteen years of Socialist rule, the ensuing economic disaster, and the assurance that once the Germans returned to their senses and gave the chancellorship to the party of Adenauer all would be well. In contrast to their ideologically inspired opponents, the CDU talked almost exclusively about the economy. Though the economy had not yet begun to rebound, the electorate believed that it had. Additionally, the CDU was viewed as more competent to manage the economy, and since the economy was central to the concern of voters, the CDU benefited.

The Shape of the Christian Democrats' Victory

The result of these two approaches was, as one would expect, the legitimization of the 1982 no-confidence vote. The CDU and FDP continued the coalition. (See Table 6.14.)

As Table 6.14 shows, the Christian Democrats augmented their strength among both the new middle class and the working class, while the Social Democrats' favor among workers plummeted substantially: "The erosion of the SPD's proletarian core was a key factor in the CDU/CSU victory."[37]

Because the Christian Democrats pilfered SPD votes from the new middle class and working class, they benefited from a partisan tide that is almost American in magnitude. They received more than one-fifth of their vote from 1980 Social Democrat voters, an amount achieved by Reagan from the Democrats in 1980, and Nixon from the Democrats in 1972. In absolute numbers, the defection of the SPD voters was the most significant shift in 1983 and it "came disproportionately from the working class occupations . . . the traditional proletarian core of the party."[38] In contrast, the Social Democrats earned defections from only 11 percent of the 1980 CDU voters.

The CDU went for the center, where most of the voters are, while the SPD chased a phantom, the hidden left. Its middle class, center to center-left foundation, which had brought the party to rule in 1969, left it for the center. Thus, the 1983 election finished the SPD-FDP coalition and ended SPD dreams of a new balance in the electorate. The new coalition triumphed in 1987 and in 1990.

Although the SPD regained some lost ground in 1987, as working-class voters drifted back, its slide continued. In 1990 its 33.4 percent was the worst performance since 1957. The descent in support by the working class was resumed; the loss of the middle class continued.

The 1983 Social Democratic campaign, searching for the hidden left, recalls the 1964 Barry Goldwater campaign in the United States, which searched for the "hidden conservatives." Ordinarily, true believers, partisan or ideological, cannot fathom a public that is less passionately committed. They look at the adoring crowds and conclude that the surveys of voter opinion are false, but they never are. Geraldine Ferraro, pushed upon a reluctant Walter Mondale in 1984 to win "the women's vote," puzzled frequently about the disparity between the wildly enthusiastic crowds and the dismal survey projections.[39] Surely, the surveys were wrong. They were not!

SOUND AND FURY, SIGNIFYING NOTHING?

The evidence of linkage, in democratic theory a principal purpose of elections, is meager. People do not generally vote ideologically or programmatically; they vote retrospectively and protectively (how good or bad things have been; how good or bad they are likely to become). In the cases of electoral change examined here, one factor in common is immense, sustained, widespread public dissatisfaction with the incumbent government. If the nation's economy, not just one's personal financial situation, appears to voters to be in good shape, the government that presided over the good fortune probably will be allowed to remain. When times go bad, governments are replaced. Economic voting is not equally pervasive in all elections for all countries: it is more prominent in Britain than in Germany or France.[40] Of major import for this book is Lewis-Beck's finding that economic voting is *directly related to coalition complexity* (the number of parties in the ruling coalition). Coalitions dampen economic voting by making it difficult for a voter to know whom to hold responsible.[41]

In the United States, the problem is solved by holding the president accountable, even though he is less likely to be responsible for the shape of the economy than are European prime ministers.

The inertia of the past is more difficult to overcome in the United States than in governments without separation of powers. Institutional fragmentation makes it "harder to change the direction of public policy."[42] Add in the additional centrifugal force of modern issueless campaigns, the decline of the anchor of partisan affiliations, and, as Paul Kirk, former Democratic National Committee Chairman, worries, "consultants, spin doctors, fat cats and photo opportunities have replaced party leadership and platforms in the perception of most voter....A lot of them think [the political process] doesn't make a goldurn difference, and it doesn't."[43]

Change (as distinguished from idiosyncrasies such as Iran-Contra) occurs more in systems with an appreciable degree of institutional concentration of power. Mrs. Thatcher is gone; the British economy has not returned, as she had hoped, to its previous position of strength at the peak of empire. But her visceral hatred of trade unions pushed the Conservatives where they probably would not have gone under more traditional leadership. The resulting industrial relations legislation was, in the British tradition of union-management relations, revolutionary. This legislation is all the more meaningful as she believed correctly that trade union political power was of major concern to the electorate in 1979. "The people" wanted trade unions brought to heel; she did it, and "the people" knew and approved. Carry the argument one step beyond, and the luster is tarnished. Because most trade union members are not especially political, what they really care about is the shop floor, where almost nothing has changed. Unions, weakened politically, have not lost their grip on the daily lives of workers.

The *Parti Socialiste* began its reign in France possessed of a coherent concept of changing French society. Two years later, these concepts were replaced by the *rigueur*, the "U-turn." Never publicly announced as a new strategy, the period of austerity was presented as a "parenthesis, a concession to the times."[44] But it was not; rather, it was an important change for the left, one that made its reelection possible. Nevertheless, Rocard the pragmatist introduced three revolutionary items in public policy. First, the *revenu minimum d'insertion* provides a guaranteed income for all legal residents of France, whether citizens or not. A guaranteed income is not merely tinkering; it is of greater scope than any of the reforms successfully implemented by any government during the Fifth Republic. Second, Rocard began the *crédit-formation*, the right for a second chance in education. In the elitist atmosphere of French education, where failing national exams has traditionally meant the end of education, the notion of adult education is genuinely advanced. Finally, the *impôt de solidarité sur la fortune* imposed a tax from 0.5 to 1.5 percent on income above 4 million francs. Taken together, these measures made good on promises by Mitterrand in his 1988 campaign to return to the traditional Socialist concern with inequality that had been neglected because of the decline of the economy. Here is another example of politicians doing what the people wanted. As we know, ideology and issues played a less substantial role in the 1988 than in the 1981 French presidential election. Nevertheless, a promise was made and kept. However, if we take the next step, the "so what" step, skepticism returns. With regard to the *revenu minimum*, Chris Howell concludes that:

> Despite the fanfare attending its arrival, its primary purpose was to plug the gaps in welfare protection which existed in the expanding gray area between employment and unemployment, and to encourage people to sign onto job training programs.[45]

The wealth tax, since it affected less than half of 1 percent of all households, was even more symbolic. The Rocard thrust, then, was not "revolutionary" and "had a negligible impact on inequality."[46]

CHAPTER 7.

Problems with Pluralism and Corporatism

If the United States has weak political parties, the same cannot be said for interest groups. They are pervasive. Theoretically, the prominence of interest groups should be welcome. If political parties are unable to invent the people, then interest groups should do so. Indeed, American citizens appear to be relying more upon groups for their cues than was once the case (see Chapter 1). However, when interest groups successfully compete with political parties for individual commitment, is the representative bargain between rulers and the ruled strengthened? A positive answer depends on the ability of the interest group to do a more precise job in inventing the people than do political parties. Furthermore, while there is near universal consensus that political parties should be strong, professional opinion is more divided about interest groups.

Whereas political parties should both channel individual preferences and be held accountable, interest groups are disconnected from formal accountability. What is good for the Democrats, Republicans, Conservatives, Labour, Social Democrats, *Parti Socialistes*, and so on, should be good for the country. But what is good for an interest group might be quite *bad* for a country. Even if interest groups accurately represent member opinion, they lack the aggregating ability that parties should have. American pluralist theory, which exalted interest groups, can be taken to task for failing to comprehend their potential for paralyzing the polity. And if people join interest groups for personal, nonpolitical reasons, organization leaders are free to pursue whatever goals they wish without fear of member reprisal.

The objections to corporatism are nearly the exact opposite. By virtually coercing a select clientele, accurate representation is assured, but its scope is very narrow. Corporatist arrangements can be inflexible. For example, the various Green and environmental parties of Europe have not been included in corporatist bargaining. Corporatist arrangements are not accused of sacrificing long-term national interest to short-term group interest; rather they are accused of the neglect of the marginal.

INDIVIDUAL CHOICE, POLITICAL STRUCTURE, AND CULTURE

The original arguments against the pluralists were developed by American economists using American models of individual choice. Since the United States is more individualist in mass and elite attitudes, less corporatist in governance, and more fragmented politically than most other industrial democracies, it is natural to wonder if other cultures would produce such self-maximizing, rational individuals. Although the evidence is far from comprehensive, there is ample reason to presume that other political cultures are inhabited by interest groups whose members are "irrational."

In the United Kingdom, not a good manifestation of corporatism or collectivism, David Marsh found that whereas the small businessman who joined the Confederation of Business did so for services (selective benefits), large firms did not.[1] West German antinuclear protestors did so because they believed themselves to be in imminent danger and because they enjoyed protesting.[2] As we have already noted, in the United States, individual motivations vary with the nature of the organization and with the nature of the decision.

The Two Modes of Pluralism

Pluralism describes a political routine with a roughly equal distribution of opportunities to amass political resources, although not the actual distribution of these resources. However, another understanding of the term, especially among European political scientists, is a system of multiple, competing interest groups that, through bargaining and compromise, contribute to the shape of public policy.

The European version enunciates a political process in which interest groups organize, attempt influence, survive, or disappear, largely without the participation or encouragement of governmental bureaucracies.

Decisions are a result of *elite* bargaining and adjustment. Elite competition helps to safeguard individual nonparticipants from governmental abuse, since no set of interests is likely to be ascendant indefinitely. A particular interest will win in some years, lose in others; win in some arenas, lose in others; win on some issues, lose on others. Therefore, pluralism is—besides being a process with at least the pretensions of balanced power—a loosely structured free-market system, with groups coming and going without negative or positive sanctions from the government. Although, depending upon the criteria employed, the United States, the United Kingdom, France, Canada, Ireland, and Italy have been called pluralist, only the United States has consistently and consensually been so regarded.

Being consistently identified as a pluralist nation does little to guarantee access to any organized group in the United States. And while business associations clearly enjoy a privileged status in American politics, the privilege is more a matter of money and prestige than of "official" sanction or regulation.[3] The very phrase "pressure group" implies that American interest groups do not have the ease of access afforded by quasi-governmental status and therefore must lobby:

> [Pressure groups] suggests a distance and a separation of function between business organizations and government that would not make sense in many countries. . . . It remains more common to think of business organizations in [the United Kingdom and the United States] as outside pressure groups than as groups incorporated into the framework of government. This tendency is strongest in the USA.[4]

What is true of business associations is even more certain for the less privileged groups: labor, consumers, civil rights organizations, and the like. With freedom to organize and no guaranteed access, pressure groups gain their advantages by creating encumbrances and cashing in on them. Since the ill-fated American reforms of the 1970s the number of such groups—and their attendant political action committees—has increased exponentially.

With free commerce in interest groups came doubts about the efficacy of interest groups for democracy. Having caused pluralist theorists to reassess the *representative* function of organizations, Mancur Olson, a widely respected author on the subject of interest groups, then caused them to reassess their political consequences. He argued that "narrow distributional coalitions"—interest groups—doing what they do best (defending their unique interests), constrain the polity's ability to make difficult choices. From this perspective, interest groups, unless they are subordinated to a more encompassing view, ensure economic decay. Olson alleges that two prototypes of economic decline—the United States and the United Kingdom—establish his point. Of the United Kingdom, Olson offers the classic description of a pluralist group pattern:

> The number and power of its trade unions need no description. The venerability and power of its professional associations is also striking.... Lobbying is not as blatant as in the United States but it is pervasive and often involves discreet efforts to influence civil servants as well as ministers and other politicians.[5]

Clearly Olson's idea of pluralism is unrelated to the *distribution* of power, but rather is related to its use: interest groups are not encompassing, therefore they pursue their special interest to the detriment of the polity.

Moreover, as Olson simplified individual motivation, so he glossed over major *institutional* differences between governments, pluralist in group structure or not. Again, the United Kingdom and the United States provide instructive examples. The United States government, a presidential, federal government with deteriorating party discipline, is, in British political scientist Richard Rose's apt words, no government at all. Echoing American Theodore Lowi's lament, Rose asserts that the president cannot "override the preferences of subgovernments [interest groups] in the name of broader national interests."[6] Because *the* government cannot govern, there often may be no government (though there will be found subgovernments, often in cooperation with other subgovernments, to serve their particular purposes).

Parliamentary democracies, especially unitary ones such as the United Kingdom, without doubt, have a government. They also have interest groups, often exceedingly powerful ones, as in Great Britain. The difference is that "the cabinet has the collective authority to hold subgovernments [interest groups] in check."[7]

The opposite is true of the American cabinet. It has become, like the other institutions of government, a holding company for interest groups; the cabinet secretaries feed into the "iron triangles" to provide yet more pull. There are fifteen cabinet jobs, the last eleven of which were added to please an interest group or special constituency. President Reagan had proposed the elimination of the Departments of Energy and Education. Congress refused, so he suggested adding a new Department of Veterans Affairs, knowing that Congress could not refuse. Bush has endorsed a sixteenth cabinet position, the elevation of the Environmental Protection Agency. The cabinet is just a crowd of interest groups.

PLURALISM, FRAGMENTATION, AND POLITICAL CONTROL

So the notion that interest groups destroyed collective purpose seems flawed. It requires the active collaboration of the government. Such a view also exaggerates the divorce between interest groups and government in the world's most pluralist democracy. As Jack Walker and Alan Ware have shown, organizations are often sponsored by the American national government.[8] Additionally, "iron triangles"—tight policy networks with congressional subcommittees at the hub—provide preferential access, albeit to groups that give them money.

Notwithstanding, fragmented sectors of the American government, including bureaucracies, are tightly aligned with interest groups. The point is that parliamentary governments are potentially capable of coordinating and subordinating the behavior of interest groups, whereas pure presidential ones cannot. They do not always succeed, of course. The French Fourth Republic was as much an "interest group society" as is the United States today, even with parliamentary government. But the potential for coordination is enhanced when power is concentrated, when the number of access points for interest groups is narrowed. According to Rose, the differences between presidential and parliamentary systems are "organic." Using the United States as an example, Rose believes that institutional power ("the state") is inferior to personal, transitory power. Thus, parliamentary systems can sometimes confront interest groups with the power of "the state," whereas the American presidential system cannot.[9]

Therefore, the American economic degeneration can be blamed partially upon narrow distributional coalitions. Paul Kennedy, like Olson, blames interest groups that, "by definition," sabotage the public good.[10]

Beyond the American case, one is hard pressed to illustrate the premise that interest groups are incompatible with broad images of the public good. In the United Kingdom, the Thatcher government took on the unions and reduced their institutionally assured access immensely.[11] Other countries—Sweden, Japan, Switzerland, Nor-

way, and West Germany—have enjoyed vibrant economies while simultaneously encouraging vibrant organizational activity. It is not
interest groups that enhance or impede a polity's ability to enunciate
and consummate its goals; rather, it is the degree of coordination imposed or encouraged by the government, and the ability or failure of
governments to weaken divisive groups.[12] In the United Kingdom,
the economic dive lamented by Olson has been abated. As A. G. Jordan and J. J. Richardson conclude: "Whether governments utilize
the capacity of groups skillfully or turn the opportunities into opposition is the test of successful governance."[13] Since Rose has insisted
that the pluralist, presidential system of the United States lacks governance, it obviously cannot meet this challenge. A more structured
pluralist, parliamentary system, the United Kingdom, does better at
pursuing a common good. Moreover, corporatist regimes are said to
be best at managing interest groups because they *incorporate* them directly and deliberately into the governing process.

Structured Pluralism: The United Kingdom

Given the power of British political parties, it is natural that interest groups generally operate through them; if not as auxiliaries,
then undeniably as major players. We have seen the extent to which
the Labour Party and trade unions are integrated structurally and financially. Labour is far more dependent upon unions than are
American democratic politicians, even more so than the German Social Democrats and German unions.

In contrast, there is no formal relationship between business interest groups and the Conservatives, as the rudiments of the modern
Conservative Party were developing before the industrial revolution
and, therefore, before the rise to political prominence of business.

From the end of World War II until 1979, both political parties, irrespective of their biases, tried to emulate the West German "concerted action," but the Labour defeat of 1979 ended the experiment
abruptly. Even before Mrs. Thatcher denounced corporatism, neither Labour nor the Conservatives had much success in reaching
consensus and sustaining it over a period of years. When unions
tried to behave as peak associations, they faced shop-floor revolts;
nor could business associations deliver their members.

The Conservative victory in 1979 and Mrs. Thatcher's reliance
upon monetary policy rather than corporatism have meant a state-
centered policy process, instead of a consultative one as in Switzerland or Japan: "The very practice of formulating economic policy

through negotiation with the affected interest could be rejected as unnecessary because of the overriding role of monetarist theory."[14]

The Confederation of British Industry and the National Economic Development Council.   The privatization programs begun in the 1980s have provided further distance between the government and interest groups. The National Economic Development Council (NEDC) was established in 1962, with membership divided among the Confederation of British Industry (CBI), the Trades Union Council, and the government. It was to be the central planning office for the British economy (significantly, it was created under a Conservative government). It produced many well-reasoned analyses of the British economy, but no one paid attention.

No groups can send plenipotentiaries to Whitehall to negotiate. The structure is provided by the government and the parties. Since Commons lacks policymaking power, members of Parliament are an unlikely target for lobbying. It all must be done at Whitehall. The multiple access points of the United States (Congressional committees, state governments, and the like) do not exist. Interest groups devote almost all their attention to senior civil servants and departmental ministers.

The CBI and the NEDC illustrate the problems for British interest groups. In spite of the willingness of pre-Thatcher governments to accord more legitimacy to functional representation than is true in the United States, the CBI is not a peak association. Recognized by bureaucrats and government ministers as a peak association, it owes its creation to the assistance and encouragement of the Labour government.[15] But the CBI could not deliver:

> Commitments made by the CBI were not seen as binding or particularly authoritative by member companies. The ability of the CBI to influence government policy was less than its members had hoped. So the CBI could neither deliver the co-operation of corporations to the government, nor deliver the co-operation of government to corporations.[16]

Undeniably, the CBI could not equal the City (the financial sector) in bureaucracy access. Thus, the NEDC never developed a power base, and Mrs. Thatcher finally abolished it, to the chagrin of the CBI, which wanted (but did not attain) a "bare-knuckle fight." Just as she had taken on, and defeated, the unions, she also took on British industry. A number of CBI affiliated corporations left the organization and it never recovered. The Thatcher revolution, presumably to reintroduce vigor into the British economy, was undertaken "against the wishes of many leaders of *organizations* representing

British Capitalists."[17] But what of the City? The Thatcher government, with its monetarist commitment, unquestionably looked to the Bank of England for advice, but Thatcher did not appear to be vulnerable to pressure. Despite vigorous and sustained opposition from the governor of the Bank of England, Thatcher stuck to her tight-money policy. Yet, there is more at work here than Mrs. Thatcher. After all, she is gone. It would be as silly to argue that she caused the dissolution of British corporatism as to argue that Reagan caused the United States' seemingly intractable problems. As John Freeman concludes:

> The quasi-corporatist bodies created under the Labour government are now defunct, and most producer groups and party leaders think it is unlikely these bodies will be created in the near future or outright oppose the idea. Thus Britain's polity remains basically pluralist.[18]

Strong Pluralism and Political Ruin: The American Savings and Loan Scandal, the Deficit, and American Interest Group Politics. Thomas Mann, less given to hyperbole than most, in a masterly bit of understatement, grieves that "when effective action on the country's most pressing problems requires the imposition of losses on organized interests, with benefits to all on the distant horizon, the odds of success in the U.S. political system are not very high."[19] Why not? Perhaps because Rose was right when he said no government exists there. Only a government strong enough to impose costs on its public could operate effectively on the savings and loan crisis or the deficit. The pluralist United States does not have that government. Mann, after tossing out pleasing disparate scenarios (rosy ones at that), settles on a realistic, if funereal, probability of the future of American politics: "A continuation of the escapism and deadlock of recent years."[20] In a similar vein, Terry Moe predicts that the "current administrative tangle may actually get worse over time." Moe thinks so for the same reasons as does Mann: the proliferation of interest groups and the attendant "structural disarray."[21]

"Structural disarray" is harsh judgment, for its remedy requires more than just electing good people. Congress and its supporters find occasion to cheer when something is done. In 1990, after ten years, a clean-air act was passed and celebrations ensued. In the same year, a budget deficit reduction plan released another "the-system-works" deluge. Nonetheless, these outcomes are "consistent with the interests of the most powerful participants at the bargaining table," and do not survive unless those participants continue to be satisfied. As John Chubb and Paul Peterson so brilliantly explain:

"Onlookers may congratulate participants for any sign of the subordination of narrow interests and immediate concerns to long range interests. But they do so only because such accomplishments are so rare."[22]

Alan Schick does exactly this in discussing the 1986 Tax Reform Act, legislation that he regards as "surprising,"[23] since it was passed over the objections of "armies of lobbyists" and "operating in a context shaped mainly by broader policy, partisan, and institutional considerations." Robert Salisbury calls this legislation "one of the most startling events in the history of public policy in the United States." His explanation is sensible: as more groups flock to Washington, no single group, or coalition of groups, will be able to achieve the market dominance possible when there were fewer competitors in the market. Because there will surely be as many groups in the future as now, Salisbury believes that group influence will, of necessity, diminish.[24] But this is a reach, although an interesting one entirely in keeping with the economic logic of the market.

Another, more cynical explanation comes from the proponents of public choice. They argue that the 1986 tax legislation occurred because Congress had flooded the market with loopholes, thus lowering the value of each loophole and the value of a congressional vote to the interest groups. It was, therefore, necessary to wipe the slate clean, to empty the market of the commodity, tax loopholes, and thus increase the value of each future loophole. As we know, the 1990 budget began the loophole-granting process anew.

Thus, a single example, so remarkable that it generated pages of praise, even though it was eroded within two years, is said to prove that "the political process worked."[25] Legislation that would be assured in other industrial democracies was judged as startling. One is reminded of the joy with which students of political parties greeted Jim Wright's centralizing efforts, and their silence when he was driven from office.

By the 1990s "America's apparently intractable governability problem" (from Walter Dean Burnham's dust jacket blurb for James A. Morone, *The Democratic Wish: Popular Participation and the Limits of American Government*) had chiseled out an intellectual habitat.[26] Morone is the latest to complain about the excesses of pluralism, yearning for "a government with the authority to make judgments ...less riddled with competing interests and agents, less fragmented."[27] As Morone correctly remarks, one must commence with the Constitution, setting aside checks and balances and separation of powers. Plainly, such hopes will not come to fulfillment.

The instance of "the system works" most recently given, the 1987 budget agreement, "illustrates how grateful even thoughtful observers can be when a country's politicians are taking only tiny steps in the right direction."[28] In 1990, as the same budget crisis reappeared, just how tiny the steps were became apparent. The disarray of American government is not caused by elite whim or disposition; it is caused by structural flaws. Systematic incentives toward short-term thinking make fiscal stability beyond hope. America does not lack an energy policy because Reagan was indisposed toward government intervention; it lacks one because pluralism provides no incentives for conservation or thinking beyond today:

> The pluralist form of interest intermediation produces dissensus and instability. Pluralism encourages interest groups to pursue their own particular interests in coalitions with other groups that are pursuing their particular interests. Such coalitions generally adopt policies that are concerned more with existing distributional inequities than with long-term collective gain.[29]

The Savings and Loan Tragedy.   The savings and loan scandal seems almost too good to be true for those scholars who, like Mann, worry about unconstrained interest groups and the debasement of national purpose. In August 1989, Congress authorized the largest bailout—government financial help to the private sector—in American history. The initially estimated cost, $115 billion to liquidate or reorganize failed savings and loan associations, exceeded by at least fifty times the earlier bailouts (New York City in 1975 and Chrysler in 1979). But the ultimate price, between $325 billion and a numbing $500 billion, is unimaginable. The per-household expense comes to about $5,000, with about 90 percent of the cost borne by individual income taxes.

The necessity for a bailout to avoid the loss of individual savings was engendered by a collaborative exploitation: savings and loan lobbyists bribed congressmen and bureaucrats who, in exchange, created the opportunities for irresponsible investment and, therefore, insolvency. Savings and loan associations were originally intended to be low-risk alternatives to commercial banks. Low-interest charges on loans and low-interest payments on investments kept the S&Ls from failing during the depression of the 1930s. Forty percent of commercial banks folded, wiping out millions of dollars in savings, but only 5 percent of the S&Ls went under. To avoid a run on the remainder, deposit insurance was begun and increased with inflation until it reached $100,000, eliminating the need for investor monitoring or S&L prudence.

No serious fissure occurred until the Federal Reserve Board, try-ing to halt the 1970s inflation, raised interest rates, sometimes to as high as 20 percent. Depositors took their money out of the S&Ls in pursuit of more lucrative opportunities. In 1982, at the urging of the savings and loan lobbyists, Congress allowed S&Ls to make unse-cured loans and to invest in commercial real estate, but the hemor-rhage continued.

By 1983 recession cooled interest rates down to normal, but the savings and loan associations had gotten a taste of escapades. They could break a huge investment into $100,000 (insured) chunks, mov-ing them in and out of markets to obtain the maximum return. With little or none of their capital invested, and with insurance against loss, savings and loan owners speculated in junk bonds, land and of-fice development, and other high-risk adventures. Especially in the Southwest, "cooked" books, insider deals with family and friends, opulent life-styles, and little investment experience characterized the new S&L ownership.

In 1986 the oil market—and consequently the value of land and real estate—in the Southwest plunged. The S&L industry suffered a net loss of $6 billion, and the figure soon rose to $20 billion. In 1987 the stock market crash and the expiration of the junk bond market slowed many of the deals that kept the savings and loans afloat.

The governmental response, principally by the Federal Home Loan Bank Board, prodded by congressmen who had been lavishly funded by the S&L PACs, was to lower the capital requirements for S&L ownership and to adopt new accounting procedures that effec-tively concealed insolvency.

A common problem in government regulation is the propensity of regulating agencies to become so identified with the regulated that they become promoters (advocates) rather than supervisors: "The Federal Home Loan Bank Board . . . [was] closer to the regulated than in any other industry in America," said John Heimann, vice presi-dent of Merrill Lynch Capital Markets.[30] The regulatory bu-reaucracy—willing captives of the savings and loans—was joined by congressmen who received substantial campaign contributions from the S&L main interest group, the United States League of Savings In-stitutions. Speaker of the House Jim Wright and majority whip Tony Coelho resigned in disgrace because of their financial dependence upon S&L PACs. The infamous Keating Five—Democratic senators Alan Cranston (California), Dennis DeConcini (Arizona), John Glenn (Ohio), and Donald Riegle (Michigan) and Republican John McCain (Arizona)—intervened with regulators after S&L owner Charles Keating (of Lincoln Savings & Loan based in Irvine, Califor-

nia) gave them $1.3 million in contributions (the Keating Five's origi-
nal defense was that they were performing "constituent service"
when intervening on Keating's behalf).

"Capture theory," the argument that all bureaucracies ultimately
fall under the supremacy of the regulated industry, the clients, is not
without exception. Some agencies are captured; some are not. They
are most likely to be captured when the interest group environment
is homogeneous, or noncompetitive. If a single powerful interest is
unchallenged, the agency will likely become captured.[31] Murray
Edelman, incorrectly alleged to have claimed that all government
regulation is symbolic,[32] genuinely and precisely delineated the precise conditions under which bureaucracies are reduced to impotence. His account closely matches the structure of the S&L
industry: "A relatively high degree of organization—rational, cogni-
tive procedures—precise information—an effective interest in specifi-
cally identified tangible resources—a favorably perceived strategic
position with respect to reference groups—relatively small
numbers."[33]

Arrayed against such a cohesive group are, for instance, consumers, or in the S&L case, taxpayers.

> Shared interest in the improvement of status through activity—an unfa-
> vorably perceived strategic position with respect to reference groups—
> distorted, stereotyped, inexact information and perception—response
> to symbols connoting suppression of threats—relative ineffectiveness in
> securing tangible resources through political activity—little organization
> for purposeful action—quiescence—relatively large numbers.[34]

S&Ls were unchallenged. Furthermore, they did not *appear* as ra-
pacious predators, but rather as benevolent handmaidens to the
American dream.

The pervasiveness of the command of the S&L interest groups
over elected and appointed public officials is well shown in the bi-
zarre behavior of those entrusted with the bailout. By 1990 the S&L
scandal had produced a second generation of scoundrels: failed institutions were being sold to yet more crooks who put up almost no
money to buy them. For example, James M. Fail put up a mere $1,000
to buy fifteen insolvent savings and loans, accompanied by a pledge
of $1.85 billion in federal aid and a $70 million loan. Fail had entered
a 1976 guilty plea (a presumptive disqualifier) to a securities fraud
charge, a fact that did not disqualify him from merging the fifteen
failed savings and loans into Bluebonnet Savings Bank, the most
profitable S&L in the nation in 1989, with the help of $275 million in
federal aid.

Mr. Fail's endeavors were guided by Robert Thompson, lobbyist and former aide to George Bush. The Fail fiasco is merely a microcosmic illustration of the fact that 60 percent of the failed savings and loans were engaged in serious fraud. Probably, an equal percentage of government officials were on the take.

> The FHLBB is...culpable. [It] officially recognized only a few of the many insolvencies....It forbore from closing economically insolvent S&Ls, instead reducing its capital requirements and using accounting gimmickry....It did not require S&Ls to report capital based on market values; therefore, it continued regulations that permitted economically insolvent institutions to remain open and to increase their risk exposure and losses....The industry made large political contributions to members of Congress in return for the postponement of legislative action that would have increased deposit insurance premiums and other payments, reduced thrifts' independence, and resulted in the removal of managers and owners of insolvent or nearly insolvent institutions. Because the dollar amounts at stake were so massive, the contributions were huge even by Washington standards....What is more, some S&L owners and managers were simply thieves....As a result, more "high rollers" gained control of S&Ls. In particular, real estate developers used thrift associations to fund their own activities.[35]

Although Charles Keating did not operate a PAC, the response of three senators to his S&L problems shows how buying time looks. Senators Alan Cranston (D-Calif), the party whip, Denis DeConcini (D-Ariz), and Donald Riegle (D-Mich) made late night and early morning telephone calls to federal regulators on Keating's behalf and urged the White House to name a Keating associate to a Federal Banking agency. Roger Martin, a member of the Federal Home Loan Bank Board, was called, at his unlisted home number, twice: once by Cranston late at night and once by DiConcini at 5:30 A.M. The urgency of these calls was, in Mr. Martin's experience, unprecedented.

In a hand-written note to his staff, for instance, Senator DeConcini outlined a plan to counter "Charlie's" negative publicity: "I think sometimes the best defense is a good offense. This is not going to go away, so we need to discredit Gray [DeConcini refers to chief Keating accuser Edwin Gray, then chairman of the Federal Home Loan Bank Board]."

Cranston, Riegle, and DeConcini kept in close and frequent contact with Keating through letters, memoranda, and personal meetings. They were kept apprised of Keating's fundraising efforts for them, and were told exactly what Keating expected. Several memos list the political favors, tabulated next to the money given. Keeping up with Keating's problems assiduously, the senators helped one another in sharing Keating's largesse.

Keating wrote of his "very serious task" in raising funds for Riegle, who "will be the next chairman of the Senate Banking Committee." DeConcini joined in these attempts, writing Riegle personal notes with Keating's checks enclosed. A Riegle aide wrote to DeConcini that a fundraising appearance in Arizona will "add to your stash."[36] The senators explained that their service to Keating was the same as would be provided for any constituent; it was normal "case work." The Senate agreed: it exonerated all but Alan Cranston.

The point is that by trying to find out if political action committees buy votes, we are probably overlooking what they are *really* buying: time. Money buys "marginal time, energy, and legislative resources."[37]

These organizations are the kind of single-issue groups that remain focused on lobbying for one issue, and are not easily swayed by selective benefits, but only by collective goods.

The Budget-Making Process

The extravagant costs of bailing out S&Ls, and the lack of central fiscal discipline it revealed, can be multiplied a dozen times, as each policy arena gets its way. The chaos of fiscal policy revealed by the S&L fiasco simply will not die. A few months after the bailout was concluded, Treasury Secretary Nicholas Brady asked for an "open-ended commitment," explaining that the original subsidy was exhausted. The idea of open-ended spending appealed to Congress, as this would let it escape unpopular votes for even more bailout billions.

Astute Congress watchers note that the preoccupation with the interests of narrowly defined groups to the detriment of any larger issue is "relatively routine" and "fits into a more general pattern of the way Congress responds to constituencies and to regulatory developments.[38] The upshot is a budget deficit that gnaws away at the American economy, eroding its international competitive capacity, and lowering the nation's standard of living."[39]

The 1990 budget-making process supports the Thomas Mann prediction to the letter: deadlock. After Congress had, in effect, refused to undertake the budget-writing task, a summit assembled. Consisting of representatives of the executive office of the president, and the leaders of both parties in the House and Senate, the summiteers labored four months. In October 1990, the results were submitted to the House, where majorities of both political parties, led by the Republican whip, rejected it. As the government prepared for closure, stop-gap spending authorizations kept bureaucracies running.

The original budget compromise included a $500 billion deficit reduction. This projected reduction was based on a predicted annual GNP growth of 3.8 percent. No responsible economist estimates a 1992–95 GNP growth rate of more than 2.5 percent, and growth has been averaging about 1.5 percent for the last several years. Federal revenues were overstated by about $30 billion. The summiteers predicted inflation at 3 percent, and interest rates for Treasury bills at 4 percent. The budget compromise was a deception. Rather than a budget surplus of $70 billion by 1995, the summiteers delivered a package that would yield a budget deficit of $250 billion by that time. Nevertheless, $500 billion was, as the lobbyists put it, "ugly." Since lobbyists operate within the committee system, they were prepared to resist. Interest groups sought to preserve their clients' benefits; insurance and real estate companies, targeted for substantial increases, fought for the status quo. The proposed luxury tax angered the Distilled Spirits Council, but not the manufacturers of private planes, as Kansas Republican and Senate Minority Leader Robert Dole, a summiteer, exempted private planes from the proposed tax. The American Trucking Association, worried about the effects of higher gasoline taxes, set up a phone bank to speak to the presidents of the 3,000 trucking companies located in the districts of House Ways and Means Committee members.

Although Congress did not write the budget, it emphatically rejected it. Today, because of a string of presidential humiliations, Congress is asserting its reactive rights more energetically than has become the custom; therefore, Republican presidents sometimes grumble about "the imperial Congress." President Bush, stung by the rejection by both political parties of his budget compromise proposal, was embarrassed by the defection of leading Republican members of the House of Representatives. Bush withdrew, saying, "Let Congress sort it out." And sort it out it did. First, general guidelines were approved, with details left to the subcommittees and committees that form the heart of the iron triangles.

While media attention was focused on income tax increases, capital gains taxes, and Medicare, the House Democrats confronted the Republican president with their "soak the rich" scheme, and minuscule deals were struck. Narrowly targeted tax breaks—"rifle shots"—are part of the culture of Congress. Part of the rebellion against the leadership was generated because the rifle shots were only available to the leadership and not the rank and file.

For example, a proposed 10-percent "luxury tax" was to be applied to all private airplanes that cost more than $100,000, to all boats that cost more than $30,000, and to all jewelry and furs priced over $500. In the Senate, the counterproposal raised the cost to $250,000 and exempted planes that were used 80 percent of the time for business. Why the change? Senate Minority Leader Robert Dole is from Kansas, where Cessna Aircraft Company and Beechcraft Aircraft Corporation are located.

The summit budget plan had set the cost floor for boats at $30,000. However, Senate Majority Leader George Mitchell is from Maine, where the boat building industry would be damaged. Therefore, the floor was raised to $100,000. Simultaneously, Mitchell secured a break for UNUM, the Life Insurance Company of Portland, the largest private employer in Maine's largest city. About $8 billion in new taxes was to be raised by changing the way insurance companies deduct new expenses for securing new policies. However, UNUM, which specializes in health and accident insurance policies that cannot be canceled, was placed, thanks to Mitchell, in a special category with companies that sell group life insurance (which UNUM does not). Thus UNUM does not pay the new tax rate.

The Fur Information Council of America lobbied for a higher threshold, arguing that 90 percent of all American furriers are small businesses, a venerated symbol, and that most furs are purchased by middle-income, middle-aged, working women. So the threshold went up to $5,000, but the Fur Information Council kept at it, and the threshold was raised to $10,000.

Return to luxury cars. What difference do you see? The threshold started and ended at $30,000. The vast majority of such cars are made in Europe and Japan. There were no lobbyists to plead their case, and the American automakers thought the threshold was just fine.

Or contemplate the proposed "sin tax" on tobacco and alcohol. In early conversations, talk of 16¢ per pack tax was common. Eventually, the tax was halved, due to intense tobacco industry lobbying and the savvy of Kentucky Senator Wendell Ford. He importuned House Ways and Means Committee Chairman Daniel Rostenkowski for a deal: if Rostenkowski would buy the tobacco tax reduction, Ford would support legislation permitting airport passenger fees for construction. Rostenkowski is from Chicago, where O'Hare Airport was in serious need of funds, and eagerly traded tobacco taxes for passenger fees. While this bargain was struck, the cigar manufacturers of southern Florida were exempted. The tax on cigarettes, but not cigars, will be increased. Sam Gibbons, a Tampa Democrat, arranged this $100 million deal.

Meanwhile, the liquor and wine industry, aided by House Majority Leader Richard Gephardt of Missouri, held down the increase in excise taxes on beer (Anheuser-Busch is in St. Louis). Senate budget bargainers were said to be more worried about protecting California's Pete Wilson, in a tough reelection campaign. As California is the nation's leading wine producer, Wilson was given "something to take credit for." Oregon's Bob Packwood could take credit for another wrinkle: wineries producing less than 200,000 gallons a year were exempt (all Oregon vineyards meet this criterion).

While these bargains were struck, museum directors had been lobbying quietly to reverse provisions of the 1986 tax reform legislation. In 1986 large donations (of art) to museums had to be declared as a tax liability as well as a deduction, thus eliminating the advantage. But led by Senator Daniel Moynihan of New York, in whose district America's greatest museums are located, persuaded his Finance Committee colleagues to revert to the pre-1986 rules, allowing a reduction of taxable income for donations of art.

So the American Congress, or at least its myriad committees, is, for the moment, more imperial than was the case before Watergate, and a string of failed presidencies has allowed it to assert itself again. By turning the budget process back to the committees, everybody—not just the leadership—got their rifle shots.

One of the most damaging rifle shots was fired by the myriad of groups opposed to increases in gasoline taxes. This tax increase not only would have raised revenue; it also would have had at least a marginal impact upon America's eagerness to consume energy at rates far greater than those of the other industrial democracies. Gas taxes in 1990 were about 25¢ per gallon; they were $3.80 in Italy, $3.10 in France, $2.10 in Britain, $2.05 in West Germany, $1.80 in Japan, and 90¢ in Canada. So why are we so remiss?

> Few, if any, organized interests have an incentive to lobby for this type of energy tax, whereas many have incentives to assail it. . . . A gasoline tax lacks allies among energy producers of any kind. . . . A decline in the use of gasoline does not lead to an increase in the demand for other fuels. . . . Therefore, *the tax offers coal and natural gas companies no clear opportunities to improve their market share.* Meanwhile, as far as the petroleum industry is concerned, reduced demand for its principal product is bad news. Others think so, too. Alongside the gasoline sellers will stand road contractors, engineers, truckers, taxicab companies, the nation's biggest automakers, and the United Auto Workers. . . . Every congressional district bulges service industries—motels, fast-food chains, shop-

ping malls, and countless other roadside businesses—for whom patronage by motorists (and, at bottom, existence of inexpensive gasoline) is the lifeblood. *Elected officials in other industrialized democracies sometimes confront similar pressure groups, but never on the same scale.*[40]

Notice the inference here: if there had been a market incentive for competitive energy producers to support an increased gas tax, they would have done so. Pluralism relies upon market incentives to provoke competing group pressures. A grim reminder of the power of interest groups is this conversation between former U.S. Ambassador to Iraq April Glaspie and Saddam Hussein:

> Glaspie: "I would ask you to examine the possibility of not charging too high a price for oil."
> Hussein: "We do not want too high prices for oil. . . . Twenty-five dollars a barrel is not a high price."
> Glaspie: "We have many Americans who would like to see the price go above $25 because they come from oil-producing states."

So the budget was a political document. The budget legislation, unnoticed at the time, declared that in the event of a recession, the spending limits were to be eliminated. In January 1991, the Treasury Department declared a recession. Vincent Wright wrote of the French Fourth Republic (1945–58) that:

> Within parliament individual members exercised great power, and because of weak party discipline were able to create havoc with governmental proposals; at budget times they would badger unstable governments into concessions in favour of their constituencies. Parliamentary initiatives delayed the adoption of the budget and all too often compromised the balance between revenue and expenditure. It was small wonder that one critic. . . could describe the parliamentary assemblies as "wasteful, incompetent, and irresponsible."[41]

Were Wright to turn his attention to the American Congress, could he discern a difference? How typical is the current American dilemma of past American experience and the experience of other industrial democracies? That all governments are now, and have always been, corrupt is not debatable. The United States has had scandals before, and European governments erupt periodically in scandal. Japanese government is surely as riddled with bribery and corruption as the United States Senate and House of Representatives. The Flick scandal in Germany touched both political parties. In France, the issue of corruption emerged in the last days of the Rocard administration when judicial officials were accused of burying evidence of illegal contributions to the *Parti Socialiste,* and local government officials were found to be in the pay of businessmen seeking building contracts. Italian corruption, led by a persistent Mafia, is on the scale of Japan's.

As we have seen, the French claim to be in the depths of a malaise, and two-thirds of them believe that public officials are dishonest, a figure that is American in its *ampleur.*[42] A flood of books proclaims France to have become a "banana republic."[43] It is unclear who is involved in the corruption. Political parties have always skimmed from government contracts, for instance. The emerging consensus is that the quantity and frequency of corruption is increasing because of the Socialist government's decentralization program.[44] Mayors and local commissions have obtained power over zoning and building permits, and are using it to enrich themselves. The departmental prefects, officials of the Ministry of the Interior, lost power. They were already losing power to mayors of large cities, many of whom held seats in parliament, and negotiated directly with administrative bureaus in Paris. But the reforms accelerated the power loss while enhancing the power of competing local elites. Most significantly, a proposal to create a unified local civil service with benefits and privileges equal to those of national civil servants was aborted. Primary responsibilities for training local civil servants remained with the *Centre Nationale de la Fonction Publique,* intimately dependent upon local pressure groups and historic defender of communal rights.[45]

The predicament in France reminds one of the blitz on Washington that ensues when a new president is sworn in: his lackeys, experienced only in the ignoble world of American campaigns, are paid off with jobs. Using the campaign organization as the primary source for recruitment leads to predictable excess. As James Pfiffner sagely remarks: "The natural choice of campaign aides...may lead to problems because the nature of governing is different in important ways from the nature of political campaigns."[46] Flexing their newly acquired muscles, they dispense contracts and grants to their political allies. Samuel Pierce, who used his position as Secretary of Housing and Urban Development during the Reagan years to dole out money to his pals, is the modern exemplar of this practice. Pierce and the French local officials were both newly empowered. Snatched from the mists of neglect, they seized the moment. John Sununu, President Bush's former chief of staff, was the latest example of egregious seizing. His persistent use of publicly funded travel for private purposes, while hardly important with regard to public policy, shows the arrogance and hubris of the newcomer.

The American tradition of political appointments has been transformed from one in which political parties (especially state and local ones) exercise influence to one in which they do not. These "good old days" were not so good. Unlike the partisan domination of Congress, partisan control of presidential appointments was primarily a device to sustain the party's organizational vitality. A laudable goal, it nevertheless made it difficult for the president to assemble loyal and effective supporters.[47] Now he can assemble loyal supporters who are ineffective and vulnerable to the heady temptations of life in a city where power is as highly valued as money. In neither case has the president's control of his agenda been enhanced.

There is, however, a difference. American corruption contributes to fragmentation. One does not need to be Machiavellian to argue that "honest graft" is not, *per se*, evil; rather, its effects can be. In the United States, corruption, like politics, is fragmented. The excessive reliance upon PAC money denigrates efforts to rejuvenate political parties, and directs the attention of decision makers toward the local and parochial. Because there are more people with power in the United States, there are more opportunities and greater opportunity costs. The system becomes more expensive. Bribing congressmen is easier than bribing the executive branch, although there are plenty of examples of executive branch dishonesty. Spiro Agnew's and Lyndon Johnson's tenures as vice president were pockmarked by examples of gross, offensive bribery. The Teapot Dome scandal, during the Warren Harding administration, ensnared cabinet officials. Attorney General Edwin Meese, during the Reagan years, was cozy with aspirants to government contracts, and John Sununu, during the Bush administration, accepted free rides on planes owned by corporations not disinterested in tax policies. The Department of Housing and Urban Development in the Reagan years had no equal, then or in the past, at handing out contracts as rewards for political loyalty.

The American Congress is hardly an island of corruption in a sea of purity. But since its committees and individual members have more power than they once did, and because it is more powerful than the legislative body in any other industrial democracy, the danger of corruption influencing policy (as distinguished from merely enriching office holders) is greater. One could argue that weak governments (the American government) offer less incentive for bribery because they have fewer goodies to dole out. A European cabinet controls more tangible resources, relative to population, than does the entire American national government. American government is less important to American society than European governments are to European societies. However, the American *subgovernments* are not less important to their particular societies. These smaller American political societies extract as many, if not more, government-allocated resources than do comparable European subsocieties. American airplane manufacturers complain about government subsidies to Airbus; but the American savings and loan industry was subsidized to the hilt, not by the American government but rather by the participants in particular, quasi-autonomous subgovernment.

In contrast, Japan, awash in financial chicanery, routinely and rationally establishes budget ceilings and spending priorities. As a result, it has established a significant deficit reduction. The major players in the Japanese budget process are the Ad Hoc Council for Administrative Reform (a chairman, three business members, two labor union members, two ex-bureaucrats, an ex-journalist, and a scholar), the Ministry of Finance, and LDP politicians (participating through their affiliation with party policy groups). The chairman of the Ad Hoc Committee was Toshio Doko, chairman of the *Keidanren* (Japanese Federation of Economic Organizations), the peak business association. The Ad Hoc Committee demanded and received a rigid budget ceiling and an increase in tax revenues.[48] Compare this process with America's Gramm-Rudman-Hollings Act, intended for the same purpose with dramatically less satisfactory results.

Pluralism, Interest Groups, and Market Failure

An exemplary illustration of the open market in interest groups is AIDS. AIDS killed 23,000 in 1989; breast cancer killed 43,000 (up from 36,000 a decade ago). Federal expenditures for AIDS research, $1.7 billion, were vastly more than those for breast cancer, $77 million, and even more than the total ($1.6 billion) for *all* cancer research. Breast cancer strikes one in eleven women and kills one-third of them. Of course, one can survive breast cancer, whereas one cannot survive AIDS. But neither can one survive pancreatic cancer. Pancreatic cancer killed 25,000 people in 1990; the survival rate is 3 percent.

Women with breast cancer, noting the success of the AIDS lobby, organized advocacy groups: "They [AIDS groups] have scored incredible coups. They've left all of us saying, 'Boy, let's learn from their techniques,' " explained a National Coalition for Cancer Research spokesperson.[49] Medical research funds, like taxes, depend upon group pressures.

AIDS became a media sensation, given the American media culture. Oprah Winfrey belted out the refrain:

Hello, Everybody. AIDS has both sexes running scared. Research studies now show that one in five—listen to me, hard to believe—one in five
heterosexuals could be dead from AIDS at the end of the next three
years. That's by 1990. One in five.

Of course, this was nonsense; 5.5 million people had not died by
1990. Notwithstanding, in the marketplace of interest groups fos-
tered by pluralism, AIDS funding, and AIDS interest groups, prospered. In 1990 the federal government allocated $1.7 billion for
AIDS, $1.6 billion for cancer, and $1.1 billion for heart disease.

Heterosexuals who do not use drugs rarely (about 5 percent of
all AIDS cases) contract AIDS in this country. The odds of a heterosexual act causing AIDS are one in 2 million. In Washington state, of
2,131 AIDS cases in 1990, 38 (0.002 percent) were a result of heterosexual contact. Of those 2,131 cases, 1,660 (78 percent) were caused
by homosexual-bisexual male activity, 98 (5 percent) were caused by
intravenous drug use, and 220 (10 percent) were the result of
homosexual-bisexual behavior plus intravenous drug use. One
would have a better chance of winning the Washington lottery than
contracting AIDS by heterosexual activity alone.

Similar techniques were used by the Natural Resources Defense
Council to inflict the 1989 Alar scare. Alar, used by apple growers to
strengthen stems, was said by the Natural Resources Defense Council to be carcinogenic. Meryl Streep was the "Oprah Winfrey" here,
used by NRDC to sell CBS on an exposé of Alar. It was a carefully coordinated hoax intended to scare consumers into buying the organic
products represented by the NRDC. Alar does not cause cancer.

Media attention drifts from topic to topic, as the public's short
attention span is honored in extreme. Ethiopian famine, for example,
is not new. But during 1984–85, NBC news aired footage of starving
Ethiopians and Tom Brokaw touched a raw nerve: Americans gave
generously to various relief agencies. By 1985 the disaster had disappeared from the media, although the famine most assuredly had not
disappeared from Ethiopia.[50] Media attention shifted to a topic closer
to home: sexual assault. The "silent epidemic" replaced AIDS on
Oprah's agenda, although the alleged increase in sexual assault was
fiction. The actual rate of reported and unreported rape fell from 150
per 100,000 in 1979 to 113 per 100,000 in 1988. Thus, one in 1,000
women is a victim of rape, whereas the media portrayal hovered
around one out of every two.[51] At about the same time, CBS's "60
Minutes" revealed yet another threat to health: sudden acceleration
incidents (SAIs), said to be a problem with certain Volvo models. The
Department of Transportation examined each incident and discov-

ered, as one might surmise, that the sudden acceleration was caused by drivers depressing the accelerator rather than the brake.

These episodes are the political equivalent of "market failure." Groups pursuing their self-interest do onerous harm to a broader public interest. The antidote is technically accurate information. Nonetheless, the interplay of groups in pluralism does place as high a value on information as happens in corporatism. Information is the currency of bureaucracy, and bureaucracy in America is not highly esteemed and, therefore, does not interest those who could balance the hysteria and fads of pluralist group conflict. They know AIDS is not a serious threat to the heterosexual community, that Alar is harmless, and that we are wasting our energy while other countries are not. These episodes illustrate pluralism's inclination toward the political equivalent of market failure. The antigas tax lobby, the AIDS lobby, and the Natural Resources Defense Council are pursuing their self-interest.

What is required, but institutionally unavailable, is America's Naohiro Amaya, a hero of David Halberstam's *The Reckoning*.[52] As he watched the fall of the Shah of Iran, Amaya was:

> slim, graying, scholarly, a senior bureaucrat in a nation in which bureaucrats wield exceptional power and influence.... Political visionary, poet, and amateur historian, [he] was chosen from among the best products of the Japanese system.... Upon graduation [from Tokyo University] he was accepted at MITI [Ministry of International Trade and Industry], one of the choice places for an enterprising young man. He enthusiastically accepted the job, because he had graduated right after the war and felt it was his duty to help his country extricate itself from economic ruin.... At MITI he gradually developed the reputation as a kind of one-man think tank.[53]

Why Not Some New Rascals?

In 1990 much was made of the anti-incumbent mood; hardly rare, but always troublesome to members of Congress. To protect themselves against electoral threat, they did the following in October 1990, when the media were fixed on budget *cutting*. The House Appropriations Committee, considering the defense bill, restored these cuts: $850,000,000 for aircraft carrier improvements at the Philadelphia Naval Shipyard (courtesy of Subcommittee Chairman Murtha of Pennsylvania); $99 million for a fiber-optic guided missile for committee member Tom Bevill's Alabama district; and $118 million for missile development from Washington's Norm Dicks (in anticipation of contracts being awarded to Seattle's Boeing Company). Congress also earmarked $3.4 million for highway construction in Pittsfield, Massachusetts, home of Silvio Conte, ranking Republican on the House Appropriations Committee. In addition, it set aside money for West Virginia University to appease Robert C. Byrd, chairman of the Senate Appropriations Committee. Washington's Brock Adams, in serious political trouble because of accusations of personal impropriety, snagged $1.5 million (for low-income housing in Seattle and Tacoma) of the $50 million "special purpose grants" attached to funding legislation for the Department of Housing and Urban Development.

Thus, while 20 percent of those surveyed by *The New York Times* believed that most congressmen deserved reelection, and two-thirds wanted new people to have a chance, fully 44 percent thought their congressmen deserved reelection and only 40 percent wanted to give a new person a chance. Pork helps incumbents win elections. To tamper with pork is to tamper with a colleague's career. It is not done.

Unquestionably, Congress is the most powerful (and most handsomely paid) legislative body among the world's industrial democracies. Most legislatures are not "directly involved in the process of governing."[54] Ours, irrespective of its reactive or proactive proclivities, emphatically is involved. A comparison of civil servants found, correctly, that whereas 58 percent of the American bureaucrats regard members of Congress as influential, only 2 percent of their British counterparts regard members of Parliament as powerful.[55]

It is instructive to read economists' prescriptions for reducing the deficit, for they all imagine that *somebody* or *something* in the political or governmental system can develop a plan and stick to it. Within the larger context of the debate about American decline (see Appendix), the reality of severe fragmentation cannot sink in. Thus, political scientist Joseph Nye, Jr., wrote that the decline can be arrested if we simply address "such domestic issues as the budget deficit, savings rate, educational system, and condition of our cities."[56] But pluralism does not recognize public goods, and no settlement among private interests can address decline, since one reason for the nose dive is unconstrained interest groups. Each interest group, operating within the rationale of the problem of the commons, pursues its own economic best interest.

To seize direction of a runaway budget process, the United States would have to abandon either separation of powers or the philosophical underpinnings of a pluralistic group process. The very conception of a capture posits a confrontation between public and private. Classic pluralism emphatically rejects the notion of "the public interest," as all policy is a consequence of pushing and shoving among competing interests: there is no state autonomy. The state is no more than a holding company for interest groups. The public interest exists above the fray, almost like Rousseau's "general will," and requires a suppression or at least a regulation of group conflict to find it.

In the United States, combine pluralist biases with (1) separation of power and federalism, (2) the destruction of political party authority by electoral and congressional reforms, (3) the absence of a career conscious, nonpolitical civil service, and (4) private control of key sectors in the economy, and you get capture. Of course, as was previously explained, capture is a fluid concept. As there is no "they" looming everywhere, neither can the case be made for inclusive capture. The drift toward capture is virtually irresistible.

Theda Skocpol and Kenneth Finegold show the irony of state autonomy in the United States. During the New Deal, the Department of Agriculture was almost "European" in that its bureaucracy had a conception of what it was about that was not derived from the needs and expectations of agricultural interest groups. However, the initially autonomous intervention by the Department of Agriculture strengthened the American Farm Bureau Federation and gave it the administrative leverage it needed to capture post–New Deal agricultural policy.[57] Consequently, "subsequent state planning efforts... were then circumscribed and destroyed by the established commercial farming interests championed by the Farm Bureau."[58]

Although the reforms of the late 1970s exacerbated the interest group problem, they did not cause it. Without any structure to combat fragmentation, the United States was destined to become the apogee of the interest group society.

The Corporatist Politics of Exclusion

Generally, corporatist governments recognize peak associations—those organizations that represent a large population of smaller organizations. For example, a peak labor organization would include the building trades, teamsters, electricians, and so on. A peak business association would include computer manufacturers, textile manufacturers, and the like. The component organizations do not engage in political activities in defiance of, or even in augmentation of, the peak association.

As the primary interest of corporatist decision making is economic wages or income policies, international trade balances, deficits, and so on, only those groups that might influence such policies are invited to participate. As John Keeler observes, others must resort to the traditional lobbying techniques of the pluralist political processes.[59] Yet, pluralist systems also exclude, albeit with less certainty. This restriction is especially true when some groups can claim a monopoly on *expertise*, as for instance in educational policy-making.[60]

At any rate, corporatism is more officially exclusive in granting the representative franchise. For example, in Austria, an informal collaboration between unions and business was institutionalized in 1957 as the *Gemeinsamer Auftrag auf der Preisen and Lohnausschuss*. Labor representation to the Commission is from the *Österreichischer Gewerkschaftsbund* and from the *Kammer für Arbeiter und Angestellte*. The *Verernigung Österreichischer Industrieller und Landwirtschaftskammern* represents business and agriculture. Any lesser organization not a member of one of these peak organizations lacks a voice in policy formation. The Austrian government merely bequeaths the structure for interest-group bargaining and ratifies the decisions reached by the participating interest groups.

Equality of Political Influence

In the European corporatist governments, labor's governmental role is generally, except in Switzerland, firmly set, and no need to show its muscle is required. Indeed, Marxist critics of corporatism allege that its fundamental goal is to deradicalize labor unions. By accepting these accords, unions are said to act contrary to the intentions that guided their origins; that is, they cooperate in the preservation of a stable, rather than an inflationary, economy by not pursuing excessive wage demands. Leo Panitch, writing of corporatism in liberal democracies, believes that unions in corporatist arrangements are instruments of oppression.[61] He is especially anxious to have proponents of corporatism lay bare their ideological bias, which he believes to be intensely antiegalitarian, and calls our attention to the incompatibility of corporatism (which assumes the existence of cooperation between labor and capital) and Marxism (which assumes their perpetual antagonism). Unions must be able to assure business and government that their members will comply with the terms of the social contract.

Corporatism, Marxism, and Labor. In classical Marxist thought the state is an instrument of oppression, initially at the bidding of the ruling class, and—in its transitional phase—of the proletariat. In corporatism, the state is not *necessarily* oppressive; on the contrary the state is liberating in the tradition of Rousseau and the collectivist romantics. Corporatism is, therefore, compatible with authoritarian or even totalitarian regimes, but it need not be so. Fascist governments may be corporatist, but so can democratic ones.

The seminal idea of corporatism is that geographical representation is inadequate and that functional representation should replace or augment it. Governments create and sanction occupational associations— farmers, electricians, computer programmers, and the like. In some forms of corporatism these organizations have been given authority for policy implementation; in others, they are legitimately influential in policy formation. In Japan, Austria, and Switzerland, for example, the distinction between public and private is uncertain. Austrian labor unions and Japanese manufacturers are as much a part of the governing process as are legislators and bureaucrats.

In Austria, a decision to strike cannot be made by an individual union acting unilaterally, but only after a protracted and complex set of negotiations between peak associations. The unions eschew the ideologically loaded subject of inequality in exchange for maximum influence "at the very highest levels in the arenas of economic and social policy most critical to Austria's strategy in the world economy; labor as a force for conservatism is of course not unique to Austria."[62]

In Switzerland, labor is equally conservative. Unions are weak, more akin to Japanese unions than those in left-corporatist governments like Sweden or Austria. Much more than business groups, unions are nonmonopolistic, and torn by internal divisions. Since 1937 the unions and employer associations have operated with "peace treaties," which amount to no-strike deals that also outlaw lock-outs and boycotts. These peace agreements rarely go beyond the local level. The federal government stays out, and the national unions and employers' associations have rights for binding arbitration. They have "Swiss" power, probably more so than unions in Japan. Here again, the Constitution provides for generally binding agreements; unions may collect dues from nonmembers and bargains struck by unions and employers bind all workers. The agreements are public law. Unions and business groups unite to keep up the (somewhat) discriminatory treatment of foreign workers (25 percent of the work force), without whom the unemployment rate would be far higher. Labor's ostensible ally, the social Democrats, committed themselves to various unsuccessful referenda to improve the status of foreign laborers. The cozy pact means there are almost no strikes.

Corporatism's politics of exclusion are not in the traditional rhetoric of Marxism, although these politics coöpt workers who might otherwise be attracted to Marxism. Labor and business are *the* incorporated groups, not the various single issue, citizen, and protest groups that scatter themselves across the landscapes of democracies. Corporatism embraces only those organizations that the economic division of labor creates; some students of corporatist societies almost define corporatism in terms of the bargain struck with organized labor.

It is most often the labor movement that extracts concessions from the government or wins settlements by allying with other interest groups. Corporatism is an alliance between *economic* interest groups. They must be able to deliver, and they—especially labor— must be willing to discourage dissent, if not indulge in coercion. As John Freeman explains:

> They must sometimes enact undemocratic rules and regulations, such as multilayered, indirect procedures for the election of leaders. While these actions promote unity within the organization, they may alienate workers and thereby delegitimize leaders' positions of authority. In turn, labor will find it difficult to forge a corporatist bargain with employers because the latter will question the former's ability to enforce such agreements.[63]

Corporatism requires the suppression of individualism, but then all organizations do so. Are any organizations compatible with democracy, or can internally undemocratic organizations serve the cause of representative government?

CORPORATISM AND DEMOCRACY

Corporatism creates major incentives for effective policy formation by granting quasi-official status to economic interest groups, and by connecting these peak associations directly to the appropriate government bureaucracies. The justification for corporatism is precisely its ability to remove policy from those without the expertise to comprehend complexity, parliaments or legislatures, and to transfer it to bureaucracies (those with a specialized expertise). Corporatism is designed to make policy immune from ideological passion, partisan preference, or shifting public opinion. The adoption of corporatist mechanisms and processes was a conscious effort to ensure continuity in economic policy:

> What permitted stability...was a shift in the focal point of decision making. Fragmented parliamentary majorities yielded to ministerial bureaucracies, or sometimes directly to party councils, where interest group representatives could more easily work out social burdens and rewards.[64]

Best or Less Bad?

Neither pluralist nor corporatist systems are superior in representing the views of members of voluntary associations. Whereas the reliance upon selective benefits is less crucial when membership is, almost, compulsory and access assured, no evidence or theory suggests that the functional representation of corporatism is more likely to be "accurate" than is the "accidental" laissez-faire mode of pluralist representation. As John Keeler suggests, in pluralist systems, elite response to members' demands is imperfect, whereas in corporatist systems, elites can afford insulation.

Is either more likely to balance narrow interests against a larger public good? Here the answer is less ambiguous. Corporatism can deliver more. As Graham Wilson puts it:

> [Corporatist] systems have aroused the interest and envy of other states for some years now. Their success in securing above-average incomes and economic growth with lower than average inflation has fueled both admiration and envy. . . . [Corporatist] systems have provided their inhabitants with thirty years of high employment, low inflation, and considerable economic growth.[65]

Corporatism provides stability of public choice; it renders public choice less vulnerable to the whims of populism, though at the cost, sometimes, of "enforced consensus."[66]

Of the United States, there is reason to agree with Robert Reich that:

> America's economy has been slowly unraveling. The economic decline has been marked by growing unemployment, mounting business failures, and falling productivity. . . . America's politics have been in chronic disarray. The political decline has been marked by the triumph of narrow interest groups.[67]

Although a bit on the alarmist side (unemployment has not been growing consistently), Reich is correct in arguing that our strong anticorporatist culture is taking its toll. The posture is perfectly illustrated by the Bush administration's determination to avoid an industrial policy. In response to yet another loss to the Japanese, this time in computer chips, President Bush's chairman of the Council of Economic Advisors, Michael Boskin, taunted: "Potato chips, semiconductor chips—what is the difference? They are all chips."

8.

Corporatism, Pluralism, and the Rational State

Corporatism is more fiscally sound than pluralism, providing for stable growth without massive debt.[1] Moreover, capture theory, so prominent in understanding American pluralism, has no application to political arrangements that do not assume an inevitable antagonism between public and private. Bureaucracies can hardly be "captured" when they provide for institutionalized participation by interest groups.

Big-spending governments, not surprisingly, incur more debt than frugal ones. Corporatist arrangements keep industrial democracies honest because they are less extravagant and can develop and implement long-range fiscal and monetary plans. They do *not* resort to "planned economies" as some of their critics allege: the vigorously free market economies of Switzerland and Japan are, nevertheless, constrained. The constraints are not imposed, but rather are a consequence of the consortium between interest groups and bureaucracies that define corporatism.

The voguish notion of "state autonomy" also seems a bit out of focus. Bureaucracies surely impose their will upon interest groups, but as interest groups are part of the bureaucracy, autonomy is an inappropriate concept. In Peter Katzenstein's brilliant phrase: "The essence of collaboration is to entangle in a densely woven fabric political actors that elsewhere choose to walk their separate ways."[2]

THE DENSELY WOVEN FABRIC

Perhaps it is the notion of a densely woven fabric that makes state autonomy more likely in corporatism rather than pluralism. Pluralism, considered either as a power balance between competing interests or as unrestrained group competition, does not augur well for an autocephalous state.

Indeed, the purest of pluralist theories imagines government to be part of the flow of demand and response. Government is not a neutral referee, a holding company, or even an arbiter of group demands. Rather, it is no more than a participant in the demand-making process. When governments allocate goods, that is, pass laws, they do not do so from a neutral position. Although governments do more than "just sit there," they are—in this manifestation—"pure analogues of the competing societal interest groups of classical pluralism."[3] How can they be captured, as they are part of the *demand* process? They are *already* captives to group demands. State autonomy becomes an oxymoron, as government is merely the passive reactor to group demands, or the active, equal partner in making these demands.

Pluralism and the Politicization of the Bureaucracy

Presumably, as participants in the capturing process, bureaucracies and the attendant interest groups seize control of another constellation of groups and bureaucracies and bend them to their will. Thus, pluralism almost *presupposes* an American institutional structure, with policy formation and implementation decentralized, fragmented, spread all-round. Iron triangles go at each other relentlessly, with the greatest accumulation of power declared to be the public interest.

While fragmentation and the attendant competing demands seem a vice to enthusiasts of corporatism, they are a virtue to the pluralists. The chaos of American government, for example, is said to trade efficiency for openness. Many points of access mean many opportunities for influence. Capturing an agency, therefore, becomes an implied right (such as the right to privacy).

Here is where the two pluralisms merge: pluralism as the opposite of corporatism, open competition, and pluralism as equal distribution of political resources both concur in the belief that, whether the system works or not, it is an open one. Whether it is relatively equal in the distribution of rewards is another matter.

Although critics of pluralism make much of inequality of resources, pluralists do not argue, seriously, that any polity provides more than a crude approximation of equality. Surely, access to the Federal Reserve System's Board of Governors is limited to those who have something to say. Deprived groups may profit from the Supreme Court's noblesse oblige, but the Council of Economic Advisors probably does not care much about oppression. Moreover, the problem is neatly finessed by consensus.

Policy disputes—politics—are merely quibbles over sets of alternatives that have been narrowed down to those within the broad accord. So, to "lose" is not really so bad: "the more fully the social prerequisites of polyarchy [representative democracy] exist, the less probable it is that any given minority will have its most valued freedoms curtailed through governmental action."[4]

Thus, politics are the tip of the societal iceberg; government is of little threat as long as the social consensus exists; it is of little threat when that consensus evaporates. In the United States, this tenet of pluralism contributes to amateurism in the bureaucracy, to its low esteem, and to its capture.

The Role of the Civil Service.   In Europe, bureaucrats believe their job to be technical. They "spotlight the technical aspects of public policy and attempt to develop agreements among a limited number of actors with continuous and specialized interests in clearly defined functional arenas. . . . By contrast, politicians, like lightning rods, attract the sparks of sporadic but vociferous claimants. They advance broad policy claims based on party program, ideology, and constituency demands. They are, in other words, not so much interest reconcilers as they are interest articulators."[5] Interest articulators— politicians—do not need capturing, as they are already articulating. Bureaucrats—self-described experts—are the better target. Experts are unlikely to be captured except by other experts.

Neither French nor Japanese bureaucracies are regarded as capturable. In France, ENA and the culture of the French administration caused French civil servants to feel "responsible for the direction of industry, generally capable of undertaking it, and entitled to do so."[6] In Japan the independence of bureaucracy is clear; the only competitors are Liberal Democratic Party (LDP) politicians, not interest groups. Like Europe, Japan and France "have long valued their civil servants."[7] In a popular French soap opera, the mother dreams of her

Table 8.1   Closeness of Interest Groups to the LDP Bureaucracy

Seeks opinion	High	Medium	Low	Very low
Frequently	74%	62%	57%	18%
To some extent	14	27	32	39
Not much; not at all	12	12	11	41

Source: Adapted from Michio Muramatsu and Ellis S. Krauss, "Dominant Party and Social Coalitions in Japan," in T. J. Pempel, ed., *Uncommon Democracies: The One-Party Dominant Regimes* (Ithaca, N.Y.: Cornell U. Press, 1990), p. 295.

daughter marrying not a doctor or a lawyer, but a civil servant! Imagine! Or imagine an American novelist allowing one of his characters to speak often to his oldest son of the day "when you will have the honor of being employed by the government!"[8] Assessments of occupational prestige in the United States do not include the option "civil servant." But in France, 40 percent of the higher civil servants had made their career choice before entering a university, and 25 percent decided during or before adolescence.[9]

Japanese bureaucrats consider LDP politicians to be as powerful as other bureaucrats. This assessment is undoubtedly aided by the entry of many retired bureaucrats into parliament (by way of the LDP). Still, "of all the groups with which higher civil servants... come into contact...'representatives of clientele groups' ranked near the bottom."[10] However, when they do seek out interest groups, they are inclined to listen more to those that are closely associated with the Liberal Democratic Party. (See Table 8.1.)

Notwithstanding, the fact that Japanese bureaucrats only avoid those groups that loathe the LDP lends credence to the belief that they are not captured. As in France, the bureaucracy is the more powerful partner in the exchange with interest groups. Even opposition politicians do not believe that business groups have much influence on policy, and even LDP politicians concede that they have a leading role.[11] The dominance of Tokyo University and, to a lesser degree, Kyoto University is even more striking: "The two universities together account for seven in ten higher civil servants overall, and their share of the pot increases to eighty nine percent at the bureau chief level and to ninety five percent at the vice-ministerial level."[12]

Thus the *esprit* of the civil service inhibits capture as much as does the institutional structure of parliamentary and corporatist governments. No better instance of this spirit can be found than the remarks of François de Combret to a conference on French industrial policy:

At the top of this [educational] hierarchical system are nestled a few elite schools—the Ecole Polytechnique, the Ecole Nationale d'Administration, and the Ecole Normale Supérieure. It is not surprising that all the French speakers at this conference come from these schools, for these educational institutions train people to become high-level civil servants. In practice only the weakest graduates head immediately to the private sector. The private sector is considered a demotion. The American system leans in the opposite direction. It inculcates the belief that public service is certainly not the only and probably not the best choice of career.[13]

But suppose that bureaucrats and politicians do not view their jobs differently. Imagine that bureaucrats are as "political" as elected politicians. Imagine them as "appointed politicians." *Then* capture by interest groups becomes more likely. That is what happens in the United States. In a fragmented institutional system, American bureaucrats must create and maintain their political support by themselves. In a political culture that glorifies individualism, and a political structure that mandates multiple points of access, administrative agencies face the same Darwinian world as do politicians.

Failed politicians do not, of course, leave office (the incumbency factor is too great), and rarely are agencies abolished. Nevertheless, limping along is different from *flourishing*. One can see the effect of a pluralist culture in the attitudes of American civil servants:

American bureaucrats must find allies where they can. This, in turn, generates an entrepreneurial style of behavior *that encourages bureaucratic commitments to clienteles*. . . . By institutional necessity, and also because of the historic absence of socialization as an administrative elite, American bureaucrats are more oriented toward traditionally political roles than bureaucrats in Europ. . . . Uncertain lines of authority encourage American bureaucrats to play political roles—to cut deals with congressmen who can protect their agencies. . . to pursue the interests of clienteles who can help to protect their programs, and to act as *advocates of interests* inadequately represented through the ostensible channels of political representation.[14]

The American system is institutionally designed on a foundation of mistrust; bureaucrats have no choice but to plunge into the power game. They care far more about power than purpose. Without strong political parties, which in Europe can develop and implement programs, mobilize parliamentary majorities, and maintain coherence even as party leaders come and go, the American system is one of personal, valueless, entrepreneurial conflict. "The bread and butter of congressional politicians and high-level bureaucrats in America is earned by the responsiveness to what each sees as relevant local constituencies, whether these are composed of electorates and local interest groups or bureaucratic clients." Therefore, the S&L crisis is aberrant only in its cost and visibility, not in the principles of the political process that it exposed.

Not only are American bureaucrats vulnerable to capture because they are institutionally required to be; they lack the core of common recruitment and socialization that would give them a strong independent identity. They do not go to the American equivalent of Tokyo University or *l'Ecole Nationale d'Administration*. *Enarques* account for 28 percent of all ambassadors, 29 percent of all departmental prefects, 42 percent of all directors of civil service, and 25 percent of all members of ministerial cabinets. About 90 percent of the *Grand Corps* are from ENA or its predecessor, the *Ecole Libre* (which became the *Institut d'Etudes Politiques*, "Science Po" in 1945).[15]

There is a strong social dimension here, also. Most of the administrative elite were reared and trained in Paris. Imagine if you can an American bureaucracy in which 70 percent of the higher civil servants grew up in Washington, D.C. While a larger proportion of higher civil servants in the United States attended prestigious universities than is true of the population at large, perhaps 20 percent, this proportion is paltry compared with France or Japan.

Because the main policymaking positions in American government are exempt from civil service requirements, and they come and go with each president, the civil service does not have much prestige. As noted in the first chapter, only the president approaches the private sector in prestige. A president can appoint about 4,000 people, most of whom have little *governing* experience, as service during the president's campaign is weighed more heavily. In Europe and Japan, in contrast, most top officials are civil servants. Most new governments among industrial democracies can assume control in a matter of days, with little fanfare. American presidents undergo an elaborate transitional period, during which the political appointees of the previous administration are replaced by new ones. Even if the same party wins two consecutive elections, the transition involves massive hirings and firings, as the presidential campaign is a personal, rather than a party, endeavor. A ten-week transitional period, subsidized by millions in government funds, and researched exhaustively by political scientists, has no parallel in Europe: "In Britain, control of government literally changes hands overnight, as the winner of a general election held on a Thursday takes over Downing Street on Friday evening."[16] The popular British sitcom "Yes Minister" has a civil servant saying of a cabinet minister: "Politicians are like children; you can't give them everything they want, or they will only ask for more."

The onslaught of the American amateurs leads, inevitably, to stupid, sometimes serious, gaffes, since the president's men are political operatives. Watergate, the HUD scandals, Iran-Contra, and John Sununu's abuse of travel are the most egregious Congressional "perks" of the Washington version of "The Beverly Hillbillies."

But, equally seriously, the populist traditions of political patronage have crippled the civil service. Entry into the civil service, as we have seen, is not from a narrow field. Examinations too are wide in range and expectation, depending on the department that is administering them:

> This truncated civil service developed features very different from fully developed counterparts in Japan and most industrial societies. Lacking access to the highest policymaking positions, the civil service acquired little prestige....The concept of the public administrator...never took hold.[17]

Public Choice: The American Ideology.   American scholars who subscribe to theories of public choice categorically disavow the notion of bureaucracies as emissaries of the public interest. Nor surprisingly, given the American administrative tradition, these scholars see bureaucrats not as instruments of an autonomous state, but rather as takers of bribes and dispensers of favors. James Buchanan and Gordon Tullock, who both developed theories of public choice at the University of Virginia, compare government officials to entrepreneurs. Their rational self-interest, like that of private sector entrepreneurs, necessitates that they become "utility maximizers"; that is, that they get theirs. How can one conclude otherwise? But America is not the world; it is merely the world of public choice. Public choice makes perfect sense in the United States. Less government means less public corruption, less gridlock. With American governmental structure programmed for perpetual deadlock, and American bureaucracy so vulnerable to capture, who could argue for an expansion of government power without simultaneously demanding radical change? Where would we start? The recruitment and socialization of civil servants? The elimination of separation of powers and checks and balances? The return of nominations to political parties? Public choice accentuates the private sector because the public sector is a scandal. If a government is rent with scandal, and if its public servants are held in low regard for the good reason that they do not represent the cream of the crop, then demands that the government rectify market failure are misguided. The current debate over the lack of American industrial policy illustrates the dilemma. Chalmers Johnson, a leading student of Japan, asks: "Why can't the U.S. Government do some of the things to increase our economic strength that the Japanese government does all the time?"[18] The answer is that we do not have, in the Japanese sense of the word, a government.

Public choice rightly argues that the less government (in its current form), the better. Without a bureaucratic sense of the public interest, as in Japan, government becomes another competitor for resources. The French bureaucracy, as we saw in the last chapter, may be losing this sense of the public, and may be less prestigious than it once was.[19] One reason may be the decline of a public ethic. Bruno Jobert and Pierre Muller write of the tendency of "sectorial" interests to carve out a special niche in the French bureaucracy in a manner similar to the American "iron triangles."[20] Ezra Suleiman is harsh in his explanation of increased corruption:

> The clearest manifestation of this disquieting tendency [corruption] is the decline of a public ethic, the blurring of the distinction between public and private interests.... The terms "public interest" or the "general interest" may have sounded noble in the days when they were frequently uttered by public servants.... Today they are used only rarely, and are often mocked.[21]

Is bureaucracy inherently incapable of disinterested decision making, or can bureaucrats be successfully socialized in a Platonic tradition?

WEAK CORPORATISM: FRANCE

How can you govern a country with more than 300 kinds of cheese? asked Charles de Gaulle. By this he meant that the French culture seems to encourage excessive fragmentation. Truly, this is the case with interest groups. Here, organization breeds counter-organization. A country in which neo-Rocardians flourish surely is fissiparous. Michel Debré, the Fifth Republic's first prime minister, anticipating Margaret Thatcher's assault on interest groups and Olson's tirades against "narrow distributional coalitions," wrote in his *Ces Princes Qui Nous Gouvernent* that the state must wage war against "feudal forces (interest groups) that divide the state and leech upon it with scarcely a thought for the nation or the citizens."

However, his mentor and patron, de Gaulle, while expressing contempt for interest groups in their parliamentary lobbying vein, was inclined toward neocorporatism. The referendum of April 1969 sought to bring interest groups into the upper house of the National Assembly as instruments of representation. However, the defeat of the referendum and de Gaulle's resignation ended the idea.

The French will fight over minutiae. In 1990–91 the *Academie Française* was rent asunder by disputes concerning the elimination of the cedilla (ç), and efforts to modify spelling eccentricities provoked a national backlash, led by the organizations of lycée teachers (those who passed the difficult *agrégation* exam). The lycée teachers picked up support from *Le Figaro,* the conservative Paris newspaper, but were opposed by the Association for Research on Spelling. Prime Minister Rocard, who appointed a High Commission on the French Language, unveiled the changes with the endorsement of his government, but the *Academie Française* split badly over the issue. Opponents of the changes, alleging that "our beautiful and rich language" was being attacked by "mediocre people," further claimed that the permanent secretary of the *Academie Française* was a puppet of the government. Several prominent center-right politicians joined the fray, and Françoise Sagan, author of *Bonjour Tristesse, A Certain Smile, Aimez vous Brahms?* led them with: "French is a superb language, there's no reason to change it." Prime Minister Rocard, who had merely wanted to do French school children a favor by removing the irksome accents, circumflexes (ô), and the like, encountered a raging horde of French intellectuals. Rocard pleaded that he, besides easing the burden on the youth, sought to combat the growing popularity of English. However, in January 1991, the *Academie* reversed itself, and the government gave up.

The Depoliticized Bureaucracy Encounters the Fragmented Groups

Most organizations cannot insinuate themselves into the civil service, one of the most professional and aloof organizations in the world. French groups, like American ones, come and go; but unlike their American counterparts, they cannot buy influence. For example, the women's liberation movement, born in 1970, sprang up when a group of women deposited a wreath with the inscription, "To the unknown wife of the unknown soldier." French bureaucrats simply cannot take such posturing seriously. Many French groups are intellectual or theoretical in intent. The 1968 students' movement was dominated by Sartre. There were heated discussions of existentialism. The campus debate ignited the workers, and strikes involving 7 million workers began.

Agricultural Spats: Wine and Champagne

French groups are ideologically fragmented: there are not "farmers," but infinite divisions of farmers. Splits and inefficiency are the rule. Agriculture offers a fine case history. The Vichy regime tried corporatism, the integration of rural interests into the state bureaucracy; but the Vichy regime was discredited. After the war, peak associations were tried, but the subsidiary groups could not be suppressed: there are 500 rural defense associations. The most important, the *Fédération Nationale des Syndicats d'Exploitants Agricole* (FNSEA), is the government's instrument for modernizing French agriculture. *Concertation* was offered only to FNSEA. However, the violent opposition of farmers to the government, FNSEA, and the Common Market led to tensions and the emergence of rival groups. The strongest is the *Mouvement de Défense des Exploitants Familiaux*, which argues for the small family farms. It is, typically French, a Communist-inspired defense of property, bitterly opposing the exodus from the countryside and the Common Market. FNSEA lives on public funds; the Ministry of Agriculture recognizes it as the peak association. Though it faced competition, the FNSEA remained hegemonic until the Socialist victory in 1981. As John Keeler explains, FNSEA enjoyed privileged access to decision makers in exchange for the usual corporatist bargain, behaving "responsibly."[22]

Corporatism was widely condemned, and Mitterrand is less inclined to buy into the FNSEA; the Socialists sought to encourage pluralism. There is a world of difference between seeking to decorporatize FNSEA and doing it. Edith Cresson, prime minister in 1991, then Mitterand's minister of agriculture, was chosen, among other reasons, for the assurance that her feminism (she was the first woman in French history to serve as minister of agriculture), her *soigné* haughtiness, and her Parisian condescension would irritate the conservative agricultural community. FNSEA, forced to accept its new downgraded status, had no choice but to accede to pluralism (other agricultural organizations presented competing views at "official" functions). However, Cresson did not succeed in creating centers of countervailing power, and the FNSEA relaxed a bit when Michel Rocard (later prime minister, subsequently replaced by Cresson) became agriculture minister. Unfortunately for FNSEA, its demands that the rival organizations be "de-recognized" went unheeded.[23]

The fragmentation of agriculture shows a quirky side to French interest group politics: modernity versus tradition. The politics of Bordeaux wine classification provide a perfect illustration. The sheer intellectual challenge of figuring out the Bordeaux system attracts the intellectual. Bordeaux is the largest wine district on earth. The whole Department of the Gironde is dedicated to winegrowing. Bordeaux is divided into these primary areas:

> Haut-Medoc and St. Emilion
> Medoc and Pomerol
> Fronsac and St. Emilion
> Graves
> Sauterne and Barsac

Each of these has its own local system of classification, without a common standard. The most famous of these was completed in 1855, based on prices the wines had fetched for the last hundred years or more: first to fifth growths, cru exceptionnels, Crus bourgeois Superiors, Crus Bourgeois, and others about which we do not care. Obviously, there is more weight placed on first through fifth growths than current quality would justify: the immortal first growths, Lafite-Rothschild, Latour, Margaux, Mouton Rothschild, and Haut Brion attract prices three times as high as lower ranked wines. Mouton Rothschild was admitted in the 1970s, the only change ever agreed to. There are some stunning wines that are not in growths one through five: Chasse-Spleen, Poujeaux, and Larose-Trintaudon are rated as Crus Bourgeois. Gloria, a legend, is unclassified. Belgrave is a fifth growth, but is no longer important. The classification remains, and will remain, untouchable, although many unofficial ones have sprung up. Rationalist corporatist planning is thus thwarted by mores.

Other wine regions are equally complex. In Champagne, for example, the government pushed successfully for an *interprofessional contract*, a web of agreements, obligations, quotas, and fixed prices that has regulated economic life in Champagne for a generation. However, in 1990 the growers and producers announced the end of the contract, and proclaimed a virtual free market in Champagne. The government could do nothing to prevent the end of fixed prices for grapes. Fixed prices are the growers' guarantees to sell a pre-fixed percentage of the harvest to selected houses (Moët, Mumm, et al., that account for 70 percent of production). These preeminent houses, which account for about 90 percent of the region's exports, own only 15 percent of the vineyards (a chief difference from Bordeaux, where each chateau owns its own vineyards).

The failure of the accords was the consequence of a dispute between the growers and the houses: the houses, producers, wanted growers to promise them at least 48 percent of each harvest; the growers want a larger share of Champenois prosperity and prestige. Many growers are already part-time producers that function like chateau owners in Bordeaux. Growers will now consolidate and expand their operations to make, bottle, and sell their wine exclusively from their own grapes.

Without the government control that characterizes other regions, quality may decline. More wine will be sold *sur latte* (a uniquely Champenois technique of making still wine bubbly by bottling it with yeast, but unriddled, undisgorged, and undosed), and sold in racks *(lattes)* to merchants. The result is, in comparison with the traditional *methode Champenois,* a disaster. There is no obligation to reveal the *sur latte* method on the bottle, and therefore, the region's reputation will suffer when consumers drink the swill (it probably will never be exported from France, but will end in the ubiquitous bistros of Paris, where owners sock it to foolish tourists). The expanded role of growers also will erode the quality of the products of the established houses, as they will be forced to sell their champagne sooner (the law requires twelve months, but most houses hold their wine for between two and five years) or compromise on grape quality. Small and medium-sized houses, unable or unwilling to compromise, will be gobbled up by the conglomerates, causing the disappearance of well-known brands (this would be impossible in Bordeaux).

The Educational Policy Arena.   The educational policy community reveals the same fragmentation, irrespective of the extreme centralization of French educational policymaking.[24] Representing teachers and auxiliary personnel is the *Fédération de l'Education Nationale* (FEN), a holding company for affiliated unions, including employees of the Ministry of Education. Its strong ties to the *Parti Socialiste* and its membership in every village in France give FEN resources rivaled only by the Catholic Church. Because it is so encompassing, FEN is deeply divided: university professors and *lycée* instructors (who have passed the *concours d'agrégation*) are dissimilar to those who have lesser positions, for example. The debate between those who wish to maintain France's rigid examination and tracking system and those who want to expand opportunity has divided the FEN (and France) forever. The affiliated *Syndicat National des Instituteurs et Pro-*

fesseurs d'Enseignement General des Colleges (elementary school teachers) and the *Syndicat National d'Enseignement Secondaire* (secondary school teachers), the two largest FEN participants, are constantly struggling for control. The secondary school teachers resist, the primary school teachers support, reduction of the elite status of the *lycée*. Mitterrand supported the primary school teachers in trying to increase the number of students taking the baccalaureate (pre-college) exam from less than half to about 80 percent. Consequently, students rioted in 1990, demanding smaller classes. Mitterrand supported the students against his prime minister, Rocard, thus politicizing the issue even more and exacerbating the intra-FEN cleavage.

FEN must also compete with other education unions, such as the *Syndicate Général de l'Education Nationale*. This union is, pedagogically, to the left of FEN in its opposition to France's authoritarian tradition in education (a custom vigorously supported by the Communists).

Industrial Policy: *Dirigisme*

In industrial policy, however, French *dirigisme* is more corporatist. There is "the Plan," in existence since 1946 and modified every five years. The French government has always had a hefty share of the economy, before Mitterrand nationalized and after he privatized. A strong government presence is not confined to the *Parti Socialiste.* There is the *Commisariat Général du Plan,* begun in 1946, which brings in businessmen, trade unionists, and civil servants to meet with the Commission staff. An independent agency reporting directly to the prime minister, the *Commisariat* compared legitimately to the Japanese Ministry of International Trade and Industry. Unlike the British National Economic Development Council, the French *Commisariat* does not merely indicate desirable goals; it enforces them. The French government, through its nationalized firms, is a massive purchaser of private sector goods and services. As a seller—again through the nationalized industries—the state controls most raw materials essential to the private sector's health, including energy. Since French banks are also nationalized, the state can play a sizable role in the allocation of investment capital. The French system is aptly called "capitalism without capitalists."[25]

Thus, the French government has "an apparatus with the capacity to put real pressure on private sector actors to conform to the government's economic strategy."[26] A double layer of influence is added when one regards the nationalized industries as an interest group, a reasonable conjecture since French nationalized industry is market-driven. The nationalized industries, even after the Mitterrand denationalizations, remain prestigious and important.[27] They are headed by former civil servants whose friendship with bureaucrats is unsurpassed.[28]

The *Conseil National du Patronat Français* (CNPF) is the umbrella organization for French employees. Unlike the other instances of French interest groups, the CNPF has become a true peak association, largely because of the patronage of the state in making it a partner in industrial development. CNPF benefits, naturally, from *pantouflage*, the exchange of personnel between the private sector and the bureaucracy, as in Japan. ENA and *l'École Polytechnique* provide the bridge: of 560 firms employing more than 1,000 people, a majority were headed by a graduate of *l'École Polytechnique* and most had ex-civil servants on their boards of directors. Public-private cooperation is also well illustrated by the French automobile industry. Privately owned Peugeot and state-owned Renault have prospered, as the civil service found ways to keep Japanese cars out of France. Yet, if France were more corporatist, it would presumably have fewer strikes. It enjoys more industrial peace than the United Kingdom or the United States, but substantially less than Japan or Germany. Trade unions are rarely consulted, even by Socialist governments, because they are too internally ruptured to be useful in resolving labor disputes.[29]

Weak corporatism explains the fragmentation and contentiousness of French organizational life, but it does not describe a weak government or unruly political parties, depictions more appropriate for the full-blown pluralism of the United States. A centralized state, with a technically competent bureaucracy, French government is not weak. The bureaucracy, imbued with the Rousseauistic notion of the general will, socialized to believe that it defends the integrity of the state, the French bureaucracy is an unlikely victim of capture.[30] Not only are bureaucrats encouraged to be aloof, but power is so heavily concentrated at the top of the national government that the development of competing spheres of influence, iron triangles, is difficult. French interest groups rely on contacts with ministers and civil servants. Unlike the interest groups of pluralist America, they eschew legislative lobbying (since the National Assembly is far less powerful than the American Congress).[31] Deputies are insulated from group pressures because they vote in tightly disciplined party blocks. Nor do they need campaign funds because campaigns are short and expenses are borne by the party organization.[32] However, the National Assembly is useful when unconnected groups want to politicize an issue. Students are especially prone to this tactic.[33]

The French government can carry out policies that would cause chaos in hyperpluralist countries. In 1989 Mitterrand ordered back into operation a nuclear plant that had been closed because of an earlier accident. In 1990 Mitterrand ordered the manufacturers of the new after-intercourse abortion pill to resume distribution. Imagine comparable decisions in the United States. France, therefore, exercises "state autonomy." As Frank Wilson explains:

> The French government finds it easier to take unpopular steps than do more responsive governments....On the other hand, the aloofness from interest group pressure leads to incomplete representation and to a setting where citizens find protest politics as regrettable but necessary.[34]

Wilson may exaggerate slightly. Ezra Suleiman (in Chapter 7) believes that these bureaucratic traditions are eroding. Keeler has shown how closely the French bureaucracy can work in certain economic sectors but not in others.[35] Jobert and Muller write that "Ces voies d'accès à l'administration sont multiples."[36] But France is far from the "interest group society." Suleiman wrote earlier that, while certain administrative bodies give special treatment to some interest groups in the name of the public interest, "There are other parts of the administration that do not maintain close ties with interest groups, and whose actions are based on a set of priorities that, if they do not represent the general interest, do not at any rate stand for the strongest groups."[37]

De Gaulle's views were in this tradition, and the power of interest groups waned after the creation of the Fifth Republic in 1958. His success in granting independence to Algeria was a brilliant tribute to his aloofness from the military and from conservative political parties. Nationalist organizations were very much opposed. Conversely, when Socialist Prime Minister Savary tried to integrate private schools into the national school system, a coalition of Catholic educators, parents, and conservative political parties forced Savary to withdraw his proposal.

The French government is not fully autonomous, for no government is. But a powerful strain of French political thought, unlike American or English, but somewhat akin to German romanticism, has been inspired by Rousseau's commitment to the general will. Organizations that interpose themselves between the government and "the people" were actually made illegal in 1791. Although the law was rescinded in 1884, it was not until 1901 that interest groups could organize without government permission. France does not have an authoritarian government, merely a strong one.

MODERATE CORPORATISM IN THE FEDERAL
REPUBLIC OF GERMANY

Occupation is of primary significance. There are, of course, the
Greens, but they are declining electorally and never were able to
crack the inner circle. Employers are organized into two national organizations: the Federal Association of German Employers (*Bundes-
vereinigung der Deutschen Arbeitgeberverbände*), the BDA, which
handles labor relations, and the Bundesverband der Deutschen Industrie, Federation of German Industry (BDI), which addresses economic policy. Workers are represented through the German
Confederation of Trade Unions (*Deutscher Gewerkschaftsbund*), that is,
the DGB.

Peak Associations

These are genuine peak associations. The BDA and BDI are pre-
Nazi, representing firms, not individuals. The BDA has forty-six formal associations representing 384 local units, and is organized into
six economic sections, each corresponding to a primary productive
category (manufacturing, construction, banking and finance, agriculture, and so on). BDI is about the same. Over 70 percent of German business beyond the smallest belongs to a trade association that
is, in turn, affiliated with the BDA and BDI.

The DGB is postwar in origin. Initially founded by those who
had been active in trade unions and socialist and Catholic left politics
during Weimar, it emerged during the allied occupation. By hard
work, patience, and consummate pragmatism, it eliminated
fragmentation and rivalry. It is a unitary federation of major national
industrial unions, with membership on its governing board shared
between Protestants and Catholics. DGB has seventeen unions, with
about 31 percent of the labor force in them. Sixty-eight percent are
industrial workers. DGB represents the majority of industrial workers. However, affiliated unions have been unwilling to follow its lead
and accept limited wage increases negotiated for them.

These three are the peak associations, but West Germany is a
moderate, not a strong, corporatist country. True, more than in the
United States, France, or the United Kingdom, groups are "an inte-
gral part of the policymaking process."[38] And surely the interest-
group system is a sizable component of the German miracle.
However, most industrial workers are not in the DGB.

Nonetheless, like the Swiss, the employers and local unions negotiate deals that are then approved by the peak associations. These

are: the *Deutscher Bauernverband* (German Association of Farmers), *Deutscher Beamtenbund* (Civil Servants), Federation of Free Professions (*Bundesverband der Frei Berufe*), and German Union of Salaried Employees (*Deutsche Angestelltengewerkschaft*).

Locally, an intricate network of industrial and commercial chambers (*Kammern*) composed of employees, provides vocational training and certification for federal and state governments. The local chambers are represented nationally by the German Industrial and Commercial Association (*Deutscher Industrie und Handelstag*). Like many economic interest groups, these associations have benefited from German administrative regulations that stipulate that ministries formally consult with affected interest groups and allow time for a response. As the department has discretion in deciding which interests are affected, a tight relationship is more advantageous.

The DGB, *the* labor union, is committed to economic democracy, "codetermination of organized workers in all economic, social, and personnel decisions." It also claims to support nationalization, but has only taken codetermination seriously. It has accomplished worker participation: in the late 1940s with the elected company councils and in the British-zone industry-wide codetermination in iron and coal (equal representation of labor and shareholders on boards determining production, investment, personnel, and so on). After the British-zone experiment, codetermination was extended to all iron, coal, and nonsteel in the Federal Republic. In 1952 labor got a third of the seats on all industrial boards, and in 1976 approached parity on the boards of all noncoal and steel industries. It was challenged but upheld by the Federal Constitutional Court. Because it has achieved a measure of codetermination, the DGB has given up on nationalization. It has moderated wage demands, and collaborates with management and public officials to ensure stable growth. Moderation in labor demands is typical of corporatist systems, so why does Germany fall shy of the genuinely strong corporatist arrangements of Switzerland or Austria?

The Failure of Concerted Action

Concerted action *(Konzertiete Aktion)*, a formalized experiment in democratic corporatism, failed. It was to be formal planning under the grand coalition of the 1960s. Three meetings were held during the final year of the Grand Coalition in 1969. But by 1969 the concerted action sessions became acrimonious, as SPD and CDU participants bickered over economic policy and the DGB renewed its efforts. When the CDU went into opposition following the election, employee groups were less willing to participate. Wildcat strikes exploded, and concerted action collapsed.

West Germany, therefore, fell back from trilateralism, preferring intensified bilateral negotiations with the national government playing the key policy initiation and coordination role. Yet, even with the new structure, the SPD could not sustain the growth, defeat stagflation, or cope with the decline of heavy industry and rise of the service vocations. Unemployment remained mired at 9 percent.

The problem faced by the SPD was the conservative, almost stodgy nature of German banking. It does not like to invest venture capital into new growth industries such as software. The bundesbank invests in security; it preaches budget cuts, deficit reduction, income tax reductions, and selective government intervention. Both political parties are about equally interventionists.

But deflation has annoyed the DGB, and it might be phasing out its commitment to collaboration, implying a further suspension of corporatism. The DGB is demanding parity in codetermination from the factory to regional, Land, and National economic councils to "equalize the existing preeminence of private economic interests in the preparliamentary stage of policy decisions." However, the SPD opposes the union federation on codetermination even as it sympathizes with it on protection against imports.

Besides these disputes, Germany's strong political party system reduces interest-group influence. Given the inevitability of coalitions due to the two-ballot system, many of the agreements struck between the parties are so binding and critical to the government's survival that other corporatist arrangements of necessity are given less priority. As Michael Huelshoff explains, "German coalition politics make it difficult to maintain momentum toward strengthening corporatist institutions."[39]

Compared with France, Germany evinces less state autonomy and, as a corollary, more corporatism. Its policy initiatives appear commonplace and incremental, leading Peter Katzenstein to portray the German government as "semi-sovereign" and incapable of "formulating and implementing large-scale policy changes."[40]

SWITZERLAND'S DEMOCRATIC CORPORATISM

No country can compare with Switzerland as an exemplar of the fiscal virtues of corporatism. Switzerland's political culture elevates interest groups to the status of legal (constitutional) participant in the policy routine. According to Katzenstein, whose work on Switzerland leaves *no* questions unanswered, Switzerland's governing mode is "democratic corporatism," the outstanding attributes of which are (1) "an ideology of social partnership, (2) centralized and concentrated interest groups, (3) voluntary and informal coordination of conflicting objectives through continuous political bargaining among interest groups, state bureaucracies, and political parties."[41]

Switzerland's government was *designed* to ensure the continuance of democratic corporatism, just as the American Constitution was intended to ensure fragmentation of power. The current model of democratic corporatism dates only from the 1930s and is hardly evocative of a deep-seated cultural imperative.[42] Unlike Japan, a country to which scholars sometimes compare it, Switzerland is not culturally, ethnically, or linguistically homogeneous. Like Belgium, with which Switzerland is also compared, there are ethnic and linguistic stresses that, given other decision rules, would surely promote political decay.[43] Switzerland's decision rules go well beyond the normal consociational ones. Belgian cabinets are short-lived; Switzerland's government is a quasi-permanent agreement between political parties, interest groups, and government.

Geographical and historical explanations of Swiss exceptionalism help to place Switzerland in contrast to the other small democracies. Unlike the frequently invaded provinces of modern Belgium, Swiss cantons were left alone, snuggled in behind mountains, offering untillable land and isolated valleys: unappetizing terrain for commerce-minded conquerors. In contrast, Belgian provinces offered bustling ports and banking centers combined with seats of both manufacturing and sources of raw materials. Spaniards, French, Dutch, and Germans licked their chops. Thus, one could argue that the Swiss tradition engendered a low-visibility federal government, since an overly powerful national government was never needed to raise an aggressive army, conduct overt foreign policy, or settle internal ethnic conflicts.

Swiss corporatism has an attitudinal component, among interest group leaders, public officials, and citizens, which consists of "vaguely but firmly held notions of the public good." Interest groups also enjoy authoritative rule over compliant memberships. Katzenstein and Steiner write often of the commitment of leading groups to *public* rather than purely *private* goods. In Olsonian language, Swiss interest groups are "encompassing" and, more often than not, they support public policies that they believe to be "rewarding for the society as a whole."[44] Cautious as we should be about inferring generalized legitimacy from elite responses, it is, nevertheless, revealing to note that one-third of the Swiss population claims to rely on interest

Table 8.2   The "Core" of Decision-making Influence

1. Swiss Federation of Labour (SGB)
2. VORORT—Peak Association of Employers
3. Association of Small Business and Trades (SGV)
4. Federal Council of Governments
5. Farmers' Association (SBV)
6. Christian Democratic Party (CVP)
7. Radical Party (FDP)
8. Social Democratic Party
9. Swiss National Bank
10. Department of the Economy (EVD)
11. Department of the Treasury (EFZD)
12. Office of Foreign Trade (HA)
13. Association of Mutual Health Insurances (KK)
14. ZVA—Second Peak Association of Employers
15. Office of Industry, Trade, and Labour
16. Administration of Finances (FV)

Source: Adapted from Hanspeter Kriesi, "The Structure of the Swiss Political System," in Gerhard Lehmbruch and Philippe C. Schmitter, *The Structure of Corporatist Policy-Making* (Beverly Hills, Calif.: Sage, 1982), p. 142.

groups to defend its interest, compared with 17 percent that count on elected officials and 8 percent that depend upon parties.[45]

The Significance of Interest Groups

Hanspeter Kriesi's list of the "core" of the influence brokers leaves little doubt about Switzerland as the paradigm of corporatism. His ordering of the influence of organizations is based upon both observation and elite interviews. (See Table 8.2.)

This is a remarkable discovery, of course: Interest groups are *more powerful* than any unit of government, *even the Bundesrat,* which is fourth. Interest groups infuse economic life: about 68 percent of the Swiss belong to an occupational interest group, a number far higher than in the United States, where less than one-fourth belong to a political party:

> Swiss democracy is geared to pressure groups; it is a form of government calculated to call such groups into existence and give them power. The system could conceivably continue for a time without parties, but without pressure groups it would not work at all.[46]

Parliament is not included among the core, nor are any of the cantonal governments. Parliament's absence is no surprise, but Switzerland's cantons were completely independent for 500 years, and the tradition of decentralization is decidedly more alive in Switzerland than in the United States or other federal systems.[47] The other countries with federal divisions of authority—Australia, West Germany, and Canada—also allow judicial review. Switzerland does not. Federal relationships may be used to provide a political order for a nation to become unified out of separate and distinct entities, as happened in Germany in the nineteenth century. Or federalism may serve as a means of combining several nations or nationalities into one political order, as happened in Switzerland and Belgium.[48]

The absence of judicial review sheds some light upon the curious exclusion of cantonal governments from Kriesi's list. Because the Constitution can be amended easily, and since the nature of Swiss federalism is more of a cooperative arrangement than a belligerent one, the Swiss political mind sees less of a regional distinction than is true in other federal systems.[49]

Business.   While labor (the SGB) is surprisingly ranked first among the core, business interests eclipse the others. The most important is the *Schweizereische Handels-und Industries-Verein* (VORORT), the peak association representing business, and arguably the most formidable quango (quasi-autonomous nongovernmental organization) extant in industrial democracies. Although the Swiss business community has divided over sensitive questions such as foreign workers or European integration, business relations are excellent due to the VORORT's ceaseless search for a workable consensus: "geographically diverse groups and different economic interests come to follow a common political point of view through frequent consultations within a centralized peak association."[50] VORORT's Zurich headquarters appear quasi-governmental; its staff, though small, is possibly more attuned to international business than are many federal bureaucrats. It savors an associational monopoly unique among European corporatist systems and possibly even stronger than Japan's *Keidanren*.[51] Jürg Steiner, assaying the VORORT's monopoly as without peers, agrees with the common Swiss folksaying that the "VORORT in Zurich sets the switches for the government in Bern."[52]

The confidence that accompanies such status is unmistakable. VORORT's staff members do not talk, as do lobbyists, about access or campaign finance. They talk as though they were, as they are, members of a governing class. Again, the *Keidanren* is the obvious counterpart. While the differences might be of no serious import, and possibly attributable to the vast cultural expanse that separates Japan's corporatism from Switzerland's, the *Keidanren* spends much money making the various Liberal Democratic Party factions happy, a task that VORORT would find unseemly.[53] Since the VORORT is much more consequential in the policy system than the "business" party, the Christian Democrats, or the older, traditionally liberal Rad-

Table 8.3   Net Direct Private Investment

Italy	-2,917
West Germany	-8,121
United Kingdom	-8,378
Sweden	-2,309
Belgium	-990
Norway	-107
Austria	-41
Canada	-824
Netherlands	-2,198
United States	-300
France	-2,116
Switzerland	+383

ical Democrats, it is superfluous to pay much attention to them, and the VORORT does not. As Steiner concludes, "The boundaries of most economic interest groups do not coincide with those of a particular party."[54]

International Business.   Among the contributors to the VORORT's renown, the international business community looms large. Business in Switzerland *is* international, and the VORORT works vigorously to maintain Switzerland's internationalism:

> Because of Switzerland's small size and exposed position in the international economy, the VORORT's stance on critical issues is distinguished by the fact that it considers the effects that particular policies would have on Switzerland's political and economic system as a whole. It focuses on policies that affect Switzerland's position in the international economy or relate to the general principles governing Switzerland's market economy.... [It] opposes the protectionist tendencies of Switzerland's domestically oriented business community.[55]

Possibly the VORORT's extraordinary station is a consequence of the rabid internationalism of the Swiss business community. There are skirmishes about major issues, but there is a central thrust to the Swiss business community. The dominance of exports is astonishing. Consider, for example, Net Direct Private Investment (amount invested or reinvested by nonresidents, minus direct investment by residents of the country), as displayed in Table 8.3.

Switzerland exports 25 percent of its Gross National Product (Japan exports about 16 percent; the United States exports 7 percent).[56] The Swiss giant multinationals that account for about half the total production—Nestle, Ciba-Geigy, Hoffman-La Roche, Alusuisse, Brown Boveri, Sandoz—have two-thirds of their sales and employees outside Switzerland.[57] As Rosecrance has depicted trading states:

"They have to live. . . . They no longer think of improving their national position through territorial gain but seek rather to use strategies of economic growth sustained by foreign trade to maintain and increase the standard of welfare enjoyed by the population."[58]

Switzerland, and the VORORT especially, will not bestow much protection on local industry and, since the home market is so tiny, the multinationals are in a sink or swim competitive position. Although most interest groups claim to speak for the illusive "public interest," the VORORT comes the closest to doing so, since the Swiss public interest really *is* in international business.

The VORORT is, of course, not a democratic organization. Much of its power (like the claims of most interest groups, but this time with justification) stems from the skills of its professional staff and their tight connections with centers of expertise in the public and private sectors. No one knows much about how it formulates its policies. There are very few, if any, meetings, votes, delegates, and so on. Yet, there is not the slightest suggestion that the VORORT distorts its members' preferences. Like the *Bundesrat*, the VORORT's "democratic centralism" is intractable. Its success is not easily obtained, because its membership is not any more monolithic than business anywhere else. Nonetheless, the VORORT is willing to stick with an issue until a consensus is obtained, and cling to this course during the extensive negotiations begun by the *Bundesrat*.

Banks. Banking accounts for 4 percent of the Swiss Gross National Product. To understand the pervasive nature of banking, consider that there is one bank branch for every 1200 Swiss (cf. 1/6000 in the United States). Swiss bankers have such a sinister reputation for international shenanigans that in the throes of the British currency crisis of the 1960s, Labourites called them the "gnomes of Zurich." The Swiss banking industry has grown truly international. It is becoming concentrated, like manufacturing. The three largest banks (Credit Suisse, UBS, Swiss Banking Corporation) have about half the domestic market. Of the total Swiss private banking market, less than one-third is domestic business. Swiss banks have between one-third and half the *total* international off-shore private banking market. But unlike the watch industry, Swiss banks as international colossi is a new phenomenon: they only shed their status as money launderers when the inflationary spiral made the U.S. dollar no longer the most respected currency in the world.

Swiss banks are very much the reserve of the big investor: 10 percent of the clients account for 90 percent of the investment. The assets of the big three banks exceed the Swiss GNP, and they have kept the foreign bond unto themselves by organizing into a massive syndicate, which doles out fixed percentages of new issues and charges huge commissions.

The Stamp Duty as a Prototype of Public-Private Bargaining

Swiss banks want to eliminate the stamp duty (16.5 percent of the total value of each transaction), but the duty contributes 8 percent of the Swiss government's revenue. The Socialist finance minister has agreed to abolish the stamp duty only if he can tax fiduciary deposits instead; bankers oppose. (Fiduciary deposits are a way to get around the 35-percent withholding tax. The money is not actually in a cash balance in Switzerland; instead, it is in a subsidiary abroad. Of course, the customer, not the bank, is at risk.)

The discord over the stamp duty shows that Switzerland's corporatism is not really like the innards of a Rolex. This quarrel between the banks and the minister of finance has been dragging on for three years, with a bank representative pouting that "the banks are not much liked or even respected in this country. They carry less political clout than the big industrial companies."

The Banks and Secrecy

But the banks are vexed not not only by a suddenly recalcitrant government. They have felt the scorn of the media and, thus, embarrassed their very proper government because of hanky panky. Elizabeth Kopp, minister of justice, resigned because her husband entangled himself in a drug money-laundering scam (money laundering is a crime only when the money can be linked to illegal drugs). Suggestions of an expanded law—opposed by the banks— are under consideration. The United States Securities and Exchange Commission threatened to ban the Swiss from dealing on the stock exchange unless the banks coughed up. Swiss banks are also routinely lambasted for catering to various authoritarian kleptomaniacs such as Marcos and Duvalier. Credit Suisse did not freeze Marcos's and Duvalier's accounts until ordered to do so.[59] Secrecy continued to erode under international pressure and virtually disappeared by the early 1990s. The Swiss government was not impotent or helpless in the face of bank pressures. Indeed, it displayed more independence than the U.S. government in the savings and loan scandal.

In 1988 the Swiss government prohibited insider trading. But the law will not make tax evasion *per se* a crime, since such a decision would need a referendum. The banks opposed, unsuccessfully, the inflationary consequences of export policy (undervaluation of Swiss-franc-helped exporters, but increased money supply and threatened inflation). The banks—saviors of the watch industry—would not agree with the prevalent assessment that interest groups are more powerful than the government, especially when Otto Stich (who really did sound like a European Social Democrat, oddly dissonant among the patois of the Swiss elite) was president. However, since executives rotate annually, their imprint upon policy is difficult to ascertain. Stich's successors did not share his skepticism toward banks.

However, the banks are in some danger of tumbling to the Tokyo-New York-London axis, and if they maintain their stodgy ways, might find themselves in the same predicament as the watchmakers a few years ago: on the edge of international eclipse. The banks show little interest in creating new financial instruments and in electronic trading. (When Zurich decided to open an exchange in traded options, forty separate work permits were required for the stock exchange.)

The Ferdinand Marcos affair is another example of corporatist smugness. As Marcos's government was discharging its death rattle, a bank (actually a minor clerk) noticed "exceptional" movement into numbered accounts and told the Federal Banking Commission. It was clear that it would be a while before a new government in the Philippines got around to a freeze request. The Banking Commission told the *Bundesrat*, which then froze Marcos's swag, so the unsavory billions remained in Zurich instead of accompanying the Marcos gang to Hawaii. Many bankers regarded this transaction as a betrayal of the secrecy tradition and the "squealing" bank as a traitor!

There is a strong possibility that the banks will have to pursue, as have Swiss multinationals, a nondomestic market (especially with the liberalization of banking and securities dealing in Europe), and will concentrate on the wholesale rather than the retail sector banking that interests the Americans and the British. If this transformation occurs, it will require the kind of government-private sector coordination that saved the watchmaking industry.

Corporatism and Economic Challenge

A similar problem faces one of the multinationals, Hoffmann-La Roche, whose Valium patent has expired. It is concentrating on antibiotics, dermatological drugs, and anticancer drugs (it went in heavily for interferon, but lost when its star faded). Hoffman-La Roche looks lustily toward the government for succor.

The Watchmaking Industry. The best illustration of the integrative role of government is the obstinate challenge faced by the watchmakers. A 1947 law, incorporated as amendments to the Constitution in 1951, shows just how seriously corporatist the Swiss culture has become. Article 31 allows the Confederation to depart from the constitutional principle of "freedom of trade and industry" and to take measures and enact regulations "in favor of specific economic sectors or professions" if the "economic sectors or professions to be protected have taken such measures to help themselves as can reasonably be expected of them."

In the 1920s the small firms that represented a large portion of total manufacturing were hit hard by foreign competition. The Confederation negotiated industry-wide agreements guaranteeing the small firms a fair share of the market. The export of watchmaking machinery was placed under federal license, with government permission required for the opening of new facilities or increase in the productivity of existing ones. The industry's interest groups contributed to a governmentally controlled crisis fund, but the money is strictly under government control. The government has shepherded the industry toward the use of the funds for research and development and for marketing surveys. The government also controls the quality of Swiss watches and prohibits the sale of substandard ones.

The Japanese brought the Swiss watch industry to its knees in the 1970s, yet it recovered and prospered. The Swiss also encountered a market assault on budget-priced watches by Hong Kong, Japan, and the United States. The problem was that these cheap watches were not inferior in performance: they were more accurate than, and almost as durable as, the carefully crafted Swiss watches. But the Swiss watch industry is dominated by the "little old watchmaker": 75 percent of sales are in the higher-priced models (but these watches make up only 18 percent of world sales). Most watchmakers were willing to use quartz, providing they could continue their line of traditional watches, but *none* were willing to go digital.

The Swiss were, on the other hand, willing to combine. The two largest watchmakers merged to form *Industries Horlogere Suisse*, creating the world's second largest watchmaking group. The bankers took over (97 percent) and ran the cartel, pumping about 500 million into advertising, new products, and upgrading facilities. By the mid-1980s the decline had been braked, and by 1984 watch exports increased by 9 percent, and by 12 percent the following year.

Seventy-five percent of Swiss watch sales are in hand-assembled instruments. These watches, while remaining immune from mass production, profited from the banks' emphasis on style and aggressive marketing. Swiss advertising made a virtue of *not* being quartz, for example. The advertising efforts moved in the direction of conceiving of Swiss watches as fashion accessories, a successful stratagem as the fashion world recoiled in horror at digital watches. Had the Swiss tried to beat the Japanese, they probably would have lost.

The banks saved the watch industry, and they would not have done so had not the bureaucracies lobbied hard. In sharp contrast to the role of banks in the development of the British financial empire, Swiss banks have involved themselves heavily in policy.

The Swiss Watch Chamber, a constituent of the VORORT, wanted money but not guidance. The banks were not initially receptive to VORORT's entreaties. VORORT lobbied the *Bundesrat*, which, in turn, successfully lobbied the banks to provide enough money to rescue the ailing companies, an investment that paid off handsomely. The government persuaded the banks to convert loans into equity, to accept write downs, and to generate new capital. The watch companies surrendered control for money. Watch imports, declining until this decade, have been able to reach beyond the European Community (which has never had as much of a Japanese presence as has the United States), establish profitable beachheads in Asia and the Pacific, and stabilize its share of the U.S. market.

Corporatism and Labor Unions

Swiss unions are politically anemic, more akin to the Japanese ones than to those in left-corporatist governments like Sweden or Austria. Much more so than is the case for business, unions are non-monopolistic, and shredded by internal disunity.[60] Then why is the *Schweizerischer Gewerkschaftsbund* (SGB) said to be the most powerful? One possibility is that unions are not *corporatist* in the usual sense. Since 1937 the unions and employer associations have operated with "peace treaties," which amount to no-strike deals that also outlaw lock-outs and boycotts. These peace agreements rarely go beyond the local level. The federal government stays out of the negotiations, and the national unions and employers' associations have rights for binding arbitration. They have "Swiss" power, probably more than do unions in Japan. Here again, the Constitution provides for "generally binding" agreements; unions may collect dues from nonmembers, and bargains struck by the unions and employers bind all workers. The agreements are thus public law. Unions and business groups cooperated to keep up the (somewhat) discriminatory treatment of foreign workers (25 percent of the work force), without whom the unemployment rate would be far higher than it is. Labor's ostensible ally, the Social Democrats, committed themselves to various (unsuccessful) referenda to improve the status of foreign laborers. The cozy pact means there are almost no strikes. Switzerland typically loses about one working day per thousand workers, about the same as does Japan.

About 20 percent of the working population belong to unions. Fifteen percent of the labor force (459,000) belong to the peak labor union. Therefore, it is corporatism of the *right*, without an income policy and without a strong left. Because of the partnership, unions have more leverage than they would have under other decision rules. If Switzerland were less consociational, unions would be worse off.

Does It Work?

Switzerland is typical of *inclusive capitalist systems*. The economic system of these countries is driven by the market and private enterprise, with government participation limited to subsidy and regulation, as opposed to ownership. Taxes are designed for the sustenance of government, rather than for the achievement of a social or political goal, such as an equitable income distribution. Other cases are the United States and Japan.

Switzerland was assiduously successful in managing the economic crisis of the 1970s. If one considers economic growth, economic stability (steady growth), rates of inflation, rates of unemployment, balances of trade, and economic diversification for the last four decades, the best performing economies, in rank order, are displayed in Table 8.4.

In 1987 the Population Crisis Committee, a research organization concerned with population control, published its Human Suffering Index, a composite index based on such factors as literacy, infant mortality, income, caloric intake, and the like, rated Switzerland as having the world's best quality of life.[61] The *Economist*, using slightly different criteria (including, for example, cultural opportunities that, one need hardly add, are of slight interest in Chad or Mozambique), concluded that the most livable countries are, in order, France, West Germany, Australia, Japan, Canada, Sweden, United States, United Kingdom, and Switzerland.[62] However one regards such lists, Switzerland is always there.

Table 8.4   Corporatism, Pluralism, and Performance

	Corporatism	Economic system
Japan	High	Capitalist inclusive
Switzerland	High	Capitalist inclusive
Norway	High	Mixed capitalist inclusive
West Germany	Medium	Capitalist inclusive
Austria	High	Mixed capitalist inclusive
United States	Low	Capitalist inclusive
Finland	Medium	Mixed capitalist inclusive
France	Medium	Mixed capitalist inclusive
Netherlands	Medium	Mixed capitalist inclusive
Sweden	High	Mixed capitalist inclusive

Source: Harmon Zeigler, "The Interrelation of Freedom, Equality, and Development," in Raymond Gastil, ed., *Freedom in the World* (New York: Freedom House, 1988), pp. 204–28.

The Role of Government: Minimalist Corporatism

Switzerland seems about as minimalist as you can get. Only 18 percent of its Gross National Product is ascribed to government expenditures, a figure lower even than that of the United States. Switzerland's marginal tax rate, 18 percent, is also lowest among industrial democracies. However, as we know from Japan, a governmental presence is not necessarily measured solely in terms of money spent and taxes collected. The Swiss national government is not moribund until jogged into action by interest groups. As in Japan and Austria, the distinction between public and private is uncertain.

The seven members of the *Bundesrat* are senior civil servants, rather than party politicians. Because the Swiss civil service is small, it relies on the expertise and manpower of interest groups to conduct research and to develop policy. Switzerland is federal, rather than unitary, with local traditions and power stronger in the cantons than in the American states. The Swiss national government is, by European standards, impoverished: it receives only 29 percent of tax revenues, compared with the European average of 58 percent.

But if interest groups subordinated by corporatism or at least structured and balanced by unitary, parliamentary governments are beneficial, and if they—inhibited by the impotence of strong pluralism—contribute to economic stagnation and decline, is this not a paradox for pluralism? For, as the linchpins of pluralism, interest groups are hastening its death. In an internationally interdependent economy, governments that can govern will prevail over those that surrender to narrow coalitions.

But one can hardly attribute the rise and decline of economies solely to the relations between interest groups and the state. British decline from the 1870s is attributable as much to the accidents of empire as to narrow distributional coalitions. As the British empire and the industrial revolution developed simultaneously, the British relied more on their colonies for commercial and industrial development than did other, less imperialistic countries. British firms continued to sell to semi-industrial colonies while other countries were competing in the more developed European market and producing more technologically sophisticated products. The seeds of decline were sown by empire rather than modes of interest-group intermediation. France has become more corporatist and has prospered; West Germany has become less corporatist and has prospered even more. Nations need an institutional articulation of a public interest.

PLURALISM, CORPORATISM, AND WHO "THEY" ARE

Nineteen-ninety provided a good opportunity to compare corporatism and pluralism with respect to economic stability, as the Iraqi invasion of Kuwait was recrudescent of the 1970s. If Kuwait's main export had been figs, would the United States have intervened to defend it from its loutish neighbor? Was Iraq any less loathsome when it invaded Iran? The primary issue is oil, not integrity. The president must protect America's oil supply or face an uncertain political future.

But why does the United States care about oil? Did we learn nothing from the 1972 and 1979 oil shocks? Would other industrial democracies have reacted as quickly as we did? Why us? Other industrial democracies did not, of course, react like us. Fortunately for the United States, they followed our lead. Had we remained silent, so would they have. They could afford to because they, after the last crisis, "did something." Each American gobbles up about 1,000 gallons of oil a year; each Japanese about 600 and each West German about 550. But West Germany and Japan have "governments" and we, in the United States, do not.

This mode of argument runs directly into another American intellectual tradition: the location and exposure of "them." At its most preposterous, "them" seekers detect conspiracies where none exist. The "paranoid style"[63] detects "them" everywhere: "secular humanists," whoever they are, "control America...control the television, the radio, the newspapers, the Hollywood movies, magazines, porno magazines, and the unions, the Ford Foundation, Rockefeller Foundation....They have infiltrated until every department of our country is controlled by the humanists. . . . Their goal is to accomplish [a dictatorship] by or before the year 2000."[64]

Academics clothe their conspiracy fantasies in jargon, but the result is the same: the "power elite" will get you if you don't watch out. Because members of the power elite wish to preserve a system that has enriched them, they work together, or collaborate, to control or integrate political demands and policy responses: "they" manage the polity. The members of the power elite come from the same social background, have similar values, know each other intimately, and conspire to preserve order and, therefore, their privileged positions.[65]

Unquestionably, a power elite would be a welcome change from the chaos of fragmented government that fiddles while interest groups abscond with the loot, but, as you might surmise, there isn't one. Rather there are *many* power elites and no coordination. John Heinz and his associates "find no identifiable set of 'core actors.' This suggests that autonomous statesmen who have the capacity to bridge . . . policy areas either do not exist or we were not able to find them."[66]

"They" are not hard to locate in corporatist systems. Japan, for instance, having learned from the last time that events in the Persian Gulf are beyond anyone's control, spent the last two decades insulating itself. By imposing strict goals on car makers and industry, Japan produced cars that were more energy efficient than ours (presumably, as the Japanese continue to expand their share of our market, we will benefit more from their ingenuity). As Japan has moved toward more information intensive industries, it has speeded the transition to nuclear power, natural gas, and coal. In 1979 it contained money supply and wages, thus avoiding the inflation that devastated our economy.

A nearly exact parallel is the Swiss and agricultural products. In 1939 Swiss agriculture supplied only 30 percent of domestic consumption of bread cereals, and it produced almost no fruits and vegetables. World War II brought home the need for self-sufficiency. By 1975, 40 percent of vegetables and 75 percent of bread and cereals were produced domestically.[67] Success was a consequence of a "self-conscious and consistent policy. . . . Every five years the Swiss formulate a plan in which they decide what Swiss agriculture should produce and in what quantites."[68]

Other industrial democracies have industrial policies and the United States does not because it is not institutionally structured, or ideologically anchored, in economic planning. Whether or not a strong market commitment is a failure depends upon one's point of view. But the lack of systematic policy is not a partisan issue, nor is it a function of the president's personality or priorities. Chalmers Johnson, echoing the Olsonian argument against narrow coalitions, argues that we have no industrial policy because "economic and intellectual vested interests stand in the way. By economic interest I mean the vast amount of money spent by private parties, both domestic and foreign, to influence legislators and administrators."[69]

George Bush's quick, well-planned response to Iraq could never be duplicated in domestic policy. He could not, even if he wished, impose an energy policy, because he could not rally the support necessary (in the House or the Senate) to impose the costs that would come with it. He does not command a majority in either the Senate or the House; *nobody* does.

The Bush energy option signaled his recognition of reality; during the Gulf War, Bush advanced the development of alternative energy sources rather than conservation. It called for pumping oil in areas previously off limits for environmental reasons, and for the deregulation of pipeline operators and electricity producers. The policy, then, is purely a market-driven one. Because the United States both consumes and produces oil, a tax imposed by a consuming nation—Japan, France, or Germany—is opposed by American producers, whereas a tax to stimulate production is resisted by consumers. Among the energy producers, oil companies bad-mouth natural gas, a potential competitor, accusing it of a history of shortages and price volatility. Natural gas producers complain about coal, which is too dirty. Coal producers, with supplies so abundant and technology so advanced that big price swings are inconceivable, speak with derision about price volatility in both oil and gas. The nuclear industry is by itself, despised by everyone. Thus, "it is hard to differentiate what is being done because it makes sense and what is being done because the policy helps someone."[70] That is, one cannot discern a difference between policy that makes sense and one that is designed merely to give an economic interest group a boost.

Policy is fragmented into small-issue areas, each with attendant interest groups, and no president can control them. No genuine government would have allowed itself to be bought by a gang of thugs masquerading as S&L officers.

The parody continues. Early in 1991 the American real estate market suffered a near collapse, due in large part to the withdrawal of the "Tokyo takeout." The real estate market had become dependent upon Japanese money; the S&L crisis stifled Japanese investors' ardor, and the crash ensued. Japan is the prevalent factor in world finance, with $240 billion in international investment (compared to a

U.S. high of $141 billion). Japan is the biggest foreign buyer of U.S. securities and property.[71] When Japan gets cold feet, the jolt is instantaneous. In contrast, the American government's capacity to manipulate the economy is handicapped by its loss of direction of the investment and money supply. Even if there were a government with political resolve, the American economy has drifted out of its purview.

It is imperative to differentiate between corruption and the political reverberations of fragmentation. The political consequences of corruption are more important than the venality that caused it. Bribery and corruption are obstacles when they impede autonomous decision making, as they do in the United States. The classic argument in favor of corruption, developed by studying the American urban political machines at the turn of the century, is that it fused legally separate governmental organizations into a functional whole, that it counterbalanced fragmentation.[72]

Corruption can debilitate a government when policy decisions can be traced to it and when the content of those decisions is inimical to the public interest. In this sense of the word, the United States is more corrupt than the countries with which it is compared. A system is corrupt if it systematically serves the interests of special groups or sectors. It may do so legally. As James Scott defines it: "Behavior which deviates from the formal duties of a public role because of private regarding wealth or status gains: or violates rules against the exercise of certain types of private regarding influence."[73]

Most of the exchanges between political action committees and American congressmen are not illegal, since Congress wrote the laws. They are insidiously corrupting, however, in that they weaken autonomy. Thus, the entire American system, in that it operates without a concept of the public interest, is corrupt. Individually venal office holders are found everywhere.

In poorer, weaker countries, "kleptocracies" have been shown to have actually hindered economic growth. Arguably, the savings and loan scandal approaches this magnitude. Its implications, in comparison with other American scandals, are vast. Not only is the cost of salvaging the industry immense but the episode speaks volumes about the ease of purchasing access in a fragmented system.

Corruption has not yet governed the shape of policy in Europe or Japan. It has surely enriched individuals and led to conspiracies of silence among governing classes. Just as the French political classes papered over the *Rainbow Warrior* episode, so they appear prepared to minimize the decline of public virtue among French civil servants.[74] And, of course, theoretically, strong political parties enjoy monopoly power over the votes of their members. Thus, bribe taking by individual legislators, as occurs in the United States, may contain less potential for harm than bribery in a strong party system.[75]

But, since the American system creates pockets of great strength, subgovernments that are as hierarchical as the government of any European democracy, corruption is not hindered by fragmentation. The cost of corruption in the American system is continued fragmentation. The world's most powerful legislative body (otherwise why bother to corrupt it?) is also the world's most decentralized and least responsive to organizational constraints. Its influence and staff continue to grow. The world's most powerful legislature is also the world's most expensive. Besides paying the world's highest salaries (see Appendix), it has the largest legislative staff in the world and, unavoidably, the world's largest legislative budget.

The danger here exceeds the danger of party monopoly. Fragmentation, and the auxiliary corruption it engenders, can prevent the implementation of decisions in the public interest. Decentralization does not ensure beneficial outcomes, indeed it almost ensures their absence.[76] The financial scandals in the United States in the late 1980s and the 1990s were of such a truly stunning level of greed and incompetence that they raise the specter, as Sophie Coignard and Jean-François Lacan said of France, of a "banana republic."[77]

CHAPTER **9.**

Is Change
Stable?

We come now to the final question: So what? We have
described and explained variations in political organizations, and
concluded that strong and durable political organizations can invent
people who are, at least theoretically, strong and durable. Individual
heroes come and go, but organizations endure. But do they endure
as inventors of people, as agents of linkage, or as inventors of policy?
Does it really matter who governs with what symbols of authority?

As Richard Rose and Ian McAllister put it: "Instability in parties
is consistent with stability among individual voters. During a lifetime
of political learning, ordinary people acquire political values [parti-
san loyalties] that are much more stable than the reactions of politicians to matters of the moment."[1] Even in the United States in 1988,
in one of the silliest elections conducted in this century, the best pre-
dictor of vote was party identification.[2] This, of course, bodes ill for
the Democrats, who have been losing (as the Republicans gain)
adherents.[3]

Perhaps the query about permutation and permanence is misdi-
rected. After all, electorates do change their minds, and then change
them back. In stable political party systems, with readily unambiguous and feasible choices available, voters choose. When Reagan and
Thatcher won, it did not herald the age of conservatism, but it did

show that voters *really* disliked the existing governments. John Goldthorpe and his associates write of the 1979 British election:

> The major sources of Labour's electoral failure...are two. The first is in fact an essentially political one: the poor performance of Labour as a party....The second source is sociological, but straightforward...a decline in the size of the working class.[4]

This is, of course, precisely the point. When governments fail, voters will replace them. But organizations matter. Labour, *as a party*, was replaced. The West German Social Democrats, *as a party*, were replaced (although personality was more apparent than in the United Kingdom). Jimmy Carter and Giscard, as *individuals*, were replaced. Linkage possibilities are greater when individualism is suppressed.

Anthony King's criteria—that to understand the impact of parties upon policy one must be able to ascertain which party is in power—applies, of course, only to the United States.[5] A discernible, readily identified opposition exists only in the United Kingdom and Germany. Nonetheless, European parties, and those who write of them, posit that they have a purpose beyond election. In the United States, parties have never had much of a policy purpose, being (even in their prereform days), more interested in winning elections than developing coherent policy. As Richard Rose puts it:

> The sole national election—the presidential race—is a contest between individuals. Issues can be important, but they are not so much related to differences between American parties as between candidates, including candidates of the same party pitted against each other in primary elections. To view parties solely as individuals or teams competing for electoral victory is to deny further purpose to parties. An election victory would be an end in itself, like victory in a boxing or football match, and not a means to larger political ends.[6]

This conclusion augurs for more party-linked policy variance in Europe, less in the United States or Japan. While there are a variety of ways of assessing this proposition, the anecdotal examples are of little interest; long-range macroeconomic outcomes are useful. Perhaps the outcome most unquestionably linked with party ideology is income transfers or subsidies, the taking of goods from one group and giving them to another. While we normally assume that transfers are in one path, from rich to poor, this may not be the case. Indeed, the claim against Reagan and the United Kingdom's Conservatives is that income gaps enlarged, the rich got richer and the poor got poorer. These vagaries notwithstanding, income distri-

Table 9.1   Income Transfers in the United States, United Kingdom,
             West Germany, and France

	1970	1975	1980	1985	1988
United States	7.17	9.42	9.38	10.13	9.86
United Kingdom	10.41	13.72	14.55	16.04	15.01
West Germany	12.67	14.63	15.15	15.63	15.51
France	17.60	22.00	21.87	26.31	26.21

Source: Adapted from James Gwartney, Walter Block, and Robert Lawson, "Measuring Economic Freedom," unpublished, 1990, Appendix 2.

bution is the heart of domestic politics: socialists *ache* to attack it directly, center parties more obliquely, and the right parties are willing to let the fittest survive.

A glance at Table 9.1 shows how much the image and the reality are in synchronization. The table arrays the total government effort (as a percentage of GNP) committed to the International Monetary Fund's category, "transfers and subsidies."

As one would expect given the political organization of the United States, nothing happened. How could it? In the United Kingdom, the Conservative Party victory meant a slightly more active government effort; in Germany, the increase evident from 1970 to 1975 continued when the Christian Democrats formed a coalition; and in France, the increases during the Giscard years were reintroduced during the last years of Mitterrand's first term. These are hardly revolutionary transformations. In France, for instance, the increase under the Socialists was identical with the increase under their center-right predecessors.

Another measure of policy change is only slightly more useful: top marginal tax rate and the income threshold to which it applies. Macroeconomic management and monetarism are one thing; the individual pocketbook nerve is another. Taxes are the policy area that the common man can understand. In Table 9.2, marginal (highest) tax rates and the income level at which they are applied are listed.

Here we encounter many of the problems that occur when we try to link policy choice and party ideology. In the United States the election of a Republican president determined to "get the government off our backs" led directly to a reduction of the tax rates. However, the tax reduction was negated by lowering the taxable income threshold. These decisions, tax and threshold reduction, were supported by the House and Senate Democrats, the "opposition." In the United Kingdom, just as in the United States, rates and thresholds were dropped; in Germany there are no discernible trends.

Table 9.2   Marginal Tax Rates and Income Thresholds in the United States, United Kingdom, West Germany, and France

	1975	1980	1985	1988
United States	70–75	70–75	50–59	33–42
	185,000	82,645	156,000	58,937
United Kingdom	41	83	60	40
	185,000	66,942	41,100	24,700
West Germany	56	56	56	56
	167,283	193,939	39,650	114,764
France	48	60	65	53
	130,109	126,722	30,700	29,929

Source: Adapted from James Gwartney, Walter Block, and Robert Lawson, "Measuring Economic Freedom," unpublished, 1990, Appendix 2.

In France the Socialist government raised the marginal tax rate and reduced the threshold, providing us with our single unclouded case of a policy change that could be properly attributed to an alteration in government. Personality and theatrics aside, the *Parti Socialiste* did induce a policy change. Alas, the vagaries of French politics mean that, as Mitterrand in the famous cohabitation agreement of 1986 (when the *Parti Socialiste* lost its legislative majority), the Gaullist prime minister, Jacques Chirac, gets more of the credit than Mitterrand! Also, Gwartney and his associates have concluded that individual economic freedom *increased* after Mitterrand's election; it spiraled more than was the case in the United Kingdom after Thatcher's triumph!

Without an organization that can structure choice and demand compliance, political parties too often succumb to personality. The two most brazen examples, France and the United States, bestow upon us forbidding questions about the separate election of a chief executive. Could political parties in either country have dismissed a leader that had headed the party for three successive election victories? London wags said Mrs. Thatcher grew fond of employing the "imperial we" (as in "we have a grandchild"). Her Tory colleagues taught her a lesson in humility. Political systems work best when hero worship is lessened by the strictures of organization. Compare the ease with which Mrs. Thatcher was dispatched with the national nightmare that accompanied the disgrace, and ultimate resignation, of Richard Nixon.

Table 9.3   Incongruity (Proportion of Policy Areas with the Content of
Policy Inconsistent with the Majority of the Public) between
Policy and Opinion in the United Kingdom, United States,
France, and West Germany

United Kingdom	56%
United States	59
France	59
West Germany	58

POLICY CONGRUENCE AND POLICY CHANGE

Another matter entirely is *congruence* (measured by matching the
content of policy with the content of public opinion), the extent to
which the government's policy matches the people's wishes; or,
more accurately, the extent to which the people's expectations come
to mirror extant policy. Generally, there is *incongruence* between what
the government does and what the people want. That is, the policy
course of a government is, as a rule, not in keeping with the proclivities of a majority. In West Germany, as in Britain, France, and the
United States, in cases of both landslides and slim victories, discrepancy between preference and policy persists; never does it reach the
50-percent level. This finding by Joel E. Brooks is troublesome.[7]
Brooks selected issues on which there was good survey information,
matched the content of public policy (governmental actions) on these
same issues, and calculated the frequency of cases indicating inconsistency between public opinion and public policy.

Brooks shows that the *institutions* of government make no difference: policy is for the most part disconnected from opinion. Strong
political parties (the United Kingdom) produce no better result than
weak ones, parliamentary governments are as disengaged as presidential ones, unitary ones as disconnected as federal ones. A summary of Brooks's findings appears in Table 9.3.

Governments do a deplorable job of inventing "the people";
they do not do what "the people" want more than about 40 percent
of the time. In the remainder of examples, they do what "the people"
do *not* want. Arend Lijphart, in an otherwise outstanding survey of
democracies, writes of democratic regimes characterized "not by
perfect responsiveness but by a high degree of it; their actions have
been in *relatively close* correspondence with the wishes of *relatively
many* of their citizens for a long period of time."[8] I suppose it depends
on what one means by "relatively close," but typically democracies
promulgate laws and policies of which a majority do not accord with
a majority of the public's opinion. One has to concede major meth-

Table 9.4   **Incongruity on Redistributive versus Nondistributive Issues**

	Redistributive	Nonredistributive
United Kingdom	54%	57%
United States	62	51
France	67	57
West Germany	81	48

odological problems in matching opinions to policies. Different methodologies can produce different results. For example, Benjamin Page and Robert Shapiro, using only examples of opinion *change*, find more congruence in the United States than does Brooks.[9] An advantage of Brooks's research is that it is comparative, thus allowing for some control over the "phantom public." The American public is the most phantomlike of all, but the European publics are more informed, more attentive, and more active.

The inconsistency between public opinion and public policy is unusually evident concerning redistributive issues, proposals to transfer income or tangible goods from one group to another. Here, except for the United Kingdom, such issues provoke more disagreement. When governments set out their tasks as righting society's wrongs, elites—as we know from research on elite and mass attitudes—are more progressive, less responsive. The stunning feature of Brooks's work is the nearly identical scores of countries with vast differences in political culture, government structure, interest group intermediation, and political party organization, as amply documented in this book. "The people" remains as illusive a notion as the divine right of kings. If the United Kingdom has the fewest institutional barriers to responsiveness (pure parliamentary government, no federalism, strong political parties) and still comes up short, then presumably there is no room for improvement. If there is a "captive public," blindly taking its cues from opinion leaders, then there must be scant cues to follow, or the common folk's perceptual screen is effectively opaque.

There are, of course, some policies that attract formidable emotional responses. Those that seek to take from one group and give to another are the best illustration. (See Table 9.4.) However, since redistributive issues are typically associated with left-wing parties, possibly during their reigns, image and reality coalesce to produce less inconsistency. (See Table 9.5.)

This proves correct, with the notable exception of West Germany, where both ruling coalitions are out of harmony with public opinion (the measure cannot be used in the United States, since one

Table 9.5   Incongruity on Redistributive Issues by Political Party

	Left	Right
United Kingdom	44%	75%
France	41	76
West Germany	80	82

cannot decide which party is in power). Redistributive issues are, however, the sole illustration of *congruity*. But redistribution is hardly a minor matter; after all, redistribution by government fiat, as opposed to natural market forces, is the encapsulation of the issue agenda that has traditionally divided the left from the right in Europe and, to a lesser extent, the United States.

These examples of congruence are therefore far from trivial: both occurred because the left party was in harmony with public opinion on the central theme of left-wing politics in Europe. Democratic frustration is lower when left governments undertake efforts at income and resource distribution: "The attainment of political power by a social democratic party appears to have a substantial impact upon issues affecting its supposed ideological raison d'être."[10] The partisan composition of the government matters. Why not in Germany? One possibility is that the left party, the SPD, because of the electoral boost given to the small Free Democrats, always governed in coalition with a decidedly more centrist party. Institutions matter, too. Coalitions reduce ideological clarity.

An issue that cannot be resolved by these data is the *order* in which the congruence occurs. Although we are accustomed to thinking of policy following opinion, those who think people are too ignorant to have opinions until elites articulate them and those who believe in captive public theories of a helpless mass pharisaically manipulated by elite conspiracies believe that mass opinion flows with elite agendas. The West German pattern provides little evidence here, since there are immense incongruities irrespective of the party in power. However, France offers the best test of the captive public theory. Not only did a *symbolically* more extreme party win but its leader executed a U-turn after two years, switching to an austerity program. Incongruity was lower (41 percent) during the reform period than in the subsequent period of moderation (57 percent). The *Parti Socialiste* was more in tune with mass aspirations when it adhered to a more orthodox socialist ideology. Yet Mitterrand, riding the economic boom, was reelected. Opinions did not shift, but they became less linked to elections, as Mitterrand's personality took center stage.

There are, then, infrequent but very significant examples of linkage (or at least consistency) between opinion and elite behavior. We should keep the successful invention of the people by left governments in the United Kingdom and France firmly in mind. Additionally, incongruity does not lead to electoral retaliation. Here is where Brooks is short of the mark, and here is where political organizations "matter."

Congruence between elite policy and mass preference says nothing about the ability of political organizations to facilitate government delivery on its promises, irrespective of linkage. Here the evidence is unambiguous. The government enacts 97 percent of its laws in Britain, 87 percent in Germany, 82 percent in France, and 33 percent in the United States (here, government is taken to mean the executive office of the president).[11] In short, governments that are woven together by the ties of party can address and attempt to solve social and economic problems. Whether what they do is congruent with popular preferences is less important than whether their actions have a discernible impact, in the direction intended, upon a specified problem.

Yet, the evidence about parties making a difference is not definitive. Changing political parties does not alter income distribution appreciably, for instance. Brooks avows that there is a "general inability of left-wing mobilization to create an increase in egalitarianism" because left-wing parties must extend their appeal beyond the working class if they are to win and, in any case, the "embourgeoisement" of such parties makes this task pleasant and natural.[12] There are simply not enough ideologically secure left voters to ensure an electoral fruition, and therefore, "no political party ever won an electoral majority on a program offering a socialist transformation of society."[13] Rose and Edward Page's astute comparison of unemployment policy in Britain and Germany portrays the German Social Democrats in no such danger: "Whether the Chancellor has been a Socialist or CDU, German policy makers have given a higher priority to stability (that is, fighting inflation) than to full employment." They conclude that "national differences appear greater than left-right differences within nations."[14]

The degree of corporatism does not matter either, whether one considers income redistribution or the broader question of economic growth, but there is no readily apparent reason why it should. Corporatism, as we have seen, contributes to more fiscal responsibility; its function is not really related to the creation of mass-elite congruence.[15]

Claims that political parties matter are generally prefaced by the supposition that they are conduits for majority supremacy, a conjecture contradicted by Brooks. Therefore, when incumbents are *perceived* as incompetent, they will be replaced. The perception of incompetence may be accurate, and incompetence may be a result of externalities (oil shocks, worldwide recession, and so on). These infrequent but important episodes are when the people are invented precisely. Personnel are replaced, policies are adjusted, and people address their quotidian tribulations. For what is important? That a government be in a position, given competent personnel, to assess shortcomings and propose solutions. If these solutions end up, as they invariably do, as incremental adjustments, what is the harm? What really matters is that people with acumen and experience are placed in positions where responsibility and power are well matched. Strong political parties, because they are not democratic (that is, because they can control the use of their name) are in a better position to do this than are weak ones.

Governments are constrained by tradition, inertia, and the external environment. In France, even if the *Parti Socialiste* had not abandoned socialism, how could spending in excess of revenues be accepted by the other members of the European Community? External pressure from other governments is intense. The Socialist government is consciously pursuing a tax policy that is not out of line with those of the other European governments, irrespective of their partisan competition. For European governments, the internationalization of domestic economies is proceeding slowly but irrevocably. Thus, Mitterrand's "temporary" *rigueur* (austerity) became permanent.[16] In the United Kingdom, economic decline began well before Mrs. Thatcher. Her noble attempts to restore Britain to its former economic hegemony could not possibly succeed. In the United States, inertia aided by fragmentation limits governmental flexibility. Both the French and British systems, then, allow political elites to "do something." Mitterrand changed his mind, and French economic policy was altered in the manner he preferred. Mrs. Thatcher's stubborn determination to take on Labour's political power resulted in new industrial relations legislation that moderated Labour's influence (and incidentally helped the center return to power within the Labour Party).

Occasionally, change happens. The inability of the American Democrats to elect a president may not matter much concerning immediate policy; the long-term impact may be more consequential. Consider the judiciary. Here the Reagan administration was atypically coherent. It wanted to institutionalize the Reagan presidency and, to a remarkable degree, succeeded. Reagan appointed close to half of all lower-court federal judges, and they are different from the appointees of other presidents.[17] The changes they bring are not revolutionary, of course, since the reliance upon precedents demands incrementalism. Margaret Thatcher's successful assault upon trade union political power falls into the same category: change is gradual but discernible. And, aggregate data notwithstanding, it is highly probable that majorities of Americans choose judicial restraint and a majority of Britons prefer a less politically intimidating trade union movement. Add in the success of the French and British Socialists in avoiding "democratic frustration" on policies concerning redistribution and we have uncommon examples of government doing what "the people" want.

These examples illustrate Sidney Hook's thesis about heroes. He writes of "eventful" and "event-making" leaders.[18] Eventful leaders do not "cause" events; rather they help events along on a course they probably would have taken anyway. Such leadership is not uncommon in industrial democracies: Thatcher, Reagan, and Mitterrand helped events along, crystallized the issue, and offered resolution. None fashioned events to suit their fancy, as do event-making leaders. Event-making leaders are virtually excluded by the constraints of democracy. Remove Lenin and there would have been no Bolshevik power seizure in 1917. Remove Thatcher and...?

But people infrequently want change. Governments need not launch auspicious "new beginnings" or "change everything" in order to be responsive. Since governmental rhetoric and incremental reality ultimately coincide, perhaps the shrinking of grandiose plans is the best example of inventing the people. The most realistic invention of the people is not one of abstract ideology; rather, it is one of simple economics. When governments reign during periods of economic prosperity, they are usually returned to office. Because the Japanese have never experienced a recession of much magnitude, and since the American House of Representatives is effectively insulated, we cannot say that the rule of economic voting is inviolate; but it is nearly so.

The irony is that short-term economic policy may be the opposite of long-term public interest. The Japanese are constantly badgering American presidents to right the economy by lowering the federal deficit, increasing individual savings rates, improving education, and pushing business to think less of short-term profit and more about long-term strategy. To do all these things, Congress and the president must *not* do what the people want. When President Bush tells the American people that "American productivity is second to none," as he did in his 1990 State of the Union address, he is telling people what they want to hear (as in "it's morning in America"), but it is not the truth. As Michael Porter ruefully laments, "The inability of the United States to gain consensus even that U.S. industry faces problems in international competition, much less on solutions, is in many ways the most disturbing sign of all."[19] What "the people" want, as indicated by their voting preferences, is a good economy. One need only examine the tracking of the question, What is the most important problem facing the U.S. today? to understand the enduring salience of the economy. However, the public's opinion, poorly informed or thought out, allows short-term preferences to operate against its long-term priorities. In the last two decades, the economy has towered over other matters—civil rights, the "social agenda," and foreign policy.[20] Previous eras did not produce such a consensus. Of course, the well-documented inconsistency in preferences does not mean that public opinion is a reliable guide to what should be done. Majorities favor a constitutional amendment requiring a balanced budget and favor massive reductions in government spending. These majorities are *not willing*, however, for the government to provide fewer services, especially those that subsidize middle-class taxpayers.[21]

Astute governments would, therefore, not do what "the people" want, but rather what the people *really* want. One need not lapse into Rousseauistic theories of the general will or Marxian concepts of false consciousness to assert that tough choices require a willingness to defy short-term demands. Economic performance, the bottom line, is likely to be satisfactory when either (1) left-oriented governments govern with clear cabinet domination and strong, encompassing unions or (2) right-oriented governments govern with a dominant cabinet majority and without powerful unions. That is, "Where leftist or rightist parties govern in *coherent systems*, they can both further their partisan interests and help generate reelectable macroeconomic outcomes. If they govern in incoherent contexts, however, they may be unable to satisfy either objective—certainly not both."[22] The American institutional context guarantees just the sort of incoherence that cannot lead to a strong economic performance.

Robinson Jeffers' poem, "Be Angry at the Sun," should provide some solace[23]:

> That public men publish falsehoods
> is nothing new. That America must accept
> Like the historical republics corruption and empire
> Has been known for years.

Be angry at the sun for setting
if these things anger you....

Let boys want pleasure, and men
struggle for power, and women perhaps for fame
and the servile to serve a Leader and the dupes to be
  duped.

In addition to the structural problems described here, consider another example of the American propensity to personalize institutions: the Twenty-Second Amendment, approved in 1947 in response to four consecutive electoral victories by Franklin Delano Roosevelt. With only one reelection to worry about, naturally an American president will think largely in terms of short-term solutions. Thus, among the industrial democracies, while there is only modest variance in responsiveness and although all governments are limited by inertia, custom, scarce resources, and international expectations, the government of the United States stands at a disadvantage. The disadvantage can be regarded as an advantage, if one is so inclined. Structural and cultural impediments to central planning, so Madisonian in their import, may be regarded as the "genius of America." Even if there were widespread demands for more economic planning, it could not be done:

> [Differences in centralization of power]...affect a nation's ability to develop a coherent, long-run structural policy. Specifically, coherency is less likely to emerge in the United States. If structural policies are essential to maximize long-term growth, Japan...is politically advantaged. If individual creativity and initiative, unconstrained by a strong central government, promote growth, the United States is advantaged.[24]

So the issue is joined. We shall see. The traditional American solution is to rely upon the electoral process; to elect good leaders. But since event-making leaders are rare, and since institutional constraint so vivid, one cannot argue that the economic mess in which America finds itself is Reagan's fault, because he was so inattentive, or Carter's fault, because he was short on charisma. An event-making leader would be frustrated by American fragmentation; probably no leader, no matter how talented, could accomplish much. John Chubb and Paul Peterson offer a gloomy analysis:

> [America's economic problems] reflect a basic incompatibility between the government institutions that the United States has developed to manage its economic affairs and the new economic challenges that it has come to face over the past two decades.[25]

The flaws that Chubb and Peterson see are, for readers of this book, familiar and need no further elaboration. They are not likely to be corrected, and the policies that those who neglect institutions propose are not liable to be adopted as a consequence. Joseph Nye, whose policy solutions were discussed in Chapter 7, fits into this category. He wants to address the deficit, the decaying infrastructure, our poor quality education, and our low savings rate. But the American system is much better at representing groups of people, interest groups, than it is at ignoring demands and seeking a broader public interest. American pluralism even denies the existence of a public interest: "We do not need to account for a totally inclusive interest, because one does not exist."[26] This utterance, by arguably the most influential pluralist theorist of his time, David Truman, guided academics to legitimate American individualism by providing it with a theory; a more natural arrangement could not be imagined.

Although representing interest groups does not create a more generally responsive America, as Brooks has shown, such representative success does contribute to governmental impotence. Chubb and Peterson imagine that the American government decided to pursue a strategic trade policy: "It would degenerate into a politically motivated program of protectionism."[27]

The frustration that drips from the pens of Chubb and Peterson is not shared by all, possibly even most, analysts. Anthony King, worrying (unnecessarily) about efforts to reform, says of the American political system that "it ain't broke."[28] King, however, is no Panglossian. He knows that America may not be able to manage its economy, but is not sure that any government can manage decline. He speculates that America is in the throes of a period of "British-style relative economic decline," and believes, correctly, that it will be "difficult for American politicians to manage or reverse."[29] If the political system "ain't broke," it does a great imitation.

Yet, the most recent assessment of the state of America's political health is decidedly negative. Added to Chapter 3's dreary conclusion that both political parties have declined in the public's eyes, the Kettering Foundation's 1991 report, *Citizens and Politics: A View from Main Street America*, provides yet more evidence of disarray. Borrowing a page from the 1988 Bush campaign, the foundation assembled focus groups in ten American cities. The foundation, listening to the groups, concluded that "the legitimacy of our political issues is more at issue than our leaders imagine." There is, of course, no surprise here; political elites routinely overestimate the happiness of the masses. The gist of "the people's" complaint is that they have been "squeezed out" by interest groups and the media. One should not take "focus groups" too seriously. Who is to say how representative they are? And how different is this carping from the usual "nobody cares" complaint? But since the last three decades have been devoted precisely to bringing "the people" back in (PACs and primary elections were designed to accomplish a shift from organizations to individuals), perhaps the true significance of this latest evidence of alienation is that the reforms have not worked as intended. Even as they destroyed political organizations, they did not empower "the people" because "the people" do not exist. They must be invented and reinvented. To destroy the organizations best suited to this task, political parties, is the political equivalent of the medieval cure for the plague, self-flagellation.

Yet, every government suffers through institutional crises. The replacement of Margaret Thatcher by John Major prompted a rash of complaints about how undemocratic the British system turned out to be; French intellectuals are, again, bemoaning the Americanization of France; Japan is tormented by perpetual scandal; and Italy has only recently modified its electoral system in response to a referendum. A Harris poll in 1988 showed 88 percent of the French were "disenchanted with politics." Sixty-one percent believed politicians to be indecisive; 68 percent believed that governments had failed to solve their problems; 20 percent claimed to have confidence in politicians; 40 percent had more confidence in business leaders.[30]

In 1597 William Shakespeare published these complacent lines:

This happy breed of men, this little world, . . .
This blessed plot, this earth, this realm, this England.

Forty-six years later, the blessed plot was immersed in civil war. Possibly each country, in each era, is inclined to paper over its problems. Shakespeare's "blessed plot," and Reagan's "morning in America" share a common origin in self-deception. Flaws are difficult to discern; they rarely spring up overnight, and thus are not liable to solution within the reign of a single "hero." As Carson McCullers wrote in *The Ballad of the Sad Café*:

There are great changes, but these changes are brought about bit by bit, in simple steps which in themselves do not appear to be important.[31]

Without durable political organizations, America must depend upon heroes—event-making or eventful as the case may be. Without organizations to recruit them, American political heroes are becoming scarce. They are becoming scarce because the institutions of American government do not encourage their entry. But even if politicians were willing to make tough choices, that is, choices with a

view toward the less than immediate future, the institutional incapacity would obviate almost all of their efforts.[32]

If, as Dr. Johnson said, second marriage is evidence of the triumph of hope over experience, American politics is testimony to the
triumph of faith over evidence.

Notes

Chapter 1   Introduction

1. Alan Ehrenhalt, *The United States of Ambition: Politicians, Power, and the Pursuit of Office* (New York: Random House, 1991), p. 10.
2. Russell J. Dalton, *Citizen Politics in Western Democracies* (Chatham, N.J.: Chatham House, 1988), p. 58.
3. Ehrenhalt, *The United States of Ambition*, p. 9.
4. Arthur Seldon, *Capitalism* (Oxford, England, and Cambridge, Mass.: Basil Blackwell, 1990), pp. 231–32.
5. Thomas Hobbes, *Leviathan*, 1651 (New York: Collier Books, 1963), p. 22.
6. Roberto Michels, *Political Parties: A Sociological Study of the Oligarchical Tendencies of Modern Democracies*, 1915, repr. (New York: Free Press, 1962), p. 70.
7. Ehrenhalt, *The United States of Ambition*, pp. 18–19.
8. Ibid., p. 258.
9. Ibid., p. 36.
10. David Broder, "A Minor Triumph: Democrats Finally Take a Policy Stand," syndicated column, 24 September 1989.
11. Samuel P. Huntington, *American Politics: The Promise of Disharmony* (Cambridge, Mass.: Harvard U. Press, 1981), p. 42.
12. Ibid., pp. 43–44.
13. Source: Gallup International Research Institutes, National Opinion Research Center, 1987–88.
14. Sidney Verba, et al., *Elites and the Idea of Equality* (Cambridge, Mass.: Harvard U. Press, 1987). pp. 85–86.
15. Richard Rose, "Presidents and Prime Ministers," in Christian Soe, ed., *Comparative Politics, 91/92* (Guilford, Mass.: Dushkin, 1991), p. 120.

16. Richard Rose, *The Postmodern President: The White Meets the World* (Chatham, N.J.: Chatham House, 1988).

17. Paul E. Peterson and Mark Rom, "Lower Taxes, More Spending, and Budget Deficits," in Charles O. Jones, ed., *The Reagan Legacy* (Chatham, N.J.: Chatham House, 1988), p. 238.

18. Paul J. Quirk, "Domestic Policy: Divided Government and Cooperative Presidential Leadership," in Colin Campbell, S.J., and Bert A. Rockman, *The Bush Presidency* (Chatham, N.J.: Chatham House, 1991), p. 69.

19. Rose, "Presidents and Prime Ministers," p. 71.

20. Theodore J. Lowi, *The Personal President* (Ithaca, N.Y.: Cornell U. Press, 1985), p. 154.

21. George C. Edwards III, *At the Margins* (New Haven, Conn.: Yale U. Press, 1989).

22. Lester G. Seligman and Cary R. Covington, *The Coalitional Presidency* (Chicago: Dorsey Press, 1989), p. 30.

23. C. Calvin MacKenzie, "Partisan Presidential Leadership: The President's Appointees," in L. Sandy Maisel, ed., *The Parties Respond: Changes in the American Party System* (Boulder, Colo.: Westview Press, 1990), p. 288.

24. Joseph LaPalombara, *Democracy Italian Style* (New Haven, Conn.: Yale U. Press, 1987), p. 210.

25. C. Calvin MacKenzie, "Partisan Presidential Leadership: The President's Appointees," in Maisel, ed., *The Parties Respond*, p. 288.

26. Hugo Young, "Margaret Thatcher—Brought Down by Her Own Strengths," *Manchester Guardian Weekly*, 2 December 1990, p. 4.

27. Ehrenhalt, *The United States of Ambition*, pp. 259, 264.

28. Hugh Bone, "An Introduction to the Senate Policy Committees," *American Political Science Review*, 50 (1956), p. 342, cited in Donald C. Baumer, "An Update on the Senate Democratic Policy Committee," *PS: Political Science and Politics*, XXIV (1991): 174.

29. Baumer, "An Update on the Senate," p. 174.

30. George Reedy, *The U.S. Senate* (New York: Crown, 1986), p. 12. Cited in Baumer, "An Update on the Senate," p. 174.

31. "Richard Neustadt Says Bush Team Is Able on Military and Foreign Affairs, AWOL on the Home Front," *Public Affairs Report*, May 1991, p. 7.

32. Lowi, *The Personal President*, p. xi.

33. Ibid., p. 115.

34. George C. Edwards III and Stephen J. Wayne, *Presidential Leadership*, 2d ed. (New York: St. Martins, 1990), p. 99.

35. Ibid., p. 97.

36. Michael Novak, *Choosing Our King* (New York: Macmillan, 1974), p. 3.

37. James David Barber, *The Presidential Character* (Englewood Cliffs, N.J.: Prentice-Hall, 1977), p. 4.

38. Reeves, Op. Cit.

39. Robert, E. Denton, Jr., *The Symbolic Dimensions of the American Presidency* (Prospect Heights, Ill.: Waverly Press, 1982), p. 52.

40. Mort Rosenblum, *Mission to Civilize* (New York: Doubleday, 1988), p. 19.

41. *Paris-Match*, 27 Janvier 1983, p. 78. The ranking is: Catherine Deneuve, Raquel Welch, Claudia Cardinale, Caroline de Monaco, Sophia Loren, Brigitte Bardot, Miou-Miou, Isabelle Adjani, Nathalie Baye, Jane Fonda, Dorothée, Jane Birkin, Sylvie Vartan, Isabelle Huppert, Sue Hellen, Christine Ockrent, Denise Fabre, Edith Cresson, and Anémone.

42. *Le Canard Enchaine,* a satirical French newspaper, explained that Englishmen suffer from "too many years in all-male boarding schools."
43. James W. Ceaser, "Political Parties—Declining, Stabilizing, or Resurging," in Anthony King, ed., *The New American Political System* (Washington, D.C.: AEI Press, 1991), p. 112.
44. Elaine Ciulla Kamark, "Structure as Strategy: Presidential Nominating Politics in the Post-Reform Era," in Maisel, ed., *The Parties Respond,* pp. 160–186.
45. Robin Toner, "Identity Is Central to Debate as Democrats Prepare for '92," *New York Times,* 21 May 1991, p. 1.
46. Ross Baker, "Democratic Weakness Stems from Their Strength," syndicated column, 27 May 1991.
47. Herbert Gans, *Middle American Individualism* (New York: Free Press, 1988), p. 39.

Chapter 2 Inventing the People

1. I wish I could claim authorship of this marvelous phrase, but Edmund S. Morgan beat me to it. (*Inventing the People* [New York: W. W. Norton, 1988]).
2. Richard Pipes, *The Russian Revolution* (New York: Alfred A. Knopf, 1990), pp. 131–33.
3. Ibid., p. 131.
4. Quoted in Georgie Ann Geyer, *Guerilla Prince* (Boston: Little, Brown, 1991), p. 129.
5. James A. Morone, *The Democratic Wish* (New York: Basic Books, 1990), pp. 114–15.
6. Ibid., pp. 83, 334.
7. Morgan, *Inventing the People,* p. 39. Italics mine.
8. James MacGregor Burns, *Leadership* (New York: Harper & Row, 1978), p. 396.
9. David Broder, "Strong Parties Could Revive Democracy," syndicated column, 4 June 1991.
10. Janos Kadar, address to the Hungarian National Assembly, 11 May 1957, quoted in Fred Willhoite, *Power and Governments* (Pacific Grove, Calif.: Duxbury, 1988), p. 105.
11. Mona Charen, syndicated column, 3 March 1989.
12. *New York Times,* 12 October 1988, p. A6.
13. Debra J. Saunders, "Voters Understand Democrats All Too Well," *Seattle Post-Intelligencer,* 27 June 1991, p. B1.
14. Max Weber, "Politics as a Vocation," in H. H. Gerth and C. Wright Mills, eds., *From Max Weber* (New York: Oxford U. Press, 1958), p. 83.
15. Morgan, *Inventing the People,* pp. 13, 38.
16. See Kay Lawson, "When Linkage Fails," in Lawson and Peter H. Merkl, eds., *When Parties Fail* (Princeton, N.J.: Princeton U. Press, 1988), p. 16.
17. Thomas R. Dye and Harmon Zeigler, *The Irony of Democracy* (Pacific Grove, Calif.: Brooks, Cole, 1988), p. 205.
18. Joseph A. Schlesinger and Mildred Schlesinger, "The Reaffirmation of a Multiparty System in France," *American Political Science Review* 84 (1990): 1077.

19. John Keeler, "Opening the Window for Reform: Mandates, Crises, and Extraordinary Policymaking," American Political Science Association, 1990.

20. Robert Harmel and Kenneth Janda, *Parties and Their Environments* (New York: Longman, 1982), p. 29. See also Janda, "A Comparative Analysis of Party Organizations: The United States, Europe, and the World," in William J. Crotty, ed., *The Party Symbol* (San Francisco: W. H. Freeman, 1980), pp. 339–58. Janda's data ended in 1962, allowing him to conclude that British political parties were not much different from American ones. Janda has the British Labour Party at –3.5 (maximum left is –5.0), the British Conservative Party at –0.75, the U.S. Democratic Party at –1.5, and the U.S. Republican Party at 2.00 (maximum right is 4.0). These data are, of course, no longer accurate, since they describe a period before the American parties were reformed, and before Margaret Thatcher was elected leader of the British Conservative Party.

21. William J. Crotty, *Comparative Political Parties* (Washington, D.C.: American Political Science Association, 1985), p. 2. Given that the Japanese Liberal Democratic Party has ruled for three decades, and the opposition has been, variously, organizationally bereft and increasingly moderate, the "consensus politics" of Japan probably place its parties between the totally vacuous American ones and the more coherent European ones. See Hans J. Baerwald, *Party Politics in Japan* (Boston: Allen and Unwin, 1986).

22. Richard Rose, *Do Parties Make a Difference?* (Chatham, N.J.: Chatham House, 1984), p. 183.

23. Paul E. Peterson and Mark Rom, "Lower Taxes, More Spending, and Budget Deficits," in Charles O. Jones, ed., *The Reagan Legacy* (Chatham, N.J.: Chatham House, 1988), p. 220.

24. Ibid., p. 214.

25. Martin Wattenberg, *The Rise of Candidate-Centered Politics* (Cambridge, Mass: Harvard U. Press, 1991), p. 114.

26. Kevin Phillips, *The Politics of Rich and Poor* (New York: Random House, 1990).

27. Ibid., p. 241.

28. Los Angeles: Times-Mirror Center for the People and the Press, 19 September 1990.

29. Frank Levy, *Dollars and Dreams* (New York: Russell Sage, 1987).

30. Ibid., p. 14, italics mine.

31. Gini coefficients measure inequality in income distribution. The numbers represent degrees of deviation from the line of "perfect equality," hence, the larger the number the greater the inequality.

32. Levy, *Dollars and Dreams*, p. 16.

33. Joseph A. Pechman, *Who Pays Taxes, 1965–85* (Washington, D.C.: Brookings Institution, 1985).

34. Peterson and Rom, "Lower Taxes, More Spending," p. 221.

35. Thomas R. Dye and Harmon Zeigler, *The Irony of Democracy* (Pacific Heights, Calif.: Brooks, Cole, 1990), p. 99.

36. Peterson and Lom, "Lower Taxes, More Spending," p. 227.

37. Russell J. Dalton, *Citizen Politics in Western Democracies* (Chatham, N.J.: Chatham House, 1988).

38. Martin Wattenberg, "The Hollow Realignment: Partisan Change in a Candidate-Centered Era." Paper presented at the annual meeting of the American Political Science Association, New Orleans, 1985.

39. Morris P. Fiorina, "The Reagan Years: Turning to the Right or Groping Toward the Middle," in Barry Cooper, Allan Kornberg, and William Mishler, eds., *The Resurgence of Conservatism in Anglo-American Democracies* (Durham, N.C.: Duke U. Press, 1988), pp. 430–60.
40. Ivor Crewe, "Has the Electorate Turned Thatcherite?" in Robert Skidelsky, ed., *Thatcherism* (London: Chatto and Windus, 1988), pp. 25–50. Anthony King reminds us that, despite Mrs. Thatcher's frightening public presence, she is cordial in personal relationships. See King, "Margaret Thatcher as Political Leader," in Skidelsky, pp. 51–64.
41. Richard Rose, *Politics in England* (Boston: Little, Brown, 1989), p. 64.
42. Ibid., p. 248.
43. *The Economist,* 17 November 1990, p. 14.
44. Ivor Crewe and Donald D. Searing, "Mrs. Thatcher's Crusade," in Barry Cooper, Allan Kornberg, and William Mishler, eds., *The Resurgence of Conservatism,* p. 286.
45. Ibid., p. 298.
46. Fiorina, "The Reagan Years," pp. 436, 430.
47. Wattenberg, *The Rise of Candidate-Centered Politics,* pp. 123–24.
48. Richard G. Niemi, John Mueller, and Tom W. Smith, *American Public Opinion* (New York: Greenwood Press, 1989), p. 12.
49. Ibid., p. 35.
50. Warren E. Miller, "The Election of 1984 and the Future of American Politics," in Kay Lehman Schlozman, ed., *Elections in America* (Boston: Allen and Unwin, 1987), pp. 293–320.
51. Crewe, "*Has the Electorate Turned Thatcherite?*" in Robert Skidelsky, ed., *Thatcherism,* pp. 33–35.
52. See Edward Pearce, *The Quiet Rise of John Major* (London: Weidenfeld and Nicolson, 1991), and Andrew Tyrie, "John Major Rose to Power as a Prime Minister Without Fingerprints," *Public Affairs Report,* 3 May 1991, p. 9.
53. Cited in Robert Shepherd, *The Power Brokers: The Tory Party and Its Leaders* (London: Hutchinson, 1991), p. 187.
54. Wattenberg, *The Rise of Candidate-Centered Politics,* p. 73.
55. Herve Hamon and Patrick Rotman, *L'Effet Rocard* (Paris: Stock, 1980).
56. *Le Figaro,* 22 June 1989, p. 6.
57. See, for example, Alain Duhamel, *Les Habits Neufs de la Politique* (Paris: Flammarion, 1989).
58. Stuart A. Scheingold, *The Politics of Law and Order: Street Crime and Public Policy* (New York: Longman, 1984), pp. 77–79.
59. See Thomas R. Dye, and Harmon Zeigler, *The Irony of Democracy,* 7th ed., (Monterey, Calif.: Brooks, Cole, 1987), p. 176.
60. Dalton, *Citizen Politics in Western Democracies,* p. 25. See also Samuel Barnes and Max Kasse, *Political Action* (Beverly Hills, Calif.: Sage, 1979).
61. See Marie-France Toinet, "Abstention: le mythe de l'americanization," *Le Journal des Elections,* September–October 1989, pp. 19–21.
62. "Les Français Face au Malaise Politique," *Le Figaro,* 12 December 1990, p. 1.
63. See also Alain Duhamel, *Les Habits Neufs de la Politique.*
64. Jérôme Jaffré, "Le RPR Doute de Lui-Meme," *Les Journal des Elections,* June–July 1990, p. 16.
65. *Le Figaro,* 11 June 1989, p. 1.
66. Duhamel, *Les Habits,* p. 119.
67. *Le Figaro,* 12 December 1990, p. 6.

68. Robert Nisbet, *The Present Age* (New York: Harper and Row, 1988), p. 23.
69. James MacGregor Burns, *Leadership* (New York: Harper and Row, 1978), p. 322.
70. Walter Dean Burnham, "Foreword," to Michael Wattenberg, *The Decline of American Political Parties*, p. xiii.
71. Jérôme Jaffré, "France au centre, victoires socialistes," *Pouvoirs* 47 (1988): 169, 172.
72. Marianne Means, "Bona Fide Racist Is Just What GOP Doesn't Need," *Seattle Post-Intelligencer,* 29 August 1990, p. A7.
73. Apparently overlooked was Chirac's "cohabitation" as prime minister during Socialist President Mitterrand's first term.
74. Quoted in Richard Rose, *Politics in England,* p. 114.
75. Peter Brimelow and Leslie Spencer, "Ralph Nader, Inc.," *Forbes,* 17 September 1990, p. 118.
76. Murray Edelman, "Symbols and Political Quiescence," *American Political Science Review,* 80 (September 1960): 701.
77. Thomas R. Dye and Harmon Zeigler, *American Politics in the Media Age* (Pacific Grove, Calif.: Brooks, Cole, 1989), p. 30.
78. Gabriel Almond and Sidney Verba, *The Civic Culture* (Boston: Little, Brown, 1965), p. 245.
79. Robert A. Dahl, *Dilemmas of Pluralist Democracy* (New Haven, Conn.: Yale U. Press, 1982), p. 1.
80. James Madison, Federalist No. 10, in Alexander Hamilton, James Madison, and John Jay, *The Federalist Papers,* Rossiter, ed. (New York: The New American Library, 1961), p. 19.
81. Angus Campbell, Philip E. Converse, Warren E. Miller, and Donald E. Stokes, *The American Voter* (New York: Wiley, 1960), p. 328.
82. Paul S. Herrnson, *Party Campaigning in the 1980s* (Cambridge, Mass.: Harvard U. Press, 1988), p. 112.
83. Philippe C. Schmitter, "Still the Century of Corporatism?" *Review of Politics* 85 (January 1974): 104.
84. Graham Wilson, *Business and Politics* (Chatham, N.J.: Chatham House, 1985), p. 12.
85. John Keeler, *The Politics of Neocorporatism in France* (New York: Oxford U. Press, 1987).
86. Henry Kariel, *The Decline of American Pluralism* (Stanford, Calif.: Stanford U. Press, 1961), p. 74.
87. Harmon Zeigler and Wayne Peak, *Interest Groups in American Society,* 2d ed. (Englewood Cliffs, N.J.: Prentice-Hall, 1972), p. 2.
88. Mancur Olson, *The Logic of Collective Action: Public Goods and the Theory of Groups* (Cambridge, Mass.: Harvard U. Press, 1965), p. 61.
89. Robert Salisbury, "An Exchange Theory of Interest Groups," *Midwest Journal of Political Science* 12 (1969): 19.
90. Harmon Zeigler, *Pluralism, Corporatism, and Confucianism* (Philadelphia: Temple U. Press, 1988), p. 64; Lawrence Rothenberger, "Organizational Maintenance and the Retention Decision in Groups," *American Political Science Review* 82 (1988): 1130–52.
91. Terry Moe, *The Organization of Interests* (Chicago: U. of Chicago Press, 1980), p. 30.
92. Schmitter, "Still the Century of Corporatism?" pp. 85–131.
93. Donald M. Hancock, *West Germany: The Politics of Democratic Corporatism* (Chatham, N.J.: Chatham House, 1989), p. 131.

94. Peter Katzenstein, *Corporatism and Change: Austria, Switzerland and the Politics of Industry* (Ithaca, N.Y.: Cornell U. Press, 1984); Katzenstein, *Small States in World Markets* (Ithaca, N.Y.: Cornell U. Press, 1985).
95. Karel van Wolferen, *The Enigma of Japanese Power* (New York: Knopf, 1989), p. 81.
96. Katzenstein, *Corporatism and Change*, p. 84.

Chapter 3   Political Parties and the Obligation of Choice

1. Fred Riggs, "Comparative Politics and Political Parties," in William J. Crotty, ed., *Approaches to the Study of Party Organization* (Boston: Allyn and Bacon, 1968), p. 51.
2. Kay Lawson, *The Comparative Study of Political Parties* (New York: St. Martins, 1976), p. 3.
3. Theodore J. Lowi, *The Personal Presidency* (Ithaca, N.Y.: Cornell U. Press, 1985), p. 203.
4. James Reichley, "The Rise of National Parties," in John Chubb and Paul Peterson, eds., *New Directions in American Politics* (Washington, D.C.: Brookings Institution, 1985), p. 176.
5. Philip Williams, "Power and the Parties: The United States," in Vernon Bogdanor, ed., *Parties and Democracy in Britain and America* (New York: Praeger, 1984), p. 10.
6. James Bryce, *The American Commonwealth* (New York: Macmillan, 1895), vol. 1, p. 5; vol. 2, p. 293.
7. Warren E. Miller, "The Electorate's View of Parties," in L. Sandy Maisel, ed., *The Parties Respond: Changes in the American Party System* (Boulder, Colo.: Westview Press, 1990), pp. 97–115.
8. Morris P. Fiorina, "The Electorate in the Voting Booth," in Maisel, ed., *The Parties Respond*, p. 120.
9. Alistair M. Cole, "La France Unie? Francois Mitterrand," in John Gaffney, ed., *The French Presidential Elections of 1988* (Aldershot, England: Gower), pp. 81–100.
10. Russell Dalton, "The German Voter," in Gordon Smith, William E. Paterson, and Peter H. Merkl, eds., *Developments in West German Politics* (Durham, N.C.: Duke U. Press, 1989), pp. 99–121.
11. Fiorina, "The Electorate in the Voting Booth," in Maisel, ed., *The Parties Respond*, p. 122.
12. Austin Ranney, "Broadcasting, Narrowcasting, and Politics," in Anthony King, ed., *The New American Political System* (Washington, D.C.: AEI Press, 1991), p. 188.
13. Paul S. Herrnson, "Reemergent National Party Organizations," in Maisel, ed., *The Parties Respond*, p. 54.
14. Ibid.
15. Paul S. Herrnson, *Party Campaigning in the 1980s* (Cambridge, Mass.: Harvard U. Press, 1988), p. 86.
16. Gerald Pomper, "An American Epilogue," in Vernon Bogdanor, ed., *Parties and Democracy in Britain and America* (New York: Praeger, 1984), p. 274.
17. Herrnson, *Party Campaigning*, p. 86.
18. Ibid., p. 85.

19. Kazee and Thornberry, in a study of thirty-six congressional candidates that 61 percent were self-starters. However, half of them had also attended party sponsored seminars. Thus, the party organization might have pricked their interest. In no case, however, did a self-starter experience organizational assessment. See Thomas A. Kazee and Mary C. Thornberry, "Where's the Party? Congressional Candidate Recruitment and American Party Organizations," *Western Political Quarterly* 43 (1990): 48–56.
20. Herrnson, *Party Campaigning*, pp. 84ff.
21. Ibid., p. 122.
22. Frank J. Sorauf and Scott A. Wilson, "Campaigns and Money: A Changing Role for Political Parties?" in Maisel, ed., *The Parties Respond*, p. 203. Italics mine.
23. Paul S. Herrnson, "Reemergent National Party Organizations," p. 64.
24. Alan Ehrenhalt, *The United States of Ambition: Politicians, Power, and the Pursuit of Office* (New York: Random House, 1991), p. 106.
25. Cornelius P. Cotter, James L. Gibson, John F. Bibby, and Robert Huckshorn, *Party Organizations in American Politics* (New York: Praeger, 1984), pp. 28, 52.
26. David Mayhew, *Placing Parties in American Politics* (Princeton, N.J.: Princeton U. Press, 1986), pp. 19, 196.
27. Samuel C. Patterson, "The Persistence of State Parties," in Carle E. Van Horn, ed., *The State of the States* (Washington, D.C.; CQ Press, 1989), p. 165.
28. Mayhew, *Placing Parties*, p. 196. They are: Connecticut, Delaware, Illinois, Indiana, Kentucky, Maryland, Missouri, New Jersey, New York, Ohio, Pennsylvania, Rhode Island, and West Virginia.
29. Ehrenhalt, *The United States of Ambition*, p. 18.
30. Patterson, "The Persistence of State Parties," p. 167.
31. Charles L. Clapp, *The Job of the Congressman* (Washington, D.C.: Brookings Institution, 1963), p. 31.
32. Richard Fenno, *Home Style* (Boston: Little, Brown, 1978), p. 113.
33. Cited in James W. Ceaser, "Political Parties—Declining, Stabilizing, or Resurging," in Anthony King, ed., *The New American Political System* (Washington, D.C.: AEI Press, 1991), p. 121.
34. Barbara Sinclair, "House Majority Party Leadership in the Late 1980s," in Lawrence C. Dodd and Bruce I. Oppenheimer, eds., *Congress Reconsidered* (Washington, D.C.: CQ Press, 1989).
35. Ehrenhalt, *The United States of Ambition*, p. 241. See also Burton Loomis, *The New American Politician: Ambition, Entrepreneurship, and the Changing Face of Political Life* (New York: Basic Books, 1988), p. xvii.
36. See Sorauf and Wilson, "Campaigns and Money," pp. 187–203.
37. E. E. Schattschneider, *Party Government* (New York: Holt, Rinehart and Winston, 1942), pp. 64, 100.
38. William J. Keefe, *Parties, Politics, and Public Policy in America* (Washington, D.C.: CQ Press, 1991), p. 80.
39. *New York Times*, p. 1.
40. Austin Ranney, "Candidate Selection," in David Butler, Howard R. Penniman, and Austin Ranney, *Democracy at the Polls: A Comparative Study of Competitive National Elections* (Washington, D.C.: American Enterprise Institute, 1981), p. 96.

41. Donald R. Matthews, "Selecting Chief Executives in Norway and the U.S.," in Mattei Dogan, ed., *Pathways to Power: Selecting Rulers in Pluralist Democracies* (Boulder, Colo.: Westview Press, 1989), p. 93.
42. Larry Sabato, *The Party's Just Begun* (Glenview, Ill.: Scott, Foresman, 1988); Paul Herrnson, "Reemergent National Party Organizations," pp. 41–66.
43. L. Sandy Maisel, Linda L. Fowler, Ruth S. Jones, and Walter J. Stone, "The Naming of Candidates: Recruitment of Emergence," in Maisel, ed., *The Parties Respond*, pp. 137–59.
44. Austin Ranney, "Candidate Selection," in Butler, Penniman, and Ranney, "Broadcasting," p. 86.
45. Quoted in Martin Wattenberg, *The Rise of Candidate-Centered Politics* (Cambridge, Mass.: Harvard U. Press, 1991), p. 33.
46. Ibid., p. 33.
47. Theodore Lowi, *The Personal Presidency*, p. 87.
48. Bryce, *The American Commonwealth*, vol. 2, p. 77.
49. Sabato, *The Party's Just Begun*, pp. 232–33.
50. Quoted in David Broder, "Take It From Those Who Know Best: Congress Is a Wreck," *Washington Post National Weekly Edition*, 14–20 January 1991, p. 24.
51. David E. Price, *Bringing Back the Parties* (Washington, D.C.: CQ Press, 1984), pp. 53–54.
52. Lowi, *The Personal Presidency*, p. 127.
53. Ceaser, "Political Parties," p. 122.
54. Stephen Kinzer, *Blood of Brothers* (New York: Putnam, 1991), p. 360.
55. David W. Brady, "Coalitions in the U.S. Congress," in Maisel, ed., *The Parties Respond*, p. 249.
56. Ibid., p. 256.
57. W. R. Hearst, Jr., "The U.S. Banks: The Billion Dollar Mess," syndicated column, 16 January 1991.
58. *New York Times*, 16 January 1991, p. 18.
59. Sabato, *The Party's Just Begun*, p. 134.
60. Times Mirror Center for The People and The Press, "The People, The Press, and Politics, 1990," pp. 2–5.
61. Wattenberg, *The Rise of Candidate-Centered Politics*, p. 38.
62. L. Sandy Maisel, "The Evolution of Political Parties: Toward the 21st Century," in Maisel, ed., *The Parties Respond*, p. 321.
63. Ibid., p. 35.
64. David S. Broder, "Broke at a Bad Time: Impoverished Parties Are Gearing Up for a Costly Contest," *Washington Post*, 2 January 1991, p. 1.
65. Norman J. Ornstein, Thomas E. Mann, and Michael J. Malbin, *Vital Statistics on Congress, 1989–1990* (Washington, D.C.: CQ Press, 1990), pp. 84–85.
66. Jürg Steiner, *European Democracies*, 2d ed. (New York: Longman, 1991), p. 76.
67. Frank J. Sorauf and Paul Allen Beck, *Party Politics in America*, 6th ed. (Glenview, Ill.: Scott, Foresman, 1988), pp. 132–33.
68. Gary C. Jacobson, *The Politics of Congressional Elections* (Boston: Little, Brown, 1987), p. 19.
69. Ibid., pp. 19–20.
70. Herrnson, *Party Campaigning in the 1980s*, p. 88.

71. Ibid., p. 86.
72. Gary C. Jacobson, *The Electoral Origins of Divided Government* (Boulder, Colo.: Westview Press, 1990), p. 15.
73. Jacobson, *The Politics of Congressional Elections*, p. 71.
74. David T. Cannon and David J. Sousa, "Party System Change and Political Career Structures in the U.S. Congress," American Political Science Association, 1990, p. 17.
75. Ibid., p. 18.
76. Jacobson, *The Electoral Origins of Divided Government*, p. 61.
77. Jacobson, *The Politics of Congressional Elections*, pp. 59, 71.
78. Albert D. Cover, "One Good Term Deserves Another: The Advantages of Incumbency in Congressional Elections," *American Journal of Political Science* 21 (1977): 536.
79. Leon Epstein, *Political Parties in the American Mold* (Madison, Wis.: U. of Wisconsin Press, 1986), p. 213.
80. David Broder, "A Minor Triumph: Democrats Finally Make a Policy Stand," syndicated column, 24 September 1989.
81. Wattenberg, *The Rise of Candidate-Centered Politics;* Wattenberg, "From a Partisan to a Candidate Centered Electorate," in King, ed., *The New American Political System*, pp. 139–76.
82. Ehrenhalt, *The United States of Ambition*, p. 116.
83. Ceaser, "Political Parties," p. 122.
84. Ehrenhalt, *The United States of Ambition*, p. 116.
85. Keefe, *Parties, Politics, and Public Policy*, p. 8.
86. David S. Broder, "Gutless Government," *Washington Post Weekly*, 6 November 1989, p. 4.
87. Bryce, *The American Commonwealth*, vol. 2, p. 79. Italics mine.
88. Ibid.
89. Ceaser, "Political Parties," p. 129.
90. Ibid., p. 130.
91. Wattenberg, *The Rise of Candidate-Centered Politics*, pp. 55–59.
92. Ibid., p. 35.
93. Rhodes Cook, "The Nominating Process," in Michael Nelson, ed., *The Elections of 1988* (Washington, D.C.: CQ Press, 1989), p. 43.
94. Ceaser, "Political Parties," p. 137.
95. Sabato, *The Party's Just Begun*, p. 133.
96. William Crotty, *Comparative Political Parties* (Washington, D.C.: American Political Science Association, 1985), p. 1.
97. Walter Dean Burnham, "The Onward March of Party Decomposition," in Richard G. Niemi and Herbert F. Weisberg, eds., *Controversies in American Voting Behavior* (New York: W. H. Freeman, 1976), p. 431.
98. Herrnson, *Party Campaigning in the 1980s*, p. 121.
99. Ehrenhalt, *The United States of Ambition*, p. 256.
100. Sorauf and Wilson, "Campaigns and Money," p. 199.
101. Bryce, *The American Commonwealth*, vol. 2., p. 81.
102. E. E. Schattschneider, *Party Government* (New York: Holt, Rinehart, and Winston, 1942), p. 64.
103. William J. Keefe, *Parties, Politics, and Public Policy in America* (Washington, D.C.: CQ Press, 1991), pp. 295–96.
104. Richard Rose, *The Postmodern President*, 2d ed. (Chatham, N.J.: Chatham House, 1991), p. 118.

Chapter 4 Party and Recruitment

1. Leon Epstein, *Political Parties in Western Democracies* (New York: Praeger, 1967), p. 9.
2. Austin Ranney, *Pathways to Parliament* (Madison, Wis.: U. of Wisconsin Press, 1965).
3. David Denver, "Britain: Centralized Parties, Decentralized Selection," in Michael Gallagher and Michael Marsh, eds., *Candidate Selection in Comparative Perspective: The Secret Garden of Politics* (Beverly Hills, Calif.: Sage, 1988), p. 53.
4. Jeffrey Archer, *First Among Equals* (London: Hodder and Stoughton, 1984), pp. 164–69.
5. Angelo Panebianco, *Political Parties: Organization and Power* (Cambridge: Cambridge U. Press, 1988), p. 140.
6. Ibid., p. 140.
7. Ibid., p. 94.
8. J. A. G. Griffith and Michael Ryle, *Parliament: Functions, Practice and Procedures* (London: Sweet and Maxwell, 1989), p. 49.
9. Ibid., p. 50.
10. Donald D. Searing, "Junior Ministers and Ministerial Careers," in Mattei Dogan, ed., *Pathways to Power: Selecting Rulers in Pluralist Democracies* (Boulder, Colo.: Westview Press, 1989), p. 142.
11. Ibid., p. 151.
12. Stuart McDonald, "Political Ambition in Britain: A Dynamic Analysis of Parliamentary Careers," Ph.D. Dissertation, U. of Michigan, 1987. Cited in Searing, "Junior Ministers," pp. 165–66.
13. Anthony Trollope, *Phineas Finn* (New York: Oxford U. Press, 1973), p. 47. Originally published in 1869. Cited in Searing, "Junior Ministers," p. 44.
14. Kurt Sontheimer, *The Government and Politics of West Germany* (New York: Praeger, 1973), p. 95.
15. Panebianco, *Political Parties*, p. 116.
16. Geoffrey Roberts, "The German Federal Republic: The Two Lane Route to Bonn," in Gallagher and Marsh, eds., *Candidate Selection*, p. 105.
17. Ibid., p. 100.
18. Ibid., p. 106.
19. Ibid., p. 108.
20. Jean-Louis Thiébault, "France: The Impact of Electoral System Change," in Gallagher and Marsh, eds., *Candidate Selection*, p. 74.
21. Jean Michel-Belorgey, *La Politique Sociale* (Paris: Seghers, 1976), pp. 33–47.
22. Henry W. Ehrmann, *Politics in France* (Boston: Little, Brown, 1983), p. 133.
23. P. J. O'Rourke, *Parliament of Whores* (New York: Atlantic Monthly Press, 1991), p. xiv.
24. Richard Rose, "Electoral Systems: A Question of Degree or of Principle?" in Arend Lijphart and Bernard Grofman, eds., *Choosing an Electoral System* (New York: Praeger, 1984), p. 81.
25. Jean-Francois Kesler, *L'ENA, La société* (Paris: Berger-Levrault, 1985).
26. Pierre Bordieu, *La Noblesse d'Etat: Grand Ecoles et Esprit de Corps* (Paris: Editions de Minuit, 1989), p. 149.

27. Mattei Dogan, "Career Pathways to the Cabinet in France," in Dogan, ed., *Pathways to Power*, pp. 43–44.
28. Richard Rose, "Electoral Systems," p. 97.
29. See Samuel Kernell, *Going Public: New Strategies of Presidential Leadership* (Washington, D.C.: CQ Press, 1986).
30. Richard Rose, "Electoral Systems," p. 109.
31. Ibid., p. 102.
32. Frederick Spotts and Theodore Weiser, *Italy: A Difficult Democracy* (Cambridge: Cambridge U. Press, 1986), p. 5.
33. Ibid., p. 6.
34. Panebianco, *Political Parties*, p. 123.
35. Douglas A. Wertman, "Italy: Local Involvement, Central Control," in Gallagher and Marsh, eds., *Candidate Selection*, p. 152.
36. See *New Statesman and Nation*, "The Intelligent Person's Guide to Electoral Reform," April 1990.
37. Samuel H. Barnes, *Representation in Italy* (Chicago: U. of Chicago Press, 1977), p. 5.
38. Joseph LaPalombara, *Democracy, Italian Style* (New Haven, Conn.: Yale U. Press, 1987), p. 216.
39. Bradley M. Richardson and Scott C. Flanagan, *Politics in Japan* (Boston: Little, Brown, 1984), p. 100.
40. Michio Muramatsu and Ellis S. Krauss, "Dominant Party and Social Coalitions in Japan," in T. J. Pempel, ed., *Uncommon Democracies: The One-Party Dominant Regimes* (Ithaca, N.Y.: Cornell U. Press, 1990), p. 289.
41. Rei Shiratori, "Japan: Localism, Factionalism, Personalism," in Gallagher and Marsh, eds., *Candidate Selection*, p. 172.
42. B. C. Koh, *Japan's Administrative Elite* (Berkeley, Calif.: U. of California Press, 1989), p. 139.
43. Hiromitsu Katoaka, "The Making of a Japanese Cabinet," in Dogan, ed., *Pathways to Power*, p. 169.
44. Thomas R. Dye and Harmon Zeigler, *The Irony of Democracy*, 8th ed. (Pacific Heights, Calif.: Brooks, Cole, 1990), p. 105.
45. Byron Shafer, *Quiet Revolution* (New York: Russell Sage, 1983), p. 531.
46. William C. Adams, "As New Hampshire Goes . . . ," in Gary R. Oren and Nelson W. Polsby, eds., *Media and Momentum: The New Hampshire Primary and Nomination Politics* (Chatham, N.J.: Chatham House, 1987), p. 55.
47. Austin Ranney, *Curing the Mischiefs of Faction* (Berkeley, Calif.: U. of California Press, 1975), p. 206.
48. Leon Epstein, *Political Parties in the American Mold* (Madison, Wis.: U. of Wisconsin Press, 1986), p. 99.
49. Theodore Lowi, *The Personal President* (Ithaca, N.Y.: Cornell U. Press, 1985), pp. 72–75.
50. Ibid., p. 73.
51. David Broder, "Yeutter will be GOP Chairman in Name Only," syndicated column of 23 January 1991.
52. Byron Shafer, *Quiet Revolution*, p. 525.
53. Ronald Brownstein, "Hollywood's Hot Love: Politics," *New York Times*, 6 January 1991, p. 16.
54. John W. Wright, ed., *The Universal Almanac* (New York: Andrews and McKeel, 1991), p. 205. On the other hand, Americans do admire some professions: clergymen, doctors, professors. The French, apparently,

loathe everyone: 35 percent have confidence in CEOs, 17 percent have confidence in intellectuals, 16 percent have confidence in politicians. See Bertrand Pecquerie, "La Democratie Consumeriste," *Journal des Elections,* September–October 1989, p. 7.

55. Ibid.
56. Len Sherman, *The Good, the Bad, and the Famous: Celebrities Playing Politics* (New York: Lyle Stuart, 1990), p. 145.
57. Russell J. Dalton, *Politics in West Germany* (Boston: Little, Brown, 1989), p. 181.
58. Harmon Zeigler and William Haltom, "More Bad News About the News," *Public Opinion,* May–June 1989, pp. 50–52.
59. Fred Graham, *Happy Talk* (New York: W. W. Norton, 1990), p. 78.
60. Michael A. Milburn, *Persuasion and Politics: The Social Psychology of Public Opinion* (Monterey, Calif.: Brooks-Cole, forthcoming).
61. Fred Graham, *Happy Talk: Confessions of TV Newsman* (New York: W. W. Norton, 1990), pp. 214–19.
62. Jonathan Yardley, "Hurray for Washington," *Washington Post National Weekly Addition,* 7–13 January 1991, p. 36 (review of Ronald Brownstein, *The Power and the Glitter: The Hollywood-Washington Connection.* [New York: Pantheon, 1990]).
63. Ronald Brownstein, *The Power and the Glitter.*

Chapter 5   The Institutional Structure of Choice

1. James G. March and Johan P. Olsen, *Rediscovering Institutions: The Organizational Basis of Politics* (New York: Free Press, 1989), p. 159.
2. George C. Edwards III and Stephen J. Wayne, *Presidential Leadership* (New York: St. Martins, 1990), p. 316.
3. Richard Rose, *The Postmodern President,* 2d ed. (Chatham, N.J.: Chatham House, 1991), p. 78.
4. T. J. Pempel, *Policy and Politics in Japan* (Philadelphia: Temple U. Press, 1982), pp. 38–39.
5. It is also used in Ireland for parliamentary by-elections (to fill vacancies), and for the election of the president, a ceremonial position.
6. The *D'Hondt formula,* used in Europe, except for Scandinavia and Italy; the *Saint-Laque* method, used in Scandinavia; and the *single transferable vote,* used in Ireland and in the Australian Senate. Voters rank order individual candidates; votes not needed for candidates who have already made the minimum quota are transferred to the next candidate until the seats are filled. Under the *largest remainder* scheme, a quota of votes is established, which party lists must achieve in order to be guaranteed a seat. The number of votes cast is divided into the number of seats to fill; parties failing to meet the quota are assigned "remainders." For example, if the quota is 5,000, and party A gets 8,200 votes, its "remainder" is 3,200 votes. If party B gets 6,100 votes, its "remainder" is 1,100. If party C gets only 3,000 votes, its remainder remains at 3,000; if party D gets 2,700 it, too, keeps all the votes for a remainder. Since two seats were won without remainders, there are two remaining ones to be allocated. Party A gets another one, because it has the largest remainder. But party B, which finished second, does not, since its remainder is less than that

of party C. Party C, which finished third (with only about half as many votes as party B), gets the other vote. Italy uses this system.

7. Arend Lijphart, *Democracies: Patterns of Majoritarian and Consensus Government in Twenty-One Countries* (New Haven, Conn.: Yale U. Press, 1984), pp. 160–63.

8. See *New Statesman and Nation*, "The Intelligent Person's Guide to Electoral Reform," April 1990, p. 2.

9. George Tsebelis, "Nested Games: The Cohesion of French Electoral Coalitions," *British Journal of Political Science* 18 (April 1988): 145–70.

10. In the American primary elections, no *strategic* withdrawals occur since the primary and general elections are separated by months, but in France there is only a week in which to maneuver. And since the same rules (first past the post) apply in both primary and general elections, also different from France, the comparison becomes even more specious. Add that the American party organizations cannot induce withdrawal, and the analogy becomes ludicrous.

11. T. J. Pempel, "Conclusion," in T. J. Pempel, ed., *Uncommon Democracies: The One-Party Dominant Regimes* (Ithaca, N.Y.: Cornell U. Press, 1990), p. 336.

12. Douglas W. Rae, *The Political Consequences of Electoral Laws* (New Haven, Conn.: Yale U. Press, 1967).

13. Joseph A. Schlesinger and Mildred Schlesinger, "The Reaffirmation of a Multiparty System in France," *American Political Science Review* 84 (1990): 1086.

14. Ibid., p. 1088.

15. Philip E. Converse and Roy Pierce, *Political Representation in France* (Cambridge, Mass.: Harvard U. Press, 1986).

16. Ibid., p. 349.

17. Clearly, he meant plurality. See Maurice Duverger, *Political Parties* (New York: Wiley, 1963), p. 217.

18. Eric M. Uslaner, "Splitting Image: Partisan Affiliations in Canada's 'Two Political Worlds,' " *American Journal of Political Science* 34 (1990): 961–81.

19. Gary Marks, *Union in Politics: Britain, Germany, and the United States in the Nineteenth and Early Twentieth Centuries* (Princeton, N.J.: Princeton U. Press, 1989), p. 218.

20. Ibid., p. 219.

21. M. Kent Jennings, Jan W. van Deth, et al., *Continuities in Political Action* (New York: Walter de Gruyter, 1990), p. 210.

22. Ibid., p. 209.

23. John D. Huber, "Values and Partisanship in Left-Right Orientations: Measuring Ideology," *European Journal of Political Research* 17 (1989): 606.

24. W. Russell Neuman, *The Paradox of Mass Politics: Knowledge and Opinion in the American Electorate* (Cambridge, Mass.: Harvard U. Press, 1986), pp. 15–17. Italics mine.

25. Donald Granberg and Sören Holmberg, "The Berelson Paradox Reconsidered," *Public Opinion Quarterly* 54 (1990): 548.

26. Richard Rose, "Electoral Systems: A Question of Degree or of Principle?" in Arend Lijphart and Bernard Grofman, eds., *Choosing an Electoral System* (New York: Praeger, 1984), pp. 73–89.

27. Ibid., p. 80.

28. I am grateful to John Keeler for bringing this interpretation to my attention.

29. Jürg Steiner, *European Democracies* (New York: Longman, 1986), p. 103.
30. Arthur B. Gunlicks, "Between Elections in West Germany, 1976–80 and 1980–83," in Karl H. Cerny, ed., *Germany at the Polls* (Durham, N.C.: Duke U. Press, 1990).
31. David P. Conradt, "The Electorate, 1980–83," in Cerny, ed., *Germany at the Polls*, pp. 44–45.
32. See note 6 for a detailed explanation.
33. Douglas A. Wertman, "Italy: Local involvement, Central Control," in Michael Gallagher and Michael Marsh, *Candidate Selection in Comparative Perspective: The Secret Garden of Politics* (Beverly Hills, Calif.: Sage, 1988), p. 146.
34. See John Keeler, "Opening the Window for Reform: Mandates, Crises and Extraordinary Policymaking," American Political Science Association, 1990, pp. 67–69; and Rein Taagepera and Matthew Shugart, *Seats and Votes*, p. 1.
35. Taagepera and Shugart, *Seats and Votes*, p. 235.

Chapter 6   An Exploration of Electoral Change

1. Russell J. Dalton, *Citizen Politics in Western Democracies* (Chatham, N.J.: Chatham House, 1988), p. 172.
2. Richard Rose, *The Postmodern President*, 2d ed. (Chatham, N.J.: Chatham House, 1991), p. 163.
3. John Keeler, "Opening the Window for Reform: Mandates, Crises and Extraordinary Policymaking," American Political Science Association, 1990, p. 39.
4. By using both votes and seats, Keeler demonstrates that the Thatcher electoral mandate was actually exceeded only by one other government, the Labour government of 1945. See Keeler, "Opening the Window for Reform," p. 38.
5. Isaac Kramnick, ed., *Is Britain Dying?* (Ithaca, N.Y.: Cornell U. Press, 1979), p. 7.
6. Cited in Peter Jenkins, *Mrs. Thatcher's Revolution* (Cambridge, Mass.: Harvard U. Press, 1988), pp. 48–49.
7. See Bo Svärlick and Ivor Crewe, *Decade of Dealignment* (Cambridge: Cambridge U. Press, 1983), p. 8.
8. Ibid., p. 17.
9. Voters who died between 1974 and 1979 were more conservative than those who entered the electorate for the first time.
10. Ivor Crewe, "Has the Electorate Become Thatcherite?" in Robert Skidelsky, ed., *Thatcherism* (London: Chatto and Windus, 1988), p. 32.
11. Ivor Crewe and Donald D. Searing, "Mrs. Thatcher's Crusade," in Barry Cooper, Allan Kornberg, and William Mishler, eds., *The Resurgence of Conservatism in Anglo-American Democracies* (Durham, N.C.: Duke U. Press, 1988), p. 286.
12. Crewe, "Has the Electorate Become Thatcherite?" p. 49.
13. Henk Overbeek, *Global Capitalism and National Decline* (London: Unwin Hyman, 1990), p. 211.
14. Presidential approval ratings invariably skyrocket immediately after an international threat.

15. Evel W. Elliott, *Issues and Elections* (Boulder, Colo.: Westview Press, 1989), p. 81.
16. Ibid., p. 103.
17. D. S. Bell and Byron Criddle, *The French Socialist Party: Resurgence and Victory* (Oxford, England: Clarendon Press, 1984), p. 103.
18. Howard Machin and Vincent Wright, "Why Mitterrand: The French Presidential Elections of April–May, 1981," *West European Politics* 5 (1982): 22.
19. *Le Point*, 25 May 1981, p. 1.
20. Roy Pierce and Thomas R. Rochon, in Howard Penniman, ed., *France at the Polls, 1981 and 1986* (Durham, N.C.: Duke U. Press, 1988), p. 185.
21. Ibid.
22. Philip E. Converse and Roy Pierce, *Political Representation in France* (Cambridge, Mass.: Harvard U. Press, 1986), p. 128.
23. Paul Hainsworth, "A Majority for the President: The French Left and the Presidential and Parliamentary Elections of 1981," *Parliamentary Affairs*, p. 441.
24. Ibid., pp. 443–44.
25. *Le Point*, 16–27 March 1981.
26. Stéphene Denis, *La Chute de la maison Giscard* (Paris: J. C. Lattes, 1981), p. 46.
27. Roland Cayrol, "The Electoral Campaign and the Decision-Making Process of French Voters," in Penniman, ed., *France at the Polls*, p. 136.
28. Peter Hall, *Governing the Economy: The Politics of State Intervention in Britain and France* (Oxford, England: Policy Press, 1986), p. 223.
29. Cited in Peter Hall, *Governing the Economy: The Politics of State Intervention in Britain and France* (New York: Oxford U. Press, 1986), p. 226.
30. Jérôme Jaffré, "France au centre, victoires socialistes," *Pouvoirs* 47 (1988): 169.
31. Adam Przeworski and John Sprague, *Paper Stones: A History of Electoral Socialism* (Chicago: U. of Chicago Press, 1986), p. 79.
32. David P. Conradt, "The Electorate, 1980–1983," in Karl H. Cerny, ed., *Germany at the Polls* (Durham, N.C.: Duke U. Press, 1990), p. 35.
33. In order for the Bundestag to remove a chancellor, it must simultaneously agree on a successor.
34. Arthur B. Gunlicks, "Between Elections in West Germany, 1976–80 and 1980–83," in Cerny, ed., *Germany at the Polls*, p. 28.
35. Ibid., p. 9
36. Conradt, "The Electorate, 1980–1983," p. 48.
37. Ibid., p. 47.
38. Ibid., p. 53.
39. Nelson W. Polsby and Aaron Wildavsky, *Presidential Elections* (New York: Free Press, 1988), p. 223.
40. Michael S. Lewis-Beck, *Economics and Elections* (Ann Arbor, Mich.: U. of Michigan Press, 1988), p. 84.
41. Ibid., p. 109.
42. Rose, *The Postmodern President*, pp. 90–91.
43. Tom Price, "Voters Have Good Reason to Be Disillusioned," syndicated column, *Seattle Post-Intelligencer*, 19 June 1991, p. A9.
44. Jean-Pierre Worms, "The Rocard Government and Reform," *French Politics and Society* 9 (1991): 3.

45. Chris Howell, "The Fetishism of Small Differences: French Socialism Enters the Nineties," *French Politics and Society* 9 (1991): 29.
46. Ibid., p. 29.

Chapter 7   Problems with Pluralism and Corporatism

1. David Marsh, "On Joining Interest Groups: An Empirical Consideration of the Works of Mancur Olson, Jr.," *British Journal of Political Science* 6 (1976): 257–71; R. King, "The Organization, Structure and Political Function of Selected Chambers of Commerce," as cited in A. G. Jordan and J. J. Richardson, *Government and Pressure Groups in Britain* (Oxford, England: Clarendon Press, 1987), p. 299.
2. Karl Dieter Opp, "Soft Incentives and Collective Action," *British Journal of Political Science* 16 (1986): 87–112.
3. Kay Schlozman and John E. Tierney, *Organized Interests and American Democracy* (New York: Harper and Row, 1986); Charles Lindblom, *Politics and Markets* (New York: Basic Books, 1977).
4. Graham Wilson, *Business and Politics* (Chatham, N.J.: Chatham House, 1985), p. 128; see also Andrew Cox, *The State, Finance and Industry* (Brighton, England: Wheatsheaf Books, 1986), pp. 198–222.
5. Mancur Olson, *The Rise and Decline of Nations* (New Haven, Conn.: Yale U. Press, 1982), pp. 77–78.
6. Richard Rose, *The Postmodern Presidency* (Chatham, N.J.: Chatham House, 1988), p. 71; Theodore Lowi, "The Public Philosophy: Interest Group Liberalism," *American Political Science Review* 61 (1967): 5–24; Lowi, *The End of Liberalism: Ideology, Policy, and the Crisis of Public Authority* (New York: Norton, 1969).
7. Rose, *The Postmodern Presidency*, p. 71.
8. Jack Walker, "The Origins and Maintenance of Interest Groups in America," *American Political Science Review* 7 (1983): 390–406; Alan Ware, *Between Profit and State: Intermediate Organizations in Britain and the United States* (Princeton, N.J.: Princeton U. Press, 1989).
9. Richard Rose, *The Postmodern President*, 2d ed. (Chatham, N.J.: Chatham House, 1991), p. 63.
10. Paul Kennedy, *The Rise and Fall of the Great Powers* (New York: Random House, 1987), pp. 524–25.
11. Joel Kreiger, *Reagan, Thatcher, and the Politics of Decline* (New York: Oxford U. Press, 1986), pp. 36–58.
12. J. J. Richardson and A. G. Jordan, *Government Under Pressure: The Policy Process in a Post Parliamentary Democracy* (Oxford, England: Basil Blackwell, 1985); Peter Riddell, *The Thatcher Decade* (Oxford, England: Basil Blackwell, 1989).
13. Richardson and Jordan, *Government Under Pressure*, 1985, p. 291.
14. Peter Hall, *Governing the Economy: The Politics of State Intervention in Britain and France* (New York: Oxford U. Press, 1986), p. 129.
15. Graham K. Wilson, *Business and Politics: A Comparative Introduction* (Chatham, N.J.: Chatham House, 1990), p. 72.
16. Ibid., p. 73.
17. Wilson, *Business and Politics*, p. 82.

18. John R. Freeman, *Democracy and Markets: The Politics of Mixed Economies* (Ithaca, N.Y.: Cornell U. Press, 1989), p. 150.
19. Thomas E. Mann, "Breaking the Political Impasse," in Henry J. Aaron, ed., *Setting National Priorities: Policy for the Nineties* (Washington, D.C.: Brookings Institution, 1990), p. 303.
20. Mann, "Breaking the Political Impasse," in Aaron, ed., *Setting National Priorities*, p. 313.
21. Terry Moe, "The Politics of Bureaucratic Structure," in John E. Chubb and Paul E. Peterson, eds., *Can the Government Govern?* (Washington, D.C.: Brookings Institution, 1989), pp. 327–28.
22. John E. Chubb and Paul E. Peterson, "The Problem of Governance," in Chubb and Peterson, eds., *Can the Government Govern?* p. 43.
23. Alan Schick, "The Surprising Enactment of Tax Reform in the United States," in Samuel Kernell, ed., *Parallel Politics* (Washington, D.C.: Brookings Institution, 1991), pp. 145–83.
24. Robert H. Salisbury, "The Paradox of Interest Groups in Washington— More Groups, Less Clout," in Anthony King, ed., *The New American Political System* (Washington, D.C.: AEI Press, 1988), pp. 203–29.
25. These were Congressman Rostenkowski's words.
26. James A. Morone, *The Democratic Wish: Popular Participation and the Limits of American Government* (New York: Basic Books, 1990).
27. Ibid., pp. 332–33.
28. Ibid.
29. Freeman, *Democracy and Markets*, p. 91.
30. *New York Times*, 6 June 1990, p. C2.
31. See James Q. Wilson, ed., *The Politics of Regulation* (New York: Basic Books, 1980), for a discussion of the conditions which lead to capture.
32. Wilson, "The Politics of Regulation," in Wilson, ed., *The Politics of Regulation*, p. 360.
33. Murray Edelman, "Symbols and Political Quiescence," *American Political Science Review* 80 (September 1960): 701.
34. Ibid.
35. George J. Benston and George G. Kaufman, "Understanding the Savings and Loan Debacle," *Public Interest* 100 (Summer 1990): 87–88.
36. *New York Times*, 18 October 1990, p. A17.
37. Richard L. Hall and Frank W. Wayman, "Buying Time: Moneyed Interests and the Mobilization of Bias in Congressional Committees," *American Political Science Review* 84 (1990): 817.
38. Jeremy Rabkin, "Micromanaging the Administrative Agencies," *The Public Interest* 100 (Summer 1990): 116.
39. Michael E. Porter, *The Competitive Advantage of Nations* (New York: Free Press, 1990), p. 531; Charles L. Schultz, "The Federal Budget and the Nation's Economic Health," in Aaron, ed., *Setting National Priorities*, pp. 19–64.
40. Pietro S. Nivola, "Déjà Vu All Over Again: Revisiting the Politics of Gasoline Taxation," *The Brookings Review* 9 (1990/1991): 33.
41. Vincent Wright, *The Government and Politics of France* (New York: Holmes and Meier, 1988), p. 133.
42. *L'Express*, 20 April 1990, p. 8.
43. Sophie Coignard and Jean-François Lacan, *La République bananière: De la démocratie en France* (Paris: Belfond, 1989); Airy Routier, *La République des loups: Le pouvoir et les affairs* (Paris: Calmann-Lévy, 1989); Alexandre

Wickham et Sophie Coignard, *La Nomenklatura française: Pouvoir et privi-léges des élites* (Paris: Belfond, 1988); Josua Giustiniani, *Le Racket politique* (Paris: Albin Michel, 1990).

44. Ezra Suleiman, "The Politics of Corruption and the Corruption of Politics," *French Politics and Society* 9 (1991): 65.
45. Douglas E. Ashford, "Decentralizing France; How the Socialists Discovered Pluralism," *West European Politics* 13 (1990): 59.
46. James P. Pfiffner, *The Strategic Presidency: Hitting the Ground Running* (Pacific Grove, Calif.: Brooks-Cole, 1988), p. 21.
47. C. Calvin Mackenzie, "Partisan Presidential Leadership: The President's Appointees," in L. Sandy Maisel, *The Parties Respond: Changes in the American Party System* (Boulder, Colo.: Westview Press, 1990), pp. 267–88.
48. Yukio Noguchi, "Budget Policymaking in Japan," in Schick, ed., *Making Economic Policy in Congress* (Washington, D.C.: AEI Press, 1983), pp. 119–44.
49. Jane Gross, "Turning a Disease Into a Cause: Breast Cancer Follows AIDS," *New York Times*, 7 January 1991, p. 16.
50. Christopher J. Bosso, "Setting the Agenda: Mass Media and the Discovery of Famine in Ethiopia," in Michael Margolis and Gary A. Mauser, *Manipulating Public Opinion* (Pacific Grove, Calif.: Brooks-Cole, 1989), pp. 153–74.
51. Neil Gilbert, "The Phantom Epidemic of Sexual Assault," *Public Interest* (1991), pp. 54–65.
52. David Halberstam, *The Reckoning* (New York: William Morrow, 1986).
53. Ibid., pp. 18–20.
54. J. A. G. Griffith and Michael Ryle, *Parliament* (London: Sweet and Maxwell, 1989), p. 516.
55. B. H. Koh, *Japan's Administrative Elite* (Berkeley, Calif.: U. of California Press, 1989), p. 210.
56. Joseph S. Nye, Jr., "We Can Stay on Top," *Money*, October 1991, p. 160.
57. Theda Skocpol and Kenneth Finegold, "State Capacity and Economic Intervention in the Early New Deal," *Political Science Quarterly* 97 (1982): 255–78.
58. Theda Skocpol, "Bringing the State Back In: Current Research," in Peter Evans, Dietrich Rueschemeyer, and Theda Skocpol, eds., *Bringing the State Back In* (Cambridge: Cambridge U. Press, 1985), p. 14.
59. John T. S. Keeler, *The Politics of Neocorporatism in France* (New York: Oxford U. Press, 1987), p. 19.
60. M. Kogan, *Educational Policy-Making* (London: Allen and Unwin, 1975).
61. Leo Panitch, "The Development of Corporatism in Liberal Democracies," *Comparative Political Studies* 10 (1977): 61–90.
62. Peter Katzenstein, *Small States in World Markets* (Ithaca, N.Y.: Cornell U. Press, 1985), p. 247.
63. Freeman, *Democracy and Markets*, p. 91.
64. Charles S. Meier, *Transforming Bourgeois Europe* (Princeton, N.J.: Princeton U. Press, 1975).
65. Wilson, *Business and Politics*, 1985, pp. 110, 113.
66. Freeman, *Democracy and Markets*, p. 90.
67. Robert Reich, *The Next American Frontier* (New York: Times Books, 1983), p. 3.

Chapter 8   Corporatism, Pluralism, and the Rational State

1. Harmon Zeigler, *Pluralism, Corporatism, and Confucianism* (Philadelphia: Temple U. Press, 1988), pp. 99–100.
2. Peter Katzenstein, "Small Nations in an Open International Economy," in Peter Evans, Dietrich Rueschemeyer, and Theda Skocpol, eds., *Bringing the State Back In* (Cambridge: Cambridge U. Press, 1985), p. 236.
3. Theda Skocpol, "Bringing the State Back In: Current Research," in Evans, Rueschemeyer, and Skocpol, eds., *Bringing the State Back In*, p. 198.
4. Robert A. Dahl, *A Preface to Democratic Theory* (New Haven, Conn.: Yale U. Press, 1951), p. 135.
5. Joel D. Aberbach, Robert D. Putnam, and Bert A. Rockman, *Bureaucrats and Politicians in Western Democracies* (Cambridge, Mass.: Harvard U. Press, 1981), p. 93.
6. Peter Hall, *Governing the Economy* (New York: Oxford U. Press, 1986), p. 279.
7. James A. Morone, *The Democratic Wish* (New York: Basic Books, 1990), p. 332.
8. Balzac, *Les Employés* (Paris: Gallimard, 1985), p. 9.
9. Ezra N. Suleiman, *Politics, Power and Bureaucracy in France* (Princeton, N.J.: Princeton U. Press, 1974), p. 117. Applications for entrance at ENA have been down in recent years, however.
10. B. C. Koh, *Japan's Administrative Elite* (Berkeley, Calif.: U. of California Press, 1989), p. 142.
11. Ibid., p. 217.
12. Michio Muramatsu and Ellis S. Krauss, "Bureaucrats and Politicians in Policymaking: The Case of Japan," *American Political Science Review* 78 (1984): 126–46.
13. Francois de Combret, "What Can the United States Learn from the French Experience?" in William J. Adams and Christian Stoffaes, eds., *French Industrial Policy* (Washington, D.C.: Brookings Institution, 1986), p. 162.
14. Aberbach et al., *Bureaucrats and Politicians*, pp. 96, 99. Italics mine.
15. Suleiman, *Politics, Power, and Bureaucracy in France*, p. 49.
16. Richard Rose, *The Postmodern President*, 2d ed. (Chatham, N.J.: Chatham House, 1991), p. 144.
17. John E. Chubb and Paul E. Peterson, "Political Institutions and the American Economy," in Samuel Kernell, ed., *Parallel Politics* (Washington, D.C.: Brookings Institution, 1991), p. 26.
18. Chalmers Johnson, "A Policy of American Abnegation," *Los Angeles Times*, 25 March 1991, p. 7.
19. Pierre Muller, in remarks at the University of Washington, 15 May 1991, argues that this is the case.
20. Bruno Jobert and Pierre Muller, *L'État En Action: Politiques Publiques et Corporatismes* (Paris: Presses U. de France, 1987), p. 1285.
21. Ezra N. Suleiman, "The Politics of Corruption and the Corruption of Politics," *French Politics and Society* 9 (1991): 58.
22. John T. S. Keeler, *The Politics of Neocorporatism in France* (New York: Oxford U. Press, 1981), p. 242.
23. The episode is exhaustively treated in Keeler, *The Politics of Neocorporatism*, pp. 319ff.

24. Frank R. Baumgartner, *Conflict and Rhetoric in French Policymaking* (Pittsburgh, Pa.: U. of Pittsburgh Press, 1989), pp. 27–37.
25. Combret, "What Can the United States Learn from the French Experience?" in Adams and Stoffaes, eds., *French Industrial Policy,* p. 164.
26. Hall, *Governing the Economy,* p. 163.
27. Jean Tournon, "Les Pressions publique: les pouvoirs publics sont le premier lobby de France," in Maurice Duverger, ed., *Jean Meynaud ou l'utopie revisitée* (Lausanne, Switzerland: U. of Lausanne, 1988).
28. Frank L. Wilson, "France: Interest Groups in a Strong State," American Political Science Association, 1989, p. 15.
29. Frank L. Wilson, "Trade Unions and Economic Policy," in Howard Machin and Vincent Wright, eds., *Economic Policy and Decision-Making in Mitterrand's France* (London: Frances Pinter, 1985).
30. Suleiman, *Politics, Power, and Bureaucracy in France,* p. 58.
31. Wilson, "Interest Groups in a Strong State," p. 6.
32. Thiery Bréhier, "Les Groupes de pression a l'Assemblée Nationale," *Pouvoirs* 34 (1985): 107–119.
33. Baumgartner, *Conflict and Rhetoric,* pp. 170–75.
34. Wilson, "France: Interest Groups in a Strong State," p. 27.
35. See John T. S. Keeler, "Situating France on the Pluralism-Corporatism Continuum," *Comparative Politics* 17 (January 1985): 6–28.
36. Jobert and Muller, *L'État En Action,* p. 188.
37. Suleiman, *Politics, Power, and Bureaucracy in France,* p. 350.
38. Russell J. Dalton, *Politics in West Germany* (Boston: Little, Brown, 1989), p. 207.
39. Michael Huelshoff, "West German Corporatism at Forty," in Peter H. Merkl, ed., *The Federal Republic of Germany at Forty* (New York: New York U. Press, 1990), p. 160.
40. Peter Katzenstein, *Policy and Politics in West Germany* (Philadelphia: Temple U. Press, 1987), p. xxiv. See also Klaus von Beyme, "Policy-making in the Federal Republic of Germany," in von Beyme and Manfred Schmidt, eds., *Policy and Politics in West Germany* (Aldershot, England: Gower, 1985), p. 21; and Richard Rose and Edward C. Page, "Action in Adversity: Responses to Unemployment in Britain and Germany," *West European Politics* 13 (1990): 66–67.
41. Peter Katzenstein, *Corporatism and Change* (Ithaca, N.Y.: Cornell U. Press, 1984), p. 27.
42. Peter Katzenstein, *Small States in World Markets* (Ithaca, N.Y.: Cornell U. Press, 1985), p. 146.
43. Arend Lijphart, *Democracies* (New Haven, Conn.: Yale U. Press, 1984), pp. 23–32.
44. Mancur Olson, *The Rise and Decline of Nations* (New Haven, Conn.: Yale U. Press, 1982), p. 48.
45. Dusan Sidjanski, "Interest Groups in Switzerland," in Robert Presthus, ed., *Interest Groups in International Perspective (Annals of the American Academy of Political and Social Science),* vol. 413 (May 1974), pp. 118.
46. Katzenstein, *Corporatism and Change,* p. 112.
47. Ulrich Kloti, "Political Ideals, Financial Interests and Intergovernmental Relations: New Aspects of Swiss Federalism," *Government and Opposition* 23 (Winter 1988): 91–102.
48. Carl Friedreich, *Trends of Federalism in Theory and Practice* (New York: Praeger, 1968), p. 30.

49. Vernon Bogdanor, "Federalism in Switzerland," *Government and Opposition* 23 (Winter 1988): pp. 91–98.
50. Ibid., p. 114.
51. Zeigler, *Pluralism*, p. 114.
52. Katzenstein, *Corporatism and Change*, pp. 116, 134.
53. Graham Wilson, *Business and Politics* (Chatham, N.J.: Chatham House, 1985), p. 93.
54. Jürg Steiner, *Amicable Agreement Versus Majority Rule* (Chapel Hill, N.C.: U. of North Carolina Press, 1974), p. 110.
55. Katzenstein, *Corporatism and Change*, pp. 112–13.
56. West Germany, however, is far ahead with 37 percent.
57. Katzenstein, *Corporatism and Change*, p. 87.
58. Richard Rosecrance, *The Rise of the Trading State* (New York: Basic Books, 1986), p. 71.
59. The discovery of the Marcos accounts was almost accidental. A minor clerk noticed "exceptional movement" in a numbered account, tipped off the federal government, which then ordered the freeze. Many bankers regarded the tipster as a traitor and Credit Suisse as lax in allowing the leak.
60. Katzenstein, *Corporatism and Change*, p. 101.
61. Population Crisis Committee, *Human Suffering Index*, Washington, D.C., The Population Crisis Committee, 1987 (single page chart).
62. *The Economist*, May 1984, p. 13. The original ranking included climate which, as it is presumably beyond government control, I omitted.
63. Richard Hofstadter, *The Paranoid Style in American Politics* (New York: Knopf, 1965).
64. Quoted in Ervin Staub, *The Roots of Evil* (Cambridge: Cambridge U. Press, 1989), p. 62.
65. William G. Domhoff, *Who Rules America Now: A Voice for the 80s* (Englewood Cliffs, N.J.: Prentice-Hall, 1983).
66. John P. Heinz, Edward O. Laumann, Robert H. Salisbury, and Robert L. Nelson, "Inner Circles or Hollow Cores? Elite Networks in National Policy Systems," *Journal of Politics* (May 1990): 356–90.
67. Katzenstein, "Small Nations in an Open International Economy," in Evans, Rueschemeyer, and Skocpol, *Bringing the State Back In*, p. 241.
68. Ibid., p. 242.
69. Johnson, "A Policy of American Abnegation," p. 7.
70. Michael C. Lynch, senior research associate at Washington International Energy Group, a consulting firm, cited in *The New York Times*, 17 February 1991, p. 17.
71. Robert D. Hormats, *American Albatross: the Foreign Debt Dilemma* (New York: Priority Press, 1988), p. 29.
72. Robert K. Merton, *Social Theory and Social Structure* (New York: Free Press, 1956), pp. 78–79.
73. On this point see James C. Scott, *Comparative Political Corruption* (Englewood Cliffs, N.J.: Prentice-Hall, 1972), p. 146.
74. Thierry Wolton, *Les Ecuries de la Vie* (Paris: Belfond, 1989), p. 307.
75. Susan Rose-Ackerman, *Corruption: A Study in Political Economy* (New York: Academic Press, 1978), p. 45.
76. Ibid., p. 212.
77. Sophie Coignard and Jean-François Lacan, *La République bananière: De la dèmocratie en France* (Paris: Belfond, 1989).

Chapter 9   Is "Change" Stable?

1. Richard Rose and Ian McAllister, *The Loyalties of Voters: A Lifetime Learning Model* (London: Sage Publications, 1990), p. 197.
2. Robert S. Erickson and David W. Romero, "Candidate Equilibrium and the Behavioral Model of the Vote," *American Political Science Review* 84 (1990): 1127–48.
3. Warren E. Miller, "The Electorate's View of the Parties," in L. Sandy Maisel, ed., *The Parties Respond: Changes in the American Party System* (Boulder, Colo.: Westview Press, 1990), p. 99.
4. John H. Goldthorpe, in collaboration with Catriona Llewellyn and Clive Payne, *Social Mobility and Class Structure in Modern Britain*, 2d ed. (Oxford, England: Clarendon Press, 1987), p. 348.
5. Anthony King, "What Do Elections Decide," in David Butler, Howard R. Penniman, and Austin Ranney, *Democracy at the Polls: A Comparative Study of Competitive National Elections* (Washington, D.C.: American Enterprise Institute, 1981), p. 303.
6. Richard Rose, *Do Parties Make a Difference?* (Chatham, N.J.: Chatham House, 1984), pp. 10–11.
7. Joel E. Brooks, "The Opinion-Policy Nexus in Germany," *Public Opinion Quarterly* 543 (1990): 408–29. "The Opinion-Policy Nexus in France: Do Institutions and Ideology Make a Difference?" *Journal of Politics* 49 (1987): 465–80; "Democratic Frustrations in the Anglo-American Polities: A Quantification of Inconsistency Between Mass Public Opinion and Public Policy," *Western Political Quarterly* 38 (1985): 250–61.
8. Arend Lijphart, *Democracies: Patterns of Majoritarian and Consensus Government in Twenty-One Countries* (New Haven, Conn.: Yale U. Press, 1984), p. 2.
9. Benjamin I. Page and Robert Y. Shapiro, "Effects of Public Opinion on Policy," *American Political Science Review* 77 (1983): 175–90.
10. Joel E. Brooks, "Democratic Frustration in the Anglo-American Polities," p. 257.
11. Richard Rose, *The Postmodern President: The White House Meets the World* (Chatham, N.J.: Chatham House, 1988), p. 80.
12. Joel E. Brooks, "Left Wing Mobilization and Socioeconomic Equality: A Cross-National Analysis of the Developed Democracies," *Comparative Political Studies* 15 (1983): 412. See also Robert W. Jackman, "Socialist Parties and Income Inequality in Western Industrial Democracies," *Journal of Politics* 32 (1980): 135–49.
13. Adam Przeworski and John Sprague, *Paper Stones: A History of Electoral Socialism* (Chicago: U. of Chicago Press, 1986), p. 1.
14. Richard Rose and Edward C. Page, "Action in Adversity: Responses to Unemployment in Britain and Germany," *West European Politics* 13 (1990): 75.
15. Harmon Zeigler, *Pluralism, Corporatism, and Confucianism* (Philadelphia: Temple U. Press, 1988), pp. 96–99. The arguments to the contrary, Peter Lange and Geoffrey Garrett, "The Politics of Growth," and "The Politics of Growth reconsidered," *Journal of Politics* 47 (1985): 792–827; 48 (1986): 257–74 are effectively refuted in Robert Jackman, "The Politics of Economic Growth, Once Again," *Journal of Politics* 47 (1985): 646–61.
16. Chris Howell, "The Fetishism of Small Difference: French Socialism Enters the Nineties," *French Politics and Society* 9 (1991): 26–39.

17. David M. O'Brien, "The Reagan Judges: His Most Enduring Legacy?" in Charles O. Jones, ed., *The Reagan Legacy: Promise and Performance* (Chatham, N.J.: Chatham House, 1988), pp. 60–101.
18. Sidney Hook, *The Hero in History* (Boston: Beacon Press, 1943), pp. 14–15.
19. Michael E. Porter, *The Competitive Advantage of Nations* (New York: Free Press, 1990), p. 535.
20. Richard G. Niemi, John Mueller, and Tom W. Smith, *Trends in Public Opinion* (New York: Greenwood Press, 1989), pp. 44–45.
21. Gary Jacobson, *The Electoral Origins of Divided Government* (Boulder, Colo.: Westview Press, 1990), pp. 107–9.
22. R. Michael Alvarez, Geoffrey Garrett, and Peter Lange, "Government Partisanship, Labor Organization, and Macroeconomic Performance," *American Political Science Review* 85 (1991): 551.
23. Robinson Jeffers, "Be Angry at the Sun," in *Selected Poems* (New York: Vintage, 1963), p. 66.
24. Roger G. Noll and Haruo Shimida, "Comparative Structural Policies," in Samuel Kernell, ed., *Parallel Politics* (Washington: Brookings Institution, 1991), p. 220.
25. John E. Chubb and Paul E. Peterson, "Political Institutions and the American Economy," in Kernell, ed., *Parallel Politics*, p. 18.
26. David B. Truman, *The Governmental Process* (New York: Knopf, 1965), p. 423.
27. Chubb and Peterson, "Political Institutions and the American Economy," in Kernell, ed., *Parallel Politics*, p. 48.
28. Anthony King, "The American Polity in the 1990s," in King, ed., *The New American Political System* (Washington, D.C.: AEI Press, 1990), p. 305.
29. King, "The American Polity in the 1990s," in King, ed., *The New American*, p. 304.
30. Les Français et la politique: "C'est la divorce," *L'Express*, 16 December 1988, pp. 6–8.
31. Carson McCullers, *The Ballad of the Sad Café* (New York: Bantam Books, 1954), p. 22.
32. Allan Schick, *The Capacity to Govern* (Washington, D.C.: Urban Institute, 1990), p. 8. Institutional incapacity is also the subject of James MacGregor Burns, with L. Marvin Overby, *Cobblestone Leadership* (Norman, Okla.: U. of Oklahoma Press, 1991).

APPENDIX *(with* David Berg)

By the Numbers

This appendix is a collection of numbers, gathered from many disparate sources. Some statistics in this assessment are ones you can find easily in a standard description of each nation; others are not. All can tell you something about each country. Included with these statistics are brief explanations, interpretations, and depictions of any unusual abbreviations. Consider these explanations a starting point. You are encouraged to chew on them, to challenge them, and to develop your own impressions.

DEMOGRAPHICS

	United States	United Kingdom	West Germany	France	Japan
Area km² × 1,000	9,373	245	249	547	378
1987 population (in millions)	243.8	56.9	61.2	55.6	122.1
Population doubling time (years)	77	347	1,000	231	139
1988 life expectancy	75.0	75.3	75.8	75.9	79.1

(continued)

(continued)	United States	United Kingdom	West Germany	France	Japan
Year 2000 life expectancy	77	77	77	77	80
% of population over 65	20	19	26	22	20
% increase population over 65 1980–2023	130	40	38	75	131
1987 birth rate/1,000	16	13	10	14	11
Year 2000 birth rate	13	11	10	12	13
1988 crude death rate/1,000	9	12	12	10	7
Year 2000 crude death rate	9	11	12	10	9
Child dependency ratio (0–14 as ratio of 15–64)	33	29	22	30	27
Heterogeneity (1–20)	12	12	6	9	4
Demographic pressures (low = low pressure)	26	19	15	16	17

Population density is greatest in Japan (12.4 times that of the United States), followed by West Germany (9.5 times the United States), the United Kingdom (8.9), France (3.9), and the United States. Other demographics—notably life expectancy and total birth rates—however, are similar. In all countries except West Germany, the birth rate exceeds the death rate, meaning each country will see its total native-born population continue to grow. Germany's declining population has vexed policy makers for years, leading to the sardonic joke that the West German government, observing a lack of Germans, simply purchased 17 million more (unification)!

The most revealing statistic is the elderly population in each country. West Germany at present has the most citizens over age 65, but in the next thirty years all five will be hit with a huge increase in the number of elderly citizens as post-World War II baby boomers enter their senior citizenship; Japan, France, and the United States will be particularly hard-hit. The graying of these countries will force a significantly greater proportion of their resources into caring for their elderly, especially in policy areas like social security and health care. The inevitable competition with spending on other age groups could create noteworthy intergenerational tension. If the birth rates of each nation do not increase to equal the increase in the over-65 population, tax burdens will be significantly higher on the youngest members of the population.

It is important to note that, while the number of elderly in each nation will skyrocket, life expectancy will increase only marginally, and death rates are expected to remain essentially unchanged. It is improbable that technological and medical advances will result in improved care. Only an increase in the number and availability of providers will be enough to meet these new demands.

Heterogeneity scores, a measure of population diversity, suggest several possible causes of many of the differences among these five countries. Japan and West Germany are relatively homogeneous. As a result, racial, cultural, ethnic, and religious differences are likely to be much less formidable in these two nations than in the other three. France, with a score of nine (with twenty being the most heterogeneous), falls near the middle. The United Kingdom and the United States, however, are relatively heterogeneous nations. This heterogeneity is disclosed in demographic pressure scores, a rough measure of a society's ability to expand or decline politically, socially, and economically. The United States and the United Kingdom have the greatest demographic pressures, limiting their ability to progress; West Germany, France, and Japan, the least. This is somewhat surprising given the extremely low population density of the United States and the comparatively low density in the United Kingdom, which should allow for easier development, and the notably high densities in Japan and Germany, which should hamper expansion. This ability to overcome demographic constraints implies the prodigious supremacy of the Japanese and German economies over those of their British and American competitors, and the importance of cultural affinity in the building of an efficient empire.

WOMEN

	United States	United Kingdom	West Germany	France	Japan
Status of women (100 is equal)	82.5	74.5	76.0	76.0	68.5
University enrollment of women (univ. pop./fem. pop. 20–24)	5.0	1.5	2.5	3.0	0.5
Females as % of civilian employment	44.8	42.4	39.0	41.6	39.6
% of females age 25–54 employed	71.7	63.4	53.6	63	56.7

(continued)

(continued)	United States	United Kingdom	West Germany	France	Japan
Female/male ratio, administrative, mgmnt.	61	29	20	10	8
Date of women's suffrage	1920	1928	1919	1944	1947
% of women in lower house	6.0	4.0	15.0	5.0	1.4
% of women in ministries	12	8	8	10	0
Date of first woman in government (U.S. Cabinet)	1933	1929	1961	1947	1989
% of women who discuss politics (men)	72 (82)	60 (73)	67 (85)	57 (70)	35 (58)

The United States delivers the most equal treatment of women; Japan the least. The "status of women" index, derived from legal, economic, and political measures of equality, shows how the countries have fared. The future looks best for American, French, and German women if university enrollment is the chosen measure; though even those numbers are underwhelming. If employment levels are the criterion, American women still lead the way, followed by the British and the French, while the Japanese and the Germans trail. These numbers may be somewhat misleading because there is no accurate way to measure how many of the women are not employed by choice, and how many are unable to find work because of their nation's treatment of women.

Politically, West German women have fared the best, and Japanese women the worst. The women in West Germany were the first to be given voting rights, and have the largest percentage elected into the lower house of government. Japan did not have its first female cabinet member until 1989; and she was widely considered a token, appointed by the Liberal Democrats in the hope of diverting the Japanese public's attention from a major scandal that had hit the party. Her tenure was to be short—she was removed by the party in 1990—although a second woman was soon named to a different post. Serious questions remain about the Liberal Democrats' sincerity, although it is widely understood to have been the politically expedient thing to do. That the lower house of parliament in Japan has no female members only serves to strengthen this argument. Margaret Thatcher, British prime minister from 1979 to 1990, and Edith Cresson, French prime minister since 1991, are the only women to have led the government of any one of these nations.

Increased political equality seems most likely to occur in the United States or West Germany where more than two-thirds of women discuss politics, though in both nations, women still lag dramatically behind men. French and Japanese women are least likely to discuss politics (though the men of these nations also trail those of the other countries). If women do not debate politics, possible areas of training and education are significantly reduced, making it more arduous for women to have a noteworthy effect on policymaking, either from within or outside the government.

FAMILY PLANNING

	United States	United Kingdom	West Germany	France	Japan
1987 birth rate/1,000	16	13	10	14	11
Teenage birth rate	50	29	8	14	4
Abortions/1,000 for women of childbearing age	139	12	8	15	84
Out-of-wedlock births (% of births)	29	19	8	18	2
Birth control score (0–29)	25	29	28	27	19
% couples using contraception	76	83	78	79	64
Per capita expenditures on family planning ($)	0.92	0.45	0.44	0.01	0.47
Total fertility rate (1988)	1.9	1.8	1.4	1.8	1.7
Total fertility rate (year 2000)	1.9	1.7	1.7	1.7	1.9
Family policy innovation (maternity leave, day care, retirement)	low	medium	medium	high	low

The birth rates in the United States, France, and the United Kingdom are somewhat alike. All show that the native-born populations of each nation will continue to grow. Japan and Germany post somewhat lower birth rates, denoting a slower rate of growth, and according to some statistics, even a decline in native-born population. It has yet to be seen exactly what effect German reunification will have on the German birth rate, though some expect it to decline in the short term, and boom once political and economic stability are regained. In Japan, however, some fear that a growing women's liberation movement will cause a further reduction in the Japanese birth rate as women discover they can be more than housewives and mothers. Many women point to the high costs of education, the scarcity of adequate child care and housing, and the difficulty of raising a child "alone" while their husbands work long hours as factors leading to the current reduction in the Japanese birth rate to its lowest level ever. The Japanese government has offered a 5,000 yen (about U.S. $38) monthly subsidy for the first two children of preschool age, doubling to 10,000 yen for a third child. The proposal incensed representatives of Japan's nascent feminist movement.

With each nation facing a significant increase in its elderly population, having a large young and able workforce will both serve the needs of economic expansion and reduce the tax burden per individual when it comes time to pay for the care of each nation's senior citizens.

A prominent difference among these countries is seen in their teenage birth rates. West Germany and France have virtually no difference between the teen and total birth rates, while Japan's teen birth rate is dramatically lower than that of the entire population. Only the United States and the United Kingdom face onerous teenage birth rates.

Abortion is a much more prominent means of avoiding parenthood in the United States and Japan than in any of the other nations. Couples in these two nations are least likely to have used some form of contraception, although Japanese couples are clearly the greatest exceptions in this category. U.S. couples lag only slightly behind their West European counterparts, and certainly not far enough behind to justify the vast difference in abortion rates. Particularly discomfiting, Americans and Japanese spend more money per capita on family planning measures than do nations who outperform them in this category. This may indicate that birth control measures are simply more expensive and less prevalent in these two countries than the other three. If the stigma of an out-of-wedlock birth is used as a justification for abortion, supporting evidence will be hard to find. The United States has the largest percentage of all births out of wedlock, Japan the smallest.

The last category in this section describes the level of family policy innovation in these five nations. Once more, Japan and the

United States trail significantly in their support of families, young children and newborns, and retirees, while only France excels.

This pattern has profound implications for the future. Newly married couples who see little institutional political, economic, or social support available when they consider beginning their families are less likely to have children. We have already seen the great need among all these nations for a new generation of workers and taxpayers to enable each to continue its current level of support.

THE CHANGING HOUSEHOLD

	United States	United Kingdom	West Germany	France	Japan
Divorce/1,000 married couples	22	14	6	4	3
% saying divorce can never be justified	22	14	13	13	21
Average household size	2.7	2.7	2.7	2.4	3.1
% of single-parent families	8	4	7	5	1
Single-parent families as % of households with children	22	13	14	11	6
% of one-person households	25	24	34	26	24
% of households unmarried or relatives living together	13	7	4	4	8
% approving single mothers	34	33	27	65	13
% "traditional" households (husband and wife)	54	62	55	65	68
% saying a woman needs a child to be fulfilled	18	22	36	71	68

The United States clearly leads the way in nontraditional families, but Americans don't seem comfortable with that role. Americans have the highest divorce rate, more than 1.5 times that of the British, and more than 3.6 times that of the Germans; yet, Americans are also most opposed to divorce. The Japanese are less schizophrenic in their beliefs, opposing divorce nearly as often as Americans while maintaining the lowest divorce rate of the five nations. Japan also has the smallest number of single-parent families, while in the United States, nearly one in four households with children is headed by a single parent, and slightly more than half of all families can be considered "traditional." But once more, despite their prevalence, Americans remain reluctant to accept the reality of single mothers; about one-third say they approve of them. The French, on the other hand, not only are much more tolerant of single mothers but also are supportive of the idea that a woman needs a child in order to be fulfilled (71 percent say she does). This could explain the wide acceptance of single mothers; better to have a child and no husband, than a husband and no child. Japanese society continues to be largely traditional, also favoring the idea that a woman needs a child, while sustaining opposition to most nontraditional family forms.

EDUCATION

	United States	United Kingdom	West Germany	France	Japan
International math test scores (high school)	52	55	59	58	65
Science achievement scores	25	80	91	71	92
Average years of schooling (precollegiate)	10.0	12.0	10.1	11.4	11.6
Days in standard school year	180	192	240	185	243
Days of education (U.S. = 1.00)	1.00	1.28	1.35	1.17	1.57
16- and 17-year-olds in school (%)	95	52	95	79	89
17- and 18-year-olds in school (%)	90	38	81	70	88
18- and 19-year-olds in school (%)	58	20	68	60	50
College enrollment per 1,000	57	22	30	30	30
% of adult illiteracy	4	1	1	1	1
Students per teacher (university)	10	11	4	25	18

(continued)

(continued)	United States	United Kingdom	West Germany	France	Japan
Students per teacher (secondary)	13	13	19	15	20
Students per teacher (elementary)	21	22	14	21	22

Japanese students score best on math and science achievement tests, while Americans are dead last. In math, the difference in achievement, while hardly significant, is noticeable. In science, American students manage to reach a level of only slightly better than one-third that of the French, the next lowest achievers. Japanese and German students run away from the rest of the field in science. These numbers have received a great deal of attention lately. George Bush has often promised to bring the United States science achievement scores to first in the world by the year 2000. If these numbers are a good indication, that pledge may be better seen as rhetoric than as reality.

Americans send more students to college than the other four countries, but they have to work less diligently to get there. Days of education is a standardized measure of the length of time spent in precollegiate educational programs. The French spend 1.17 times as many days on precollegiate education; the Japanese 1.57 times as many. This means that using the standard American 180-day school year, Americans would have to go to school more than ten additional months to cover the same amount of material as the French. The numbers are even more astounding for the other nations. To match the British, nearly seventeen more months would be required, the Germans twenty-one more, and to match the Japanese, Americans would need thirty-four additional months! The ability to compete at any level in a global economy is clearly linked to education, and the United States is entering the twenty-first century at a considerable disadvantage.

Last, there is the question of adult literacy. The United States scores worst in this category. Four percent of adults cannot read or write; conservatively, that adds up to seven million American adults. The numbers show about one-half million British, French, and Germans, and nearly one million Japanese are in the same situation. Estimates of functional illiteracy, the ability to read only the most basic materials and nothing more, are even higher.

GETTING AROUND

	United States	United Kingdom	West Germany	France	Japan
Cars/1,000	580	330	450	410	250
Persons per car	1.8	2.9	2.2	2.6	4.2
% living in largest city	12	20	18	23	22
% living in cities over 500,000 population	77	55	45	34	42
Kilometers per person per day in cars	52	21	23	21	8
Kilometers per person per day in bus or train	1	4	5	6	10
% of oil use met by imports	37	0	95	96	100
Annual oil consumption per capita (pc), in gallons	1,067	462	567	508	622
Annual gasoline consumption pc, gallons	484	176	206	151	133
% of gas sales unleaded	98	37	61	15	99
Days oil reserves will last	99	80	135	77	132
Cost of one gallon of gas (1990) in U.S. $	1.35	3.80	3.75	4.60	3.90
Gas tax (per gallon) U.S. $	0.25	2.00	1.90	2.90	1.50
Traffic deaths/ 100,000	18.1	8.8	12.5	17.3	10.1

There is no doubt about it, Americans are car crazy. Whereas the difference in cars per thousand people displays the vast gap in the absolute number of cars in each country, other numbers may be more informational. The fewest number of persons per car can be found in the United States and Germany. This may be an indicator of the lack of use or availability of mass transit systems (in the United States), or it may simply show that the people of these countries love their cars. Support for the former theory can be found in examining the number of kilometers spent in daily transit by the people of each nation. In terms of mileage, Americans rely on their cars for transportation far more than do people of the other four nations, covering 52 kilometers per person per day in cars. This is about 2.5 times their closest competitor in this area, the Germans, and 6.5 times the country with the most developed mass transit system, Japan. Americans travel an average of only one kilometer per person per day in a form of mass transit, while the Japanese average ten times that amount. What makes these disparities more extraordinary are the population dynamics of the cities in these countries. More Americans live in cities over a half million in population than citizens of any of the other four nations, an ingredient that should make it easier for Americans to use mass transit and thaumaturgically reduce the number of kilometers between workers and their jobs. Obviously, this has not happened in the United States.

American dependence on private transportation sources rather than public transportation is also revealed in annual oil consumption per capita statistics. Americans use 72 percent more oil per capita than the Japanese, the next worst offender in this area. Their automobiles burn more than twice as much gasoline as those of the almost equally car-obsessed Germans. The War in the Persian Gulf has made oil use and oil imports more important to all five of these countries. In terms of oil imports, the Japanese, French, and Germans are in the most delicate position and have the most to lose. Japan has no internal sources of oil, and must rely completely on imports for its oil supply. France and Germany are only slightly better off in this area. Americans import just over one-third of their oil, a figure that has increased substantially since oil prices declined in the late 1970s. It became cheaper to import oil than to pump it ourselves. The United Kingdom is best off; all British oil needs can be met by internal oil sources. None of these countries could survive a major disruption in the world's oil supply, however. France, the United Kingdom, and the United States would all find themselves in economic disarray within one hundred days if their oil supply were cut off.

If all these countries are dangerously dependent on the world oil market, why haven't greater strides been taken to make private transportation prohibitively expensive, forcing people into mass transit? Everywhere but the United States, they have. Gas prices are nearly three times more expensive in the United Kingdom, Germany, and Japan, and nearly 3.5 times higher in France. Each of the other four nations has imposed gas taxes that would provoke rioting in the streets in the United States. Much of these revenues go toward the development of mass transit, something the Americans have, as yet, been unwilling to consider.

ENERGY AND THE ENVIRONMENT

	United States	United Kingdom	West Germany	France	Japan
Nuclear electricity (% of total)	19.5	19.3	34	69.9	23.4
Nuclear power production (megawatt hours per capita [pc])	2.1	1.0	2.2	4.3	1.7
Carbon dioxide emissions from fossil fuels (tons pc)	5.11	2.73	2.98	1.70	2.12
Carbon emissions from fossil fuels (tons per $, GNP)	276	224	223	133	156
Paper/cardboard consumption, kilos pc	277	160	208	150	225
Energy consumed, kilos pc	9,489	5,363	5,829	3,831	3,625
Electricity consumption pc (kwh)	11,193	5,484	6,697	5,888	5,793
Crude petroleum consumption pc (barrels)	19.2	8.8	8.8	8.6	9.4
Natural gas consumption pc (cubic meters)	7,047	1,147	1,031	585	344
Coal consumption pc (metric tons)	3.1	2.1	3.2	0.6	0.8
Energy consumption growth rate 65–80%	2.3	0.9	3.0	3.7	6.1
80–88%	0.9	0.8	−0.2	0.4	1.9
% change in pc solid waste generation (1980–85)	+3	+11	−9	+5	−3
Environmental consortium summary evaluation	poor	poor	good	fair	poor

France has the most well-developed nuclear energy system of the five nations. Nearly 70 percent of its total energy consumption needs are met by nuclear sources. The British, largely because of the easy availability of oil and coal, have the least well-developed nuclear energy capacity. Once more, Americans come through as the biggest overall environmental abusers. The United States ranks first in the absolute number of tons per capita of carbon dioxide emissions, while also being the least efficient fossil-fuel burner. America burns more fossil fuels per dollar of gross national product than any of these nations. France, due to its well-developed nuclear system, does best here, while Japan is not too far behind. Most significant about carbon dioxide emissions is their relationship to the greenhouse effect; the idea that the sun's heat is being increasingly trapped within the earth's atmosphere by carbon dioxide emissions, resulting in overall global warming. Environmentalists will be caught on the horns of a dilemma: France, the most nuclear-reliant country, is the cleanest. Its low rates of carbon dioxide emissions are a consequence of its use of nuclear energy. France, therefore, contributes the least to the greenhouse effect.

In general, America ranks as the least efficient energy user. Americans consume far greater amounts of paper and cardboard per capita. They also consume 63 percent more energy per capita than the next least efficient nation, West Germany, and 161 percent more than Japan, the most efficient nation. This great disparity may be a result of America's geographical advantage over the other four nations. The United States has a much larger source of natural resources because of its greater size. It is harder to believe Americans will run out of resources, and American citizens aren't constantly reminded, except perhaps by oil, of the need to import these natural resources. The United States, it is often argued, lacks an energy policy. Cynics respond that the United States does indeed have an energy policy: "We burn oil." We shall see who is right.

Japan ranks as one of the most efficient energy users, yet its energy consumption growth rate is considerably higher than the other nations. This anomaly may be explained not by arguing the Japanese are becoming less efficient, but simply that their industrial sector is expanding at a far greater rate than the other nations. From 1965 to 1980 this was certainly the case. From 1980 to 1988 that assertion is slightly more suspect. Germany, a very strong industrial producer, actually had a negative growth rate from 1980 to 1988.

Despite the impression that some of these nations are more environmentally conscious than others, it would not be accurate to categorize any as genuinely environmentalist. Only West Germany gets a "good" rating in overall environmental efforts; only France rates as "fair." The environmental conditions in the United States, United Kingdom, and Japan are most perilous; all rate as poor.

STAYING ALIVE

	United States	United Kingdom	West Germany	France	Japan
Heart disease per 1,000	389	315	328	221	211
Heart disease deaths per 100,000	218.1	104.5	159.5	76	41.9
Cigarettes smoked per person per year	2,285	1,695	1,910	1,680	2,515
% of women who smoke	24	32	29	26	14
% of men who smoke	30	36	44	49	66
Lung cancer per 100,000	54	55	35	33	26
Deaths by accidental poisoning per 100,000	54	29	37	59	3

Americans suffer from more cases of heart disease and more serious cases of heart disease than any other of the five countries. Nearly 39 percent of Americans will suffer some form of heart disease, and 36 percent more of them will die from that heart disease than in the next more afflicted nation. This disparity may be a result of diet, though exactly what can be done to improve things remains subject to great debate. Japan fares best in heart disease and in heart disease deaths, and is the most likely of the five nations to have a diet significantly different from that of the United States. The differences between these two extremes are less clear.

Lest we get the impression that the Japanese are pictures of health, cigarette smoking is more prominent in Japan. Some have wondered if so many Japanese smoke so much, why don't more die from smoking-related ailments like cancer? The best answer for this is that they simply haven't smoked long enough yet. Cigarettes were popularized in Japan just after World War II. This means that they have only been smokers of this magnitude for a little over 40 years. Most medical experts agree that many of the effects of smoking, most notably cancer, aren't seen until forty years after a smoker picked up the habit. If this is indeed the case, cancer deaths in Japan should begin to climb soon.

VICES

	United States	United Kingdom	West Germany	France	Japan
Chocolate, pounds per capita (pc) per year	9.5	15.4	15.2	9.5	3.3
Alcohol, % of total private consumption	1.4	2.0	3.3	2.0	1.3
Food, % of private consumption	11.0	14.5	17.6	17.9	19.9
Ratio of food to alcohol	7.9	7.3	5.3	9.0	15.3
Wine consumption (liters pc)	5.0	13.0	25.0	73.0	1.6

The British and the Germans love their chocolate; the Japanese have yet to pick up this dietary vice. The Germans also love their alcohol. In terms of spending on alcohol compared to all other private consumption spending, Germans spend 3.3 percent of total private consumption on alcohol. They spend a little over five times that amount on food. Japan spends less per person on alcohol, but more per person on food, for an overall 15.3 to 1 ratio. No one, however, can compare to the French when it comes to wine. The French drink three times as much wine per person as the Germans, nearly six times as much as the British, 14.6 times the American consumption, and 45.6 times that of the Japanese! Possibly the quality of French wine explains this passion. Most residents of France rarely drink the expensive exports, but have access to a diversity of country wines that are cheap and delicious. The low wine consumption by Japanese is understandable, given the quality of Japanese wines. But why Americans are so abstemious is a puzzle: American varietal wine is now competitive in quality with French wine, although American everyday wine is not.

CRIME

	United States	United Kingdom	West Germany	France	Japan
Murders per 100,000	8.71	1.37	4.51	4.63	1.47
Violent death as a % of youth death	78	62	70	71	69
Male youth homicide rate	22.0	3.0	3.0	4.0	2.5
Rapes per 100,000	35.7	2.7	9.7	5.2	1.6
Robberies per 100,000	205	45	46	109	2
Drug offenses per 100,000	320.1	10.1	103.8	52.5	1.6
Serious assault per 100,000	290.2	219.7	107.6	70.0	19.6
Prison population per 1,000	43	10	8	8	5

Crime is something else at which Americans excel. They are—at the very least—twice as likely to be murdered than citizens of any of the other four nations. The disparity in violent youth deaths as a percent of all youth deaths is not as great, but the United States still sets an unfortunate pace. The remarkably high male youth homicide rate in the United States is more appalling. The number in inner cities is even higher; in some American inner cities the average male life span is less than it is in many third-world nations. Rape is at least 3.5 times more common in the United States than in these other nations, robberies twice as common, drug offenses 3.2 times more common, and cases of serious assault 1.3 times more common (2.7 if we omit the British).

American rates of imprisonment are also number one, at least 4.3 times greater than any of the other nations. This immense imprisonment rate may represent part of the problem. Americans have come to demand harsher penalties and longer sentences for serious offenses, yet they also show no desire to pay for the greater number of prisons such sentences require. Prisons have ceased to be centers of rehabilitation as their populations have become more crowded, and have started to become higher institutions of crime. The problem is cyclical: commit a crime, go to jail, learn how to commit other crimes, go back to jail, and so on. It is not realistic to think we can simply lock up all offenders and expect them to emerge as model citizens, nor is it realistic to think that we can leave them in prisons for life. The numbers clearly indicate the problem is more intractable. Japan has the least number of crimes per person of the five nations, and its rates of imprisonment are also the smallest.

HEALTH AND WELFARE

	United States	United Kingdom	West Germany	France	Japan
Per capita health spending	2,050	750	1,110	1,039	925
Per capita prescription drugs	106	41	98	81	116
Doctors per 1,000	1.8	1.4	2.8	2.2	1.5
Population per doctor	418	619	370	403	644
Population per hospital bed	184	133	175	92	87
Population per hospital (1,000)	35	25	58	20	13
Population per nurse	211	209	129	137	219
Infant mortality per 1,000 (1987)	11	9	8	8	6
Infant mortality (by year 2000)	10	6	5	7	5
% of infant deaths occurring on first day of life	38	26	19	17	26
% saying the health care system must be "completely rebuilt"	29	17	12	10	6

America is the home of high-technology medicine. Health spending per capita in the United States is considerably greater than that in its nearest competitor. One possible cause of this disparity is technology. Americans demand the most advanced technology in health care, and such technology does not come cheap. Infant mortality, while subject to some of the benefits of technology, remains high in the United States compared with the other four nations, especially when looking ahead ten years. One of the most significant causes of America's high infant mortality rate is a lack of adequate prenatal care. Many expectant American mothers receive only cursory prenatal care, some getting their first prenatal care as they enter labor. The miracles of technology only go so far. Americans can learn a great deal by examining the prenatal and infant care systems in place in any one of the other four nations.

For the most part, American citizens recognize the inadequacies of their current health care system; 29 percent believe the system must be completely rebuilt. Americans tend to want a level of state intervention in health care comparable with that of the other four nations, but still want to retain high-tech care and individual choice. What must be remembered is that in a system of socialized medicine, high technology means a higher cost to everyone, whether or not they use the technology. Currently, individual medical bills can be overwhelming. Under socialized medicine, those costs would be spread over the entire population. As Americans are very reluctant to pay for the services they now receive, it is unlikely that they will be any more likely to want to pay for someone else's health care, which is what rebuilding the system would entail.

THE ECONOMY AND LIVING COSTS

	United States	United Kingdom	West Germany	France	Japan
Inflation rate (1980–87)	4.3	5.7	2.9	7.7	1.4
Inflation rate (1990)	6.1	9.3	2.9	3.3	3.8
Inflation rate (1991 estimate)	4.5	6.3	3.3	3.3	3.1
Inflation rate (1992 estimate)	3.9	4.8	3.4	2.9	2.6
% of growth in money rate (1988)	6.0	19.5	8.3	8.3	6.5
% of GNP growth (1870–99)	240	86	116	60	98
% of GNP growth (1900–29)	170	36	77	57	146
GNP growth (1950–85)	200	129	374	306	1,223
Average GNP growth (1965–87)	1.5	1.7	2.5	2.7	4.2
Average GNP growth (1980–90)	2.8	2.5	2.2	2.3	4.3
GNP growth (1990)	−0.1	1.0	3.8	2.4	5.1
GNP growth (1991, estimated)	−0.3	−0.5	2.9	2.1	3.6
GNP growth (1992, estimated)	2.5	2.1	2.5	2.8	3.7
GNP per capita (pc), U.S. $ (1987)	18,413	11,718	18,471	15,224	19,322
GNP pc 1990 (1980 U.S. $)	14,070	12,111	16,111	14,760	12,960

(continued)

(continued)	United States	United Kingdom	West Germany	France	Japan
Net domestic purchasing power (Tokyo = 100)	200	154	225	135	100
Purchasing power parities (PPPs)	100	62	75	68	74
GNP pc adjusted by PPPs	18,200	12,000	13,300	13,000	13,000
Market exchange rates (U.S. = 100)	100	79	100	86	121
GNP pc adjusted by market exchange rates	18,200	9,250	18,400	13,100	23,100
Average GNP pc growth (1950–90)	1.9	2.2	3.2	3.2	5.9
Average GNP pc growth (1960–90)	2.0	2.1	2.8	3.1	5.5
Average GNP pc growth (1970–90)	1.7	2.0	2.2	2.3	3.8
Average GNP pc growth (1980–90)	1.8	2.2	1.5	1.8	3.9
GNP pc projection, year 2020 (1975 "international dollars")	19,000	11,000	24,000	20,000	31,000
Living costs (1989)	New York 100	London 95	Bonn 101	Paris 90	Tokyo 126
Per diem State Dept. allowance (U.S. $)		London 175	W. Berlin 160	Paris 180	Tokyo 195
Average cost of a Big Mac (U.S. $)	2.20	2.30	2.56	3.14	2.32
Cost of 100 condoms (U.S. $)	92	39	76	58	125
Cost of "the pill" (13 cycles, U.S. $)	216	43	105	30	
Cost of IUD (U.S. $) avg.	300	145	101	16	225
Average 3-room apartment rent (U.S. $)	New York 1,150	London 860	Frankfurt 540	Paris 750	Tokyo 1,430
Floor area of dwellings per sq. mtrs.	134.8	91.1	93.8	85.5	80.9
Prime office rents (Tokyo = 100)	New York 38	London 65	Frankfurt 25	Paris 40	Tokyo 100
CEO annual income (U.S. $, after taxes)	429,000	122,000	112,000	118,000	178,000
Average hourly wages	11.50	11.25	12.50	10.00	13.30
Net hourly earnings	10.70	9.00	8.00	9.00	6.60
Total hourly labor costs	14.75	15.00	23.00	16.00	16.00

(continued)

(continued)	United States	United Kingdom	West Germany	France	Japan
Average weekly hours worked	39.0	36.5	40.0	40.5	47.0
Working hours per year per person employed	1,867	1,754	1,723	1,730	2,013
Working hours per year per person aged 16 to 64	1,300	1,199	1,100	1,098	1,420
Holidays per year (public holidays and annual leave)	20	32	40	37	15
% of workforce self-employed	7	8	9	15	17
% of workforce in industry	31	38	44	35	34
% of workforce in services	66	59	50	56	55
Advertising, % GDP	1.60	1.37	0.75	0.61	0.92
Advertising, $ pc	360	263	200	90	250
TV advertising (% of total)	36	33	8	25	29
Personal savings rate (% of disposable income)	4.5	1.0	12.2	14.9	16.4
% increase in personal savings rate (1972–89)	6	10	12	16	18
Gross savings (% of GNP) (1860–1938)	18	16	—	20	12
Gross savings (1950–59)	18	16	28	19	30
Gross savings (1960–84)	18	18	24	21	33
Savings, % of GNP (1981–87)	3.9	6.2	10.7	19.6	20.2
Gross savings rate, 1960–84, as ratio to pre-war savings (West German ratio to pre-WWII Germany)	0.96	1.47	1.19	1.75	2.79
People per bank	7,300	85,900	13,700	63,200	17,900
Central bank independence (1 = least, 4 = most)	3	2	4	2	3
Pension and life insurance (% of GNP)	76	105	29	19	32
Market share of top 10 life insurance companies (%)	38	58	59	65	82

(continued)

(continued)	United States	United Kingdom	West Germany	France	Japan
Stock market capitalization (% of GDP)	60	63	30	35	148
Stock market volatility (% of deviation from average rate of return)	18.7	26.2	18.8	23.8	19.4
Misery index (inflation + unemployment)	12.2	15.8	9.3	12.3	5.9
Misery index (inflation + twice unemployment)	18.3	22.3	15.7	21.3	8.0
Tourism (billions of U.S. $ spent by tourists)	34	11	9	17	3
Billions of U.S. $ spent by country to promote tourism	39	20	30	14	25
Tourist arrivals (millions)	40	18	16	50	13
Economist 1990 ranking of the economy	9	11	1	6	2
1991 (predicted)	8	11	3	6	2
1992 (predicted)	8	12	6	4	1

Consumer prices in France inflated meteorically from 1980 to 1987. Britain can expect to endure the most rapid increase in prices for the next few years. Japan has maintained the lowest rate of inflation throughout the period. In terms of gross national product (GNP), the total dollar value of all finished goods and services, Japan has been the most consistently strong performer, while Britain has been considerably less impressive. The United States and the United Kingdom are both in the midst of a recession (a decrease in GNP for three consecutive months), though all countries expect the rate of growth in GNP to decrease from 1990 to 1991. The world economy, except for Germany (weighted down by its acquisition of the impoverished eastern *länder*) is expected to pick up again in 1992. Germany is currently, and will be for some time, trying to cope with the economic stresses of reunification. Once it overcomes those obstacles, expect Germany to return to the top.

Japan is the wealthiest of the five nations, with a GNP per capita of $19,322 (measured in U.S. dollars). The United Kingdom is poorest with a GNP per capita of $11,718 (U.S. dollars). When consumer prices in each nation are taken into account (purchasing power parities), the U.S. GNP per capita of $18,200 is greatest, while the United Kindgom continues to trail at about $12,000. When international market conditions are considered, Japan comes in with a GNP per capita of $23,100, and the United Kingdom again lags behind with $9,250. These measures suggest that while Americans may have the highest standard of living, the Japanese are in the best condition internationally. This gap is expected to increase dramatically in the next thirty years, when it is estimated that Japan will have a GNP per capita of $31,000, while the British and American GNP per capita will remain effectively unchanged. German and French incomes are also expected to increase, though not as momentously as the Japanese. This measure does not, however, consider market strength or consumer prices; it is simply a measure of economic growth. It is important to remember that among the five countries living costs are highest in Japan. Something that costs $100 in New York would cost $126 in Tokyo and only $90 in Paris using international currency.

Real estate prices may be the best indicator of the cost of living in a given country. If that is so, Tokyo (with Oslo) is the most expensive city in the industrial democracies. Renting an apartment in Tokyo is 25 percent more expensive than in New York. Adding to the injury, the size of the residence is likely to be smallest in Tokyo. Frankfurt has the most inexpensive rents of the five cities in this comparison, and New Yorkers are likely to have the largest living space. Frankfurt also provides the apartment renter with the most living space per dollar spent, while that number in Tokyo is nearly twice that of London, the next most costly city. Prime office rents match the residential housing market. Tokyo is an almost inconceivably expensive place to do business, while Frankfurt is comparatively cheap. Notice that the cost of a Big Mac is more stable than other prices. Is uniformity a virtue?

German workers are paid gross salaries that, on average, are 40 percent higher than those of the next highest nation, France. British and Japanese workers receive the lowest gross wages. Net hourly earnings are greatest in the United States, while Japanese workers earn the least after taxes and deductions. Japanese workers average 47 hours per week on the job, making them the most workaholic of the five countries, while the British work the least, averaging only 36.5 hours per working week. In terms of total working age population (16 to 64), the Japanese have enough work for each person to spend 1,420 hours at work, while the French have the least work available, 1,098 hours per person. Germans take the most holidays in the course of a year, followed closely by the French, while American workers get "only" twenty holidays each year.

The entrepreneurial spirit seems highest in Japan, where 17 percent of the workforce is self-employed. By this measure, the United States is the least innovative nation; only 7 percent of American workers are self-employed. West Germany employs 44 percent of its workforce in industrial jobs, the most among the five, and 50 percent of its workforce in service jobs, the least of the five. The United States reverses those rankings, with industrial jobs for 31 percent of the workforce and service jobs for 66 percent. Most economists agree that the future lies in service, not industrial jobs, so the United States may be in the best position here.

Advertising is most prominent in the United States. American firms spend a larger percent of the total Gross Domestic Product (GDP) on advertising, as well as spending the largest amount per capita. (GDP is the total value of all finished goods and services for domestic consumption.) French companies spend the smallest percentage of GDP on advertising, while also spending the least per person. Television ads make up 36 percent of all U.S. advertising, while the Germans are least likely to use TV; only 8 percent of all German advertising is done on television.

The Japanese lead the way in personal savings rate, followed by the French and the Germans. The British and, especially, the Americans don't save—they spend. A low savings rate suggests a larger number of citizens in debt, or close to it. Money that comes in on payday goes right back out when the bills are due. All five nations have increased their personal savings rate since the early 1970s, though Americans lag considerably behind the others. The Japanese and French have not only continued to lead the way in absolute rate of savings, they have also experienced the greatest increase in savings rate.

It is intriguing to note the low number of persons per bank (or small banks) in the United States compared with the other nations. West German and Japanese banks, while dwarfed by their French and British counterparts, are still considerably larger than American banks. It is easy to see the difficult position in which American banks find themselves. If a large bank and a small bank make the same loan, the small bank will have more to lose if the loan goes into default. To compete with the larger banks, small banks have to risk more to provide the same rate of return. Once in financial trouble, they will also have less to fall back on, and will find themselves in more serious danger.

British and Americans are financially more prepared for retirement and death than citizens of the other three nations. The British have more money stowed away in pensions and life insurance policies than their nation produces in a given year. Americans have not reached that level, but they aren't too far from it. Japanese, West Germans, and French spend comparatively little in these areas. Because the French and Germans are secure beneath an expansive welfare net, they can afford to relax. And the Japanese, because they save at prodigious rates, can also afford to relax. The Americans obviously rely upon corporate schemes, rather than governmentally induced, or individually planned, savings. As with American banks, American insurance companies tend to be much smaller than their equivalents in the other nations. The top ten American life insurance companies hold less than 40 percent of all policies. The next smallest amount is found in the United Kingdom, where nearly 60 percent of all policies are held by the top ten companies. The Japanese system is the most monopolistic in this regard; more than 80 percent of all policies are held by the top ten life insurance providers.

Overall, economic conditions in the United Kingdom are the poorest. Using a misery index (similar to stagflation, the misery index provides a score combining inflation and unemployment), Japan appears to be the most stable economically, while the economies of the United Kingdom and France are in somewhat more precarious positions. *The Economist*, a weekly news and opinion journal (published in London, with a free-market orientation), ranks the economies of thirteen leading industrial nations by their GNP growth rates, their consumer price inflation rates, and their current account balances. Presently, the economies of West Germany and Japan rank among the healthiest of the thirteen nations, while the United States and the United Kingdom are among the most sickly economies on the list. The only major shift *The Economist* predicts in the next few years is a gradual decline for Germany. Until the problems accompanying reunification are mastered, Germany's economy will decline slightly.

GOVERNMENT AND THE ECONOMY

	United States	United Kingdom	West Germany	France	Japan
Income distribution	1980	1979	1978	1975	1979
top 20%	39.9	39.7	39.5	42.2	37.5
bottom 20%	5.3	7.0	7.9	5.5	8.7

(continued)

(continued)	United States	United Kingdom	West Germany	France	Japan
Transfers and subsidies (% of GNP, 1988)	9.9	15.0	15.5	26.2	1.5
Billionaires (total)	99	7	38	7	40
Billionaires (adjusted for population)	40	17	62	12	32
Pretax, pretransfer Gini index	.446	.418	.404	.462	.365
Posttax, posttransfer Gini	.383	.324	.389	.422	.318
Gini reduction	.063	.094	.015	.040	.047
(% of decrease)	(14)	(22)	(4)	(9)	(13)
Defense (% of 1987 budget)	25.6	12.9	3.2	6.3	1.0
Defense (% of GNP)	6.6	5.3	3.2	4.1	1.0
R&D as % of GNP	2.6	1.9	3.2	2.6	3.0
Nondefense R&D as % of GNP	1.8	2.3	2.6	2.3	2.8
% of GDP spent on education (1987)	6.8	5.2	4.6	5.8	5.6
% of GDP spent on vocational education	0.2	0.9	1.0	0.8	0.1
% of GDP spent on housing, social security, welfare (1987)	31.3	31.6	33.0	38.5	22.0
% of GDP spent on health	11.1	6.2	8.1	8.5	6.7
Public health (% of total)	40.8	86.2	78.1	79.2	72.9
Unemployment benefits (% of GNP)	0.34	0.95	1.08	0.75	0.25
Labor-market spending (% of GNP)	0.85	2.5	2.4	3.0	0.75
% of economy under gov't ownership	32	48	36	54	31
Subsidies as % of GDP (1980)	0.43	2.32	1.59	2.51	1.32
Subsidies as % of industrial output (1986)	0.5	2.0	2.1	3.0	1.0
% of world's biggest 500 industrial concerns	33	9	6	6	22
Index of Social Progress	5	3	1	2	4
1990 trade balance (billions)	−100.4	−32.0	64.3	−9.4	64.2

(continued)

(continued)	United States	United Kingdom	West Germany	France	Japan
Tax on int'l trade (% of trade, 1988)	3.1	0.14	0.01	0.05	1.7
1990 current account balance (billions)	-96.4	-28.7	44.0	-8.2	37.6
1991 current account balance (% of GNP, estimated)	-1.3	-1.7	+1.3	-0.8	+0.9
Budget deficit (% of GNP)	2.2	—	—	2.1	—
Budget surplus (% of GNP)	—	1.7	0.01	—	2.7
Public debt as % of GNP	39.0	30.0	23.8	26.6	24.6
Gov't interest payments (% of GNP)	2.4	3.7	2.7	2.8	4.0
Per capita aid (U.S. $) to developing countries	40	31	63	92	46
Total foreign aid (% of GNP)	2.1	3.0	3.8	7.1	3.0
% believing Third World has too much influence in United Nations	42	31	13	25	12
Economic stability	51.55	43.00	52.73	48.06	56.54
Rank	10	21	7	11	1

Although recent income distribution numbers are difficult to come by, most estimates show things haven't changed much from the early 1980s. The changes that have been seen have largely exacerbated the rich-poor gap—more money to the top 20 percent, and less money to the bottom 20 percent. Japan has the most equitable distribution of wealth among the five nations, while France is the most inequitable. Although it is indubitably misleading to describe income distributions in any of these nations as equitable, some are better than others. The United States is home to the largest population of super-rich, represented by billionaires in this compilation, while West Germany has the greatest number of super-rich adjusted for population. France works hardest at increasing income equity, while Japan does the least. This may be a result of the natural divisions of these countries' economies; the French may know they have more to do, and the Japanese may feel less compelled to act. Or, as free marketeers believe, the market—the invisible hand—may be the best equalizer.

A second way of measuring income equality is to use a Gini index. Scores on the Gini index range from 0 to 1; a score of zero represents complete income equality, one represents complete inequality. Using this method, gross income inequality still is rated worst in France, and best in Japan. After taxes and transfer payments are included, net income inequality rankings change little. What these posttax, posttransfer numbers do show is that the United Kingdom has the most progressive system, and Germany the least progressive. The British are able to reduce income inequality by 22 percent, and the Germans by only 4 percent.

If defense spending is a valid indicator, Americans are the most militaristic people of the five, both when spending is considered as a percentage of budget and when it is calculated as a percentage of GNP. The Japanese spend least on defense: They committed themselves to economic development and a minimum role for the military, spending only one percent of their GNP.

Looking to the future, Japan and Germany seem to be in the best position, at least where research and development spending is considered. The United States does tolerably well when all research and development (R&D) spending is included, but follow behind the other nations when defense-related R&D is excluded. The United Kingdom does not fare particularly well in either category. The United States spends a larger percentage of its gross domestic product (GDP) on education than the other nations, but other statistics in this cluster question how well that money is spent (see the section on "Education"). Germany spends the smallest amount of its GDP on education. The United States spends the most money for the least satisfactory outcome:

> Ironically, in the one area of investment where we do not have an investment shortfall—education—we have a performance gap, rooted in the kindergarten through high school level. American students perform poorly on internationally standardized math and science tests. High drop-out rates, inadequately prepared graduates, and an ever increasing shortage of Americans trained in science will have severe ramifications for the future of American industry.*

General public welfare spending shows several interesting differences among the five nations. The French spend the largest percentage of their GDP on housing, social security, and welfare, while the Japanese spend the least (consistent with the above income equality numbers). The U.S. government spends more of its GDP on

---

*Washington, DC, Council on Competitiveness, *Competitiveness Index, 1990,* p. 7.

health spending than do the other four countries, while the British spend the least. In spite of the apparent abundance of U.S. health spending and the apparent dearth of British spending, public health care in the United Kingdom makes up a larger percentage of total health spending than in all the other countries—in the United States considerably less health spending comes from the government than from private hands. The United States may spend more overall, but the cost of U.S. health care is so much more than in the other nations that spending goes significantly less far. Despite the conventional wisdom of the 1980s, the United States provides a comparatively small amount of unemployment benefits to its population; only Japan designates a smaller percentage of its GNP to unemployment compensation, and the Japanese unemployment rate is one-third that of the Americans. Germany and Britain provide the largest percentage of GNP to their unemployed, about three times greater than the United States, with virtually equal unemployment rates.

The French government is more active in its economy, and the Americans less active, than any of the other nations. More than 50 percent of the French economy is based on state-run enterprises, while just over 30 percent of the Japanese and American economies come from state-run sources. The French also expend a greater percentage of their GDP on subsidies than the other nations, spending an amount equal to nearly six times as much as the Americans. The British also spend a great deal on subsidies; the British total is just over 90 percent of the French allocation. Subsidies in industrial output change the rankings very little. The French still expend the most, the Americans still the least. One consequence of this intervention—or absence of intervention—is seen in international economic competitiveness. A country that provides a larger amount of subsidies to its own industries will make those industries more able to compete on an international scale by reducing those companies' operating costs. A consequence of this action may, however, be trade restrictions by other nations on products of the subsidized industry; usually this delicate balance is addressed in terms of *protectionism* and *fairness*. Too much subsidization allows an industry to unfairly impinge on the workings of the free market, to handcuff the invisible hand.

Balance of trade is another area where the United States lags. In 1990 the United States imported $100.4 billion more worth of material than it exported. West Germany and Japan are at the other extreme; both exported over $64 billion more worth of material than they imported. Numbers for overall 1990 current account balance are not much better; the United States posted figures putting its economy $96.4 billion further in debt, while Germany had earnings of just over $44 billion. In 1991, as a percentage of GNP, the Germans will once again have the best current account balance.

The budget deficit of the United States continues growing; the Americans and the French are almost equal, with a budget deficit of 2.2 percent and 2.1 percent, respectively (for those who fear the United States is losing its edge, in absolute dollar terms, it is far and away still number one). Japan will have the largest budget surplus of the five nations at 2.7 percent of its GNP, followed by Britain with a respectable 1.7 percent surplus, and West Germany, which just comes out ahead. The lead in public debt goes to the United States; West Germany fares best in this category.

Despite other budget problems, the French still provide the largest amount of foreign aid, both per capita and as a percentage of GNP. The British and Americans are the most self-centered of the five, spending 3.0 percent and 2.1 percent of their GNP, respectively, on foreign aid. A provocative aside is seen in public attitudes toward Third World nations and the amount of government foreign aid. Americans are most likely to believe Third World countries have too much influence in the United Nations, while the West Germans and Japanese are at the other end of the spectrum. Consistent with these attitudes, the American government is comparatively tightfisted. However, foreign aid is consistently the least popular public spending program, judging from survey evidence.

Overall, the Japanese economy is widely considered to be the most stable performer in the world. Only two other nations in this survey fall in the top ten, West Germany (7) and the United States (10). France (11) just misses that cutoff, while the United Kingdom (21) has a long way to go before it is considered economically stable.

THE REACH OF THE STATE

	United States	United Kingdom	West Germany	France	Japan
Central gov't total expenditure (% of GNP, 1987)	23.3	38.9	30.1	45.1	17.4
Total gov't spending (% of GNP, 1979)	23	43	47	45	31
Total gov't spending (% of GNP 1989)	34	39	45	49	33
% change	+48	−9	−4	+9	+6

(continued)

(continued)	United States	United Kingdom	West Germany	France	Japan
Central gov't expenditure as % of total gov't expenditure	32	12	26	40	22
Central gov't expenditure as % of total nondefense gov't expenditure	37	20	54	55	25
Total public expenditures as % of GNP	35.3	44.9	43.4	49.4	26.9
State enterprise (% share of fixed capital formation)	4.5	18.3	13.0	14.0	11.8
Gov't enterprises (% of total)	15	49	54	12	30
% of gov't enterprise in key areas*	60	12	9	58	23
% of managers believing governments should actively help domestic firms internationally	74	80	40	90	48
% of managers believing domestic firms should be prepared to pay higher prices to domestic suppliers	24	22	13	31	33
Gov't employees (% of population)	8.1	13.2	8.6	4.8	4.4
Central gov't employees (% of work force)	5.5	19.2	15.2	25.1	7.6
State and local employees (% of work force)	12.8	12.2	10.6	7.5	1.8
% increase in job creation (1960–88)	75	7	–5	16	37
Ratio of workers to adult population	0.62	0.58	0.47	0.50	0.60
Yearly salaries, members of lower house ($)	120,700	42,700	63,800	78,250	102,600
Gov't-sponsored bills enacted (% of laws)	33	97	87	82	77
Gov't-sponsored bills (% of all legislation)	4	81	81	91	86

*Agriculture, airlines, radio and television broadcasting, construction material manufacture, chemicals and fertilizers, fishing or mining, hotels and/or theaters, energy production, pharmaceuticals, and real estate (including housing).

(continued)

(continued)	United States	United Kingdom	West Germany	France	Japan
Top personal income tax rates	28	40	53	57	50
VAT rates (US = NYC)	8	18	15	19	3
Payroll tax for all social security (%)	7.15	9.00	17.75	14.81	10.95
Tax as % of GDP	31	38	40	43	30
Central gov't tax revenue as % of all tax revenue	65	85	70	95	74
Central gov't tax (% of GDP)	20	34	26	42	20
Gov't net worth as % of GNP	21	18	50	16	48
Mfg. imports as % of GDP	7.3	17.0	14.4	28.4	2.3
Mfg. imports (% of GDP in mfg.)	37.8	78.0	44.7	59.2	8.3
Share of nonoil world exports (% of 1973)	15.2	6.0	14.0	7.9	7.9
Share of nonoil world exports (1990)	13.8	5.9	13.8	8.6	9.2
% change	-9.2	-1.6	-1.4	+8.8	+16.5
Export growth rate (1980-88)	1.2	3.1	4.6	3.4	5.3
Total merchandise exports, 1990 (bn)	400	170	420	210	300
% share of world total	11.4	5.3	12.1	6.2	8.2
Import growth rate (1980-88)	8.9	4.9	3.3	2.6	5.0
Export concentration	0.110	0.152	0.136	0.085	0.209
Exports and imports (% of GNP)	18	49	49	37	12
% of U.S. exports	—	5.6	4.6	3.1	11.2
% of EEC† imports	19	52	52	60	13
% of EEC exports	24	50	55	62	18
% of OECD‡ imports	62	85	81	81	50

†EEC: European Economic Community, comprising Belgium, Denmark, France, West Germany, Greece, Ireland, Italy, Luxembourg, Netherlands, Portugal, Spain, and the United Kingdom.

‡OECD: Organization for Economic Cooperation and Development, comprising Australia, Austria, Belgium, Canada, Denmark, Finland, France, West Germany, Greece, Iceland, Ireland, Italy, Japan, Luxembourg, Netherlands, New Zealand, Norway, Portugal, Spain, Sweden, Switzerland, Turkey, United Kingdom, and the United States.

(continued)

(continued)	United States	United Kingdom	West Germany	France	Japan
% of OECD exports	63	79	84	80	61
Intra-industry trade (0 = none, 100 = complete)	60	78	66	82	25
Gov't stability (low = stable)	31	41	23	31	13
Democratic stability (low = stable)	0.36	0.58	0.62	0.19	0.13
Average turnout in national elections (%)	52	77	87	74	73
Deaths from internal political violence (1948–77)	434	0	61	164	60
Last revolution or coup	1861	1688	1933	1958	1940
Corporatism (1 = weak, 2 = moderate, 3 = strong)	1	1	2	1	3

As observed previously, the French government is more involved in that nation's economy than any of the governments of the other four nations; the Japanese is the least entangled (at least financially). The British central government spends only a fraction of that country's total government expenditure (12 percent), while the French central government accounts for 40 percent of all that nation's government expenditure. Total public expenditures as a percentage of GNP are also highest in France, although the United Kingdom approaches that percentage. This British "comeback" suggests the extent of government beyond the central core in the United Kingdom, and the extent of local autonomy over spending.

The governments of West Germany and the United Kingdom sponsor the greatest number of total government enterprises, while the United States and France are relatively uninvolved at this level. Yet, when government enterprise in key areas is taken into consideration, the numbers reverse themselves: governments in the United States and France are most involved; West Germany and the United Kingdom least involved. The United Kingdom and West Germany seem most willing to intervene broadly in economics, while the United States and France seem more interested in surgical intervention. The United Kingdom (13.2 percent) employs the largest percentage of its population in government jobs, while the Japanese (4.4 percent) occupy the other extreme. France (22.1 percent) employs the greatest portion of its workforce in central government sponsored jobs, the United States (5.5 percent), the least. When state and local employees are brought into the equations, the United States (12.8 percent) is the most active, Japan (1.8 percent), the least active. The U.S. national bureaucracy is small compared to its state and local civil service (a pattern unique to the Americans), while the French state and local bureaucracy is dwarfed by its national counterpart. France's central government tax revenues eclipse those of the other countries.

The United States president is the most impotent executive among these five nations. Only one-third of all laws passed in the United States are enacted with the sponsorship of the executive branch. Only *four percent* of all bills introduced into the U.S. Congress are sponsored by the president. In the United Kingdom, 97 percent of the bills approved in Commons are enacted with the leadership of the prime minister; and in France, 91 percent of all bills introduced to the legislature are introduced with executive sponsorship. Excluding the United States, an average of 86 percent of all enacted bills are enacted with government blessing, and 85 percent of all legislation introduced is executive supported. This extraordinary discrepancy is a result of two main factors: (1) The United States has the weakest political parties in any of the five nations and (2) the U.S. president and U.S. Congress both exist as predominantly autonomous powers—neither owes the other anything.

Despite prevailing public opinion, the U.S. government has the lowest income and social security taxes of the five (though many people feel the United States is the most "taxing"). The top personal income tax rate of 28 percent in the United States is one-half that of France, home of the highest top personal income tax of the five. The U.S. social security tax is only 40 percent of the highest social security payroll tax, found in West Germany. Overall, Japan and the United States have the smallest tax burden, while France has the largest tax income as a percentage of GDP. If only central government taxes are included, France remains the highest taxing nation, with the United States and Japan the least.

International trade also presents some intriguing distinctions among the five nations. Of the five, France imports the largest percentage of its GDP in manufactured goods, nearly twice that of second-place Germany, while Japan imports the least, less than 10 percent that of the French. Manufacturing imports as a percentage of GDP in manufacturing presents more unexpected information. The British import 78 percent as much manufactured goods as they produce (for every $100 produced domestically, $78 more is imported), while for Japan the number is 8.3 percent. This is a fitting indication of the weakness of the British manufacturing industry and the verve of Japanese industry.

In terms of overall nonoil exports, the United States has suffered the greatest losses in the period from 1973 to 1990, losing just over 9 percent of its share of world exports, while France gained nearly 9 percent, and Japan gained over 16 percent. In the period from 1980 to 1988, the United States (1.2 percent) had the smallest export growth rate of the five, Japan (5.3 percent) the largest. In the same period, total U.S. imports grew at a rate of 8.9 percent, while France registered the smallest increase in imports at 2.5 percent.

Export concentration is a measure of the number of countries to which exports are sent; a score of 1.0 indicates all exports were sent to one nation, while a score of 0.0 shows that all countries that received exports from that nation received an equal amount. Japan has the highest export concentration, and France the most diverse export market. In the event that any one of its major markets were lost, France would be in the best position, while Japan would be hurt the most. West Germany and the United Kingdom are the most reliant on international trade, as indicated by their value as a percent of GNP, while Japan is the most self-sufficient nation of the bunch.

Besides concentration of trade, it is also engaging to see where each country is exporting its goods to, and where it is importing its goods from. The United States sends more than twice as much of its exports to Japan as to its next largest trade partner of the five, Britain. France receives the smallest amount of American exports. France imports 60 percent of its international trade from other European Economic Community (EEC) nations, just ahead of West Germany (52 percent) and the United Kingdom (52 percent), while non-EEC countries Japan and the United States get less than 20 percent of their imports from EEC nations. France also targets 62 percent of its exports to other EEC countries, followed once more by West Germany (55 percent) and Britain (50 percent). The United States (24 percent) and Japan (18 percent) trail far behind. Among the Organization for Economic Cooperation and Development (OECD) nations, the United Kingdom (85 percent) is the most significant importer, while Japan (50 percent) imports the least amount of goods. West Germany is the most significant OECD exporter, exporting 84 percent of its goods to other OECD nations, while Japan at 61 percent is the least significant exporter.

As a summary measure, government stability is provocative to compare. Using a variety of measures, it has been calculated that Japan has the most stable government, and has the most stable democracy. The United Kingdom is said to have the least stable government, but West Germany has the least stable democracy. Among the numbers influencing these rankings are economic stability, frequency of party change in government, number of parties in government, voter participation, and amount of government involvement in the economy. Voter participation numbers can be summed up by saying the United States is woefully apathetic. Of course, these measures of stability should not be taken too seriously; all these governments are very stable and very democratic.

Government involvement in the economy is more complicated, though the best general measure is to see how corporatist a system is. The United States, United Kingdom, and France are all weak corporatist states least organized in this manner; West Germany is considered moderately corporatist; and only Japan is considered to be a strong corporatist state. The main body of the text fleshes out these distinctions with more precision.

PRODUCTIVITY

	United States	United Kingdom	West Germany	France	Japan
Union membership, % of active population	15	38	34	17	22
Union membership, % of nonagricultural employees (1970)	30	50	30	18	35
Union membership, % of nonagricultural employees (1990)	18	45	42	22	24
% change (1970–90)	–40	–10	+40	+22	–31
Strike days lost per 1,000 workers	180.2	79.3	1.4	26.8	4.3
Centralization in wage bargaining (centralized = 1; decentralized = 16)	15.1	11.5	6.1	10.5	13.0
Union centralization (organizational unity, power in collective bargaining, scope of collective bargaining; high = centralized)	0.30	0.43	0.53	0.23	0.17

(continued)

(continued)	United States	United Kingdom	West Germany	France	Japan
Labor organization index (sum of standardized membership and centralization)	0.86	1.93	1.73	0.81	0.41
% favoring worker participation in management	39	48	51	76	58
Hourly compensation for mfg. workers (U.S. = 100)	100	75	130	93	91
Real hourly compensation	99	137	136	128	127
% ranking good salary most important	16	37	28	36	7
% ranking job security most important	19	20	28	21	23
% ranking feeling of accomplishment most important	50	25	22	26	38
Wage sensitivity to unemployment (high = rigid)	0.19	1.90	1.80	1.65	0.24
Unemployment (Dec. 1990)	6.1	6.5	6.6	9.0	2.1
% of unemployment "long-term"	6	45	42	48	20
Employment as % of working-age population	74	68	62	60	71
% economically active youth	64	75	61	40	41
GDP output per hour	132.4	148.1	132.4	141.2	170.5
Average annual GDP growth rate per worker, 1979–86 (%)	1.0	1.8	1.3	1.6	2.5
Growth in GDP per hour, 1979–89 (%)	1.09	2.95	1.88	3.24	3.06
GDP per hour projected growth rate, 1979–2020 (%)	2.27	2.57	3.93	3.49	4.65
Manufacturing labor productivity growth, 1978–83 (%)	2.0	3.8	2.8	3.7	5.8
1983–88	4.0	4.6	2.7	2.9	5.9

(continued)

(continued)	United States	United Kingdom	West Germany	France	Japan
Total labor productivity (includes self-employed) growth, 1980–88	2.0	3.2	5.1	5.9	8.9
Passenger car production, monthly (× 1,000)	590	95	362	248	658
Passenger car production (% of world total)	23	8	10	8	26
Steel production metric tons per year	80	16	39	19	105
Steel production per capita, kilos	448	254	481	258	553
Steel quality, % of oxygen steel (higher % = higher quality)	59	71	82	81	71
% of continuous casting (steel)	44	55	80	81	91
Productivity improvement (1960–73)	2.8	4.0	5.4	5.9	9.9
(1973–79)	0.9	0.1	5.0	4.8	3.8
Per capita output change 1983 (1970 = 100)	102.5	120.4	128.9	128.6	135.2
Total factor productivity change, 1950–79 (%)	1.09	1.63	2.78	2.53	2.97
Annual growth rate of capital stock, 1950–79 (%)	3.61	3.29	5.28	4.11	8.36
Annual growth rate capital-labor ratio, 1950–79 (%)	2.44	3.55	5.66	4.18	7.11
Rates for borrowing on equipment and machinery (%)	11.2	9.2	7.0	8.1	7.2
Industrial robots (× 1,000)	25	10	15	11	180
Industrial production, 1990 (1982 = 100)	130	112	125	117	145
Industrial production (% change last year, 1990)	−1.4	−2.8	5.7	−0.8	6.3
Private investment as % of GNP	10	16	21	21	24

(continued)

(continued)	United States	United Kingdom	West Germany	France	Japan
Public investment as % of GNP	1.6	1.9	2.4	3.1	6.7
Investment in U.S. (% of GNP)	—	5.7	1.8	1.3	0.5
Investment in U.S. (% of U.S. GNP)	—	2.1	0.5	0.2	0.8
Inflows of foreign investment (% of GNP)	28.2	7.6	0.9	3.0	0.2
Foreign investment income, 1990 (billions)	0	2	12	0	28
Share in Nobel Prize winners 1970–79	53.8	17.5	2.5	1.3	—
European patents issued (1990)	5,800	1,500	6,000	2,100	4,500
European Management Forum competitiveness ranking	2	15	4	16	1
Economist cumulative ranking 1991	9	10	2	5	1

The United Kingdom has the highest percentage of union membership of the five nations, while the United States has the lowest rate. In the past twenty years, for nonagricultural employees, that number has increased most in West Germany (up 40 percent) and decreased most in the United States (down 40 percent). At present, the United Kingdom still has the largest percentage of union membership among nonagricultural workers, while the United States still has the smallest amount of nonagricultural unionization. Despite this small unionization rate, the United States leads the group in days lost due to strikes per thousand workers. West Germany loses just over one day of work per thousand workers, while the United States loses just over 180 days per thousand. Many Americans may not be in unions, but those who are union members are quite aggressive about their demands. Centralized bargaining is most prominent in Germany, though its score cannot be considered to reflect much centralization. The United States is the home of the least centralized bargaining; and that number does reflect a high degree of decentralization. In sum, unions are strongest in the United Kingdom (in spite of Mrs. Thatcher) and weakest in Japan. The Labor Organization Index (see note 20, Chapter 9) establishes this point well.

Those favoring worker participation in management are most common in France, where 76 percent of those surveyed approved of the idea, and least common in the United States, where only 39 percent favored the option. These numbers suggest the reluctance of American workers to do much more than go to work and collect a paycheck; they are content to let management do whatever it feels necessary. West German manufacturing workers receive the best wages of the group, while the British wages are smallest. In real hourly compensation, including benefits, British workers excel, ranking just higher than the Germans, while Americans bring up the rear.

Japanese workers are least likely to rank salary as the most important part of their jobs, while 37 percent of the British and 36 percent of the French feel that a good salary is most important. West Germans tend to value job security more, as do the Japanese. Fifty percent of Americans consider getting a feeling of accomplishment the most important part of their jobs; second place here goes to the Japanese at 38 percent. This diversity of opinion in how workers think about their jobs could explain some of the differences among these five nations found in other areas.

Unemployment is most serious in France, where 9 percent of the workforce was unemployed at the beginning of 1992. Forty-eight percent of the French unemployed were long-term unemployed; workers with little hope of finding a job any time soon. The United States, with an unemployment rate of 6.1 percent at the end of 1991, has the fewest long-term unemployed; only 6 percent of American unemployed fit this category. Long-term unemployment numbers hint at how much the unemployment rate in a particular nation is treatable. A nation with a very high degree of long-term unemployment is likely to be more forbearing of its current unemployment rate. If the U.S. unemployment rate were 9 percent, Americans would be furious because a very small percentage of those unemployed would be long-term. The French are more likely to accept that fact and work toward other types of economic remedies. Each nation has its own level of "permanent" unemployment. As the overall unemployment rate falls, a larger percentage of the unemployed will fall in the permanent category, and it will be trickier to diminish unemployment further. Only when the ratio of long-term to short-term unemployment is low is there a danger of economic instability.

Economic output per hour is highest in Japan, while Germany and the United States have the lowest GDP output per hour. The Japanese also had the highest average annual growth rate in productivity from 1979 to 1986, while the Americans had the least productivity increase. Growth in GDP output per hour was greatest in France over the last decade, though Japan and Britain were not far behind; the United States once more trailed the field. Using that growth rate, economists predict that through 2020 the Japanese economy will continue to grow at a faster rate than any of the other five countries, while the U.S. growth rate will lag behind. Manufacturing productivity growth continues to favor Japan, while West Germany and France are struggling. Total labor productivity figures suggest the United States is in a seriously troubled position. From 1980 to 1988 the total labor productivity growth rate in the United States was a paltry 2 percent, while the Japanese posted a stunning 8.9 percent increase over the period. As American productivity continues to lose ground to these other nations, the U.S. economy will find itself in a more precarious position. Only if American productivity growth is able to keep pace with its competitors will Americans be able to continue to compete fairly in international trade; an area in which the United States is already losing a considerable amount of ground.

The United States already trails Japan in total passenger car production. In an average month, American car makers produce 590,000 cars—but Japanese car makers produce 658,000 cars, about 12 percent more. On a world scale, Japan is now the source of over one-quarter of all passenger cars produced. Steel production numbers are no more encouraging. Once more, Japan produces an absolute amount greater than the United States, while both Japan and Germany produce more steel per capita. Each of the other four nations produces higher quality steel than the United States. The implications of this American backsliding are numerous. Among the most important ramifications is the need for American firms to import steel in order to produce goods for export. Importing the raw materials for production greatly reduces the profitability of that production, as well as doing little to reduce the trade deficit Americans currently face. Overall, United States productivity continues to lag far behind that of the other nations in this survey. Every nation outdistanced the United States in the period from 1960 to 1973, and all but the United Kingdom repeated the achievement from 1973 to 1979. There appears to be no silver lining in this evergrowing cloud.

Especially dismal is the forecast for the future: rates for borrowing on equipment and machinery are highest in the United States, further decreasing American industries' ability to modernize and improve their competitiveness. The edge in industrial robots, at one time a largely U.S. innovation, is clearly to the Japanese. About the best thing U.S. industries have going for them is that the United

Kingdom is struggling in some areas more than they are. Investment in the economy is lowest in the United States, further handicapping the American ability to catch up with, let alone pass, the other four nations. Japanese private investment occurs at a rate 2.4 times that of the United States, while the disparity in public investment (4.2) is even greater. Even the United Kingdom outpaces the United States here. The United States does have the greatest amount of foreign inflows of investment of the five nations, but this also means the highest amount of dividends are going back to the investing nations. All in all, the Japanese economy is in the best condition of the five, the West German economy second best, the Americans and the French hold positions in the middle of the pack, and the United Kingdom is last.

MORALITY

	United States	United Kingdom	West Germany	France	Japan
Believe in God (% yes)	98	81	80	65	62
How important is God in your life? (% not very)	8	40	42	50	42
% attending church once a month or more	60	23	35	17	12
% saying homosexuality can never be justified	65	43	42	47	52
% saying extramarital affairs never justified	64	51	46	25	44

Nearly all Americans (98 percent) believe in God; and only 8 percent of Americans say that their belief in God is not very important in their lives. The next most "religious" country in these terms is the United Kingdom, while the French and the Japanese are the least religious of the five nations. Five times as many Americans attend church at least once a month as Japanese, and nearly twice as many Americans as West Germans. While other effects of this American religiosity are difficult to identify (teen birth rates, for example, cannot be explained by this category), Americans are certainly more critical and moralistic than any of the other nations. Sixty-five percent of all Americans condemn homosexuality as unjustifiable. The next highest in this category are the Japanese at 52 percent. No other population is above 50 percent. Sixty-four percent of Americans believe that extramarital affairs can never be justified. Besides the United States, only the United Kingdom squeaks in above 50 percent on this issue, and the French come in at a "shocking" 25 percent. For a nation supposedly based on freedom and equality by people escaping persecution, Americans are an intolerant and judgmental lot.

FINAL JUDGMENTS

	United States	United Kingdom	West Germany	France	Japan
% of males saying they are satisfied with life	85	86	85	74	73
% of females	84	87	83	73	77
% of males saying they are "very happy"	30	25	15	13	14
% of females	32	28	13	15	18
Suicides per 100,000	12.4	18.0	17.0	21.8	21.1
Male youth suicide rate (per 100,000)	21.0	10.0	17.0	15.5	12.0
% very proud to be _____ (nationality)	76	53	21	66	30
% willing to fight for country	74	68	47	48	32
Military personnel per 1,000	9.6	5.9	8.1	10.2	2.0
Battle deaths, 1800–1980 (thousands)	664	664	5,353	1,965	1,371
Last foreign invasion	1812	1066	1944	1940	1945
% of households owning microwave oven	61	30	16	8	n/a
Sales of sound recordings, pc	25	35	27	19	24
TV sets per 1000	798	333	373	394	580
Newspapers per 1000	268	414	350	212	585
Economist (U.K.) "nirvana" rank	8	9	2	1	4

(continued)

(continued)	United States	United Kingdom	West Germany	France	Japan
International Living (USA) "nirvana" rank	1	16	21	10	7
United Nations quality of life score (rank)	0.961 (17)	0.970 (10)	0.967 (11)	0.974 (8)	0.996 (1)

American, British, and West German citizens are the most likely of the five countries to say they are satisfied with life, though Americans are most likely to say they are "very happy." These numbers are partially supported by suicide rates. The overall American suicide rate is the lowest of the five, but the male youth suicide rate is the highest. The overall suicide rates of France and Japan intimate unhappiness and discontent, as expressed in their survey responses, but the German and British suicide rates are considerably higher than might be expected. Obviously, suicide is a very complex problem, and is not only caused by being unhappy or dissatisfied. Finally, why aren't the Japanese happier? Have they sacrificed too much for international economic hegemony?

Americans are also the most patriotic of the five populations; 76 percent respond that they are very proud to be Americans, and 74 percent are willing to fight for their country. French are the next most patriotic, but the British are the next most likely to fight for their country. The West Germans, understandably, given the devastation of WWII and the horrors of excessive nationalism, are the least patriotic; though they may be more proud to be Germans than West Germans. The Japanese are least likely to be willing to fight for their country. These last two numbers are quite likely reflections of the post-World War II limitations put on these two nations, and of course the devastation of the war itself. West German battle deaths are astounding.

Americans love their televisions, too. In the United States are nearly 800 televisions per every 1,000 people. The British have the smallest number of televisions per thousand, 333. Newspapers are most common in Japan where there are 585 newspapers produced per 1,000 citizens; France, at 212 per 1,000, and the United States, at 268 per 1,000, trail the field in this source of information. These numbers are particularly important when you consider that studies have shown that the more television you watch, the *less* informed you are likely to be, while the more newspapers you read, the more informed you are likely to be. The comparative ignorance of Americans is consonant with their habits of information acquisition.

So, what does this all mean? The concluding "final judgment" is up to you. But others have come up with their own "nirvana" rankings, combining a number of statistics to try to determine the "best" place to live—most disagree in their results. *International Living,* an American publication, prefers the United States; *The Economist* opts for France, while the more focused United Nations survey selects Japan. Last-place votes go to the United Kingdom (from *The Economist*), West Germany (from *International Living*), and the United States (from the United Nations). Average rankings give the nod to Japan, the United States, and France.

Name Index

Subject Index

Composition by Point West, Inc., Carol Stream, Illinois
Printed and bound by McNaughton & Gunn, Inc., Saline, Michigan
Edited by Dana R. Gould, Hoffman Estates, Illinois
Designed by Willis Proudfoot, Mt. Prospect, Illinois
Production supervision by Robert H. Grigg, Chicago, Illinois
The text is set in Palatino